Wendy Mayer and Bronwen Neil (Eds.)

**Religious Conflict from Early Christianity to the Rise of Islam**

# Arbeiten zur Kirchengeschichte

Begründet von
Karl Holl† und Hans Lietzmann†

Herausgegeben von
Christian Albrecht und Christoph Markschies

## Band 121

# Religious Conflict from Early Christianity to the Rise of Islam

Edited by
Wendy Mayer and Bronwen Neil

DE GRUYTER

ISBN 978-3-11-048850-0
e-ISBN 978-3-11-029194-0
ISSN 1861-5996

**Library of Congress Cataloging-in-Publication Data**
A CIP catalog record for this book has been applied for at the Library of Congress.

**Bibliographic information published by the Deutsche Nationalbibliothek**
The Deutsche Nationalbibliothek lists this publication in the Deutsche Nationalbibliografie; detailed bibliographic data are available in the Internet at http://dnb.dnb.de.


Printing: Hubert & Co. GmbH & Co. KG, Göttingen
♾ Printed on acid-free paper
Printed in Germany

www.degruyter.com

# Preface

Founded in 1997 under the direction of Professor Pauline Allen, the Centre for Early Christian Studies at Australian Catholic University (comprising sixteen full-time academic staff and twelve honorary fellows) constitutes a significant focus for New Testament and late-antique scholarship as well as representing the largest concentration of Patristics scholars within Australia. In addition to its links with colleagues in traditional centres of scholarship (UK, Europe and North America), the Centre intentionally reaches out via its networks to colleagues in South Africa and the Asia–Pacific region (particularly Japan, Korea, Russia and South America), resulting since 2004 in fruitful professorial exchanges and mutually successful grants in Australia, Japan and Korea, as well as collaborative and linked research projects. Since 2009 the fruits of focusing the collective expertise of the Centre on broad research themes of contemporary relevance – to date, poverty and crisis management – have been demonstrated by the publication of two collected volumes: *Prayer and Spirituality in the Early Church*, vol. 5, *Poverty and Riches*, eds. Geoffrey D. Dunn, David Luckensmeyer, and Lawrence Cross (Strathfield: St Pauls Publications, 2009); and *Ancient Jewish and Christian Texts as Crisis Management Literature: Thematic Studies from the Centre for Early Christian Studies*, eds. David Sim and Pauline Allen, LNTS 445 (London–New York: T&T Clark, 2012). The present volume, which includes a guest contribution by a colleague at the University of Ottawa, constitutes the fruits of collaborative focus on a third topic of current global interest, religious conflict.

All of the chapters in this volume have been subjected to peer review and in some cases chapters have been revised on the basis of reviewers' comments. The fact that the bulk of the volume constitutes the collective research of scholars within a single Centre, however, inevitably results in both strengths and weaknesses. Firstly, the authors in this volume view religious conflict largely through the lens of Christianity, which is an artefact of the Centre's research focus. Secondly, to our regret the commitments of two members whose research focus is the second and third centuries CE led to their withdrawal from the project, leaving a critical gap which Pierluigi Piovanelli kindly agreed to fill. We are deeply grateful to Professor Piovanelli for coming to our rescue at the last minute and excited to include the contribution of a scholar whose interests and intellectual curiosity very much coincide with our own. Thirdly, there is an uneven focus on the eastern half of the Mediterranean world, as well as, fourthly, a bias towards the expression or study of religious conflict in or through narrative. In regard to the first of these two partialities, the geographic focus reflects the choices of the contributors. Pauline Allen and Bronwen Neil, in particular, situate their research comfortably in both worlds. In regard to the second, with the exception of Alan Cadwallader, whose larger project on Chonai (Kolossai) draws on both material and textual evidence, and Michael Theophilos, who works at the intersection of text and artefact in relation to Second Temple Judaism and Early Christianity – and perhaps Wendy Mayer, whose recent study with Pauline Allen of the churches of late-antique Antioch (mod. Antakya) engaged with archaeological scholarship – the bulk of the members of the Centre for Early Christian Studies are trained primarily in the interpretation (and, in some cases, editing) of texts. These constraints shape the character of the volume, but do not, we hope, devalue its contribution. It remains a testament to the quality of the research produced by scholars of the Centre for Early Christian Studies, much of it ground-breaking, and to the wisdom of its Director in bringing together the still largely separate disciplines of New Testament Studies, Patristics, and Late Antiquity.

Wendy Mayer and Bronwen Neil — March 2013

# Contents

# Abbreviations

| | |
|---|---|
| AB | Anchor Bible |
| *ABR* | *Australian Biblical Review* |
| ABRL | Anchor Bible Reference Library |
| AKG | Arbeiten zur Kirchengeschichte |
| *AntT* | *Antiquité Tardive* |
| BCNH | Bibliothèque copte de Nag Hammadi |
| BETL | Bibliotheca Ephemeridum Theologicarum Lovaniensium |
| BNTC | Black's New Testament Commentaries |
| *BSac* | *Bibliotheca Sacra* |
| *Byz* | *Byzantion* |
| *BZ* | *Byzantinische Zeitschrift* |
| BZNW | Beihefte zur *Zeitschrift für die neutestamentliche Wissenschaft* |
| *CBQ* | *Catholic Biblical Quarterly* |
| CCCOGD | *Conciliorum oecumenicorum generaliumque decreta*, eds. G. Alberigo et al., Corpus Christianorum, 2 vols. (Brepols: Turnhout, 2006–2010) |
| CCSA | Corpus Christianorum Series Apocryphorum |
| CCSG | Corpus Christianorum Series Graeca |
| CCSL | Corpus Christianorum Series Latina |
| *CIG* | *Corpus Inscriptionum Graecarum* |
| CPG | Clavis Patrum Graecorum |
| CPL | Clavis Patrum Latinorum |
| CSCO | Corpus Scriptorum Christianorum Orientalium |
| CSEL | Corpus Scriptorum Ecclesiasticorum Latinorum |
| *CTh* | *Codex Theodosianus* |
| *DOP* | *Dumbarton Oaks Papers* |
| FChr | Fontes Christiani |
| FOTC | Fathers of the Church |
| GCS | Griechische Christliche Schriftsteller |
| GCS NF | Griechische Christliche Schriftsteller, Neue Folge |
| GNS | Good News Studies |
| *GRBS* | *Greek, Roman and Byzantine Studies* |
| *HE* | *Historia ecclesiastica* |
| *HThR* | *Harvard Theological Review* |
| *HTS* | *Hervormde Teologiese Studies* |
| ICC | International Critical Commentary |
| IJO | Inscriptiones Judaicae Orientis |
| *JECS* | *Journal of Early Christian Studies* |
| *JEH* | *Journal of Ecclesiastical History* |
| JK | Philippe Jaffé, *Regesta Pontificum Romanorum*, vol. 1, *A S. Petro ad a. MCXLIII*, rev. F. Kaltenbrunner (rev. edn.; Leipzig: Veit, 1885) |
| *JQR* | *The Jewish Quarterly Review* |
| *JRS* | *Journal of Roman Studies* |
| *JSJ* | *Journal for the Study of Judaism* |
| JSJSup | Supplements to the *Journal for the Study of Judaism* |
| *JSNT* | *Journal for the Study of the New Testament* |

| | |
|---|---|
| JSNTSup | *Journal for the Study of the New Testament*, Supplement Series |
| *JTS* | *Journal of Theological Studies* |
| LCL | Loeb Classical Library |
| LNTS | Library of New Testament Studies |
| LSTS | Library of Second Temple Studies |
| MGH | Monumenta Germaniae Historica |
| MGHAA | Monumenta Germaniae Historica, Auctorum Antiquissimorum |
| MGHEpp | Monumenta Germaniae Historica, Epistolarum |
| MGHSRM | Monumenta Germaniae Historica, Scriptores Rerum Merovingicarum |
| NBA | Nuova Bibliotheca Agostiniana |
| NHC | Nag Hammadi Codex |
| NHMS | Nag Hammadi and Manichean Studies |
| *NovT* | *Novum Testamentum* |
| NovTSup | *Novum Testamentum*, Supplements |
| NTIC | New Testament in Context |
| NTOA | Novum Testamentum et Orbis Antiquus |
| NTR | New Testament Readings |
| *NTS* | *New Testament Studies* |
| NTT | New Testament Theology |
| OCM | Oxford Classical Monographs |
| OECS | Oxford Early Christian Studies |
| OECT | Oxford Early Christian Texts |
| OLA | Orientalia Lovaniensia Analecta |
| *OLP* | *Orientalia Lovaniensia Periodica* |
| PG | Patrologia Graeca |
| PL | Patrologia Latina |
| PO | Patrologia Orientalis |
| PLRE | *Prosopography of the Later Roman Empire*, 3 vols., ed. John R. Martindale et al. (Cambridge: Cambridge University Press, 1971, 1980, 1992) |
| PTS | Patristische Texte und Studien |
| *REByz* | *Revue des Études Byzantines* |
| SBLDS | Society of Biblical Literature Dissertation Series |
| SBLSS | Society of Biblical Literature Seminar Series |
| SC | Sources Chrétiennes |
| SCJ | Studies in Christianity and Judaism/Études sur le christianisme et le judaïsme |
| SCSS | Studies in Critical Social Sciences |
| *SE* | *Studia Evangelica* |
| SEG | Supplementum Epigraphicum Graecum |
| *SJT* | *Scottish Journal of Theology* |
| SNTSMS | Society for New Testament Studies Monograph Series |
| SNTW | Studies of the New Testament and its World |
| SP | Sacra Pagina |
| STAC | Studien und Texte zu Antike und Christentum |
| SUNT | Studien zur Umwelt des Neuen Testaments |
| TCH | The Transformation of the Classical Heritage |
| *ThG* | *Theologie der Gegenwart* |
| TTH | Translated Texts for Historians |

| | |
|---|---|
| UNT | Untersuchungen zum Neuen Testament |
| *TZ* | *Theologische Zeitschrift* |
| *VC* | *Vigiliae Christianae* |
| WBC | World Biblical Commentary |
| *WTJ* | *Westminster Theological Journal* |
| WUNT | Wissenschaftliche Untersuchungen zum Neuen Testament |
| *ZNW* | *Zeitschrift für die neutestamentliche Wissenschaft* |

Wendy Mayer

# Religious Conflict: Definitions, Problems and Theoretical Approaches

The almost constant awareness today in the western media of conflict associated with religion is reflected in a rapidly growing scholarly literature on the topic. At the forefront of such studies is a natural preoccupation with its most visual, newsworthy, and disruptive aspect – its expression in physical violence.[1] Religious conflict is a much larger phenomenon, however, than religiously-motivated violence, while even religious violence itself is not simple. The latter encompasses not just the physical domain (violent acts), but also the discursive (violent, i.e., hostile/hate-filled speech),[2] raising questions about the precise relationship between these two forms, how each should be addressed, and the degree to which each is harmful to society. The motivation for such violence, moreover, is often complex, leading to the conclusion, on the one hand, that violent "religious" conflicts in late antiquity, for instance, were rarely purely religiously motivated. On careful examination they can be shown to owe as much, if not

---

1 See, e.g., Brent D. Shaw, *Sacred Violence: African Christians and Sectarian Hatred in the Age of Augustine* (Cambridge–New York: Cambridge University Press, 2011); Charles B. Strozier, David M. Terman, James W. Jones, and Katherine A. Boyd, eds., *The Fundamentalist Mindset: Psychological Perspectives on Religion, Violence, and History* (Oxford: Oxford University Press, 2010); William T. Cavanaugh, *The Myth of Religious Violence: Secular Ideology and the Roots of Modern Conflict* (Oxford: Oxford University Press, 2009); Thomas Sizgorich, *Violence and Belief in Late Antiquity: Militant Devotion in Christianity and Islam*, Divinations: Rereading Late Ancient Religion (Philadelphia, PA: University of Pennsylvania Press, 2009); Bryan Rennie and Philip L. Tite, eds., *Religion, Terror, and Violence: Religious Studies Perspectives* (New York: Routledge, 2008); James F. Rinehart, *Apocalyptic Faith and Political Violence: Prophets of Terror* (New York: Palgrave, 2006); Michael Gaddis, *There Is No Crime for Those Who Have Christ: Religious Violence in the Christian Roman Empire*, TCH 39 (Berkeley–Los Angeles–London: University of California Press, 2005); Jessica Stern, *Terror in the Name of God: Why Religious Militants Kill* (New York: Ecco, 2003); David G. Bromley and J. Gordon Melton, eds., *Cults, Religion, and Violence* (Cambridge–New York: Cambridge University Press, 2002). The close relationship between conflict and violence is a key premise in the National Science Foundation-funded project "The Dynamics of Religions and Conflict" (DRC) conducted by the Center for the Study of Religion and Conflict, Arizona State University, 2008 – 2011 (csrc.asu.edu/research/projects/dynamics-religions-conflict), as also in a recent European-based project, the results of which are published as a manual: Erik Eynikel and Angeliki Ziaka, eds., *Religion and Conflict: Essays on the Origins of Religious Conflict and Resolution Approaches* (London: Harptree Publishing Ltd., 2011).

2 This is the focus of Michael Gaddis' analysis of religious violence in late antiquity, in Id., *There Is No Crime*, where he labels it "extremist discourse." It is also a focus of the Spanish projects discussed in section 2.2 below.

more, to political considerations, local conditions, and the personal motives of the chief protagonists.[3] Conversely, it has been argued that in contemporary conflicts more generally – for example, in the case of those viewed as politically or ethnically motivated – the definition of religion brought to bear is idealised and impoverished, and that the religious element has, in consequence, often been underestimated.[4] To complicate matters, religious violence can, particularly in the case of New Religious Movements (NRMs), be self-directed and free from any association with conflict.[5] Conversely and manifestly, not all religious conflicts are violent.

As we can see simply from looking at this single most obvious aspect (violence) and as will become clearer in sections 2 and 3 below, on the one hand study of religious conflict is both topical and a rich field that offers a wide range of avenues for investigation. On the other, it is clear that what we mean by religious conflict requires careful definition, if we are to tease out the assumptions that underlie our approaches to it in our effort to seek solutions. Consequently, in section 1 we first provide a working definition of the topic. In section 2 we outline in brief the theoretical approaches that have been brought to bear in recent decades, including discussion of a number of significant research projects with specific relevance to the time period that is the focus of this volume (the first to ninth centuries CE). Paying particular attention to that time period, in section 3 we then discuss how this research has brought about a paradigm shift and is in the process of raising a variety of new questions.

## 1 Defining religious conflict

Conflict occurs when something is contested. When we couple religion with conflict, we might expect that what is contested is ideology or morality (i.e., belief).

---

**3** See the conclusions of Johannes Hahn, *Gewalt und religiöser Konflikt. Studien zu den Auseinandersetzungen zwischen Christen, Heiden und Juden im Osten des Römischen Reiches (von Konstantin bis Theodosius II)*, Klio Beihefte NF 8 (Berlin: Akademie Verlag, 2004). The approach taken by the social scientists engaged in the DRC project referred to in n. 1 posits the influence on religious conflict of cultural, psychological, social, political and economic conditions.

**4** See the introduction to Ronald L. Grimes, Ute Husken, Udo Simon, and Eric Venbrux, eds., *Ritual, Media, and Conflict* (Oxford: Oxford University Press, 2011), 4–5. I am indebted to Bronwen Neil for alerting me to the contribution of Ritual Studies to this discussion.

**5** See the discussion in James R. Lewis, ed., *Violence and New Religious Movements* (Oxford: Oxford University Press, 2011). Violence in these cases does not always manifest as mass suicide, but the example of NRMs cautions against drawing a direct line between religious violence and religious conflict.

But this is not necessarily the case,[6] and religious conflict is best described as a more complex phenomenon that engages a combination of contested domains, including power, personality, space or place, and group identity.[7] These contested domains should not be confused with enabling factors or conditions, which, as mentioned above, can be political, social, economic, cultural and psychological. When both of these aspects are taken into consideration, we should be open to the possibility that, as a religion develops over time and/or as different enabling conditions come into play, different contested domains are accorded priority. A distinction should also be drawn between the root cause/s of the religious conflict (what is contested) and the way in which the conflict is discursively or narratively framed. That is, what a conflict is said to be about may differ significantly from what is actually being contested. We should be similarly open to the possibility that what is contested may be reframed retrospectively, just as it is also possible that what is not a conflict becomes viewed or framed as a conflict in hindsight and vice versa.

Our primary definition – that religious conflict is a complex phenomenon that engages a combination of contested domains (ideology/morality, power, personality, space/place, and group identity), in turn enabled by a range of other conditions (political, social, economic, cultural and psychological) – gains further clarity when we turn to consider what religious conflict is not. The model developed by the Religious Rivalries Seminar conducted by the Canadian Society of Biblical Studies is helpful in this regard with its categorisation of four ways – coexistence, cooperation, competition and conflict – in which religions in the same environment (or marketplace) interrelate.[8] While this model is limited in

---

**6** Neither is contested morality/ideology exclusive to religious conflict. See the ground-breaking work of the cognitive linguist George Lakoff, *Moral Politics: How Liberals and Conservatives Think* (2nd edn; Chicago–London: University of Chicago Press, 2002), further developed in Id., *The Political Mind. Why You Can't Understand 21st-Century Politics with an 18th-Century Brain* (New York: Viking, 2008), in which contested morality is located in the domain of political conflict.

**7** Understanding religious conflict in this way takes away the debate as to whether a conflict is or is not religiously motivated or "ausschließlich auf religiösen Gegensätzen beruhte" (the research question addressed by Hahn, *Gewalt und religiöser Konflikt*; see n. 3). For an example in which personality is a contested domain see the chapter by Pauline Allen; and for an example where conflict is itself contested see the chapter by David Sim in this volume.

**8** First outlined by Terry Donaldson, "Concluding Reflections," in: *Religious Rivalries and the Struggle for Success in Caesarea Maritima*, ed. Terence L. Donaldson, SCJ 8 (Waterloo, Ont.: Wilfrid Laurier University Press, 2000), 331–39; summarised by Richard Ascough, "The Canadian Society of Biblical Studies' Religious Rivalries Seminar: Retrospection, Reflection and Retroversion," *Studies in Religion/Sciences Religieuses* 32/1–2 (2003): 153–73 at 158.

that it refers only to conflict that occurs between or within religious groups,[9] it does help us to distinguish, on one level, between the potentially blurred categories of conflict and competition.[10] When we apply our primary definition, competition turns into conflict at the point when a particular domain/s become/s contested. Where this becomes complicated is that the two categories are not necessarily exclusive. If we consider the case of two religions competing for converts in the religious marketplace, the two groups can be focused towards each other in conflict, while simultaneously maintaining an outward focus towards potential converts as competitive rivals. Similarly we should be open to the possibility that two distinct religions or two groups within the same religion could cooperate in some areas (e.g., charity), while being in conflict in others (e.g., ideology and/or ritual). In this model only coexistence and conflict are mutually exclusive, in that coexistence implies that the religious groups involved engage in no direct interaction.

These considerations require us to clarify two aspects of our definition: the agents involved; and what precisely identifies a conflict as religious. While individuals may be the chief protagonists, the coupling of religion with conflict implies that the agents involved are not individuals, but collective individuals, i.e., groups or communities. Martyrs or religious leaders, for instance, self-identify and operate as part of a larger system. If we accept this premise, then we can posit on the basis of the studies already mentioned that the agents in religious conflict are two or more groups that derive from identifiably separate religions, separate factions within the same religion (that result from splintering, i.e., sectarianism), the same faction within a religion (where splintering has not yet occurred – and may or may not, in fact, eventuate), and secular authority, the latter of which may also wield religious authority. Our definition of the second aspect (what identifies a conflict as religious) is related to how one defines religion and determines how broadly or narrowly we focus our investigation. At the beginning of this section we talked about the coupling of religion and conflict and it is this view, we suggest, that offers a useful definition that is not restrictive. Conflict is

**9** One of the parties drawn into religious conflict, particularly as a target when violence or the threat of violence is involved, can be secular authority (the government/state). See, e.g., the case of the Justus Freemen described by Jean Rosenfeld, "The Justus Freemen Standoff: The Importance of the Analysis of Religion in Avoiding Violent Outcomes," in: *Millennialism, Persecution, and Violence: Historical Cases*, ed. Catherine Wessinger (New York: Syracuse University Press, 2000), 323–46.

**10** Blurring between competition and conflict is prevalent, e.g., in the Christian cult of the saints as demonstrated by a variety of case studies in *An Age of Saints? Power, Conflict and Dissent in Early Medieval Christianity*, eds. Peter Sarris, Matthew Dal Santo, and Phil Booth, Brill's Series on the Early Middle Ages (Leiden: Brill, 2011).

religious when a conflict occurs in which religion is also involved. This avoids questions of the nature: when is a conflict religious and when is it political/ethnic, since it allows that a conflict can be both. It also avoids questions about degree, that is, whether a conflict is primarily religious or primarily political/ethnic, since under this definition all conflicts are religious in which, whether in large degree or small, religion is involved.

To sum up, then, for the purposes of studying this phenomenon in as open a way as possible religious conflict can be said to occur when the following conditions are satisfied:

(1) two or more collective agents are involved and the agents derive, for example, from separate religions, separate factions within the same religion, from within the same faction in the same religion, and/or secular authority;
(2) a domain – e.g., ideology/morality, power, personality, space/place, group identity – is contested, singly or in combination;
(3) there are enabling conditions – e.g., political, social, economic, cultural and psychological; and
(4) religion is involved (the degree to which it is involved is deemed irrelevant).

# 2 Recent theoretical approaches

## 2.1 Contemporary theories and approaches

The approaches to religious conflict are diverse and determined to some degree by the chronological focus. Studies of contemporary religious conflict emerge for the most part from the disciplines of religious studies and the social sciences and focus on a variety of aspects: root causes (thoughtworld/ideology); enabling conditions; and the important corollary of conflict, resolution/reconciliation. Sara Savage and her team at Cambridge University, for instance, apply cognitive psychology to understanding neurological causes of fundamentalisms and to developing educational programs that encourage the use of different brain pathways that lead to greater religious tolerance.[11] Similarly, Catherine Wessinger, Jean Rosenfeld, and other experts in New Religious Movements (NRMs), partic-

**11** See, e.g., Sara Savage, "Four Lessons from the Study of Fundamentalism and Psychology of Religion," *Journal of Strategic Security* 4 (2011): 131–50; Ead., "Towards Integrative Solutions to Disputes between Conservative and Liberal Christians," *Journal of Psychology and Christianity* 27 (2008): 320–28; and Sara Savage and José Liht, "Mapping Fundamentalism: The Psychology of Religion as a Sub-discipline in the Understanding of Religiously Motivated Violence," *Archive for the Psychology of Religion/Archiv für Religionspsychologie* 30 (2008): 75–91. A similar application of psychology is reflected in Strozier et al., *The Fundamentalist Mindset* (n. 1).

ularly within the United States, have successfully employed their understanding of the elements common in the internal thoughtworld of millenialist religious movements to avert violence in a recent NRM-state conflict.[12] As this particular field has continued to develop, new and broader questions are being asked about the relationship between New Religious Movements and violence, focusing not just on groups that inflict, but also on groups that are the targets of violence.[13] An approach that derives from sociology and the Frankfurt school of Critical Theory, epitomised by Rudolf Siebert,[14] addresses the question of resolution from a different perspective. In this view religion is intimately linked with economic and social struggle,[15] of which religious conflict, resulting in pain and suffering, is an inevitable product. Conflict Theory, applied by Geoffrey Dunn in this volume, is an older sociological theory aligned with this approach. One outcome of recent developments in Critical Theory of relevance to our focus in this volume is a negative critique of Rational-Choice Theory, a theory based in economics and mathematics, which underpins Rodney Stark's controversial analysis of the rise and success of Christianity.[16]

An interest in the origins of religious conflict, coupled with its resolution, is the focus of a different group of scholars, who approach these aspects from the combined perspectives of historical and gender studies and the political and social sciences.[17] This work is of particular interest in that, like the research of Sara Savage and contemporary psychologists, it is aimed at providing a theoretical and practical framework from empirical studies.[18] One aspect that the contribu-

12 See the articles in *Millennialism, Persecution, and Violence: Historical Cases*, ed. Catherine Wessinger (New York: Syracuse University Press, 2000), especially Jean Rosenfeld, "A Brief History of Millenialism and Suggestions for a New Paradigm for Use in Critical Incidents: A Presentation to the Los Angeles Police Department," 347–351; and Ead., "The Justus Freemen Standoff" (n. 9).

13 See the articles in Lewis, *Violence and New Religious Movements* (n. 5).

14 See Rudolf Siebert, *Manifesto of the Critical Theory of Society and Religion*, SCSS, 3 vols (Leiden: Brill, 2010).

15 See Siebert, *Manifesto*, vol. 1, 11: "...the critical theory is a social theory, which understands modern civil society as an antagonistic totality of non-equivalent exchange processes." Siebert's central concern in these three volumes is to address the consequences of these processes, pain and suffering.

16 Rodney Stark, *The Rise of Christianity: A Sociologist Reconsiders* (Princeton, NJ: Princeton University Press, 1996); critique by George Lundskow, "The Concept of Choice in the Rise of Christianity: A Critique of Rational-Choice Theory," in Warren S. Goldstein, *Marx, Critical Theory, and Religion: A Critique of Rational Choice*, SCSS 6 (Leiden: Brill, 2006), 223–48.

17 See Eynikel and Ziaka, *Religion and Conflict* (n. 1).

18 Erik Eynikel, "Introduction," in: ibid., xv. Eynikel points out here the tendency in general debate concerning religious conflict to either neglect or overemphasise beliefs and discourses, in

tors to this manual emphasise is the importance to the three monotheistic religions of canonical texts,[19] an element in religious conflict that is theorised within social psychology via social dominance theory and intratextuality.[20] The discipline of ritual studies offers an entirely different way of approaching the phenomenon of religious conflict. The interdisciplinary project that gave rise to the volume *Ritual, Media, and Conflict*[21] set out to address a gap in existing research, "ritual's capacity for mediating or provoking conflict," with specific reference to the way in which "media technologies are changing the dynamics of conflict and shaping strategies for deploying rituals and ritualized processes in situations of conflict."[22] Not all ritual is religious – ritualisation also marks the human life cycle – and not all of the chapters in their collaborative volume might seem at first glance to couple conflict with religion. Religion constantly lurks, however, in the background. Importantly, this study points out the utility of maintaining a broad definition of religion, which allows the drawing into consideration of aspects of conflict that might not otherwise be acknowledged to have religious relevance. A separate conference organised by Robert Langer, one of the participants in the Ritual, Media, and Conflict project, the results of which were published in a special issue of the journal *Die Welt des Islams*, demonstrates the interrelatedness of some of these theoretical approaches to the study of one aspect of religious conflict, authoritative discourse.[23] Of special interest here is the application to Islam of the categories "orthodoxy" and "heterodoxy" (heresy), categories

---

addition to emphasising only the destructive force of religion (e.g., violence, and religion as the cause of conflict).

**19** Eynikel and Ziaka, *Religion and Conflict*, 17–48. For further discussion of the role of canonicity in relation to heterodoxy/orthodoxy and social conflict see the chapter by Pierluigi Piovanelli in this volume.

**20** Outlined in Joanna Collicutt, "Bringing the Academic Discipline of Psychology to Bear on the Study of the Bible," *JTS* n.s. 63 (2012): 1–48 at 29.

**21** For the different disciplines from which the participants draw, which include cultural and social anthropology, communications, theatre, performance studies, sociology, art history, and archaeology, as well as religious studies, see Grimes et al., *Ritual*, ix–xvi. The research, jointly funded by the Netherlands Organization for Scientific Research and the German Research Foundation, is the result of collaboration between the Faculty of Religious Studies at Radboud University Nijmegen and the Ritual Dynamics Collaborative Research Center at the University of Heidelberg.

**22** Grimes et al., *Ritual*, 4–5.

**23** See, e.g., Jan Scholz, Tobias Selge, Max Stille, and Johannes Zimmermann, "Listening Communities? Some Remarks on the Construction of Religious Authority in Islamic Podcasts," *Die Welt des Islams* 48 (2008): 458–509.

previously thought to be Eurocentric and invalid outside of a Christian context.[24] In their contribution Langer and his co-author, Udo Simon, review previous criticisms and theorise about the applicability of categories of right and wrong belief as analytical tools, producing an important position piece for not just Islamic studies but assessment of this phenomenon in other religions.[25] Although they draw no explicit connection, their approach aligns with the theories of psychologists concerning a constituent element in conflict, in-group and out-group dynamics.[26]

## 2.2 Approaches to religious conflict in the period 50–850 CE

Some of these same theoretical approaches appear in recent studies of religious conflict in the period that stretches from the beginnings of Christianity to the beginnings of Islam. Rightly or wrongly – we will discuss this in section 3 – until recently a distinction has for the most part been drawn between the phenomenon in the period before the emperor Constantine the Great (that is, before Christianity was recognised by the state as a religion) and the period after Constantine (c. 313 CE onwards). This division goes hand in hand with the view that Christianity related to other religions differently before and after this defining event, the earlier period being characterised by rivalry and struggle for success, the later period by a position of dominance in regard to other religions. For approaches specific to this first period we turn again to the work of the Religious Rivalries Seminar of the Canadian Society of Biblical Studies,[27] in addition to the

---

**24** This is the view from the perspective of contemporary Islamic Studies. See Robert Langer and Udo Simon, "The Dynamics of Orthodoxy and Heterodoxy. Dealing with Divergence in Muslim Discourses and Islamic Studies," *Die Welt des Islams* 48 (2008): 273–88 at 273. That the categories are not unique to Christianity or Eurocentric is demonstrated by John B. Henderson, *The Construction of Orthodoxy and Heresy: Neo-Confucian, Islamic, Jewish and Early Christian Patterns* (Albany, NY: State University of New York, 1998), who documents the commonalities between the heresiological and heresiographical trends in these four religions, with which discourses in Hinduism and Buddhism also coincide. The discourses he analyses emerge from the Rabbinic Jewish tradition (1st century CE onwards), early Christianity (4th century CE onwards), eleventh-century Sunni Islam, and the Ch'eng Chu school of Neo-Confucianism in early imperial China.

**25** Langer and Simon, "The Dynamics of Orthodoxy and Heterodoxy."

**26** See Collicutt, "Bringing the Academic Discipline," 28; and Ifat Maoz, "Social-Cognitive Mechanisms in Reconciliation," in: *From Conflict Resolution to Reconciliation*, ed. Yaacov Bar-Siman-Tov (Oxford: Oxford University Press, 2004), 225–37 at 231–32.

**27** Published in three collective volumes: Terence L. Donaldson, ed., *Religious Rivalries and the Struggle for Success in Caesarea Maritima*, SCJ 8 (Waterloo, Ont.: Wilfrid Laurier University Press,

research of Peter Lampe,[28] and the recent critique of Rodney Stark's thesis by George Lundskow among others.[29] It is important to note that until very recently religious conflict per se has rarely been a topic of investigation with regard to this earlier time period and thus has received little in the way of focused theoretical reflection.[30] More commonly individual or tangential aspects of this phenomenon have been the topic of investigation, such as religious polemic (particularly apologetics and *adversus*-literature), the parting of the ways between Christianity and Judaism, martyrdom, tolerance, legislation about religion, the relationship between religion and politics, and persecution.

What is significant about the Religious Rivalries Seminar is that it approached – primarily from the disciplines of social history, New Testament studies and archaeology – the topic of religious rivalry in the first two centuries of the Common Era from the perspectives of Christianity and the urban social setting, utilising specific urban case studies – Caesarea Maritima in Palestine, Smyrna and Sardis, and North Africa – to explore this phenomenon.[31] Within their model of the religious marketplace, derived from Critical Theory and its antecedents,[32] conflict is not their primary focus. Given their interest in Christianity and

2000); Richard Ascough, ed., *Religious Rivalries and the Struggle for Success in Sardis and Smyrna*, SCJ 14 (Waterloo, Ont.: Wilfrid Laurier University Press, 2005); and Leif Vaage, ed., *Religious Rivalries in the Early Roman Empire and the Rise of Christianity*, SCJ 18 (Waterloo, Ont.: Wilfrid Laurier University Press, 2006). The Seminar ran from 1995 to 2003.

**28** Peter Lampe, *From Paul to Valentinus: Christians at Rome in the First Two Centuries*, trans. Michael Steinhauser from 2nd German edn., revised and updated by Peter Lampe (Minneapolis, MN: Fortress Press, 2003).

**29** Lundskow, "The Concept of Choice" (n. 15). Lundskow's is not the only critical response to Stark's thesis, which are numerous, but it serves as representative. Stark's thesis is also consciously addressed by the four essays in Part 3 of Vaage, *Religious Rivalries and the Rise of Christianity.*

**30** More common is a preoccupation with religious pluralism, identity, and competition or cohabitation as seen in a number of projects in which Nicole Belayche has been a key participant: e.g., "Cohabitations et contacts religieux dans les mondes hellénistique et romain" (Centre Glotz, 2007–2010), and the resultant publication, *L'oiseau et le poisson: cohabitations religieuses dans les mondes grec et romain*, eds. Nicole Belayche and Jean-Daniel Dubois, Religions dans l'histoire 6 (Paris: Presses de l'Université Paris–Sorbonne, 2011). Cf. Nicole Belayche and Simon C. Mimouni, eds., *Entre lignes de partage et territoires de passage. Les identités religeuses dans les mondes grec et romain: "Paganisms", "judaïsmes," "christianismes"*, Collection de la Revue des Études Juives 47 (Peeters: Leuven, 2009).

**31** See Ascough, "Retrospection," 155–56. As Donaldson, *Religious Rivalries in Caesarea Maritima*, 3, points out, their interest was primarily in religions not as isolated entities, but as social and urban phenomena.

**32** Borrowed from John North, "The Development of Religious Pluralism," in: *The Jews Among Pagans and Christians in the Roman Empire*, eds. Judith Lieu, John North, and Tessa Rajak

in the period in question, their primary focus is the struggle for success.[33] In this context, urban societies are viewed as plurireligious and conflict is viewed as one of four possible modes of religious interaction.[34] A significant finding to emerge from the detailed case studies was the predominance of evidence of co-existence and cooperation, and the slender evidence for competition and conflict. In Caesarea Maritima, for instance, there was no clear evidence of sustained conflict with "outsiders," but clear evidence of Christians competing with one another.[35] At Smyrna evidence for competition and conflict was greater, but again, in many cases was found to occur within a designated group.[36] From the study of North Africa what again stood out was evidence of inner-group conflict within a wider context of religious coexistence.[37]

These findings are matched in large part by those of Peter Lampe for the same time period (the first two centuries CE) based on another specific urban case study, Rome. There, through application of a social-historical analysis, the elicited conflict is identified as inner-group, in which the contested domain is charity and the enabling condition social stratification.[38] Fractionation, a term which Lampe applies to this period with reference to the natural emergence and development in Rome of independently worshipping Christian groups based around house-churches (*tituli*) – that is, the religion is comprised of small

(London: Routledge, 1992), 174–93. See Donaldson, *Religious Rivalries in Caesarea Maritima*, 5–6. The metaphor of the religious marketplace implies cost-benefit analysis, an element in Rational-Choice Theory utilised by Rodney Stark (see the summary of this theory at Lundskow, "The Concept of Choice," 225–29), while notions of religious competition and struggle derive ultimately from Marx, Durkheim and Weber.

**33** Ascough, "Retrospection," 157–58.

**34** Note that the concept of cohabitation adopted by Nicole Belayche and her collaborators is not inconsistent with the four "modalities of interaction" proposed here, cohabitation implying simply that the religions inhabit the same social and geographic space. It is also important to note that underlying the marketplace model adopted by the Religious Rivalries Seminar is an anthropological paradigm that views religion in the Hellenistic and republican periods as embedded in the domains of politics and kinship, whereas the social shift that occurred with the rise of the Roman empire was accompanied by a shift to religious pluralism, which enabled choice. See Donaldson, *Religious Rivalries in Caesarea Maritima*, 5–6.

**35** Ascough, "Retrospection," 158–59.

**36** Ascough, "Retrospection," 165.

**37** Ascough, "Retrospection," 167. For a similar location of conflict in this period within a single religious group (between two factions, within the same faction or between a group and its founder) see the chapters by Ian Elmer, Michael Theophilos and A.M. Smith, and David Sim in this volume.

**38** Lampe, *From Paul to Valentinus*, 90–99.

units rather than unified,[39] offers another approach of interest to the question of pre- and post-Constantinian conflict, since it implies an organic movement in the first centuries of Christianity from scattered, independently worshipping groups without any central control to the development of centralisation and unification. Of further interest is his thesis that fractionation is associated with social status – fractionation is greater when the social status of the individuals who adhere to a religion, in this instance Christianity, is lower; conversely, agglomeration and unification increase in relation to the increase in social status of its constituent members.[40] Lampe further associates fractionation with tolerance of other theological opinions (ideologies),[41] and views as an enabling condition in increasing unification the development of monarchical episcopacy and presbyterial governance.[42]

Lundskow, like the scholars of the Religious Rivalries Seminar, returns to the question of success, but takes a longer-term view of the process. Appealing to class- and culture-based theory – an approach from within sociology – Lundskow argues that the success of (orthodox) Christianity was due to external politics, not to the intrinsic quality of its beliefs or membership criteria (the marketplace analogy).[43] As Christianity rose gradually, paganism died gradually, and Christianity succeeded because it "became a direct expression of the power interests of the ruling class," eventually becoming a religious monopoly. A contributing factor to its success was its assimilation, rather than replacement or destruction of traditional pagan cultural traditions.[44] There was nothing distinct about Christianity till much later; instead there was a great deal of religious blending.[45] This theory has indirect implications of interest to the question of religious conflict, particularly in light of the recent paradigm shift in archaeological and historical scholarship concerning early post-Constantinian developments in inter-religious relations, namely that the Christian discourse of temple (and synagogue) destruction obscures a more eirenic reality.[46] It also aligns with

**39** The phenomenon is discussed in detail in Lampe, *From Paul to Valentinus*, 357–408 (Part 5).

**40** See Lampe, *From Paul to Valentinus*, 372.

**41** Lampe, *From Paul to Valentinus*, 385–96.

**42** Lampe, *From Paul to Valentinus*, 397–408.

**43** Lundskow, "The Concept of Choice," 224.

**44** Ibid.

**45** Lundskow, "The Concept of Choice," 230–39.

**46** See, e.g., Jitse Dijkstra, "The Fate of the Temples in Late Antique Egypt," in: *The Archaeology of Late Antique 'Paganism'*, eds. Luke Lavan and Michael Mulryan, Late Antique Archaeology 7 (Leiden: Brill, 2011), 389–436. We reached a similar conclusion in regard to Antioch in Wendy Mayer and Pauline Allen, *The Churches of Syrian Antioch (300–638 CE)*, Late Antique History and Religion 5 (Leuven: Peeters, 2012).

recent scholarship on identity differentiation and boundary-setting between Christianity and its parent religion, Judaism.[47] Of more direct relevance is Lundskow's theorising of the role in Christianity's success of spirituality – a unifying *nomos* (accepted set of ideals and morals) – and social conflict. *Nomos* is viewed as holding a social group together during intolerance and persecution, but is inseparable from class and struggle.[48] Lundskow's approach is in the end a Critical Theory approach, similar to that of Siebert's analysis of contemporary religion.

Among a cluster of recent research projects on the topic that originate in Spain, the previously defining watershed of 313 CE runs strong even when the phenomenon (and its absence) is reframed using the categories religious "tolerance" and "intolerance." The project *Conflicto y convivencia en el cristianismo primitivo: retórica religiosa y debates escatológicos* (2009),[49] for instance, adopts a paradigm of religious plurality and tolerance for the first three centuries CE and of religious coercion associated with intolerance from the fourth to seventh centuries. The same paradigm, which views Christianity's exclusivist character coupled with its empowerment in the fourth century as a driving force behind Christianity's interaction with other religions in the period after 313 CE, informs the joint project of Mar Marcos and José Fernandez Ubiña: *Multiculturalismo, convivencia religiosa y conflicto en la Antigüedad tardía (ss. III–VII)* (2007–2009),[50] funded in a second phase: *Estrategias clásicas y cristianas para la resolución de conflictos en la Antigüedad Tardía* (2010–2012).[51] In all of these proj-

---

47 See, e.g., Judith Lieu, *Christian Identity in the Jewish and Graeco-Roman World* (Oxford: Oxford University Press, 2004); and Daniel Boyarin, *Borderlines: The Partition of Judaeo-Christianity*, Divinations: Rereading Late Antique Religion (Philadelphia, PA: University of Pennsylvania Press, 2004). Boyarin appeals to wave theory to describe a range of Judaisms (and Christianities) more closely or distantly related along a continuum.

48 Lundskow, "The Concept of Choice," 243–46.

49 Led by Mercedes López Salvá, it involved eleven researchers from Universidad Complutense Madrid, Universidad de Cantabria, Universidad de Granada, Universidad de León, Consejo Superior de Investigaciones Cientificas (Spain), and Harvard University (Department of Classics, and the Divinity School). See Mercedes López Salvá, ed., *De cara al Más Allá. Conflicto, convivencia y asimilación de modelos paganos en el cristianismo antiguo* (Zarazoga: Libros Pórtico, 2010).

50 See their outline of the project in Mar Marcos and José Fernández Ubiña, "Multiculturalismo, convivencia religiosa y conflicto en la Antigüedad Tardía," in: *La investigación sobre la Antigüedad Tardía en España: estado de los estudios y nuevas perspectivas*, ed. M.V. Escribano Paño, Mainake 31 (Univ. Málaga, 2009), 187–96. It generated two sub-projects, each led by one of the investigators: *Pluridad religiosa y conflicto en el Imperio romano (s. III–IV): convivencia y exclusión* (Marcos); and *Diversidad cultural y uniformidad religiosa en el Antigüedad Tardía. La genealogía de la intolerancia cristiana* (Ubiña).

51 Anticipated in Marcos and Ubiña, "Multiculturalismo," 189.

ects the topic is pursued through the disciplines of philology, history and literary studies. While there is some theorising in the publications that have thus far resulted from the project, conscious reflection is focused for the most part on the validity and definition of the categories tolerance and intolerance.[52]

This same paradigm – that the period after 313 CE took a coercive turn in state-religion and inter-religious relations characterised by violence – is operative in two ground-breaking monographs by Michael Gaddis and Tom Sizgorich, respectively.[53] The approach in both studies is primarily historical and concerned with discourse. Gaddis appeals to a shift in the ideologies of martyrdom and resistance to explain the violence that occurred at a variety of levels when Christianity became a universalising power.[54] Sizgorich applies social scientific theories of inter-communal boundary construction and policing to the late Roman and early Islamic worlds as a means of understanding "why militant forms of piety...became such crucial resources for communal self-fashioning among early Christian and early Muslim communities."[55] In dividing his study into two parts – post-Constantinian Christianity and early Islam – he in effect expands the paradigm to include a new defining shift in inter-/intra-religious relations of particular relevance (the middle decades of the seventh century and the

**52** See Mar Marcos, "'He Forced with Gentleness': The Emperor Julian's Attitude to Religious Coercion," *AntT* 17 (2009): 191–204; Ead., "De la convivencia a la exclusión: Reflexiones sobre el discurso de la tolerancia religiosa en el Cristianismo antiguo," in: *Actas del XII Congreso Español de Estudios Clásicos*, vol. 1 (Madrid: Ed. Clásicas, 2009), 631–37; Mar Marcos and Ramón Teja, eds., *Tolerancia e intolerancia religiosa en el Mediterráneo Antiguo. Temas y problemas*, thematic issue of *Bandue. Revista de la Sociedad Española de Ciencias de las Religiones* 2 (2008); José Fernández Ubiña and Mar Marcos, eds., *Libertad e intolerancia religiosa en el Imperio romano*, Instituto Universitario de Ciencias de las Religiones Anejo 18 (Madrid: Publicaciones Universidad Complutense de Madrid, 2007).

**53** Gaddis, *There is No Crime*; Sizgorich, *Violence and Belief* (n. 1). Shaw, *Sacred Violence* (n. 1), follows in their footsteps. Prior to the emergence of an interest in religious violence in the mid 2000s, the only previous analysis relating to this period was an isolated study from the 1970s: Timothy E. Gregory, *Vox Populi: Popular Opinion and Violence in the Religious Controversies in the Fifth Century A.D.* (Columbus, OH: The Ohio State University Press, 1979).

**54** See Gaddis, *There is No Crime*, xi: "...this study is not about institutions. It is, rather, about mentalities, the ideologies, moral postures, and emotional dispositions of violent actors, victims, critics, and observers. In these areas too the Christian Roman Empire laid down patterns and precedents. It saw the fruition of an ideology of martyrial resistance, and the transformation of martyrdom from commemoration of violence suffered to justification for violence inflicted – from dying for God to killing for God. Its emperors and bishops responded in turn by laying out a centrist ideology of coercive consensus that would be invoked time and again over the centuries by those in power..."

**55** Sizgorich, *Violence and Belief*, 4. The theories, introduced in Chapter 2 (esp. 48–51), are drawn from anthropology, sociology, and identity studies and centre on the role of narrative.

rise of Islam). To these studies can be added three different, very recent approaches to the phenomenon: Adam Schor's appeal to Social Network Theory to explain an enabling condition in religious conflict,[56] Tina Shepardson's application of theories from social geography to explore the contested domains of space and place,[57] and Beth Digeser's study that explores the less obvious role of non-polemical language and ideology as triggers for religious persecution.[58] The agency of seemingly ordinary language in violent conflict, in contrast to the more obviously inflammatory use of publicly-chanted slogans, is a topic raised by Brent Shaw in his recent monolithic historical and archaeological study of the "Donatist" controversy in North Africa.[59] An additional feature of this work is employment of the language of dissent, a development recently introduced by scholars of late antiquity in an attempt to avoid perpetuating the "orthodox/heterodox" discourse of the dominant literary sources.[60]

---

**56** Adam Schor, *Theodoret's People: Social Networks and Religious Conflict in Late Roman Syria*, TCH 48 (Berkeley–Los Angeles–London: University of California Press, 2011). Schor follows in the footsteps of Liz Clark's now classic analysis of the Origenist controversy: Elizabeth A. Clark, *The Origenist Controversy: The Cultural Construction of an Early Christian Debate* (Princeton, NJ: Princeton University Press, 1992).

**57** Christine Shepardson, *Controlling Contested Places: Fourth-Century Antioch and the Spatial Politics of Religious Controversy* (Berkeley: University of California Press, forthcoming). For an earlier exploration of some of the ideas now incorporated in Chapter 4, see Ead., "Controlling Contested Places: John Chrysostom's *Adversus Iudaeos* Homilies and the Spatial Politics of Religious Controversy," *JECS* 15 (2007): 483–516. For a similar project and approach see the chapter by Alan Cadwallader in this volume.

**58** Elizabeth DePalma Digeser, *A Threat to Public Piety: Christians, Platonists, and the Great Persecution* (Ithaca–London: Cornell University Press, 2012). Digeser sets out her approach in the Preface (ix) as follows: "What is the relationship between philosophical religious thought and violence? In attempting to understand religious violence, sociologists, and other social scientists often assume that material conditions and economic interests are the real motivations for violence directed against particular religious groups. If ideas make a difference at all we see them as rationalizations, justifications, or explanations for violence, not as motive forces in themselves. This book turns the conventional wisdom on its head, for it argues that ideas about correct ritual and metaphysical doctrine inspired people to bring about Rome's last and longest effort forcibly to repress Christianity. And it involves philosophers and theologians as the primary sources of these ideas even though they themselves never called for forcible repression of their doctrinal opponents..."

**59** See Shaw, *Sacred Violence*, 409–89 (Chapters 9–10).

**60** See, e.g., Guy Stroumsa, "Religious Dynamics between Christians and Jews in Late Antiquity (312–640)," in: *Cambridge History of Christianity*, eds. Augustine Casiday and Frederick W. Norris, vol. 2 (Cambridge: Cambridge University Press, 2007), 149–72; Sarris et al., *An Age of Saints?*; Chapter 6 ("The Dilemma of Dissent") referring to theological conflicts, in: Jonathon Conant, *Staying Roman: Conquest and Identity in Africa and the Mediterranean, 439–700*, Cambridge studies in medieval life and thought: fourth series 82 (Cambridge–New York: Cam-

# 3 Shifting paradigms, old problems, and new questions

Studies of religious conflict in the period between the emergence of Christianity and of Islam as religions have been conducted predominantly from the perspective of Christianity,[61] and the studies offered in the present volume are no exception. It is this perspective that is largely responsible for the interpretive categories heterodoxy/orthodoxy and for the differentiated view of inter-religious relations in the periods pre- and post-Constantine and post-rise-of-Islam. Lurking behind the first is the perennial issue of the bias of the surviving sources, and the historical forces that led to the transmission of some and the suppression or dwindling into obscurity of others. Lurking behind the second is the persistence of a mode of interpretation that views certain moments in history (in this case, the birth and death of Christ, Constantine's adoption of Christianity, the fall of Rome, and the Arab conquest) as defining and disruptive.[62]

If the bias brought to the study of religious conflict in this period by the often unconscious wearing of "Christianity-coloured glasses" is proving more resistant to change, in other areas the paradigms that lie behind how this subject is approached are – in some cases, rapidly – undergoing alteration. As Richard Ascough notes, when the Religious Rivalries Seminar initially formulated their approach, in their adduction of "Christianity v. Judaism" as a model for rivalry they

bridge University Press, 2012); and Phil Booth, *Moschus, Sophronius, Maximus: Asceticism, Sacrament and Dissent at the End of Empire* (Berkeley: University of California Press, forthcoming). The same approach informs the third International Graduate Conference of The Center for Eastern Mediterranean Studies (CEMS) at Central European University, "Tradition and Transformation: Dissent and Consent in the Mediterranean," Budapest, May 31–June 1, 2013: "Taking into account the dynamic sociohistorical setting of religious and cultural processes, [this conference] seeks to approach the manner in which the permanently competing communities questioned, structured and performed their own beliefs and religious practices by disclosing heresies and shaping their orthodoxies." (cems.ceu.hu/cemsconference2013, accessed 13 March 2013, where the assumed focus is Judaism, Christianity, and Islam).

**61** This is even the case with Daniel Boyarin and a number of other Jewish scholars who analyse this period (e.g., Hagith Sivan), described by Steven Fine in his review of Hagith Sivan, *Palestine in Late Antiquity* (2008), *Review of Biblical Literature*, published online 10/17/2009, www.bookreviews.org, as viewing rabbinic sources through "Christianity-colored glasses." For a discussion of this problem see the lengthy review article by Jörg Rüpke, "Early Christianity out of, and in, Context," *Journal of Roman Studies* 99 (2009): 182–93.

**62** For a discussion of the influence of Edward Gibbon and other historians in this regard see Clifford Ando, "Narrating Decline and Fall," and Stefan Rebenich, "Late Antiquity in Modern Eyes," in: *Blackwell Companion to Late Antiquity*, ed. Philip Rousseau (Oxford: Blackwell Publishers, 2009), 59–92.

were, as they subsequently realised, unduly influenced by the *adversus Judaeos* literary tradition.[63] Their recognition that this strand of Christian discourse was "as concerned with inner-Christian conflict and self-definition as with engaging with the 'other' in debate"[64] has in recent, as yet unpublished papers, been further refined into a thesis that removes the "other" from Christian discourse of this kind entirely.[65] What these scholars confirm is an increasing recognition that religious conflict that self-identifies – and was thus previously viewed – as inter-religious is now proving on careful analysis to be primarily intra-religious, dissolving the formerly pervasive oppositional dichotomies Christians and Jews, and Christians and pagans.[66] The note of caution the Religious Rivalries Seminar raised against reading such "rivalry" discourse as primarily concerned with self-definition,[67] on the other hand, reminds us of the importance of locating such discourse carefully within its cultural and social setting.

Another paradigm that is in the process of changing is the approach to the history of this period. The scholarship of late antiquity has done much to drive the shift from a predominantly economic and political view of history to a cultural, social one in which nations, societies, and communities do not rise and fall, but undergo transformation.[68] The impact of this change for how we now view the seventh century and the rise of Islam is profound. Driven by recent archaeological research, scholars now see events that were previously viewed as catastrophic (on the basis of literary sources) as effecting an administrative change in the eastern half of the Mediterranean world that had a relatively

---

**63** Ascough, "Retrospection," 167–68. Although, see the chapter by James McLaren in this volume on the origins of this discourse.

**64** Ibid., 168. See the chapter by Sarah Gador-Whyte in this volume, which arrives at a similar conclusion.

**65** So Douglas Boin, "How a Sectarian Dispute within Hellenistic 'Judaism' Gave Rise to the Late Antique World of 'Christians and Pagans'," informal talk, Dumbarton Oaks, Harvard University, Washington, DC, 10 October 2012 (to be published in *JECS*); and Ulrich Volp, "Conflict or Consolidation: The *Apocriticus* by Macarius Magnes – a Pagan-Christian Slanging Match or Intra-Christian Validation?," paper delivered at the Annual Meeting of the North American Patristics Society, Chicago, 24–26 May 2012. Similar arguments concerning Christian discourse of this kind are presented by Stroumsa, "Religious Dynamics," 154; and Rebecca Lyman, "Heresiology: The Invention of 'Heresy' and 'Schism'," in: *Cambridge History of Christianity*, vol. 2, 296–314 at 296–97.

**66** To which, for the early Islamic period, we should now add as dichotomies to be treated with suspicion Muslims and Jews and Muslims and Christians.

**67** Ascough, "Retrospection," 168.

**68** See the chapters in *A Companion to Late Antiquity*, ed. Philip Rousseau, Blackwell Companions to the Ancient World (Oxford: Blackwell Publishers, 2009).

soft impact. Economies and trade, for the most part, continued to prosper.[69] This change in the historical view undermines the impression of conflict and apocalypse promoted by the dominant discourse[70] and aligns more closely with the findings of the Religious Rivalries Seminar regarding the prevalence of evidence for actual religious coexistence and cooperation, as well as Lundskow's thesis of transition and assimilation.[71] Collectively, these shifts in the way we view the phenomenon of religious conflict, the historical period, and the discourse undermine the paradigm of periodisation (that there are distinct differences in religious interaction before Constantine, after Constantine and following the advent of Islam). Behind this lurks other assumptions that also require reconsideration – namely, that polytheism ("paganism") is generally tolerant, while Christianity is exclusionist and intolerant, the latter linked to its requirement that adherents hold to a defined set of sacred truths (Christianity as a "religion of the book"). Similarly, Lampe's fractionation thesis implies a period of agglomeration and unification in the centuries before Constantine, while unification, centralisation, and religious dominance in the period after Constantine imply increasing inner-group conflict and sectarianism. The thesis of tolerance, of importance for how one views the first to third centuries CE, has with varied success for several decades been undergoing challenge.[72]

---

**69** See, e.g., *Money, Power and Politics in Early Islamic Syria: A Review of Current Debates*, ed. John Haldon, (Farnham: Aldershot, 2010); Alan Walmsley, "Economic Developments and the Nature of Settlement in the Towns and Countryside of Syria-Palestine, ca. 565–800 CE," *DOP* 61 (2007): 319–52; and Jodi Magness, *The Archaeology of the Early Islamic Settlement in Palestine* (Winona Lake, IN: Eisenbrauns, 2003). These works provide radically revised chronologies for this period, as well as demonstrating how previous assumptions of decline distorted the reading of extant ceramic and numismatic evidence.

**70** For the influence and role of apocalyptic discourse see the chapters by Sarah Gador-Whyte and Damien Casey in this volume.

**71** This holds true for the period from the fourth to eighth centuries. As Daniel King notes in his review of Sizgorich, *Violence and Belief* (*Bryn Mawr Classical Review* 2010.08.36), despite the author's paradigm of the period after Constantine as being characterised by violence, "it is... clear that inter-communal religious violence was not a particularly common or easily conjured phenomenon...'peaceful coexistence and intercommunal exchange was the norm rather than the exception' (201)." See also the chapter by Bronwen Neil in this volume regarding the early response by Christians to Islam.

**72** Starting, e.g., with John A. North, "Religious Toleration in Republican Rome," *Proceedings of the Cambridge Philological Society* 25/5 (1979): 85–103; and Peter Garnsey, "Religious Toleration in Classical Antiquity," in: *Persecution and Toleration. Papers Read at the Twenty-Second Summer Meeting and the Twenty-Third Winter Meeting of the Ecclesiastical History Society*, ed. W.J. Shiels, Studies in Church History 21 (Oxford: Blackwell, 1984), 1–27. For more recent discussion see the articles in Marcos and Teja, *Tolerancia e intolerancia*; and in *Politiche religiose nel mondo antico e tardoantico: poteri e indirizzi, forme del controllo, idee e prassi di tolleranza. Atti del convegno*

To sum up, the very language that scholars of this period use to discuss religious conflict – for example, dissent, struggle, rivalry, success, triumph, resistance, suppression, coercion – reflects a variety of underlying assumptions about the character of different religions and how they (including secular authority) interacted. As we seek a deeper understanding of this topic, awareness of those assumptions and the larger paradigms with which they are associated is clearly critical. Locating the gap between the discourse promoted by our sources and what we can retrieve concerning what actually occurred – no easy feat in itself – emerges as another important consideration, while approaches to the issue from the point of view of boundary setting and identity formation raise the question – "What conflict?" – from the perspective of the individual, not the community. The warnings of the Religious Rivalries Seminar, and now also Jörg Rüpke,[73] about neglect of the social and cultural context of conflict are in respect to all of these issues particularly apposite. One wonders whether taking the definition that we propose and viewing religious conflict in this period from the perspective of contested domains, tracing the priority accorded to different domains in different locations over the progression of time,[74] might not offer a way forward that avoids the problems of periodisation and takes many, if not all, of these issues into consideration. This would help us to answer one question that previous approaches raise: where conflict sits within the evolution of a religion – if in the context of conflict evolution is, in the first instance, a valid model.

Comparison of approaches to contemporary religious conflict and to the same phenomenon in the period from 50 to 850 CE helps also to highlight in the case of the latter both the narrowness of focus to date and the lack of adequate theorisation. The mechanisms involved in the resolution of religious conflict and the role of religion in reconciliation, for instance, prevalent in studies of contemporary religious conflict, are aspects scarcely addressed in analysis of this earlier period.[75] Similarly, the role of both media and ritual, the latter of which has broad potential, has received scant attention.[76] In relation to both

*internazionale di studi, Firenze, 24–26 settembre 2009*, eds. Giovanni A. Cecconi and Chantal Gabrielli, Munera 33 (Bari: Edipuglia, 2011), esp. Barbara Scardigli, "Tolleranza religiosa di Costanzo II?," 275–86.

**73** Rüpke, "Early Christianity out of, and in, Context" (n. 61).

**74** An approach taken in the chapter by Pauline Allen in this volume, who applies it to a single geographic focus.

**75** A rare exception is phase two of the project led by Mar Marcos and José Fernández Ubiña, referenced in section 2.2 above (nn. 49–50), of which the results have yet to be published. See also the chapter by Ray Laird in this volume.

**76** An exception in the area of media is the chapter by Wendy Mayer in this volume.

the contemporary world and the early Christian/late antique/early Islamic past, on the other hand, studies of religious conflict have largely ignored its expression as a rural phenomenon. How does religious conflict – and, indeed, does it – impact rural dwellers and rural communities? Does the phenomenon differ significantly in a rural environment?[77] So far, to a large degree it has been explored as a phenomenon germane to the urban context.[78] In both fields, too, the focus on violence (one extreme of religious conflict) obscures broader questions about what occurs before or apart from violence: the mechanisms at play in how conflict originates in the first instance, how it manifests in its early stages, the phenomenon of splintering into sub-groups (sectarianism) within a religion, and precisely what factors are operative in conflict escalation and de-escalation. Can – and should – religious conflict be viewed as something that occurs on a sliding scale? Or is this yet another model that is restrictive? These are only some of the many questions that arise. In regard to understanding the phenomenon as it manifested in the period between the origins of Christianity and the origins of Islam, we have in many respects progressed only a short distance beyond the beginning. In the range of approaches they pursue, the chapters in this volume both adopt some of the existing paradigms and attempt to push the boundaries a little further. In this respect they nudge us further towards opening up our understanding of the mechanisms at play when religion and conflict come together.

---

**77** Here we except study of New Religious Movements that form their own isolated rural communities (e.g., the Justus Freemen, and Branch Davidians), referring rather to rural communities whose rationale is social, political and/or economic.

**78** Donaldson, *Religious Rivalries in Caesarea Maritima*, 3, in arguing the case for an urban focus acknowledges that religion was by no means restricted to the city, but continues: "the development, spread and interaction of religious movements took place primarily in urban settings in the Greco-Roman world...It was in the city that one found the necessary concentration of people and resources to support a religious infrastructure..."

Ian J. Elmer

# Setting the Record Straight at Galatia: Paul's *Narratio* (Gal 1:13 – 2:14) as Response to the Galatian Conflict

People who have even a passing familiarity with the Pauline corpus tend to know four things about Paul: (1) that he experienced a conversion on the road to Damascus; (2) that he became a missionary and apostle to the Gentiles; (3) that he was a figure of controversy; and (4) that he wrote letters. Furthermore, they have an instinctive sense that these four features are somehow linked – that is, that Paul's sometimes divisive role in the nascent Christian movement as *the* apostle to the Gentiles resulted from the combination of these aspects of his personal story. This intuition is not without foundation, for in his letter to the Galatians – one of his earliest – Paul writes a remarkable autobiographical *narratio*, an ancient rhetorical device, which serves to yoke his call to be *the* apostle to the Gentiles with his conversion experience and his subsequent conflicts with other members of the Christian communities in Judaea, Syria and Galatia (Gal 1:13 – 2:14).[1] This linkage further seems to imply that it was his peculiar understanding of the import of his conversion and call that stood at the heart of the conflicts described in Galatians.

Although commentators differ about the exact details of the situation that occasioned Paul's letter to the churches in Galatia, all agree that Paul wrote to counter what he considered to be a significant conflict with rival missionaries who were disturbing his Gentile converts at Galatia.[2] Traditionally these interlopers have been called "Judaisers," primarily on the basis of Paul's own language, which alludes to similar opponents who espoused a Law-observant gospel and

---

1 What makes Galatians so significant for understanding Paul's place in the early Church is that it may be the very first of our extant New Testament writings and, therefore, provides our first glimpse of the events that shaped Paul's life and mission. For the early dating of Galatians see, for example, James D.G. Dunn, *A Commentary on the Epistle to the Galatians*, BNTC (London: A&C Black, 1993), 19; and James L. Martyn, *Galatians: A New Translation with Introduction and Commentary*, AB 33a (New York: Doubleday, 1997), 19 – 20. Compare Ben Witherington III, *Grace in Galatia: A Commentary on Paul's Letter to the Galatians* (London: T&T Clark, 2004), 8 – 13, who argues that Galatians must be dated no earlier than 49 CE and no later than 53 – 54 CE (his preferred dating of 1 Corinthians).

2 See the surveys of the competing theories offered by Martyn, *Galatians*, 117 – 26; E. Earle Ellis, "Paul and His Opponents," in: *Christianity, Judaism and Other Greco-Roman Cults*, ed. Jacob Neusner (Leiden: E.J. Brill, 1975); and Francis Watson, *Paul, Judaism and the Gentiles: A Sociological Approach*, SNTSMS 56 (Cambridge: Cambridge University Press, 1986), 59 – 72.

had previously tried to "force the Gentiles [those who had converted to the Jesus Movement at Syrian Antioch] to live like Jews" (τὰ ἔθνη ἀναγκάζεις ἰουδαΐζειν Gal 2:14); that is, to adopt adherence to the Mosaic Law (Gal 3:10), including the practice of circumcision (Gal 5:2–4; 6:12–13), as well as the observance of the Sabbath and the Jewish feast days (Gal 4:8–11).[3]

As to the basis of the rival missionaries' warrant, they appear to have resorted to two avenues of authority. First, they apparently appealed to scripture, particularly the story of the Abrahamic covenant (Gal 3:6–29; 4:21–31), at which the institution of circumcision was imposed on God's chosen people (Gen 17:1–27). Second, the fact that Paul finds it necessary to detail the nature of his conversion and call and his relationship with the apostolic authorities at Jerusalem (Gal 1:11–2:14) may imply that these missionaries also claimed a direct commission from the Jerusalem church, while casting doubts on Paul's own claims to apostolic authority.

Few scholars are willing to accept that Paul's autobiographical reminiscences in Galatians 1:13–2:14 have an apologetic intent, and even fewer are willing to directly link the Judaisers to the earlier conflicts in Jerusalem and Antioch. Some commentators have suggested that Paul's apostleship was never an issue at Galatia.[4] Some have argued that the Judaisers did not even view themselves as opponents of Paul.[5] Others have even questioned the methods used to identify the missionaries as "Judaisers" with connections to Jerusalem and their message as a Jewish Christian "gospel," preferring less incendiary descriptions of Paul's Galatian rivals, such as "agitators," "troublemakers" or "influencers."[6]

---

3 This identification has a long history dating back to the second century, when Marcion first inferred that Paul's opponents were fanatical Jewish Christians from Jerusalem (Tertullian, *Adv. Marc.* 5.2–4). This view was further supported by both John Calvin and Martin Luther during the Reformation. Since then most Protestant exegetes have held to some form of this theory. See the discussion in Walt Russell, "Who Were Paul's Opponents in Galatia?," *BSac* 147 (1990): 329–50; Frank J. Matera, *Galatians*, SP 9 (Collegeville, MN: Liturgical Press, 1992), 7–11; and Richard N. Longenecker, *Galatians*, WBC 41 (Dallas, TX: Word Books, 1990), xliii, lii–lv.

4 Beverly Roberts Gaventa, "Galatians 1 and 2: Autobiography as Paradigm," *NovT* 28 (1986): 309–26; and Bernard Lategan, "Is Paul Defending his Apostleship in Galatians? The Function of Galatians 1:11–12 and 2:19–20 in the Development of Paul's Argument," *NTS* 34 (1988): 411–30.

5 Martyn, *Galatians*, 431–66; George Howard, *Paul: Crisis in Galatia – A Study in Early Christian Theology*, SNTSMS 35 (Cambridge: Cambridge University Press, 1990), 1–19; and Robert Jewett, "The Agitators and the Galatian Congregation," *NTS* 17 (1970): 198–212 at 205.

6 The issue of method was first raised by J.B. Tyson, "Paul's Opponents in Galatia," *NovT* 10 (1968): 241–54, which became the stimulus for further discussions pursued by George Lyons, *Pauline Autobiography: Towards a New Understanding*, SBLDS 73 (Atlanta, GA: Scholars Press, 1985); John M.G. Barclay, "Mirror-Reading a Polemical Letter: Galatians as a Test Case," *JSNT* 31 (1987): 73–93; Id., *Obeying the Truth: A Study in Paul's Ethics in Ga-*

Indeed, such is the diversity of views that even by the early 1970s, a survey by John J. Gunther revealed that there had been at least eight major theories proposed for the identity of Paul's opponents at Galatia, and further hypotheses have been added in the years since.[7]

In this brief chapter, I do not propose to revisit or attempt to resolve the conundrum of the identity of Paul's opponents at Galatia – a subject that I have addressed at length elsewhere.[8] Rather my purpose here is to investigate the circumstances surrounding the literary composition of the letter to the Galatians, with a particular focus on Paul's *narratio* in Galatians 1:13–2:14.[9] Broadly speaking, I am trying to ascertain what Paul's purpose was in rehearsing the details of his conversion and call, and his commerce with members of the Jerusalem church. Was his purpose apologetic? Was he trying to set the record straight in the face of contrary versions being retailed by his opponents at Galatia? And, if so, does this suggest any link between the various events he describes?

---

*latians* (Edinburgh: T&T Clark, 1988), 1–35; Charles H. Cosgrove, *The Cross and the Spirit: A Study in the Argument and Theology of Galatians* (Macon, GA: Mercer University Press, 1987), 31, 39–40; James L. Martyn, "A Law-Observant Mission to Gentiles: The Background of Galatians," *SJT* 38 (1985): 307–24 at 310–13; Id., "Events in Galatia: Modified Covenantal Nomism versus God's Invasion of the Cosmos in the Singular Gospel. Response to Dunn and Gaventa," in: *Pauline Theology*, vol. 1, *Thessalonians, Philippians, Galatians, Philemon*, ed. Jouette M. Bassler (Minneapolis, MN: Fortress Press, 1991), 160–79 at 160–63; and Jerry L. Sumney, *"Servants of Satan", "False Brothers" and Other Opponents of Paul*, JSNTSup 188 (Sheffield: Sheffield Academic Press, 1999), 77–85, 134–59.

**7** John J. Gunther, *St. Paul's Opponents and Their Background: A Study of Apocalyptic and Jewish Sectarian Teachings*, NovTSup 30 (Leiden: E.J. Brill, 1973), 1–5. A thorough examination of all the issues and the methodological approaches used to interpret Galatians has been recently offered by Moisés Silva, *Interpreting Galatians: Explorations in Exegetical Method* (2nd edn.; Grand Rapids, MI: Baker, 2001). See also Mark D. Nanos, *The Irony of Galatians: Paul's Letter in First-Century Context* (Minneapolis, MN: Fortress Press, 2002), 110–92; and Id., ed., *The Galatians Debate: Contemporary Issues in Rhetorical and Historical Interpretation* (Peabody, MA: Hendrickson, 2002), which brings together many of the more significant articles on Galatians published in the late twentieth century.

**8** Ian J. Elmer, *Paul, Jerusalem and the Judaisers: The Galatian Crisis in Its Broadest Historical Context*, WUNT 2.258 (Tübingen: Mohr Siebeck, 2009).

**9** James D.G. Dunn, *Jesus, Paul and the Law: Studies in Mark and Galatians* (Louisville, KY: Westminster Press, 1990), 108, makes the point that how individual scholars interpret the biographical statements in Galatians 1–2 is determinative of the differing theories concerning the identity of Paul's opponents at Galatia.

# 1 The writing of Galatians

We noted above that two of the few things that casual readers of the New Testament know about Paul are that he wrote letters and that he was a divisive figure – sometimes directly resulting from what he wrote in his letters. His notoriety as a letter writer appears to have been well-established during his lifetime. In 2 Corinthians, Paul suggests that one of the criticisms current amongst his opponents at Corinth was that his letters were more powerful and impressive than his personal presence (2 Cor 10:10). Paul himself admits that sometimes his letters could cause offense and sorrow (2 Cor 7:8; 10:9). After Paul's death, the author of 2 Peter warns against misconstruing the meaning of Paul's letters which, Peter admits, are "hard to understand" (2 Peter 3:16). And, the author of 2 Thessalonians alludes to letters, possibly forged in Paul's name, which may have shaken or disturbed the Pauline community at Thessalonica (2 Thess 2:2; cf. 3:17).

Paul's letter to the Galatians is perhaps the most polemical of all the Pauline correspondence. This too is a puzzle. We noted at the outset that Paul's opponents, whom he never explicitly identifies, were preaching a "different gospel." Despite recent attempts to suggest otherwise, we must assume that his opponents at Galatia were fellow Christians.[10] James L. Martyn observes rightly that the term "gospel" is so significant to Paul that he would not have used it here unless his opponents were also using it and, therefore, these opponents could not be anything other than Christian missionaries.[11] This conclusion can be confirmed by Paul's claim that the Galatian troublemakers were preaching a gospel message that was clearly at odds with the one he preached (Gal 1:6–9), and he suggests that their motive in doing so was to avoid being persecuted for Christ (Gal 6:12). This is a highly polemical assertion that probably provides little concrete data about the agitators' motivations, but it does reveal a great deal about

**10** Most notably, Nanos, *Irony*, who has argued that Paul's Galatian opponents, whom he calls the "influencers," were "members of the larger Jewish communities of Galatia entrusted with the responsibility of conducting Gentiles wishing more than guest status within the communities through the ritual process of proselyte conversion" (6). For earlier proponents of this theory, see Johannes Munck, *Paul and the Salvation of Mankind*, trans. Frank Clarke (London: SCM Press, 1977), and Anthony E. Harvey, "The Opposition to Paul," *SE* 4 (1968): 319–32.

**11** Martyn, *Galatians*, 109. Nanos, *Irony*, 141–42, 284–316, attempts to answer this point by noting that the term was widely used in Paul's time by Jewish groups outside Christianity. While this may be true, Nanos does not take seriously the fact that the term remains one of particular significance to Paul, especially within the context of Galatians, which focuses almost exclusively on the whole issue of Paul's gospel and his right as an apostle to proclaim that gospel.

their religious affiliations.[12] These accusations can only make sense if we assume that Paul's opponents were fellow Christian missionaries.

We might ask, then, why did Paul react so violently to the message of the Judaisers at Galatia? Elsewhere, we find Paul ready to counsel tolerance in the face of conflicting interpretations of the Christian message (cf. 1 Cor 8:1–13; 10:14–33; Rom 14:1–15:13). In attempting to answer the question of Paul's motivation, we should not underestimate the importance of the crisis facing Paul. According to Paul, the Galatians were in danger of "falling from grace" (Gal 5:4) as a result of his opponents who had "bewitched" (Gal 3:1) and "unsettled" (Gal 1:7; 5:12; cf. 6:12–13) the communities. Moreover, when Paul wrote Galatians it seems that the Judaisers were well established and were enjoying some success (Gal 1:6; 3:1; 4:21; 5:4.7). Indeed, many of Paul's Gentile converts were apparently adopting some aspects of Law-observance (Gal 4:10–11), and Paul expresses astonishment at the rapidity with which the Galatians had deserted the gospel he preached (Gal 1:6).

Such is the severity of the crisis that it is not enough for Paul to simply reassure the Galatians, he must also confront the situation head on. Despite being distant from his community, he chose to write a letter laying out the case against this "different gospel" – but that fact too does not necessarily mean that we can take what Paul writes at "face value."

It has long been recognised that the problem that confronts us in examining the Galatian conflict is that the letter to the churches in Galatia is just that, a letter.[13] It is an occasional piece of correspondence that was not intended to convey a comprehensive historical account of the dispute that compelled its composition. Moreover, Galatians divulges only one side of the conversation, Paul's. Consequently, the data that can be drawn from Galatians is fragmentary and coloured by Paul's own perspective on the events. Moreover, the debate itself is twice removed from the text of Galatians, since Paul is not even directly addressing his opponents, but only those members of his community who have been influenced by those adversaries, of whom Paul has only heard reports.

Having said that, however, we must also note that, despite the relative brevity and the bitter tone of this letter, as well as the urgency of the crisis engendered by the conflict, we should not assume that Galatians is a spontaneous composition on the part of Paul. At a very mundane level, commentators rarely

---

**12** Sumney, *"Servants of Satan"*, 136; Helmut Koester, *Introduction to the New Testament*, 2 vols. (Philadelphia, PA: Fortress Press, 1982), 2.119; and Dieter Lührmann, *Galatians: A Continental Commentary*, trans. O.C. Dean Jr (Minneapolis, MN: Fortress Press, 1992), 123.

**13** Vincent M. Smiles, *The Gospel and the Law in Galatia: Paul's Response to Jewish-Christian Separatism and the Threat of Galatian Apostasy* (Collegeville, MN: Liturgical Press, 1998), 1.

consider how letters were written in the ancient world. Understanding how the letter was written is an important first step in determining how one can interpret the meaning and intent of the letter.

In Paul's day most letters were composed with the aid of a professional scribe and, in Paul's case, most likely with the collaboration of co-workers.[14] Evidence from Paul's correspondence suggests that his letters were composed collaboratively. Many of Paul's letters are prefaced by greetings, not just from Paul, but from various co-workers who were with him at the time, and who may have had some role in composing or writing down the letters (1 Thess 1:1; 2 Thess 1:1; 1 Cor 1:1; cf. 16:21–24; 2 Cor 1:1; Phil 1:1; Col 1:1) – and in these cases the letter is usually written in the second person. Paul's letter to the Galatians has no such greeting from co-workers, and it is written in the first person. Paul does, however, acknowledge that he is not alone when he writes, and he sends greetings from "all the brothers" who are with him (Gal 1:2), adding his hand-written "signature" to the letter conclusion (Gal 6:1; cf. 1 Cor 16:21; Col 4:18; 2 Thess 3:17; Phlm 19). This latter addition would seem to indicate that the body of the letter was written in another hand, probably that of the professional scribe who may or may not have been one of Paul's co-workers.[15]

Pauline Christianity was a collaborative effort; it was a movement, not simply the sole work of a single individual. Paul probably spent very little time in any one place – except Corinth and Ephesus where he seems to have spent about eighteen months and two or three years respectively. For the most part, his communities were run and administered by fellow workers. The network of communities and communications between these churches and Paul were maintained by travelling emissaries. Hence, the composition of all the Pauline letters, Galatians included, was probably also the product of a collaborative enterprise.

What these observations suggest is that the process by which Paul and his team composed the letter to the Galatians was far more complex than we

---

**14** E. Randolph Richards, *Paul and First Century Letter Writing: Secretaries, Composition and Collection* (Downers Grove, IL: InterVarsity Press, 2004), 59–80; Id., *The Secretary in Paul's Letters*, WUNT 2/42 (Tübingen: Mohr Siebeck, 1991), 189–94; Richard N. Longenecker, "Ancient Amanuenses and the Pauline Epistles," in: *New Dimensions in New Testament Study*, eds. Richard N. Longenecker and Merrill C. Tenny (Grand Rapids, MI: Zondervan, 1974), 281–97; Jerome Murphy-O'Connor, *Paul The Letter Writer: His World, His Options, His Skills*, GNS 41 (Collegeville, MN: Michael Glazier/Liturgical Press, 1995), 1–14; and, more fully, Stanley E. Stowers, *Letter Writing in Greco-Roman Antiquity* (Philadelphia, PA: Westminster Press, 1986).

**15** Ben Witherington III, *The Paul Quest: The Search for the Jew of Tarsus* (Downers Grove, IL: InterVarsity Press, 1998), 99–109. Cf. Murphy-O'Connor, *Paul the Letter Writer*, 6–7, 16–33. I have discussed the issue of Paul's secretaries in greater detail elsewhere; see Ian J. Elmer, "I, Tertius: Secretary or Co-Author of Romans," *ABR* 56 (2008): 45–60.

would normally assume, involving several drafts before the final copy. Letters could not be simply dictated. When it came to sketching out a rough copy of a text, the secretary's tools in trade included a wax tablet upon which he transcribed the letters of each word with a metal stylus. Even if the secretary was transcribing a final copy directly on to papyrus leaves, the process would have been no faster.[16] Consequently, whether the author was composing a draft or a final text, he or she would have been required to dictate the missive, not just word by word, but syllable by syllable.

In part due to this complex and time-consuming process of composing and transcribing, letters in the ancient world were highly stylised and structured. More specifically, with direct reference to Paul's letter to the Galatians, given the severity of the crisis facing Paul, it should not surprise us that this letter would be a carefully crafted composition. And, indeed, in recent years much has been made of Paul's style of argumentation, and tomes have been written about Paul's knowledge and use of the ancient conventions of rhetoric, especially in the case of Galatians.[17] If we are to recover the circumstances pertaining to the composition of Galatians it is vitally important to pay close attention to the literary structure of the letter.

Galatians is relatively unique in the Pauline corpus, in that it appears to be a single and self-contained correspondence. Unlike some other Pauline letters, such as 2 Corinthians, Philippians and Romans, this letter does not appear to

---

**16** See further, Richards, *Paul and First Century Letter Writing*, 59–80; and Elmer, "I, Tertius," 51–54.

**17** The first significant contribution to this line of enquiry was made by Hans Dieter Betz, "The Literary Composition and Function of Paul's Letter to the Galatians," *NTS* 21 (1975): 353–79; Id., *Galatians: A Commentary on Paul's Letter to the Churches in Galatia*, Hermeneia (Philadelphia, PA: Fortress Press, 1979). His work on Galatians influenced other scholars; e.g., J.D. Hester, "The Use and Influence of Rhetoric in Galatians 2:1–14," *TZ* 42 (1986): 386–408; George A. Kennedy, *New Testament Interpretation through Rhetorical Criticism*, Studies in Religion (Chapel Hill, NC: University of North Carolina Press, 1984); David E. Aune, *The New Testament in Its Literary Environment* (Philadelphia, PA: Westminster Press, 1987); Burton L. Mack, *Rhetoric and the New Testament* (Philadelphia, PA: Fortress Press, 1990); Margaret M. Mitchell, *Paul and the Rhetoric of Reconciliation: An Exegetical Investigation of the Language and Composition of 1 Corinthians* (Louisville, KY: Westminster John Knox, 1991); Stephen M. Pogoloff, *Logos and Sophia: The Rhetorical Situation of 1 Corinthians*, SBLDS 134 (Atlanta, GA: Scholars Press, 1992); and R. Dean Anderson Jr., *Ancient Rhetorical Theory and Paul* (Kampen: Kok Pharos, 1996). For a brief overview and discussion, see Pieter J.J. Botha, "The Verbal Art of the Pauline Letters: Rhetoric, Performance and Presence," in: *Rhetoric and the New Testament: Essays From the 1992 Heidelberg Conference*, eds. Stanley E. Porter and Thomas H. Olbricht, JSNTSup 90 (Sheffield: JSOT, 1993), 409–28; and David G. Horrell, *An Introduction to the Study of Paul* (London: Continuum, 2000), 48–50.

be an amalgam of various letter fragments or contain any significant manuscript differences. Similarly, Galatians clearly addresses a single issue with a complex structured argument. It is the product of a highly skilled communicator – or more likely team of communicators – who has utilised the conventions of ancient rhetoric to construct a consistent attack on the issues raised by troublemakers at Galatia.[18] As we shall see in the following pages, Paul's autobiographical *narratio* in Galatians 1:13 – 2:14 is a key component of the rhetorical structure of Galatians.

## 2 Paul's autobiographical *narratio*

In terms of Galatians' rhetorical genre, Betz has reasoned that the epistle is primarily a typical "apologetic letter" in which Paul sets out to defend himself against opponents who, according to Paul, are making false accusations against him.[19] By contrast, Lyons has argued that Galatians is primarily "deliberative" in nature and does not respond directly to any attack upon Paul's character.[20] However, other commentators have drawn attention to Paul's use of the rhetorical device of the *narratio* (Gal 1:13 – 2:14), which was a common feature of not just ancient apologetic pieces, but also deliberative speeches.[21] A *narratio* of the kind found in Galatians 1:13 – 2:14 could be included when such would serve to correct mistaken impressions about the speaker and, thereby, improve his standing and encourage his audience to be sympathetic to the arguments that were to follow.[22] The ancient rhetorician, Quintilian, advised rhetors that statements about external matters that are nonetheless immediately relevant to the matters at hand

**18** This point is made by T. David Gordon, "The Problem at Galatia," *Interpretation* 41 (1987): 32 – 43 at 33 – 34, who is followed by Russell, "Paul's Opponents," 338.

**19** Betz, *Galatians*, 14. Betz's identification is followed by Hester, "The Use and Influence of Rhetoric in Galatians 2:1 – 14;" Brinsmead, *Galatians*, 42 – 55; and Gerd Lüdemann, *Paul, Apostle to the Gentiles: Studies in Chronology*, trans. S.F. Jones (Philadelphia, PA: Fortress Press, 1984), 46 – 48.

**20** Lyons, *Pauline Autobiography*, 25 – 27, 119.

**21** Philip F. Esler, *Galatians*, NTR (London: Routledge, 1998), has responded to Lyons' argument by suggesting "makers of deliberative (political) speeches frequently had to present their own character favourably as a way of persuading their audience of the merits of their case" (65). Similarly, David E. Aune, *The New Testament in Its Literary Environment*, Library of Early Christianity (Philadelphia, PA: Westminster Press, 1987), 203, 207, who characterises Paul's letter as an "eclectic combination of various rhetorical techniques," which is best understood as a "deliberative letter with some apologetic features."

**22** Witherington, *Grace in Galatia*, 95.

could be introduced *via* a *narratio* when making a deliberative speech.[23] So we need not argue the case for Galatians being apologetic or deliberative.

A *narratio*, even in a deliberative speech, had two functions.[24] First, the purpose of a *narratio* was not simply to inform or remind the auditors of past events, but to recall those past events as lessons for the future. In this way the rhetor could persuade his auditors by placing the facts of his case in a certain context and presenting them in the manner most conducive to his point of view. Quintilian (*Inst. Or.* 4.2.87) observes that it was the correct and accepted convention in a *narratio* to chronicle the relevant events surrounding an issue in chronological order so as to provide the proper context.

Furthermore, a *narratio* afforded the rhetor the opportunity to either attack the character of an opponent or eulogise an ally. Lyons agrees with the first, arguing that the *narratio* in Galatians has to do with Paul's concern to establish "his divinely determined ethos, not defending his personal or official credentials."[25] Put otherwise, Paul's opponents need not have made any accusations against Paul for Paul to want to stress his authority and offer himself as an example to the Galatians of one who formerly stood against similar onslaughts from Judaising opponents. However, Lyons seems unaware of the second option, that Paul must have recalled his earlier dealings with Jerusalem in order to attack the character of his opponents because they were directly linked with others who had previously attacked him.

In a *narratio* the rhetor could resort to pejorative language in order to dispose his auditors to his point of view and against that of his opponents. Throughout the *narratio*, Paul responds directly to his opponents' views on the Law from the perspective of their shared Christian traditions (Gal 1:7.13 – 14; 2:15). Nevertheless he casts his fellow Christians in the role of adversaries and credits them with duplicitous motives. We may be scandalised to imagine that one of the great founding fathers of Christianity would act so underhandedly. But the first century is not the twenty-first. We should not judge Paul by our standards. First-century Mediterranean society was highly competitive. The contemporary rules of rhetoric condoned a no-holds-barred approach to social interaction.

With this in mind, it is no surprise that Paul labels his previous opponents at Jerusalem as "false brothers" who were "secretly brought in to spy on our freedom" by "those reputed pillars." In the subsequent incident at Antioch, Peter and Barnabas are accused of "hypocrisy" and cowardice in the face of the inter-

**23** *Inst. Or.* 3.8.10 – 11; cf. Dio Chrysostom, *Or.* 40.8 – 19; 41.1 – 6.

**24** Betz, *Galatians*, 61 – 62; Esler, *Galatians*, 64 – 65; and Witherington, *Grace in Galatia*, 97.

**25** Lyons, *Pauline Autobiography*, 133. See also Cosgrove, *The Cross and the Spirit*, 133; and Witherington, *Grace in Galatia*, 71 – 73, both of whom agree with Lyons on this point.

ference of the factional and divisive "men from James." Similarly, Paul's present opponents at Galatia are cast as "troublemakers" and "agitators" who are motivated by fear of persecution. Such derogatory and emotional language could not be accidental. It must have been intended to raise animus against the viewpoint of those whom Paul perceived to be his adversaries.[26]

To return to the proposal that Paul's opponents had directly attacked Paul, it should be noted that Paul explicitly signals his readers' familiarity with some version of events in his past. First, it is significant that Paul introduces the account of his past with the formula, "You will have heard, no doubt, of my earlier life in Judaism..." (1:13), which must signal that the Galatians had been informed of his career as a zealous Jew. Further, he implicitly signals that this knowledge could only be derived from his opponents. In support of this view, we might cite Paul's rhetorical question "why am I still persecuted if I am still preaching circumcision?" (Gal 5:11), which many scholars read as an indication that Paul's opponents must have told the Galatians that Paul still taught circumcision.[27]

The accusation that Paul still taught circumcision seems a rather difficult claim to defend. Surely the Galatians, who had been the recipients of Paul's gospel, would be well aware of Paul's position vis-à-vis circumcision. A far better understanding of 5:11 is that Paul's opponents had accused him of being inconsistent in having preached circumcision at other times and places, despite the fact that he was now preaching a circumcision-free gospel.[28] Pheme Perkins points out that Paul's defence is couched within "the context of an intra-Christian conflict" and, therefore, we might assume that the Judaisers are making claims about "some element in his earlier activity as a Christian missionary."[29]

Elsewhere Paul admits to a level of flexibility in the course of his apostolic career (1 Cor 9:20; cf. Rom 15:1). In the interests of missionary expediency, Paul appears to have adopted differing but appropriate lifestyles according to the community to whom he ministered. It may be possible that Paul's opponents could cite actual examples of Paul's willingness to accommodate his faith-prac-

---

**26** Betz, *Galatians*, 61.

**27** Tyson, "Paul's Opponents," 248–49; Jewett, "Agitators," 208; Watson, *Paul, Judaism and the Gentiles*, 55; Bruce, *Galatians*, 236; and Betz, *Galatians*, 268.

**28** So Witherington, *Grace in Galatia*, 373; and Pheme Perkins, *Abraham's Divided Children: Galatians and the Politics of Faith*, NTIC (Harrisburg, PA: Trinity Press International, 2001), 99–100.

**29** Perkins, *Abraham's Divided Children*, 100. Cf. Betz, *Galatians*, 269, who suggests that Paul's indifference towards circumcision in Galatians (3:28; 5:6; 6:15) could be read as either critical or supportive of circumcision.

tice to his audience. There is no significant evidence to suggest that following his conversion Paul ever returned to the practice of Law-observance.[30]

In the light of this discussion, it would seem that the reference to Paul preaching circumcision, if genuine, could only have been to Paul's pre-Christian period – although this conclusion is far from certain.[31] On that basis, we might imagine that the Judaisers had attempted to discredit Paul by telling his Gentile converts of his former persecution of the church.

Steve Mason raises the possibility that Paul himself had once been a "Judaiser." While we cannot be certain that Paul sought to force Gentile converts to "live like Jews" as he now accuses Peter and the Galatian opponents of doing, it does seem clear that he was (prior to his conversion) involved in the "violent harassment of Jesus' followers (Gal 1:13) out of zeal, as he puts it, for the ancestral traditions (Gal 1:14)."[32] This description of Paul's pre-conversion activities mirrors the sort of "Judaising" activity attributed to Judas Maccabaeus and Razis in 2 Maccabees (8:1; 14:38), who sought to purge Hellenistic practices from amongst the Judaean population. Paul raises the issue of his former Judaising activity because he wants to make the point that "the Judaisers are doing something he has neglected, for the same mindset was part of his background; but he has deliberately abandoned Judaising for the sake of the Gospel."[33]

Paul's statement in 5:11 does imply that Paul feels that he must respond to a distorted version of events from his past. If we were to ask what events these might be, the only answer possible would be those events surrounding his conversion and his early commerce with the Law-observant Jerusalem church, which are the subject of the early chapters of the letter.[34] Paul's narration of his early career does not simply stop at his pre-Christian phase, however; but goes on in precise detail to describe events that followed his conversion. A significant aspect of the Judaisers' message must have been the record of the events surrounding Paul's early association with the Jerusalem apostles, Peter, James and John, including the Council at Jerusalem. Why else would Paul report the performances of both the false brothers and Peter in supporting James' pro-circumcision putsch at Antioch, if their duplicity were not directly related to the current behaviour of the Judaisers at Galatia?[35]

---

**30** Betz, *Galatians*, 269; and Dunn, *Galatians*, 278–80.

**31** Matera, *Galatians*, 182.

**32** Steve Mason, "Jews, Judeans, Judaising, Judaism: Problems of Categorization in Ancient History," *JSJ* 38 (2007): 457–512 at 469.

**33** Mason, "Jews, Judeans, Judaising, Judaism," 469.

**34** Martyn, *Galatians*, 476–77.

**35** Dunn, *Galatians*, 72–78.

Given the links Paul draws, we might assume that just as Paul's disagreements with the gospel and the ministry of his Galatian opponents leads to *ad hominem* attacks on their character, so they too must have been equally critical of Paul, attacking both the content of his gospel and his right as an apostle to preach it. If these were not at issue, why would Paul make them so? It seems highly unlikely that Paul would have raised both the subject of his own authority and the spectre of his past controversies at Jerusalem and Antioch, if these were not already central to the debate.

Here again, we might refer to Quintilian (*Inst. Or.* 4.2.43) who counsels the rhetor that one "should never say more than the case demands." There is no doubt that Paul was a skilful rhetorician, who could twist a story to his own ends. He does it repeatedly, not just in Galatians, but in his other letters as well. We have to always read between the lines to determine precisely what actually did occur. But we must also remember that all of Paul's autobiographical material is press-ganged into the service of his rhetoric, and especially into his campaign against others who seemed to have been spreading counter versions of the same story.

This practice of providing only the most relevant details also explains why Paul's description of these earlier events in Jerusalem and Antioch is brief and to the point. Paul is not providing his entire *curriculum vitae* or attempting to compose his autobiography. He is arguing a specific case, which requires historical contextualisation. Moreover, it is likely that he is responding to direct accusations about his gospel and his apostolic status that require a relevant reply. Again, this approach is nothing less than would be expected of one following the conventions of ancient rhetoric, which required a *narratio* to be clear, brief, plausible, and devoid of all material that was not absolutely germane.[36]

In retailing his version of his two visits to Jerusalem, Paul focuses only on the relevant facts. He asserts that he first went to Jerusalem in order to get "acquainted" with Peter (Gal 1:18), not to be "taught" or "receive" the content of the gospel he preached (1:12) or the "call" to preach it (Gal 1:15 – 16).[37] Both his gospel and his apostolic commission (Gal 1:15) are the products of the revelation (Gal 1:12) he received three years prior to his initial meeting with Cephas and James

---

**36** See the discussion of this important point in Robert G. Hall, "Historical Inference and Rhetorical Effect," in: *Persuasive Artistry: Studies in New Testament Rhetoric in Honor of George A. Kennedy*, ed. Duane F. Watson (Sheffield: Sheffield Academic Press, 1989), 308 – 20. Cf. Witherington, *Grace in Galatia*, 96.

**37** Matera, *Galatians*, 68 – 69 and Martyn, *Galatians*, 171 – 72.

(Gal 1:15–17) and fourteen years before the council meeting that recognised the legitimacy of his apostleship among the Gentiles (Gal 2:1–10).[38]

According to Paul, at some stage after the conference in Jerusalem, Peter came to Antioch, where he joined fully in the social and faith life of the community (2:11–12). However, with the arrival of some people who had been sent as envoys of James from Jerusalem, Peter withdrew from table fellowship with the Gentiles (2:12). Paul claims that it was fear of the "circumcision party" that led not only Peter, but also Barnabas and all the Jews to separate themselves from the Gentile converts (2:12–13). Infuriated by what he saw as "hypocrisy" on Peter's part, Paul accuses Peter (2:14), a Jew who till the arrival of James' people lived like a Gentile and not like a Jew, of forcing the Gentile converts at Antioch "to live like Jews."

Paul is determined to set the record straight by explaining what kind of relationship existed between himself and the Jerusalem triumvirate, James, Cephas, and John. He is resolute in his willingness to demonstrate that no rift exists between him and them and, thus, that the gospel he preaches was not at variance with apostolic teaching. Paul seeks to establish that at the Jerusalem council his gospel was recognised by the "pillars" as divinely authorised (Gal 2:7–9).

Paul asserts that he went to Jerusalem the second time to "present" his gospel to the Jerusalem apostles, not to seek their approval. Clearly, he is attempting to argue that he did not go to Jerusalem to seek apostolic sanction for his gospel, in the sense of an inferior seeking the blessing of a superior, but merely to present the details of his gospel message, which was to provide the subject for a conversation amongst equals. Moreover, he carefully distinguishes between the leadership at Jerusalem and a faction of "false brothers" at Jerusalem, as well as the "men from James" at Antioch who were the primary cause of trouble in the two conflicts. But Paul also implies that it was as a result of the pressure brought to bear by this "circumcision party" (Gal 2:12) that both James and Peter failed to act in accordance with the "truth of the gospel" (Gal 2:5.14) and it was they who reneged on the agreement reached at Jerusalem.

Given this situation, we can only conclude that Paul's peculiar emphasis on apostolic authority implies that he is trying to avoid a trap laid by his Galatian opponents, which would allow it to be said that, as a result of the meeting with the "pillars," Jerusalem has jurisdiction over Paul's gospel and his apostolate. It seems clear enough that Paul cannot ignore the connections between the Gala-

---

**38** Similarly, John Howard Schütz, *Paul and the Anatomy of Apostolic Authority*, SNTSMS 26 (Cambridge: Cambridge University Press, 1975), 128–58.

tian troublemakers and his erstwhile opponents at Jerusalem and Antioch who had similarly challenged the content of his Law-free gospel and his right as an apostle to preach that gospel among the Gentiles. And despite his attempt to drive a wedge between his opponents and the apostolic triumvirate at Jerusalem, and even discredit Peter and James by association, Paul implies wittingly or unwittingly that they all sought to undermine his apostolate by forcing his Gentile converts to accept circumcision and adhere to the Law.[39]

It may be true that, in Galatians (2:1–14), Paul attempts to present his relationship with the Jerusalem apostles as amicable, accusing the false brothers at Jerusalem and the people from James at Antioch as the real cause of the division. But Paul never completely exonerates James and Peter of the charge of having conspired with the pro-circumcision party at Jerusalem and Antioch; and he draws a connection between the apostolic authorities in Jerusalem and the troublemakers at Galatia. He accuses James of acting with duplicity in sending a delegation to Antioch to undo the agreement forged at Jerusalem. He cites Peter's hypocrisy in yielding to James' initiative, despite Peter's previous acceptance of the mixed table fellowship at Antioch. And, he implicitly groups the "pillars" with the Christian-Jewish missionaries at Galatia, charging them all with seeking to impose circumcision on the Gentiles out of fear of persecution and in the interests of their own self-aggrandisement.

This tenor of compulsion and coercion is further emphasised by Paul's charge that the troublemakers were attempting to "compel" (ἀναγκάζουσιν) the Galatian Gentile converts to submit to circumcision (6:12). Paul was clearly familiar with these people. He had encountered others from this pro-circumcision putsch elsewhere, as he testifies in his opening biographical comments. He relates how the "false brothers" at Jerusalem had wanted to have the Gentile Titus "compelled" (ἠναγκάσθη) into submitting to circumcision (2:3). Their aim too had been to both "spy on the liberty we have in Christ Jesus and to make us slaves" (2:4). Similarly in Antioch some time later, Peter, out of fear of this "circumcision party," backed a new policy intended to "compel (ἀναγκάζεις) the Gentiles to live like Jews" (2:14). We observe that Paul's use of the verb ἀναγκάζω (Gal 2:14) to describe Peter's actions mirrors both that of the false brothers at Jerusalem and the troublemakers at Galatia. That Jerusalem and its leadership figures in this pro-circumcision putsch can be detected further in Galatians.

First, we should note that in Paul's letters there are a mere ten explicit references to Jerusalem, half of which occur in Galatians (1:17.18; 2:1–2; 4:25.26; cf.

39 So Esler, *Galatians*, 138. Similarly, Martyn, *Galatians*, 462–66; Sumney, *"Servants of Satan"*, 137; and Witherington, *Grace in Galatia*, 448–49.

Rom 15:19.21.26.31; 1 Cor 16:3).[40] The names of the pre-eminent leaders of the Jerusalem church – Cephas (Gal 1:18; 2:9.11.14; cf. 1 Cor 1:12; 3:22; 9:5; 15:5) or alternatively Peter (Gal 2:7.8), Jesus' brother James (Gal 1:19; 2:9.12; cf. 1 Cor 15:7), "brothers of the Lord" (1 Cor 9:5), and John (Gal 2:9) – appear more often in Galatians than any of the other Pauline texts. Similarly, we find Barnabas (2:1.9.13; cf. 1 Cor 9:6; Col 4:10), an erstwhile member of the earliest Jerusalem community (Acts 4:36; 9:27), figuring prominently with the aforementioned Jerusalem triumvirate in Paul's opening autobiographical narrative (Gal 2:1.9.13). Later Jerusalem reappears as a figure of derision "for she and her children are in slavery" to the covenant from Mount Sinai (4:25). This claim echoes Paul's earlier attack on the false brothers at Jerusalem (2:4), whose attempt to "make us slaves" by imposing circumcision on the Gentiles is later extended to the James party, and then to Peter, Barnabas and the rest at Antioch (2:13), who were attempting to "compel the Gentiles to live like Jews" (2:14). This repeated focus on the apostolic community suggests that the spectre of the Jerusalem church and its leadership haunts the pages of this letter like no other in the Pauline corpus.

This description of the "Judaising" behaviour of Paul's opponents is striking, not only because of the parallels Paul draws between the three episodes, but also because it seems to run counter to the overwhelming scholarly consensus that Jews did not actively proselytise Gentiles. Those Gentiles who did become Jewish proselytes tended to have sought out conversion proactively, usually on the basis of close, personal or familial ties with local Jewish communities.[41] Martin Goodman notes that it was in the interest of Diaspora Jewish communities to encourage Gentile sympathisers whose links with the local synagogues could only lend support to Jews who were often marginalised because of their distinctive customs and ethnicity.[42] However, there is no evidence to suggest that such sympathisers were ever "compelled" to become proselytes or adopt the full gamut of Jewish ritual and custom.

Jewish synagogues welcomed Gentile God-fearers without demanding circumcision as a condition for attending assembly. God-fearers were embraced by the synagogue, surrendering their worship of idols, giving their children Jew-

**40** Romans (9:33; 11:26) contains two further references to "Zion," both of which are scriptural quotes dealing with messianic themes drawn directly from Isaiah (28:16; 59:20–21). Another relevant, alternative term is "Judaea," which occurs infrequently in the Pauline corpus; but, here again, Galatians (1:22) is represented along with 1 Thessalonians (2:14) and 2 Corinthians (1:16).
**41** Martin Goodman, *Mission and Conversion: Proselytising in the Religious History of the Roman Empire* (Oxford: Clarendon, 1994), 84–88; cf. Perkins, *Abraham's Divided Children*, 13; and Nanos, *Irony*, 117.
**42** Goodman, *Mission and Conversion*, 87–88.

ish names, receiving instruction in Torah, observing Jewish Sabbath and Holy days, and even serving as generous patrons without converting and receiving circumcision.[43] If a male God-fearer wanted to become a Jewish convert, then circumcision would be required; but if a Gentile Christian wanted to attend synagogue, there was no such requirement and no likelihood that they would be coerced into doing so. At Galatia, however, Paul's rivals appear to have demanded that Gentile converts to the Jesus movement accept the practice of circumcision and complete Law-observance as a requirement for inclusion in the Christian community. We must assume that what we are dealing with here is not a Jewish phenomenon *per se*, but a Christian Jewish one, which can find no other precedent than those cited by Paul himself and laid at the feet of his opponents at Galatia, as well as in Jerusalem and Antioch previously.

The sense that we get from Paul's *narratio* that he is dealing with a single group of opponents is further supported by possible recurring echoes throughout the rest of Galatians.[44] When Paul claims that the members of the pro-circumcision putsch are only acting in the interests of self-aggrandisement (Gal 4:17), he appears to be consciously reiterating the motives he earlier attributed to James, Peter and John, who thought themselves important and reputed pillars of the church (Gal 2:6.9).[45] When Paul suggests that not even those who are circumcised keep the Law (Gal 6:13), he may also have in mind the hypocrisy of Peter, Barnabas and the Antiochene Jews who defected to the circumcision party under the onslaught of James' people from Jerusalem. And when he accuses his opponents of preaching circumcision for fear of persecution, he may be alluding to the cowardice of Peter who abstained from sharing table fellowship with the Gentiles for fear of the circumcision party (Gal 2:12).

---

**43** See the discussion in Paula Fredriksen, "Judaism, the Circumcision of Gentiles, and Apocalyptic Hope: Another Look at Galatians 1 and 2," *JTS* n.s. 42 (1991): 532–64.
**44** Esler, *Galatians*, 138.
**45** Paul refers to James, Peter and John as "the ones reputed to be important" (2:6; cf. 2:2) and "reputed pillars" (2:9), to which he adds the comment, "whatever they were makes no difference to me; God does not judge by external appearances" (2:6). Later (6:3), Paul counsels the Galatians that "if anyone who is nothing thinks himself something, he is deceiving himself." This implies that in his earlier statements about James, Peter and John, Paul is sarcastically inferring that the triumvirate *thought of themselves* as important and, in the pursuit of self-aggrandisement, styled themselves as the pillars upon which the Christian movement stood. See C.K. Barrett, "Paul: Councils and Controversies," in: *Conflicts and Challenges in Early Christianity*, ed. Donald A. Hagner (Harrisburg, PA: Trinity Press International, 1999), 42–74 at 43–44.

# 3 Conclusion

In this chapter we have examined one aspect of Paul's response to the Galatian crisis that stands behind the composition of Paul's letter to the churches in Galatia. We have explored Paul's use of the ancient rhetorical strategy of the *narratio* in Galatians 1:13 – 2:14. As a result of this examination, we have speculated that the Jerusalem apostles are the primary focus, and that the issue of circumcision and Law-observance, which had proved a divisive element in his previous dealings with Jerusalem, was also central to the problems at Galatia. Accordingly, Paul makes skilful use of his own life story to effectively tar all of his opponents with the same brush. Paul seeks to demonstrate that his opponents at Galatia and his adversaries at Jerusalem and Antioch, and possibly also James and Peter, are all of one mind and all have in Paul's opinion conspired to undermine the truth of the gospel that he preaches. The clear implication here is that the demands of the three groups – the false brothers at Jerusalem, the circumcision group at Antioch and the missionaries at Galatia – were identical.[46]

If nothing else, Paul's *narratio* points to a long-standing conflict between two factions within the early church, divided not simply along ethnic lines, but ideological ones as well. Moreover, it seems similarly clear from reading between the lines of the *narratio* that the issue of Paul's status as an apostle and the story about how he came to assume that title were key components in the battle. Paul relates the story of his conversion and subsequent commerce with Jerusalem and Antioch most likely because his opponents have been circulating a very different version of the same episodes. For his opponents, this story underpins both their attack on Paul's apostolate and the Law-free gospel he sponsors. Paul is forced to provide another perspective that neatly avoids the inference that his apostleship and his gospel are derivative of either Jerusalem or Antioch.

Paul's response is an ingenious one. He and his collaborators enter the fray with a carefully composed letter prefaced by a different version of the same story by which they thought to set the record straight on Paul's past. By utilising the ancient rhetorical strategy of the *narratio*, Paul is able to turn his version of the contentious story to good purpose by demonstrating how the central issue at Jerusalem and Antioch is the same as that which occasioned the Galatian crisis. Moreover, he can "set the record straight" by demonstrating how he alone stood for the "truth of the gospel" when all others, including James and Peter, failed.

---

**46** So, correctly, Watson, *Paul, Judaism and the Gentiles*, 61.

James S. McLaren

# Early Christian Polemic against Jews and the Persecution of Christians in Rome by Nero

The fire that resulted in much of the city of Rome being severely damaged in 64 CE played a significant role in the changing architectural landscape of the city. Nero quickly seized the occasion as an opportunity to commence work on a massive palatial palace, the *Domus Aurea*, and on redesigning other parts of the city.[1] In large part due to his questionable legacy among influential members of the Roman elite, subsequent rulers readily demolished and reused Nero's palatial structure in their various building projects. A prime example was the decision by Vespasian to construct the Flavian amphitheatre on public land that Nero had acquired for his personal use in the new palace. In contrast to the limited extant evidence of Nero's building activity in the aftermath of the fire, its impact on the Christian community in Rome and on the shape of early Christian writings was profound and enduring. In what follows it will be argued that a very significant role should be assigned to the fire in the history of the Christian community in Rome and, more significantly, to the dynamic of the way Jews were depicted in the New Testament. First, we will review the details of the fire and note key observations regarding the Christians and their link to the fire. We will then examine two major questions associated with the Christian involvement in the aftermath of the fire: how did the Roman authorities identify the Christians and why did they identify the Christians as being responsible for the fire? We will conclude by proposing that what the Christians experienced in the aftermath of the fire had a direct impact on the depiction of Jews, especially in the synoptic Gospel tradition.

## 1 The fire in Rome

During the night of either the 18th or the 19th of July in 64 CE the fire broke out near the southeast end of the Circus Maximus in Rome.[2] It quickly spread beyond

---

1 Tacitus, *Ann.* 15.42–43. References for all works cited, unless otherwise stated, are to the text published in LCL.

2 Tacitus, *Ann.* 15.38–44, provides the most detailed account of the fire. See also Suetonius, *Nero* 38. and Cassius Dio, *Roman History* 62.16.1–18.5.

the Circus and engulfed other sections of the city. The fire was eventually brought under control on the sixth day at the base of the Esquiline, only for another fire to commence near the Aemilian estates of Ofonius Tigellinus, the praetorian prefect.[3] Many parts of the city, including Nero's recently constructed palace, were affected by the extent of the fire.[4] According to Tacitus, of the fourteen districts into which the city was divided three were totally destroyed, seven were badly damaged and only four remained unscathed (*Ann.* 15.40.2). Much of Rome, therefore, lay in ruins and a major reconstruction program of both public buildings and private dwellings was required.[5]

A key aspect of the surviving accounts of the fire is the role played by Nero. Tacitus reports that Nero was away at Antium when the fire started and that he only returned when the fire reached his house (*Ann.* 15.39.1). Once in the city Nero offered practical assistance, allowing people to seek respite on the Plain of Mars and around the monuments of Agrippa (*Ann.* 15.39.2). In the aftermath of the fire Nero oversaw some of the reconstruction work, including offering to pay for buildings designed in a fire-retardant manner, making plans for the removal of rubble, the acquisition of new materials and the provision of fresh water (*Ann.* 15.43.1–4). However, these positive comments regarding Nero's behaviour are strongly outweighed by criticism of his involvement in the whole incident. Suetonius provides a very negative account of Nero's role. He claims that the fire was started at the behest of Nero, out of his displeasure for the urban sprawl within the city and his desire to acquire land for the construction of his new palace (*Nero* 38.1).[6] Nero requisitioned much of the booty from the rubble and the funds raised to pay for the reconstruction work (*Nero* 38.3). Adding further insult, Nero performed the "sack of Ilium" as the fire spread across the city (*Nero* 38.2).[7]

While Tacitus avoids making similar overt, direct criticism of Nero's involvement, he does include information that calls into question the precise nature of

3 See Tacitus, *Ann.* 15.40; cf. Suetonius, *Nero* 38.2, and Cassius Dio, *Rom. Hist.* 62.17.1, regarding the duration of the fire.

4 Tacitus, *Ann.* 15.41; Suetonius, *Nero* 38.2; Cassius Dio, *Rom. Hist.* 62.18.2.

5 Cassius Dio's account focuses on a description of the sense of despair experienced by the people (62.16.3–18.1), even comparing the fire to the time the city had been sacked by the Gauls (62.17.3; 62.18.2). See also Tacitus, *Ann.* 15.38.3–7. It is important to note that fires were a frequent occurrence in Rome. During the reign of Augustus there were nine recorded fires and then a further five while Tiberius was emperor. The most recent fire prior to the one in 64 CE took place in 54 CE. See Howard V. Canter, "Conflagrations in Ancient Rome," *Classical Journal* 27/4 (1932): 270–88.

6 Cassius Dio, *Rom. Hist.* 62.16.2, also names Nero as responsible for ordering the fire.

7 See also Cassius Dio, *Rom. Hist.* 62.18.1.

the role the emperor played in the whole incident. At the outset he notes that there were several versions regarding how the fire started, including the view that it was Nero's plan (*Ann.* 15.38.1). He also reports the "rumour" that Nero performed on stage while the fire spread through the city (*Ann.* 15.39.3). Adding further to the negative view of Nero's involvement, Tacitus states that Nero desired to found a new city, using his own name (*Ann.* 15.40.2) and, most important of all, when Tacitus turns to describing the reconstruction work he commences with an account of Nero's new palatial palace and related works (*Ann.* 15.42). Tacitus then explains that, despite Nero's efforts to win favour in the aftermath of the fire by organising various offerings to the gods, the public perception was that the emperor had been responsible for the fire starting (*Ann.* 15.44.1–2). Tacitus states that in order to counter this persistent view Nero laid the blame on the Christians (*Ann.* 15.44.2). His account of what happened next is as follows:

> Therefore, to scotch the rumour, Nero substituted as culprits, and punished with the utmost refinements of cruelty, a class of men, loathed for their vices, whom the crowd styled Christians. Christus, the founder of the name, had undergone the death penalty in the reign of Tiberius, by sentence of the procurator Pontius Pilatus, and the pernicious superstition was checked for the moment, only to break out once more, not merely in Judaea, the home of the disease, but in the capital itself, where all things horrible or shameful in the world collect and find vogue. First, then, the confessed members of the sect were arrested; next, on their disclosures, vast numbers were convicted, not so much on the count of arson as for hatred of the human race. And derision accompanied their end: they were covered with wild beasts' skins and torn to death by dogs; or they were fastened on crosses, and when daylight failed were burned to serve as lamps by night. Nero had offered his gardens for the spectacle, and gave an exhibition in his Circus, mixing with the crowd in the habit of a charioteer, or mounted on his car. Hence, in spite of a guilt which had earned the most exemplary punishment, there arose a sentiment of pity, due to the impression that they were being sacrificed not for the welfare of the state but to the ferocity of a single man.[8]

In the present context, there are two significant observations to make regarding the way Nero resolved the perception that he was responsible for starting the fire.[9] First, it was widely acknowledged that the Christians were used as a scapegoat, a means of laying responsibility for what had happened on someone other than the emperor. The Christians had not played any part in the fire. Tacitus

---

**8** Tacitus, *Ann.* 15.44.2–5, trans. John Jackson, LCL 322 (Cambridge, MA: Harvard University Press, 1937).

**9** Other significant features of the way the incident is described include the nature of the punishment used by Nero, the introductory comments on the Christians provided by Tacitus, and the comment regarding life in Rome. Note also the observations made by Peter Lampe, *From Paul to Valentinus: Christians at Rome in the First Two Centuries*, trans. M. Steinhauser (Minneapolis, MN: Fortress Press, 2003), 82–84.

makes this very clear in several ways: the introductory remark about the need for Nero to find a way of dispelling the rumour that he had ordered the fire; Nero taking the initiative to put forward the Christians as the ones responsible; and, in the comment about the punishment being for crimes other than the fire.[10] Second, Nero was in a position to identify people that were known by the name "Christians." In other words, the Christians were a distinguishable group among the numerous mix of people that resided in Rome. Furthermore, they could be targeted as a scapegoat for causing the fire without fear of any notable backlash for Nero. Tacitus refers to public ambivalence regarding the precise nature and extent of the punishment inflicted upon the Christians.[11] However, there is no suggestion of any doubt regarding the initial decision to punish the Christians; Tacitus indicates there was public consensus at the time that the decision was entirely justified (*Ann.* 15.44.2, 4).

# 2 The decision to punish Christians

From the account of Tacitus there are two major questions regarding Nero's decision to blame the fire on the Christians in Rome that require discussion. Why did Nero target the Christians as opposed to any other group? Second, how did Nero identify the Christians? At first glance it appears that Tacitus provides answers to both questions. As noted above, Tacitus claims that the Christians were used as a scapegoat and they were deemed worthy of being punished. What is not explained, however, is why the Christians were chosen above any other section of the population of the city of Rome. In terms of the means by which the Christians were identified, Tacitus states that the first people to be punished "confessed." There is, however, no information provided about how these initial offenders were identified. It is appropriate, therefore, to explore these two questions regarding the process by which Nero used the Christians as the scapegoats for the fire. Aware that the discussion of these questions is entering into an area where the source material is silent, the principle that guides what follows is to

---

**10** Suetonius does not describe the retributions that followed the fire. He does, however, briefly mention Christians being punished under the initiative of the emperor in the context of a list of various groups that all warranted punishment (*Nero* 16.2). It is also mentioned in the context of construction work (*Nero* 16.1) that Tacitus specifically associated with the fire (*Ann.* 15.43.1).
**11** Tacitus links this ambivalence with the exaggerated public behaviour of Nero (*Ann.* 15.44.5).

draw insight from placing the incident within the wider social and political context of life in early imperial Rome.[12]

We commence with the question of why Nero chose to blame the Christians. The context for the choice of Christians as the scapegoat is relatively straightforward, a readiness to lay blame on people deemed to fall under the broad label of being *foreigners*. In general terms, as well as referring to a person's country of origin, the label could also apply to any customs, practices and beliefs carried out that were not deemed to be Roman in origin or those viewed as not being supportive of the Roman way of life. While the population of Rome was cosmopolitan and both the authorities and the public at large were generally tolerant of diversity in the city, there was a persistent belief that foreigners and foreign customs and beliefs were, at the very least, inferior to all things identified as being Roman.[13] Compounding the situation for people exhibiting customs, practices and beliefs deemed to be foreign to the Roman way of life was that they acted as an easy foil in times of trouble. Along with persons of no or very minor social standing, such as slaves, and people associated with certain professions, such as astrologers, foreigners were often targeted as the cause of disruption and disorder in Rome.[14] The course of action normally taken involved short-term expulsion from Rome of the offending people. Occasionally it also involved banning the activity of the foreign custom, possibly even to the extent of destroying places of worship.[15]

---

**12** On the silence of the source material, especially regarding the question of how the Christians were identified, see Fergus Millar, *The Emperor in the Roman World* (Ithaca, NY: Cornell University Press, 1977), 554, and James C. Walters, "Romans, Jews, and Christians: The Impact of the Romans on Jewish/Christian Relations in First-Century Rome," in: *Judaism and Christianity in First-Century Rome*, ed. Karl P. Donfried and Peter Richardson (Grand Rapids, MI: Eerdmans, 1998), 175–95 at 180.

**13** See Benjamin H. Isaac, *The Invention of Racism in Classical Antiquity* (Princeton, NJ: Princeton University Press, 2004); David Noy, *Foreigners at Rome: Citizens and Strangers* (London: Duckworth, 2000), esp. 31–47; and Martin Goodman, *Rome and Jerusalem: The Clash of Ancient Civilizations* (London: Penguin, 2007), 156–60.

**14** See Noy, *Foreigners* 39–47; and Leonard V. Rutgers, "Roman Policy toward the Jews: Expulsions from the City of Rome during the First Century C.E.," in: *Judaism and Christianity*, 93–116 at 107–109. It is important to note that some of the examples of action taken relate to occasions where there was an actual incident and/or issue that was deemed to require intervention. See Tacitus *Ann.* 2.85; 12.52; Suetonius, *Tib.* 36; and Josephus, *A.J.* 18.65–84. A key recent event that helped form the backdrop to the expulsion in 19 CE was the unexpected death of Germanicus.

**15** The reference to the destruction of the Isis temple made by Josephus could be a literary creation as part of an attempt to show how the followers of Isis were punished in a harsher manner than the Jews (*A.J.* 18.79).

In other words, when Nero made the decision to find a scapegoat, the obvious choice was to find such a culprit among the foreigners that resided in the city. Tacitus makes it clear that the Christians fitted this general profile. In his explanation of the group he notes that it originated in Judaea and that it was brought to the city (*Ann.* 15.44.3). Furthermore, the Christians had a track record for being un-Roman: they were known for "their vices" and to be a "pernicious superstition." However, what is not clear is why Nero settled on the Christians as opposed to any other potential target among the followers of some foreign customs and practices or one of the dubious professions. Although Tacitus indicates that the Christians were despised, a view also expressed by Suetonius (*Nero* 16.2), there is no particular reason evident from a Roman perspective as to why they should be singled out and chosen by Nero. In fact, Tacitus' brief introduction to the Christians indicates that they were a relatively new group and that their appearance in Rome was particularly recent. While their status as newcomers meant the Christians were unlikely to have much traction among people with social and political influence in Rome, it is also difficult to see how they would immediately appear as a good option to be the scapegoat.[16]

For further clarification we need to turn to the second question, the means by which Nero was able to identify the Christians. Although not an issue for Tacitus it is very important to consider how Nero identified the Christians, especially in the light of what has been noted regarding why he chose them. As well as being a relatively new addition to Rome there is no evidence to indicate that the Christians had established a presence within the physical landscape of the

---

**16** It is important to comment briefly here on the decision of Claudius to expel Jews in 49 CE. According to Suetonius (*Claud.* 25.4), in order to quell trouble involving Chrestus and Jews Claudius decided to expel Jews from the city. See also Cassius Dio, *Rom. Hist.* 60.6.6; Orosius, *Ad. pag.* 7.6.15–16; and Acts 18:1–3. While this has often been viewed as a reference to trouble between Christians and some members of the wider Jewish community in Rome, there is no clear reason to support such an interpretation. Chrestus is most likely the name of an individual rather than a reference to Jesus and there is no reason to presume Aquila and Priscilla were Christians. For those who favour the incident involving a dispute among Christians and Jews see Walters, "Impact," 177; Lampe, *Paul*, 11–16; and E. Mary Smallwood, *The Jews under Roman Rule from Pompey to Diocletian* (Leiden: Brill, 1976), 212. Cf. Rutgers, "Roman Policy," 105–106; and Edwin A. Judge, "The Origins of the Church at Rome: A new Solution?," in: Id., *The first Christians in the Roman World*, ed. James Harrison, WUNT 229 (Tübingen: Mohr Siebeck, 2008), 442–55 at 445. By implication, the reference to Christians in relation to the fire acts as our first extant occasion where they are part of public affairs. This is certainly the situation within the narrative of Tacitus, given that he provides his introduction for readers to the group in book 15. See also Dixon Slingerland, "Chrestus: Christus?," in: *The Literature of Early Rabbinic Judaism: Issues in Talmudic Redaction and Interpretation*, ed. Alan J. Avery-Peck (Lanham, MD: University Press of America, 1989), 133–44, regarding the identification of Chrestus.

city, let alone within the community at large. While it is possible that Paul's arrival in Rome had marked both an increased level of activity and a greater level of public attention being placed on the group, it did not extend to a definable footprint for which any evidence survives.[17]

In terms of the actual process by which the culprits were identified Tacitus states that the first Christians punished were those who "confessed." These people provided names of others, presumably as the result of being tortured in the process of confessing their standing as Christians. The key issue, therefore, was for the Roman authorities to be able to lay their hands on some people who called themselves Christians. One possibility was for a search to be undertaken among people already imprisoned. It was not, however, a reliable option. The broader social and political context of life in Rome indicates that there was, however, another well-established means by which Nero could be highly confident that he would achieve a successful outcome in his quest to locate Christians.[18] Although the vast majority of such activity centred on the alleged behaviour of wealthy, elite members of Roman society, vis-à-vis the emperor,[19] the significance of this culture of *delatores* and *accusatores* is that when Nero decided to use the Christians as his scapegoat there was an accepted process in place by which they could be identified. What is not clear is the exact order by which the action unfolded. It is possible Nero first selected the Christians and then some people acted as informants, providing the necessary information, or Nero declared that he needed a scapegoat and someone proposed that is should be the Christians. If the latter, the people who acted as the informants may have already identified the Christians so that Nero was provided with a complete solution, or they may have acted only once the choice of the culprit was known.

Although the specific identity of those who informed on the Christians is a matter of speculation, there is good reason to support the view that it was members of the Jewish community residing in Rome. Such a view has no direct support from Tacitus' account. Indeed, one of the notable features of the way he describes the incident is that no link is made between the Christians and the Jewish community. Nor does Tacitus refer to the Christians as a group that had its ori-

**17** This stands in stark comparison to evidence regarding the presence of Jews through their customs, epigraphs and special privileges granted by various Roman authorities. See Leonard V. Rutgers, *The Hidden Heritage of Diaspora Judaism* (Leuven: Peeters, 1998).

**18** See Steven H. Rutledge, *Imperial Inquisitions: Prosecutors and Informants from Tiberius to Domitian* (London: Routledge, 2001).

**19** For example, see Tacitus, *Ann.* 1.74.1–2; 3.25.1; 3.28.3–4; 4.36.1; and 6.29.1.

gins from among the Jewish way of life.[20] While this feature is unusual from both a Christian and a Jewish perspective, it is important not to presume it means that the Romans regarded Christianity as a group that had separated from the larger Jewish community by the mid first-century CE. Rather, it simply reveals that Tacitus, and possibly Nero and his advisers, did not view the Christians as part of the Jewish way of life. If so, why identify members of the Jewish community as the people that assisted Nero in his decision to use the Christians as the scapegoat for the fire?

One of the explanations previously offered as to why Jews would assist Nero is that they hoped to see the Christians punished for trouble they had caused for the Jewish community.[21] It is a line of argument that is not viable for one key reason, the manner of Nero's treatment of the Christians. Past experience, including recent first-hand experience under Claudius, showed that the Roman authorities normally employed short term measures against the offenders. While a growing concern about the character of Nero combined with the severity of the damage caused by the fire may have resulted in hope for a more substantive type of punishment, there was no reason to think it would be as vicious as what Tacitus describes. Angst and concern about the activity of this new group may have developed, especially after the arrival of Paul. It may have encouraged members of the Jewish community to try to distance the Christians from themselves and to see the fire as an opportunity to implicate the Christians in the hope that they may be forced to leave the city, even if only on a temporary basis. Instead, what makes members of the Jewish community the likely informants in this incident is their concern to protect their own position in Rome. The immediate political context in which the Jewish community found itself confirms that there were very strong grounds for self-preservation to be a genuine concern.[22]

It did not require a creative imagination for any of the foreign or minority groups to think that the emperor would seek to identify a scapegoat for the fire. There was a persistent rumour that he had been responsible for what happened. Nero had undertaken a number of actions in order to win public appro-

---

**20** See Edwin A. Judge, "Judaism and the Rise of Christianity: A Roman Perspective," in: *The first Christians*, 431–41 at 432, 435. There is no basis to presume that the Roman authorities needed to go through a process of distinguishing between the Christians and the Jews. However, this view is prevalent within much of the existing discussion. For example, see Walters, "Impact," 179–80; Lampe, *Paul*, 11–16; and Smallwood, *Jews*, 217.

**21** See William H.C. Frend, *Martyrdom and Persecution in the Early Church* (Oxford: Oxford University Press, 1965), 164–65; and Marcel Simon, *Verus Israel: A Study of the Relations between Christians and Jews in the Roman Empire*, trans. H. McKeating (Oxford: Oxford University Press, 1964), 117; cf. the cautionary comments of Smallwood, *Jews*, 217–19.

**22** Contra Walters, "Impact," 180–82, and Smallwood, *Jews*, 219.

val, all to no avail. For the Jewish community, there was good reason for them to think that they would come under consideration as a potential scapegoat. Two of the three previous emperors had found reason to expel members of their community from the city. There were, therefore, grounds to believe that false accusations could be made against them and, once levelled, there would not be an opportunity to offer a response. It is, however, recent events specific to the time since Nero had become emperor that are of particular relevance. They provide a context of increased anxiety and concern as to how Nero would deal with the current situation.[23]

The Jewish community in Rome found themselves coming to the direct attention of the emperor simply by their association with issues pertaining to their homeland. There are three separate incidents that would provide cause for concern regarding how the emperor might view the Jewish community in the aftermath of the fire. The first was the presence in Rome of two Jewish priests who had been sent there by Felix.[24] Exactly when they were sent to Rome and the nature of their offence is not clear. The important point to note here is that they were imprisoned in Rome awaiting trial.[25] The second incident was the resolution of a dispute regarding civic rights in the city of Caesarea Maritima.[26] Unable to resolve the matter at a local level, the governor dispatched representatives to Rome for Nero to adjudicate. The third incident was the resolution of the dispute regarding extensions made to the height of the wall surrounding the Temple.[27] Josephus attributes the decision of Nero to the influence of his wife, Poppaea. It is important not to label her involvement as that of a sympathiser of the Jewish cause. In supporting the view of the high priest and his associates, she was opposing the view of the Herodian ruler. On this occasion Jews were in dispute with fellow Jews and the governor. The tensions and complications associated with this incident are, in part, evident from the decision that the high priest and the treasurer of the Temple were required to stay in Rome.

---

**23** Further exacerbating the situation was uncertainty regarding the nature of any counsel Nero was receiving following the death of Burrus and the retirement of Seneca in 62 CE (Tacitus, *Ann.* 14.51–56).

**24** Josephus, *Vita* 13.

**25** It is not clear whether the matter was resolved before or after the fire in 64 CE. Note also that Josephus depicts that the means of obtaining a favourable outcome lay through a Jewish actor and Nero's wife, Poppaea. It is also possible that the punishment of a bandit leader sent to Rome by Felix, Eleazar b. Dinaeus, was carried out during Nero's reign (Josephus, *A.J.* 20.161).

**26** Josephus, *A.J.* 20.173–78, 183–84.

**27** Josephus, *A.J.* 20.189–98. On the dating of the incident see James C. VanderKam, *From Joshua to Caiaphias: High Priests after the Exile* (Minneapolis, MN: Fortress Press, 2004), 470–75.

All of these incidents were recent occasions where Nero's attention had been drawn to Jews in a way that left them open to being characterised as a disruptive influence.[28] It was not a context in which the Jewish community in Rome could feel confident that they could predict how Nero would behave in the aftermath of the fire. To opt for a proactive approach to the current situation would be an understandable decision. Whether they took the initiative and provided Nero with the idea of blaming the Christians or they waited until it became known that Nero was seeking a scapegoat and then helped identify Christians as suitable targets is not possible to establish.[29] Whatever the precise timing of their involvement, though, in order to protect their own position it is understandable that Jews readily helped make this relatively new, peculiar group the target of Nero's desire to find a scapegoat.[30]

## 3 The fire within early Christian polemic

The fire and the subsequent actions of Nero in the vicious way he punished the Christians is notable by its absence from subsequent Christian writings. There are several references to Nero as an enemy of God and as an evil ruler, often

**28** This attention does not, however, amount to what has been labeled judeophobia. See Peter Schäfer, *Judeophobia: Attitudes toward the Jews in the Ancient World* (Cambridge, MA: Harvard University Press, 1997). See Erich S. Gruen, *Diaspora: Jews amidst Greeks and Romans* (Cambridge, MA: Harvard University Press, 2002), 15–53; and Rutgers, "Roman Policy," 111–15.

**29** There is one further option to note, although it lacks credibility: Nero had already named the Christians, so that the Jews simply helped with the process of locating them. There is no reason why the Christians would have already acquired a profile within the community at large, let alone within the imperial court. Rather, as part of proposing the Christians as a possible scapegoat it would have been necessary to explain how they were a group that was worthy of public ridicule and punishment. The very limited level of knowledge regarding the Christians displayed by Tacitus, and the general level of ignorance exhibited by Pliny the Younger when he encountered the presence of Christians in Bithynia (Pliny, *Ep*. 10.96), reinforces the likelihood that Christians did not have a public profile among Roman authorities in the mid first century CE; cf. Lampe, *Paul*, 15, 16, 83.

**30** A possible, further dimension of the motivation for self-protection included depicting the Christians as a group that had no direct link with the Jewish way of life in order to help ensure they were not mistakenly lumped together. Given the reference in Tacitus to the origins of the group, in Judaea, it could be easily assumed that the Christians were in some manner or another connected with the Jewish way of life. As such, part of the process of informing on the Christians as a group worthy of being punished may have included a claim that they were not a subgroup of the wider Jewish community. In this context, the socio-ethnic profile of the early Christian community in Rome would have had an important bearing on the relative success or otherwise of such a line of argument. See Judge, "Origins," 454; cf. Smallwood, *Jews*, 215.

in tandem with reference to Domitian.[31] There is, however, no version of the incident in later Christian tradition.[32] It is in the New Testament depiction of Jews where the impact of the fire and the identification of the Christians as the culprits are most immediately evident. The crucial factor for recognising this impact is the order in which we read the various writings that constitute the New Testament. Rather than follow the canonical order, it is important to view the writings in their chronological order, commencing with the earliest texts.

A clear divide exists in the depiction of Jews between texts written prior to the fire and in those written after the fire.[33] In the former there is very little evidence of any overt or implied criticism of Jews, let alone reference to them as part of the subject matter. By contrast, in the latter there is significant criticism of Jews and they play a prominent role in much of the subject matter in the synoptic Gospels and in Acts of the Apostles. Jews hardly feature in the writings of Paul, which all predate the fire. While he indicates that there were direct interactions between Jews and Christians, in his capacity as someone who tried to suppress the new movement and as someone who was subsequently on the receiving end of such attacks, Paul does not dwell on such topics.[34] Indeed, they are cited primarily in order for Paul to substantiate another point to his readers. When speaking of rivals and/or opponents Paul's attention focuses on other people he regards as distorting the message of Christ as saviour.[35] In fact, there is only one occasion where Paul is openly critical of Jews (1 Thess 2:13–16). In drawing a parallel between the experience of the believers in Thessalonica and of those in Judaea Paul blames the Jews for attacking Christians, killing Jesus and forcing Christians to flee Judaea. While an explicit example of a neg-

---

**31** For example, see Tertullian, *Apol.* 5.3; 21.25 (CCSL 1.95, 127); Eusebius, *HE* 2.25.3–4 (citing Tertullian); 3.17; 3.20.6–7 (citing Tertullian) (*Eusèbe de Césarée. Histoire ecclésiastique (Livres I–IV)*, ed. Eduard Schwartz and Gustave Bardy, SC 31, Paris: Éditions du Cerf, 2001, 92, 121, 124); and Lactantius, *Mort.* 2.6. In part, the absence of the story from Eusebius' history is due to the fact that he did not use non-Christian Roman sources to construct his narrative.

**32** It is possible that some allusions to the role played by Jews have survived in 1 *Clem.* 5.6 and in a fragment of Melito of Sardis' *Apology* quoted by Eusebius, *HE* 4.26.9. See Smallwood, *Jews*, 218.

**33** In what follows the general scholarly consensus regarding Markan priority will be followed, along with the view that the Gospel was written no earlier than the late 60s CE. See Raymond E. Brown, *An introduction to the New Testament* (New York: Doubleday, 1997), 5–15. It will also be accepted that Rome is the provenance of Mark's Gospel. See Brian J. Incigneri, *The Gospel to the Romans: The Setting and Rhetoric of Mark's Gospel* (Leiden: Brill, 2003).

**34** See Gal 1:13; 3:4–6; and 2 Cor 11:23–33.

**35** For example, see Gal 2:1–14; 6:12–13; 1 Cor 1:10–17; 3:1–23; and 2 Cor 10:1–11:15. For further discussion on Paul's opponents in Galatians see the chapter in this volume by Ian Elmer.

ative depiction of Jews, it is important not to exaggerate its importance. Paul does not repeat the view in any of his later writings. In fact, the only occasion where Jews are subject to direct attention, Romans 9 – 11, presents Jews as people assured of a future in divine salvation history.[36]

In a number of the texts dated after the fire Jews feature prominently and do so in a largely negative manner. Here we focus on the earliest text to be written in the aftermath of the fire, Mark's Gospel. Throughout the account of Jesus' public ministry various Jews are presented as questioning and even opposing his activity.[37] Then, within the account of Jesus' arrest and execution various Jews play a particularly significant role, actively working to ensure that he is executed.[38] The three other canonical Gospels refine and develop the manner in which Jews are depicted as opposing the activity of Jesus, while in Acts of Apostles the main protagonists trying to attack the activity of Jesus' followers are various members of the Jewish community, not Roman officials.[39] This dramatic change, whereby Jews became a direct part of the subject matter and are consistently cast as opponents of Jesus and his followers, is best explained as part of the experience of the Christian community in Rome. The earliest layers of tradition regarding the death of Jesus give no hint of an interest in attacking Jews.[40] However, while the author of Mark's Gospel tried to help his community deal with the trauma of the recent persecution, anger at what had just transpired was given voice in the way that Jesus' public ministry and his execution was recorded. The Jews who had been informants against the Christians in 64 CE became the inspiration for how Jews would be remembered in relation to the career of Jesus. The experience of Christians in Rome was retrospectively written into the story of Jesus. It was a decision that had profound consequences that are still being experienced today. Furthermore, ongoing reflection is required as to how best to move beyond those consequences in a search for meaning regarding both the underlying story and the way it was depicted in the Gospel narratives.

---

**36** See A. Andrew Das, *Paul and the Jews* (Peabody, MA: Hendrickson, 2003).

**37** For example, see Mark 2:16 – 17.18 – 20.24 – 28; 3:1 – 6; 6:1 – 6.14 – 29; 8:14 – 21; 10:2 – 9; 11:27 – 33; 12:1 – 12.13 – 17.18 – 24.38 – 40.

**38** See Mark 14:1 – 2.10 – 11.43 – 50.53 – 65; and 15:1 – 32.

**39** For example, see Acts 18:12 – 17. Other pertinent examples include Acts 13:5; 13:50; 14:1 – 2; 17:1.5; 17:15 – 17; and 18:1.12. In terms of the other Gospel narratives note the depiction of the plot to kill Jesus (Matt 26:3 – 4; Luke 20:20; and John 11:48 – 53).

**40** See Phil 2:6 – 11, esp. v.8; 1 Cor 11:23 – 26; and 15:3 – 4. Even though the material designated as the Q tradition could be cited as further evidence that interest in depicting Jews in a negative manner post-dates the fire, it will not be discussed due to ongoing uncertainty regarding its existence.

Michael P. Theophilos and A.M. Smith*

# The Use of Isaiah 28:11–12 in 1 Corinthians 14:21

## 1 Introduction

The ecclesial practice and theological debate concerning glossalalia was a primary source of dispute between the church in Corinth and its founder. In 1 Corinthians, Paul employs various rhetorical and literary devices in an attempt to address the significant rift which was rapidly developing and consequently eroding his authority and the veracity of his interpretation of the gospel. One such method Paul employs is the quotation of authoritative Old Testament texts to bolster or illustrate his argument against his opponents at Corinth. Exegetes who discuss Paul's use of the Old Testament predominantly fall into two categories. On one hand, there are maximalists who affirm that Paul knew, and sought to evoke in the mind of his readers, the wider scriptural context of his Old Testament source for some discernable theological purpose.[1] On the other hand, minimalists argue that Paul's citations are to be understood as they stand in his text, that is, without reference to the wider context of the Hebrew scriptures.[2] Without doubt these debates will continue for some time. It seems that the most fruitful way forward is for commentators to offer a series of detailed studies on each proposed citation, allusion or echo. It is in this regard that the current investigation of Isaiah 28:11–12 in 1 Corinthians 14:21 is undertaken.

* A.M. Smith was an academic colleague and dear friend who passed away in 2005. Before this, we had both been researching the use of the Hebrew scriptures in early Christian literature, and had intended to embark on many collaborative future publication endeavours, but this aspiration was cut short. This paper honours our initial joint efforts in this regard.

**1** See for example Richard Hays, *Echoes of Scripture in the Letters of Paul* (London: Yale University Press, 1989); Francis Watson, *Paul and the Hermeneutics of Faith* (London: T&T Clark International, 2004).

**2** Günther Bornkamm, *Paul* (New York: Harper & Row, 1971); Herman N. Ridderbos, *Paul: An Outline of his Theology* (Grand Rapids, MI: Eerdmans, 1975); Denys E.H. Whiteley, *The Theology of St. Paul* (Oxford: Blackwell, 1964).

# 2 The *status quaestionis*

## 2.1 Author and recipients

In Stanley E. Porter's comments on method and terminology in discussion of the use of the Old Testament in the New Testament, he provocatively asks: "if one is writing to an uninformed audience who does not know the source text, does that mean that the echoes are no longer present? If they are clear to another audience, does that mean that the text itself is now different, or only the audience?"[3] In noting that a citation or allusion is not dependent on the recipient, Porter highlights the importance of the author's identity in the process of interpretation. Indeed, one could imagine an author alluding to an Old Testament text with which his recipients were unfamiliar, however it strains credibility to suggest that an uninformed author wrote to informed recipients.[4] In this manner, we will concentrate on the author's meaning.

Pauline authorship of 1 Corinthians is undisputed,[5] however Paul's background and conceptual framework are much debated. Sufficient for our discussion is to note that on several occasions Paul identifies himself as a Jew (Rom 9:3; 11:1; 2 Cor 11:22). Furthermore, if Acts provides even the slightest hint of Pauline identity, then one could suggest that he received a thorough Jewish education in Torah (Acts 21:9; 22:3; 26:4–5; cf. Phil 3:5).[6] Therefore in regard to Paul's

---

3 Stanley E. Porter, "The Use of the Old Testament in the New Testament: A Brief Comment on Method and Terminology," in: *Early Christian Interpretation of the Scriptures of Israel: Investigations and Proposals*, eds. Craig A. Evans and James A. Sanders (Sheffield: Sheffield Academic Press, 1997), 79–96 at 83.

4 The perceived recipients (and their perceived ability to recognise the reference and broader context) could of course influence the author's motive for including such an allusion. See discussion below.

5 Cf. 1 Cor 1:1; 16:21. Archibald Robertson and Alfred Plumber, *A Critical and Exegetical Commentary on the First Epistle of St. Paul to the Corinthians*, ICC (2nd edn.; Edinburgh: T&T Clark, 1911), xvi, argue that "both the external and the internal evidence for the Pauline authorship are so strong that those who attempt to show that the apostle was not the writer succeed chiefly in proving their own incompetence as critics." Even the Hegelian critic of the Tübingen school said of the Pauline *Hauptbriefe* (Romans, 1–2 Corinthians, Galatians) that "they bear so incontestably the character of Pauline originality, that there is no conceivable ground for the assertion of critical doubts in their case:" Ferdinand C. Baur, *Paul, the Apostle of Jesus Christ: His Life and Work, His Epistles and His Doctrine*, vol. 1, trans. Eduard Zeller (Edinburgh: University of Edinburgh Press, 1846), 246.

6 For issues in reconstructing the Pauline identity from material in Acts see discussion in Henry J. Cadbury, *The Book of Acts in History* (London: A&C Black, 1955); Robert Jewett, *Dating Paul's Life* (London: SCM Press, 1979); Gerd Lüdemann, *Das Frühe Christentum nach den Traditionen*

use of Isa 28:11–12 in 1 Cor 14:21, it seems plausible to suggest that he was in a position to understand the contextual background of Isaiah 28. This, of course, does not automatically affirm Paul's utilisation of its wider context, but only that it is at least a possibility which commends itself on the basis of the author's identity.

However, questions may be raised as to the extent of the Corinthians' contextual awareness of Paul's Isaianic quotation given that they were (1) predominantly Gentile (1 Cor 12:2; Acts 18:4), and (2) relatively new converts. Although it is difficult, if not impossible, to reconstruct the Corinthian mind, there are several indications that the Corinthians may well have had the potential to understand more than what is normally afforded them.[7] In a recent article, Christopher M. Tuckett has demonstrated that "it may not be unreasonable to postulate a certain amount of knowledge of the OT scripture on the part of the Corinthians."[8] The reasons for this conclusion are formulated from the knowledge Paul seems to assume in his correspondence (1 Cor 15:3; 5:7; 10:1–13) and the mixed Jew/Gentile composition of the Corinthian church (Acts 18:7–8).[9]

## 2.2 Occasion of 1 Corinthians

There are three particular issues which occasioned the writing of 1 Corinthians. First, during Paul's third missionary journey, approximately four to six years after founding the church on his previous visit, he had written a previous letter (cf. 1 Cor 5:9) which was misunderstood by the Corinthians (5:10–13). He thus writes to clarify himself on a number of issues. Second, Paul received news from the household of Chloe (1:11) that there were divisions among the believers in Corinth. Presumably the report included other problems addressed in the letter. Third, as is evident from 7:1 ("now concerning the matters about which you wrote...") Paul is responding to issues raised by the letter *from* (at least some of) the Corinthians delivered by Stephanus, Fortunates and Achaicus (16:17). On the

*der Apostelgeschichte* (Göttingen: Vandenhoeck & Ruprecht, 1987); Ignatius H. Marshall, *The Acts of the Apostles* (Sheffield: JSOT Press, 1992).

7 Christopher D. Stanley, "'Pearls Before Swine': Did Paul's Audiences Understand his Biblical Quotations?," *NovT* 41 (1999): 124–44.

8 Chistopher M. Tuckett, "Paul, Scripture and Ethics. Some Reflections," *NTS* 46 (2000): 403–24 at 410.

9 Ben Witherington, *Conflict and Community in Corinth: A Socio-Rhetorical Commentary on 1 and 2 Corinthians* (Grand Rapids, MI: Eerdmans, 1995), 22–23, explores the variety in race and economic status in the Corinthian church.

basis of Paul's polemical tone it would seem that, not only had the Corinthians fallen into what Paul perceived as misconduct, but they seemed to be at odds with their founding apostle on a number of issues.[10]

One of the abuses that Paul addresses concerns the χαρίσματα in public worship (1 Cor 12–14). From even a cursory reading of these chapters it is evident that some members of the community abused (according to Paul) the gift of γλῶσσαι, taking it as a sign of their superiority over others, and as a result disregarded other believers in the worshipping assembly. Paul specifically challenges this abuse in 1 Cor 14 and attempts to demonstrate its destructive effect on unbelievers (14:20–25). At the climactic point of his argument, Paul introduces a quotation from Isa 28:11–12 to support and bolster his argument. However, problems immediately arise since the explanation of the quote in verse 22 seems antithetical to the illustration provided in verses 23–25. The text seems to contradict itself: for in verse 22 Paul explains that tongues are a sign for unbelievers and prophecy for believers, whereas in verses 23–25 he demonstrates both the negative effects of tongues and the positive effect of prophecy on unbelievers!

## 2.3 Proposed solutions to Paul's use of the Old Testament

On the basis of this difficulty William Barclay omitted the second assertion about prophecy altogether, without even commenting on his oversight.[11] John Phillips, similarly perplexed about the apparent contradiction, reverses the order of the references to believers and unbelievers in order to create agreement with the illustration that follows in verses 23–25.[12] However, this is done without the slightest support of manuscript evidence. Others have sought more credible ways of dealing with the difficulties. All such attempts have to come to grips with three basic difficulties: (1) Paul's use of Isa 28:11–12; (2) the precise meaning of "σημεῖον" in verse 22; and (3) the apparent antithetical statements in verse 22 and the illustration that follows in verses 23–25.[13] In one such attempt, Peter Roberts nevertheless concludes that there is "little similarity between the situation which evoked Isaiah's words, and the circumstances which caused Paul to

**10** Gordon Fee, *The First Epistle to the Corinthians* (Grand Rapids, MI: Eerdmans, 1987), 2–7.
**11** William Barclay, *The Letter to the Corinthians* (Edinburgh: St. Andrew Press, 1984), 146–47.
**12** John B. Phillips, *The New Testament in Modern English* (London: Collins, 1959), 363.
**13** Peter Roberts, "A Sign – Christian or Pagan?," *Expository Times* 90 (1979): 199–203 at 199.

quote them here."[14] Taking support from Bernhard Anderson's work[15] on Isa 7, Roberts argues that tongues are a "sign of divine or spiritual activity"[16] which denotes the presence of God. That is, tongues are the sign of divine activity for which unbelievers look, while prophecy is the true sign of the activity of God in the church.[17] In this way, he concludes that "there seems to be little similarity between the situation which evoked Isaiah's words and the circumstances which caused Paul to quote them here, except for the strange tongues and their ineffectiveness."[18]

Bruce Johanson is also skeptical of the original context's formative influence on Paul's narrative. He suggests that verse 22 is a rhetorical question that Paul placed in the mouths of his opponents. Those who are "spiritual" in the church ask: "Are tongues, then, meant as a sign not for believers but for unbelievers...?" Paul then moves to correct this view, showing that unbelievers saw tongues as madness.[19] Although there is some legitimacy for this alteration of punctuation, the hypothesis is not without problems. Gordon Fee has demonstrated that Johanson's argument breaks down on two accounts.[20] First, Paul's use of ὥστε in verse 22 cannot bear the grammatical weight which is afforded it by an interrogative, and second, there is no contextual indication that Paul is responding to a division over this issue.

Joop Smit also maintains that the importance of the original context of Isa 28:11–12 is "entirely irrelevant."[21] He prefers to envision the quote as referring exclusively to the ecstatic speaking of the pagans at Corinth, perhaps the Cybele–Attis cult, followers of Dionysus or the devotees of Apollo. In this view, tongues are a sign of the Hellenistic frenzies that were commonplace in Paul's day, and are not a suitable indicator of Christian practice.[22] However, such an approach ignores the positive value that Paul places on tongues in 1 Cor 14:18, and as such is not viable within the broader scope of chapter 14.

---

**14** Roberts, "Sign," 201: "It is tempting, too, to treat the succeeding verses as an exposition of this quotation, rather than as further comment on the situation of Corinth."

**15** Bernhard Anderson, *The Living World of the Old Testament* (London: Longmans, 1978), 310.

**16** Roberts, "Sign," 200.

**17** Roberts, "Sign," 200–202.

**18** Roberts, "Sign," 201.

**19** Bruce C. Johanson, "Tongues, A Sign for Unbelievers?: A Structural and Exegetical Study of 1 Corinthians XIV.20–25," *NTS* 25 (1979): 180–203 at 193.

**20** Gordon Fee, *God's Empowering Presence* (Peabody, MA: Hendrickson Publishers, 1994), 646.

**21** Joop F.M. Smit, "Tongues and Prophecy: Deciphering 1 Cor 14:22," *Biblica* 75 (1990): 175–90 at 186.

**22** Smit, "Tongues," 186–87.

### 2.4 A new approach

Unlike the above-mentioned proposals, our contribution will seek to demonstrate that Paul did in fact have the origional context in mind (although carefully defined) when he quoted Isa 28:11–12 in 1 Cor 14:21. It will be shown that the original meaning of judgement was not only recognised by intertestamental Judaism, but that Paul actually utilised/formed a text which shared more affinities with the Masoretic Text than the Septuagint. We propose that much of the ambiguity of the text is resolved if the context of Isaiah is taken seriously. Thus we begin with an assessment of the broader context of Isaiah 28:11–12.

## 3 Isaiah 28:11–12 in literary context

Isaiah 28:11–12 forms part of the larger unit of 28–33, in which Isaiah expands the theme of judgement (introduced in chapter 7) and rebukes Judah for her foolishness in trusting the nations instead of Yahweh.[23] This section (Isa 28–33) is sandwiched between pronouncements against the nations (Isa 24–27) and a collection of eschatological prophesies (Isa 34–35). Isaiah opens the unit with a scathing rebuke of Ephraim's drunken leaders, and speaks of the fall of the Northern Kingdom into the hands of the Assyrians. As has been noted by several commentators, there was some danger that Jerusalem's foreign-policy makers would make an alliance with Egypt (30:3; 31:1). Isaiah saw this as foolish, because he believed help from Egypt was completely unreliable and Egypt could some day seek to turn against Judah (30:3–7; 33:3). The prophet considers it inconceivable that Israel would commit themselves to fickle Egypt instead of to God Almighty.[24] Isaiah aims at exposing the blindness and drunkenness of Israel's leaders and holds firm to the hope that they will somehow turn to God's purposes.

Isaiah 28–33 forms a tripartite structure: chapters 28–29 set the scene of foolish leaders being taunted by outside enemies; chapters 30–31 describe the unwise counsel given, that is, dependence on Egypt, and its folly; and chapters 32–33 point to the true solution when Yahweh will reign in righteousness and rule in justice.[25] Chapter 28 forms two further sub-units. First, verses 1–4 announce God's woe on the Ephraimite leaders, wherein they are described as

23 Isaiah 28–33 is editorially unified by the introductory "woe" formula (28:1; 29:1.15; 30:1; 33:1).
24 John N. Oswalt, *The Book of Isaiah: Chapters 1–39* (Grand Rapids, MI: Eerdmans, 1986), 504.
25 Oswalt, *Isaiah*, 505.

full of pride and "laid low with wine" (28:1). Here Isaiah speaks of their ultimate downfall as they will be trampled underfoot by "one who is powerful and strong like a hailstorm and a destructive wind" (v2). Second, and contrastingly, the scene changes in verses 5 – 29, which go on to describe Yahweh using foreigners for judgement on his people.[26]

Isaiah is appalled at the state of Israel's leadership. Not only are their political leaders incompetent (vv1 – 4), but Israel's spiritual leaders are depicted as being intoxicated, staggering under the influence of wine. No longer do prophets see visions and priests render decisions based on a correct application of the law (v7). Rather Isaiah observes them stumbling around in their vomit, where there is no spot without filth. John A. Motyer suggests that this is a picture from a banquet that Isaiah actually attended, where he witnessed the drunken stupor of Israel's religious leadership.[27]

An analysis of verses 9 – 13 also reveals a tripartite structure (vv9 – 10, 11 – 12, 13). Motyer notes that these units are unified by identical wording in verses 10 and 13 and are connected by the similar word כִּי (lit. "for").[28] In verses 9 – 10 the drunken priests and prophets notice the prophet and start to ridicule him for his simplistic message. Their arrogance is vivid as they ask: "who is he trying to teach? To whom is he explaining his message?" They assume that they are more mature than children weaned from milk or infants that are taken from the breast. The irony is that they are to be treated as children, as they have not understood and applied Yahweh's commands.[29]

In their conceit, the priests and prophets mock Isaiah's message with simple repeated words: "כִּי צַו לָצָו צַו לָצָו קַו לָקָו קַו לָקָו זְעֵיר שָׁם זְעֵיר שָׁם." However the meaning of these words is not clear. A literal translation – "it is precept upon precept, precept upon precept, line upon line, line upon line, here a little, there a little" (NRSV, NIV) – seems unlikely. The fact that צַו and קַו cause interpretive confusion is evidenced in the lack of coherence in the various translations in the Jewish tradition. For example, the Septuagint translators saw צַו as "tribulation" or "distress," whereas the Isaiah Targum takes צַו as "commandment." The Syriac Peshitta interprets the phrase: "filth upon filth...vomit upon vomit." Furthermore, the Great Scroll of Isaiah (1QIsa[a]) changes the ו to a י, possibly indicating that

26 Marvin A. Sweeney, *Isaiah 1 – 39: With an Introduction to Prophetic Literature* (Grand Rapids, MI: Eerdmans, 1996), 361.

27 John A. Motyer, *Isaiah: An Introduction and Commentary* (Leicester: InterVarsity Press, 1999), 231.

28 Motyer, *Isaiah*, 231.

29 Samuel H. Widyapranawa, *The Lord is Savior: Faith in National Crisis. A Commentary on the Book of Isaiah 1 – 39* (Grand Rapids, MI: Eerdmans, 1990), 169.

the scribe did not know what the original meant.[30] An alternate explanation suggests that the symmetrical repetition of each phrase seems to point to the fact that these words were used as nonsense syllables employed intentionally without meaning.[31] David Stacey concurs and affirms that the verse is "untranslatable" and lacks coherent meaning.[32] This "gibberish" is probably a continuation of the Israelite mockery as taunt: "This is how he sounds, 'blah, blah, blah'."[33]

There is a marked change in direction in verses 11–12. Israel has not listened to the clear message of God spoken through the prophet; rather, they scorned this message in their drunkenness and reduced his speech to mere "gibberish." Isaiah now announces that because of their hardness of heart, God will speak even more clearly, by sending a nation of "foreign lips and strange tongues" to communicate his message of wrath. That Yahweh distances himself from his people is evidenced in the phrase "this people."[34] No longer are the Israelites seen as Yahweh's beloved people of the covenant. They have continually disobeyed their covenantal obligations and as a result face their due judgement.

In verse 12 it is revealed that the leaders have still not heeded Yahweh's clear message. They have not given the weary rest, but instead ruled carelessly. John D.W. Watts notes that the promise of Canaan being a resting place was based on the condition that they obeyed Yahweh's commandments.[35] But as is blatantly obvious, Israel has failed to remain faithful to the covenant, and thus Yahweh enacts judgement. That this judgement takes the form of "foreign lips and strange tongues" (i.e., the Assyrians) should not be seen as a surprise. In the covenantal curses of Deuteronomy 28–30 Israel had been warned that if they disobeyed the commands that Yahweh had given them, then "a nation whose language [they could] not understand" would be brought in to destroy them (Deut 28:39).[36] In Isaiah 28:12 Israel had not listened, so Yahweh was now going to send the Assyrians to speak his clear message of judgement.[37]

---

**30** Wayne Grudem, "1 Corinthians 14:20–25: Prophecy and Tongues as Signs of God's Attitude," *WTJ* 41/2 (1979): 381–96.

**31** Francis Brown, Samuel R. Driver, and Charles A. Briggs, *A Hebrew and English Lexicon of the Old Testament* (Oxford: The Clarendon Press, 1907), 875.

**32** David Stacey, *Isaiah 1–39* (London: Epworth Press, 1993), 172. Richard Hays, *First Corinthians* (Louisville, KY: John Knox Press, 1997), 240, argues that "it may be nothing more than a string of nonsense syllables."

**33** Stacey, *Isaiah*, 172.

**34** John D.W. Watts, *Isaiah 1–33* (Waco, TX: Word Books, 1985), 363.

**35** Watts, *Isaiah*, 364.

**36** Oscar P. Robertson, "Tongues: Sign of Covenant Curse and Blessing," *WTJ* 38 (1975): 43–53 at 45.

**37** Cf. Isa 18:2.

In verse 13 the tables are turned on the Israelite leaders. Yahweh's word to them becomes exactly the same nonsense words that the drunken rulers had mocked Isaiah with in verse 10. God's judgement on them is to speak to them in words they cannot understand.[38] In this confusion they "go and fall backward" and are "injured, snared and captured." Instead of the word of the Lord acting to guide his people, here it is depicted as operating as judgement through obfuscation.[39]

## 4 Isaiah 28:11–12 in intertestamental Judaism

Within intertestamental Judaism the text of Isaiah 28:11–12 (MT) is fairly stable, with only one known variant occurring in 1QIsa[a]. Here the Great Scroll of Isaiah differs from the Masoretic Text's anomalous אָבוּא "to be willing" and has אבה "they were willing/desirous."[40] Emil Kautzsch notes that an aleph was sometimes added at the end of a word to a final û, î or ô.[41] However he believes that Isa 28:12 is not so much an example of Arabic orthography as it was an early scribal error.

The Septuagint differs from the Masoretic Text in several important regards. The most significant change is from יְדַבֵּר אֶל־הָעָם הַזֶּה ("He [God] will speak to this people") in the Masoretic Text, to λαλήσουσιν τῷ λαῷ τούτῳ ("they [the Assyrians] will speak to this people") in the Septuagint. Instead of this text being one of judgement on the Ephraimites (as in MT), the Septuagint changes it into an example of Ephraim's courageous endurance against the invaders. In the Septuagint, Ephraim refuses to listen to the Assyrian's instructions, while in the Masoretic Text they refuse to listen to the clear command of the Lord.[42]

The Isaiah Targum translates Isa 28:11–13 very differently.[43] The Targum changes verse 11 to refer to the Israelites who scoffed at the prophets with odd speech and mocking tongues. Such behaviour was to be met with harsh judgement from the Lord. Verse 13 offers an interpretation of this event:

---

**38** Widyapranawa, *Lord*, 170.

**39** See further Grudem, "1 Corinthians," 382.

**40** Ludwig Koehler and Walter Baumgartner, *The Hebrew and Aramaic Lexicon of the Old Testament* (New York: E.J. Brill, 1994), 3.

**41** Emil Kautzsch, *Gesenius' Hebrew Grammar* (Oxford: Clarendon Press, 1910), 81.

**42** David E. Lanier, "With Stammering Lips and Another Tongue: 1 Cor 14:20–22 and Isa 28:11–12," *Criswell Theological Review* 5 (1991): 259–85 at 262.

**43** The common tendency was for the Targums to be interpretive. See John Bowker, *The Targums and Rabbinic Literature* (Cambridge: Cambridge University Press, 1969), 5.

> And this will be the cup of their retribution, because they transgressed the word of the Lord, even because they were commanded to perform the law, and what they were commanded they did not wish to do; therefore they will be handed over to the Gentiles, who do not know the law. And because they went in their own pleasure and did not desire to perform my pleasure, therefore they will hope for help in the time when I bring distress upon them, and there will be neither help nor support for them. And because my sanctuary was little in their eyes, to serve there, therefore they will be left as little among the Gentiles, where they will be exiled; that they may go and stumble backwards, and be broken and caught and taken.[44]

Roy Harrisville, Edward Engelbrecht and Karl Sandnes have traced the dependence of 1QH 2:18[45] and 1QH 4:16,[46] Qumran thanksgiving hymns, to Isa 28:11–12.[47] Sandnes demonstrates that the Qumran community used Isaiah 28:11–12 for the keywords in formulating these hymns.[48] Both texts link disobedience, tongues and judgement. In 1QH 2:18bf the subjects of the verse come to ruin because they exchanged their understanding and knowledge for lips of uncircumcision and a foreign tongue. In 1QH 4:16, the subjects have all their works turned into folly because they listened to lying prophets who spoke with strange lips, and did not give ear to God's word. In both cases tongues brought ruin on the subjects because of their disobedience.

The evidence from intertestamental Jewish literature is diverse and varied. However, significant for our discussion is to note how Qumran and the Targum preserve the Masoretic Text's context of judgement, while the Septuagint pictures these verses as an example of Israel's valiant endurance against the Assyrians' accusations. It seems determinative that Paul employs a text which is much closer to the Masoretic Text than the Septuagint. We will return to this in due course.

---

**44** Translation from Bruce Chilton, *The Isaiah Targum* (Wilmington, DE: Michael Glazier Inc., 1987), 51.

**45** "Thou hast put teaching and understanding, that he may open a fountain of knowledge to all men of insight. They exchanged them for lips of uncircumcision, and for a foreign tongue of a people without understanding, that they might come to ruin in their straying." Translation from Geza Vermes, *The Dead Sea Scrolls in English* (Maryland: Penguin Books, 1962), 154.

**46** "They come to enquire of Thee from the mouth of lying prophets deceived by error who speak (with strange) lips to Thy people, and an alien tongue that they may cunningly turn all their works to folly. For (they harken) not (to) Thy (voice), nor do they give ear to Thy word." Vermes, *Dead Sea Scrolls*, 162.

**47** Roy Harrisville, "Speaking in Tongues: A Lexicographical Study," *CBQ* 38 (1976): 35–48 at 42–43; Edward A. Engelbrecht, "To Speak in a Tongue: The Old Testament and Early Rabbinic Background for a Pauline Expression," *Concordia Journal* 22 (1996): 295–302 at 299–300; Karl O. Sandnes, "Prophecy – A Sign for Believers (1 Cor 14:20–25)," *Biblica* 77 (1996): 1–15 at 9.

**48** Sandnes, "Prophecy," 9 ff.

# 5 Background context and discussion of 1 Corinthians 14:20–25

As noted above, the general scholarly consensus regarding 1 Corinthians is that it was authored by Paul while in Ephesus somewhere between 52–58 CE in response to the state of the church in Corinth. The letter is situational and responds to the primary question of what it means to be "spiritual."[49] One of the final issues that Paul addresses in the letter concerns the place of spiritual gifts in the community of worship (12:1–14:40). The fact that Paul devotes three chapters to this matter seems to indicate the extent of the abuses occurring at Corinth.[50]

1 Cor 12:1–14:40 mimics the tripartite structure that Paul used in his previous argument regarding idol meat (chs. 8–10). The opening section (12:1–31a) addresses the issue of spiritual gifts in general, using the human body as a metaphor to show how there are many different, yet complementary, gifts in the church. In the middle section (12:31b–13:13), Paul describes the preeminence of love. Initially this chapter seems to be out of context, but it actually provides the normative principle that Paul sees governing all the spiritual manifestations. Only in the closing section (ch. 14), does Paul give specific directions for regulating the various spiritual gifts, especially the gifts of tongues and prophecy. Here Paul seeks to bring the disorderly self-centered practices under control so that the whole church may be built up.[51]

## 5.1 Immediate context 14:1–19

Having laid the foundation in chapters 12 and 13, Paul moves to address his main concern regarding the condition of Corinthian "worship meetings." In this chapter Paul shares his vision for the community of worship, a community that on the one hand fully embraces the spontaneous leading of the Spirit but on the other, a community that is not chaotic or unintelligible. His solution to this precarious balance is to insist on love (which he developed in ch. 13) and to emphasise

49 Fee, *Corinthians*, 5–6.

50 Richard Hays, *First Corinthians* (Louisville, KY: John Knox Press, 1997), 206.

51 Hays, *Corinthians*, 206.

the necessity of conducting the worship service so that people are built up,[52] arguing for intelligibility above unintelligibility.[53]

In verses 1–5 Paul argues for the use of the spiritual gifts in a manner of love. Paul holds in tension both the need to desire spiritual gifts, and the need to edify through intelligible speech. He does this by outlining the benefits of tongues and prophecy. Tongues are a speech directed toward God, which edify the pray-er (and not anyone else, for they are incomprehensible speech). Prophecy, on the other hand, benefits the whole church, and is therefore beneficial for strengthening, encouraging and comforting (vv3–4).

In verses 6–12, Paul demonstrates the uselessness of unintelligible speech through four examples. In verse 6, Paul asserts that it would be non-beneficial to the Corinthian church if he came to speak to them in tongues without bringing a revelation, or knowledge, or a word of instruction. In verse 7, he shows that a distinction of notes (intelligibility) is important in order to recognise a melody. Paul shows in verse 8 that only a clear sound (intelligible) of the trumpet will prepare the army ready for battle. And in verse 9, Paul illustrates his point by referring to the example of language barriers.[54]

Thirdly, in verses 10–13, Paul argues for the use of the mind to communicate intelligibly in the public worship assembly.[55] The tongue-speaker should pray that his tongue may be interpreted (v13). Only then can the rest of the church agree and say "Amen" (v16). Without denying the importance of speaking in tongues (cf. v18), Paul states his preference: that he would rather speak five intelligible words in the public assembly than speak ten thousand words in a tongue (v19).

## 5.2 Exegesis of 14:20–25

In verse 20 there is a turn in the argument marked by the vocative Ἀδελφοί, and the abrupt exhortation for them to cease behaving as children. Having established the pointlessness of speaking in tongues without interpretation in the church assembly, Paul now moves on to describe the effects of tongues on the unbeliev-

---

**52** Hays, *Corinthians*, 206–207, argues that edification is the central idea of this chapter, and notes that the verb οἰκοδομέω (to build up) and the noun οἰκοδομή (building up/edification) occur seven times, especially in the summary statements of verses 5, 12, 26.

**53** Fee, *Corinthians*, 652.

**54** Anthony C. Thiselton, *The First Epistle to the Corinthians* (Grand Rapids, MI: Paternoster Press, 2000), 1101.

**55** Thiselton, *Corinthians*, 1107.

er. He starts off by exhorting the Corinthians to correct their thinking about speaking in tongues (v20). He then modifies Isaiah 28:11–12 to make his point that tongues do not lead to repentance and are therefore not helpful to unbelievers. Based on this quote, Paul makes two assertions: (1) that tongues are a sign not to believers but to unbelievers; and (2) that prophecy is not for unbelievers but believers (v23). Paul then goes on to illustrate the relative effects of tongues (v23) and prophecy (vv24–25) on unbelievers.[56] Paul uses a typical A–B–A' pattern in his argument here. He exhorts the Corinthian believers to (A) stop thinking like children (stated in the negative), then (B) tells them to be innocent in evil (stated in the positive),[57] and (A') instructs them to become mature in their understanding (stating the positive of A). Their understanding that tongues are a sign of their transcendent spirituality reveals their childishness. Although Paul uses παιδία here, it is possible that he alludes to 3:1, where he explained that he could not address the Corinthians as spiritual people (πνευματικοῖς), but as mere infants (νηπίοις). In instructing the Corinthians to grow up and become mature in their understanding, Paul may have had in mind the immediate context of the following Isaianic quotation, in which the Ephraimite leaders ask: "Who is he trying to teach? To whom is he explaining his message? To children weaned from their milk, from those just taken from the breast?" (Isa 28:9). Here Ephraim assumed that they were more mature than children weaned from milk and infants taken from the breast. Both texts call for an understanding and search for mature believers to apply the message of God. Furthermore, both texts have an ironic application of babies.[58]

In verse 21, Paul introduces his quote from Isaiah with ἐν τῷ νόμῳ γέγραπται ("in the law it is written…"). The term νόμος (law) can refer to scripture in general as is evidenced by Rom 3:19 (cf. Jn 10:34; 12:34 and 15:25).[59] Although Paul demonstrates freedom in interpretation of law (cf. Gal), the scriptures remained a sacred book and an authority which Paul could quote. As such, the introductory formula "γέγραπται" ("it is written") was intended to add force to Paul's argumentation.

---

**56** Fee, *Empowering*, 236.

**57** Thiselton, *Corinthians*, 1119, is right to prefer "wickedness" here, as being innocent in matters of "evil" could imply remaining aloof to understanding the evil forces that contend against the good. On the other hand, "wickedness" entails rejecting knowledge of divisive strategies which promote one's evil purposes, including the manipulation of what is seen as being "spiritual" to promote self interests.

**58** Lanier, "Stammering," 270–71.

**59** Robertson and Plummer, *Corinthians*, 316.

But why does Paul choose Isaiah 28:11–12 and quote it here? The most obvious reason is that it is selected because it speaks about "strange tongues."[60] However, it seems that Paul does more than cite a text which refers in some way to other tongues. Up until now Paul has been arguing for the superiority of prophecy over uninterpreted tongues in the context of the worship assembly. Now Paul goes on to demonstrate that tongues are completely destructive for the unbeliever, and uses the context of Isaiah 28:11–12 to show that unintelligible tongues are God's sign of judgement on unbelievers – a sign that is not suitable for the unbelievers attending the worship assembly. To make his point Paul does not merely quote the Old Testament text, but adapts it in numerous ways. It is to this issue that we now turn.[61]

Adaptations to MT/LXX

| Masoretic Text (MT) | Septuagint (LXX) | NA[27] |
|---|---|---|
| כִּי בְּלַעֲגֵי שָׂפָה וּבְלָשׁוֹן אַחֶרֶת יְדַבֵּר אֶל־הָעָם הַזֶּה׃ אֲשֶׁר אָמַר אֲלֵיהֶם זֹאת הַמְּנוּחָה הָנִיחוּ לֶעָיֵף וְזֹאת הַמַּרְגֵּעָה וְלֹא אָבוּא שְׁמוֹעַ | διὰ φαυλισμὸν χειλέων διὰ γλώσσης ἑτέρας, ὅτι λαλήσουσιν τῷ λαῷ τούτῳ λέγοντες αὐτῷ Τοῦτο τὸ ἀνάπαυμα τῷ πεινῶντι καὶ τοῦτο τὸ σύντριμμα, καὶ οὐκ ἠθέλησαν ἀκούειν. | ἐν ἑτερογλώσσοις καὶ ἐν χείλεσιν ἑτέρων λαλήσω τῷ λαῷ τούτῳ καὶ οὐδ' οὕτως εἰσακούσονταί μου, λέγει κύριος. |

| Translation | Translation | Translation |
|---|---|---|
| Truly, with stammering lip and with alien tongue he will speak to this people, to whom he has said, "This is rest; give rest to the weary; and this is repose;" yet they would not hear. | by reason of the contemptuous *words* of the lips, by means of another language: for they shall speak to this people, saying to them, "This is the rest to him that is hungry, and this is the calamity:" but they would not hear. | "By people of strange tongues and by the lips of foreigners I will speak to this people; yet even then they will not listen to me," says the Lord. |

Christopher Stanley notes that "determining the precise relationship between the wording of 1 Cor 14:21 and the text of the Septuagint is one of the greatest challenges in the entire corpus of Pauline citations."[62] Paul's version[63] differs

**60** Roberts, "Sign," 201.

**61** In addition to the discussion below, see the lengthy discussion in Christopher D. Stanley, *Paul and the Language of Scripture: Citation Technique in the Pauline Epistles and Contemporary Literature*, SNTSMS 74 (Cambridge: Cambridge University Press, 1992), 198 ff.

**62** Stanley, *Paul*, 197.

from both the Septuagint and the Masoretic Text but appears to share more affinities with the latter text.[64] David Lanier demonstrates that Paul's use of coordinating conjunctions and prepositions corresponds much more closely with the Masoretic Text than the Septuagint.[65] However, there is also evidence that Paul used a similar version to Aquila, as Origen says that "εὗρον τὰ ἰσοδυναμοῦντα τῇ λέξει ταύτῃ ἐν τῇ τοῦ Ἀκύλου ἑρμηνείᾳ κείμενα."[66]

Paul's text is unique in several ways. In place of the Septuagint/Masoretic Text's "stammering lips" and "strange tongues," his quotation inverts their order in order to aid his argument in focusing on the issue of tongues. He therefore places "other-tongues" (ἑτερογλώσσοις) in the first place as a focus of attention.[67] Second, in place of "stammering lips" (LXX/MT), Paul has "lips of others." Within the context of 1 Cor 14, the "others" refers to the Corinthian believers who are speaking in tongues as a sign of their spirituality. These tongues, as we will see shortly, have a negative effect on the unbeliever.[68] Thirdly, Paul uses λαλήσω ("I will speak") (cf. MT), as opposed to the λαλήσουσιν ("they will speak") of the Septuagint. Paul puts the speech into the mouth of God and reveals that it is no longer the Assyrians babbling, but Yahweh himself who speaks and thus brings judgement. Paul reiterates this emphasis by concluding the quote with the formula λέγει κύριος ("says the Lord").[69] Lanier also notes that Paul's addition of μου agrees with the shift to first person in the main verb and as such is closer to the Masoretic Text.[70] Interestingly, Paul does not quote the entirety of verses 11–12, deleting God's message of comfort: "This is rest; give rest to the weary; and this is repose." Presumably this was omitted in order to focus on the negative effect of uninterpreted tongue-speaking. Paul therefore seems to be "heightening the connection between God's use of unintelligible tongues to rebuke his people and their obstinate refusal to heed and

---

**63** A few variants do exist. "Other tongues" (ἑτερογλώσσεις) is changed to "other tongues" (ἑτέραις γλώσσαις) in F G Vulgate ("in aliis linguis") Tertullian, and (ἕτερον) [a A B 17 and other cursives], and is rendered (ἑτέροις) by D E F G K L P A. See discussion in Robertson and Plummer, *Corinthians*, 317.

**64** See discussion below.

**65** Lanier, "Stammering," 268.

**66** *Philocalia* 9. Greek text cited in Robertson and Plummer, *Corinthians*, 316: "I found the equivalent of this saying in the translation of Aquila."

**67** Fee, *Empowering*, 239.

**68** Fee, *Empowering*, 239.

**69** Cf. Rom 12:19; 14:11; 2 Cor 6:17–18. Stanley, *Paul*, 174, suggests that this is added to "emphasize the divine authority inherent in the original pronouncement."

**70** Lanier, "Stammering," 270.

obey."[71] Lastly, Paul differs from the Masoretic Text's "they would not hear," and instead has "but even then (after having heard the tongue-speech) they (the unbelievers) will not listen to me." Here Paul also differs from the ἀκούειν ("hear") of the Septuagint and has εἰσακούσονται ("obey"), agreeing more with the שְׁמוֹעַ of the Masoretic Text. Paul makes the connection clear; tongues will certainly not result in obedience. Rather, tongues will have the opposite effect on the unbeliever, thereby fulfilling the quote.

So far, so good? Apparently so. However, serious exegetical problems arise in verses 22 onwards where Paul seems to make two antithetical statements. Several centuries later our own Chrysostom wrote: "the difficulty at this place is great, which seems to arise from what is said."[72] Modern commentators have had no less a difficult time in arriving at a consensus. Simon Kistemaker notes that "this text has been problematic for every interpreter."[73] Anthony C. Thiselton admits that this has been "acknowledged to be...the most difficult verse in the epistle,"[74] and Richard Hays finds only "great confusion" in this section of Paul's use of the Hebrew scriptures; he concludes, "it seems best to acknowledge that Paul's argument here is somewhat garbled."[75]

The problem is twofold. The first relates to the precise meaning of "sign" (σημεῖον) and the second concerns the relationship between the assertions in verse 22 and the illustrations that follow in verses 23–25, especially how the second assertion relates to the second illustration.[76] It is clear that Paul is citing Isaiah 28:11–12 to show that "other tongues" are a "sign" for unbelievers. It is not, however, immediately clear what this means.

In regard to the meaning of "sign," two main possibilities have been suggested: either (1) a sign of judgement, or (2) a sign of grace. The first option is certainly favoured on the basis of the historical context of the Isaianic quotation. Even Roberts, who is skeptical of the Hebrew Bible's conceptual influence admits "it would be difficult to deny that the strange-tongue Assyrians were meant to be a sign of judgement to Judah."[77] However, a legitimate question arises as to how Paul can speak positively of tongues elsewhere, when here σημεῖον refers to

---

**71** Lanier, "Stammering," 270.
**72** Chrys., *1 Cor. hom.* 36 (PG 61.307.25–27): Πολλῆν ἐνταῦθα ἐκ τῶν εἰρημένων τὴν ἐπαπόρησιν ἴδοι τις ἄν.
**73** Simon Kistemaker, *Exposition of the First Epistle to the Corinthians* (Grand Rapids, MI: Baker Books, 1993), 500.
**74** Thiselton, *Corinthians*, 1122.
**75** Hays, *Corinthians*, 240.
**76** Fee, *Empowering*, 239–240.
**77** Roberts, "Sign," 200.

judgement. It is important to note in this regard that the semantic domain of σημεῖον in the Old Testament can also include a positive element. At several points in the history of Israel a "σημεῖον" was both a positive action towards those who obeyed God and a negative response towards those who disobeyed. This is seen for example in the signs that Moses and Aaron performed before the Israelites in the plague narrative of Exod 4–11. These were positive signs to the Israelite believers, but negative signs for the Egyptians.[78]

Karl Sandnes demonstrates that Paul's use of ὥστε in verse 22 actually introduces the conclusion of what was referred to in the quotation.[79] Here tongues function as a sign of judgement on the unbelieving Israelites in Isaiah 28:11–12. Paul now applies this to the unbelievers who attend the worship meetings in Corinth. Because of the Corinthians' misuse of tongues, the unbelievers cannot understand God's message and thus are under judgement. However, *unlike* the Ephraimites in Isaiah 28, the unbelievers are not deserving of such judgement, as they have not even had the opportunity of hearing the clear message of the gospel. This is precisely Paul's point. Because uninterpreted tongues function as a sign of judgement, they cannot be met with belief. Rather, the unbeliever will think that those who are speaking in tongues are mad (v23). Thus the scriptural quotation is fulfilled, "even then (after hearing the tongues) they will not listen to me."[80] The arrogance of the Corinthians' spiritual superiority, through the gratuitous use of tongues, is leading to the damnation of unbelievers. This occurs because the tongue-speakers are pronouncing an inappropriate signal of judgement upon those who are visiting and who have not yet had an opportunity to believe.

The residual problem however is how one reconciles verse 22b (prophesy for believers) with the following illustration of prophecy functioning for the benefit of bringing unbelievers to faith. The solution seems to be in the careful manner in which Paul has constructed these verses, in particular verse 22. In most discussion it is assumed that 22b is dependent on εἰς σημεῖόν.[81] This can be illustrated as follows:

**78** Cf. the occasion when the earth purportedly opened and swallowed Korah and those associated with the rebellion; Num 26:10 "...served as a warning sign."

**79** Sandnes, "Prophecy," 10.

**80** Fee, *Empowering*, 240.

**81** Joachim Jeremias, "Chiasmus in den Paulusbriefen," *ZNW* 49 (1958): 145–56 at 147. See discussion in Johanson, "Tongues," 186.

ὥστε αἱ γλῶσσαι εἰσιν
εἰς σημεῖόν
οὐ τοῖς πιστεύουσιν
ἀλλὰ
τοῖς ἀπίστοις

δὲ ἡ προφητεία
οὐ τοῖς ἀπίστοις
ἀλλὰ
τοῖς πιστεύουσιν

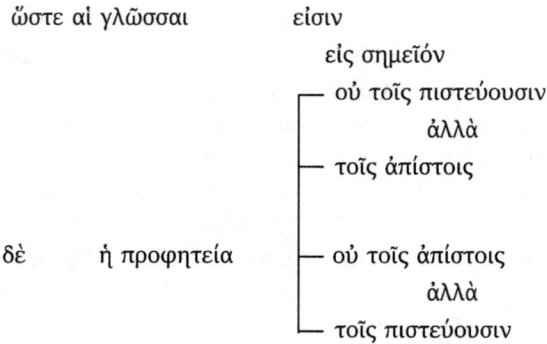

However, given that there is no repeated εἰς σημεῖόν in 22b, the grammatical structure can more accurately be represented with the grammatical dependency of 22b on εἰσιν not σημεῖόν.

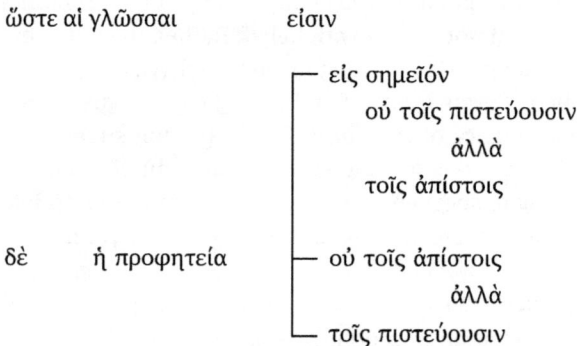

ὥστε αἱ γλῶσσαι εἰσιν
εἰς σημεῖόν
οὐ τοῖς πιστεύουσιν
ἀλλὰ
τοῖς ἀπίστοις

δὲ ἡ προφητεία
οὐ τοῖς ἀπίστοις
ἀλλὰ
τοῖς πιστεύουσιν

In this sense, it is not stated that prophecy is a to be a "σημεῖον" (sign) to believers, but only that prophecy is *for* believers. That is, it is for believers to participate in because of the positive effects on the unbelievers. It thus then functions positively in verses 23–25 for unbelievers precisely because prophecy is for believers (i.e., they are prophesying). Paul, then, is encouraging the Corinthian believers to continue this practice *for the sake of* offering a positive signal to unbelievers. After hearing "the secrets of his heart" being laid bare, the unbeliever will think that the believers have knowledge which only a divine being could reveal and thus "will bow down before God and worship him, declaring 'God is really among you'" (v25).

# 6 Conclusion: Paul's hermeneutical use of Isaiah 28:11–12

This paper has argued that Paul understood the judgement context of Isaiah 28:11–12 and purposely used it to illustrate his point to the Corinthian church. This is evidenced by the fact that Paul shaped his version of Isaiah to conform more closely to the Hebrew text, and that the original meaning makes sense of this passage that is otherwise riddled with complications. However, it is important to acknowledge that the two contexts also differ to a degree – however, this seems to be part of Paul's irony. In Isaiah 28, tongues were a foreign human language which were a sign of God's judgement. In 1 Corinthians 14, tongues are a gift of the Holy Spirit indicating the arrival of the new age. In Isaiah, the "hardening of hearts" occurred because Ephraim had rejected the clear word of the Lord. In Corinth, the "hardening of hearts" occurred because of the result of unloving, selfish actions of immature believers.[82] In this regard Roberts says "it quickly becomes clear that the two situations are not parallel. It is hardly fair to judge and condemn unbelievers on the basis of an unintelligible message uttered by Christians, in the same way that one might condemn unbelieving Judah."[83] This, however, is exactly the point Paul is making. The judgement *is* unfair and therefore the practice should be stopped. It is illegitimate to bring judgement on unbelievers because they, unlike Judah have not had a chance to repent.[84] Paul shows the Corinthian believers that they have not acted in love. They have used their uninterpreted tongues to destroy others. Paul's criterion for appropriate worship is edification through intelligibility. Thus we may conclude with Bengel who said: "quatenus prophetia ex infidelibus credentes facit; lingua loquens infidelium sibi relinquit."[85]

---

**82** See discussion in Lanier, "Stammering," 280.

**83** Roberts, "Sign," 200.

**84** Lanier, "Stammering," 280. However, in another regard, as Thiselton, *Corinthians*, 1121, has noted, the two contexts match well "those who were 'wise' in their own eyes dismiss the plain message as childish."

**85** "Prophesy makes believers of unbelievers; the speaking tongue leaves the unbeliever to himself." Cited in Thiselton, *Corinthians*, 1122–23.

David C. Sim

# Conflict in the Canon: The Pauline Literature and the Gospel of Matthew

## 1 Introduction

The very notion of "the canon" in either the Jewish or Christian traditions raises complex problems of terminology and definition.[1] In its usual sense, the term "canon" refers to a fixed and closed collection of sacred and holy scriptures which cannot be altered by omissions or additions.[2] As is well known, the evolution of the specific Christian canon (or New Testament) was a long and protracted process which began with a quite fluid concept of authoritative texts before hardening into a much more rigid collection of scriptural documents. The Pauline corpus, including some of the Deutero-Pauline epistles, had emerged by the early second century CE as important and authoritative Christian texts. Ignatius of Antioch knew many of the Pauline letters and made constant reference to them,[3] and a little later the author of 2 Peter in 3:15–16 refers to them specifically as scripture (αἱ γραφαί). There is solid evidence that the four New Testament Gospels, which Irenaeus recognised as a unified and authoritative collection around 180, had already achieved that status by the 140s.[4] By contrast, other Christian documents were vigorously debated by the various churches before being either included in or excluded from the corpus of Christian scriptures. The Book of Revelation was eventually accepted on the basis of its (dubious) Johannine connections, while another popular early Christian apocalypse, the *Shepherd* of Hermas, was ultimately excluded.[5] While it is not possible to say

1 See the recent survey of these issues in Lee Martin McDonald, "What Do We Mean by Canon? Ancient and Modern Questions," in: *Jewish and Christian Scriptures: The Function of 'Canonical' and 'Non-Canonical' Religious Texts*, eds. James H. Charlesworth and Lee Martin McDonald, T&T Clark Jewish and Christian Text Series (London: T&T Clark, 2010), 8–40.

2 Eugene Ulrich, "The Notion and Definition of Canon," in: *The Canon Debate*, eds. Lee Martin McDonald and James A. Sanders (Peabody, MA: Hendrickson, 2002), 21–35.

3 Robert M. Grant correctly argues that Ignatius shows familiarity with Romans, 1 and 2 Corinthians, Galatians, Ephesians, Philippians, Colossians, 1 Thessalonians, and perhaps 1 and 2 Timothy as well. See Id., *The Apostolic Fathers*, vol. 1, *An Introduction* (London: Thomas Nelson and Sons, 1964), 57.

4 For discussion, see Graham N. Stanton, "The Fourfold Gospel," *NTS* 43 (1997): 317–46.

5 For discussion of the process by which texts were finally accepted or rejected, see Everett Ferguson, "Factors Leading to the Selection and Closure of the New Testament Canon: A Survey

with precision when the Christian canon was finally settled, most scholars would accept that we can speak of a final and closed canon by the end of the fourth century or the early fifth century.[6]

The concept of a Christian canon does not simply involve the selection of a closed corpus of authoritative texts; it also presupposes that these texts possess a theological integrity or theological unity. The canonical texts convey by different media and genres and in diverse ways the same basic theological message. The texts, both individually and as a corpus, are considered to be, amongst other things, divine revelation, the word of God, inspired by the Holy Spirit and inerrant. Their orthodoxy and theological similarity is validated by the fact that these texts were ultimately viewed as God's (or Christ's) gift to the church.[7] Yet, whatever the claims about the theological unity of the various New Testament texts, either in antiquity or in modern times, opposing voices have been raised against this neat schema. Modern scholarship in particular has questioned the canonical approach to the Christian scriptures, preferring to interpret the documents on their own terms with no assumptions of theological integrity. When this approach is followed, then new interpretive possibilities emerge. It may well be the case that some of the texts that eventually became part of the canon were indeed critical of other documents that also found their way into the Christian corpus of scripture. These cases of conflict between certain New Testament texts were then overlooked or masked as the process of canonisation created a new paradigm of harmony and unity.

In this study I wish to revisit this issue of conflict in the canonical Christian documents. I will begin by noting briefly what previous scholarship has identified in this respect, and then move on to a further possible case that has heretofore been largely ignored. This involves the conflict between the Gospel of Matthew and the Pauline epistles. Over the last decade and a half I have argued in many publications that Matthew contains anti-Pauline material, and that such anti-Paulinism witnesses a further instance of intra-canonical conflict. This critique of Paul by the evangelist has been overlooked to some extent because of the continuing influence of the canonical paradigm even within critical scholar-

of Some Recent Studies," in: McDonald and Sanders, *The Canon Debate*, 295–320; and Lee Martin McDonald, "Identifying Scripture and Canon in the Early Church: The Criteria Question," in: McDonald and Sanders, *The Canon Debate*, 416–39.

6 Lee Martin McDonald, *The Biblical Canon: Its Origin, Transmission and Authority* (Peabody, MA: Hendrickson, 2007), 285–421.

7 See Dorina Miller Parmenter, "The Bible as Icon: Myths of the Divine Origins of Scripture," in: *Jewish and Christian Scripture as Artifact and Canon*, eds. Craig A. Evans and H. Daniel Zacharias, LSTS (London: Continuum, 2009), 298–309.

ship. I do not intend here to repeat the detailed arguments in support of this hypothesis, but I will consider some of the critical responses to my work and attend to some of their major arguments.

## 2 Other possible conflicts in the canon

Perhaps the most famous advocate of conflict in the canon comes from within the church itself. Martin Luther's detailed analysis of the New Testament corpus led him to the view that the epistle of James was nothing less than an attack on Paul's doctrine of salvation by faith alone (cf. Jas 2:14–26). For a Paulinist like Luther, this was completely unacceptable and he had no hesitation in describing the letter of James as "an epistle of straw." In his 1522 German translation of the Bible, Luther placed James as well as Hebrews, Jude and Revelation at the very end of the Christian canon in order to emphasise their comparative lesser status.[8] Despite the longstanding Christian tradition that had argued for unity within the canon, Luther saw a clear case of conflict within it. Luther's assessment of James as a critique of Pauline theology still continues to dominate modern discussions of this epistle. While most scholars still accept that Luther was correct to see in James an anti-Pauline polemic, other exegetes have recently questioned this interpretation.[9]

Further possible conflicts within the Christian canon have been proposed in terms of the Gospels, in particular the intentions of the later evangelists who used Mark as a major source. We may begin with the Gospel of John, which is markedly and obviously different in many ways from its Synoptic counterparts and even contradicts them at certain points. The Church Fathers explained the major theological differences and chronological discrepancies between John and the other Gospels by alleging that the fourth evangelist either wrote to supplement the three other Gospels[10] or that he was moved by the Holy Spirit to pro-

---

**8** Raymond E. Brown, *An Introduction to the New Testament*, ABRL (New York: Doubleday, 1997), 744.

**9** For a statement that James was an anti-Pauline tract, see Martin Hengel, "Der Jakobusbrief als antipaulinische Polemik," in: Id., *Paulus und Jakobus: Kleine Schriften III*, WUNT 141 (Tübingen: Mohr Siebeck, 2002), 511–48. The opposing view can be found in Matthias Konradt, *Christliche Existenz nach dem Jakobusbrief. Eine Studie zu seiner soteriologischen und ethischen Konzeption*, SUNT 22 (Göttingen: Vandenhoeck & Ruprecht, 1998), 210–13, 241–46; and Jürgen Zangenberg, "Matthew and James," in: *Matthew and His Christian Contemporaries*, eds. David C. Sim and Boris Repschinski, LNTS 333 (London: Continuum, 2008), 104–22 at 117–20.

**10** Eusebius, *HE* 3.24.5–15 (*Eusèbe de Césarée. Histoire ecclésiastique (Livres I–IV)*, eds. Eduard Schwartz and Gustave Bardy, SC 31, Paris: Éditions du Cerf, 2001, 130–32).

vide a more spiritual gospel.[11] This traditional view that John composed his text to complement and supplement the earlier Gospels was challenged in the early twentieth century by Hans Windisch, who argued that the evangelist viewed the Synoptics as so inadequate both theologically and christologically that he created his own narrative in the hope of replacing these inferior accounts.[12] According to Windisch, there was a clear conflict in the canon which the early church had tried to explain away. Needless to say, Johannine scholarship has for the most part not followed Windisch, and many exegetes accept the Patristic positions that John wrote to supplement or even strengthen the Synoptic portraits of Jesus.[13]

The Gospel of Luke too may reflect a dispute between its author and its major sources, one of which was Mark. The evidence in this case is tied up with the evangelist's distinctive prologue (Luke 1:1–4), which mentions the sources on which he based his own account of Jesus' ministry. Luke states that since many have undertaken to compile a narrative (about Jesus), it seems good to him also (κἀμοὶ), having investigated everything carefully (ἀκριβῶς), to write an orderly (καθεξῆς) account, so that Theophilus might know the truth (τὴν ἀσφάλειαν) of what he has been informed. This statement raises the question of the evangelist's view of his source material. How does he relate his own work to those of his predecessors? Does he respect these accounts or does he criticise them? Either view is possible. On the one hand, Luke's use of κἀμοὶ appears to place his own work very much within the tradition of his sources, in which case there is no criticism at all of these earlier efforts.[14] On the other hand, however, most scholars do perceive in this passage some dissatisfaction on the part of Luke with these antecedent texts. The very fact that he took the trouble to write his own account when others were available indicates that he

**11** Euseb., *HE* 6.14.7 (*Eusèbe de Césarée. Histoire ecclésiastique (Livres V–VII)*, ed. Gustave Bardy, SC 41, Paris: Éditions du Cerf, 1955, 107).

**12** Hans Windisch, *Johannes und die Synoptiker: Wöllte der vierte Evangelist die älteren Evangelien ergänzen oder ersetzen?*, UNT 12 (Leipzig: J.C. Hinrichs, 1926). In agreement with Windisch is Martin Hengel, *The Johannine Question* (London: SCM, 1989), 193–94 n. 8.

**13** Thomas M. Dowell, "Why John Rewrote the Synoptics," in: *John and the Synoptics*, ed. Adelbert Denaux, BETL 101 (Leuven: Peeters, 1992), 453–57; and Richard Bauckham, "John for Readers of Mark," in: *The Gospels for All Christians: Rethinking the Gospel Audiences*, ed. Richard Bauckham (Edinburgh: T&T Clark, 1998), 147–71.

**14** So John Nolland, *Luke 1–9:20*, WBC 35A (Dallas, TX: Word Books, 1989), 5–6, 11–12; and Loveday C.A. Alexander, *The Preface to Luke's Gospel: Literary Convention and Social Context in Luke 1.1–4 and Acts 1.1*, SNTSMS 78 (Cambridge: Cambridge University Press, 1993), 115–16, 133–36.

saw them as deficient to some extent.[15] In addition, since he describes his own Gospel as the result of careful investigation with an emphasis on accuracy and order, it is difficult to avoid the conclusion that those sources that preceded him were viewed by Luke as not being characterised by these qualities.[16] There appears to be a veiled critique certainly of Mark and perhaps of Q as well. Just like John and James, Luke presents a further tantalising possibility of a conflict between the Christian canonical documents.

When we turn to Matthew's Gospel, the situation is a little different. While Johannine and Lucan scholars have long debated the intentions of those evangelists regarding Mark, Matthean specialists have largely avoided the question of Matthew's attitude towards the earlier Gospel. Of the few who have discussed this issue, Ulrich Luz has suggested that Matthew wrote to supplement Mark and to make Mark's well-known story of Jesus relevant to his Jewish Christian community.[17] By contrast, Richard Bauckham and Graham Stanton have argued in the opposite manner. Both of them have maintained, without providing any real evidence, that Matthew was dissatisfied with Mark and attempted to replace that source.[18] For these scholars Matthew's intention to replace Mark reflects a conflict within the traditional Christian canon. I find myself in complete agreement with Bauckham and Stanton on this issue, and recently published a full-scale defence of the view that Matthew did indeed see Mark as seriously deficient and that he wrote his own Gospel in order to replace the earlier text.[19]

# 3 Matthew and Paul

A further possible canonical conflict involving Matthew's Gospel concerns the apostle Paul and his epistles. That certain sections of Matthew reflect an anti-

**15** See, for example, François Bovon, *Luke 1: A Commentary on the Gospel of Luke 1:1–9:50*, Hermeneia (Minneapolis, MN: Fortress Press, 2001), 19; and Barbara Shellard, *New Light on Luke: Its Purpose, Sources and Literary Context*, JSNTSup 215 (London: Sheffield Academic Press, 2002), 261–62. Cf. too Stanton, "Fourfold Gospel," 342, and Richard Bauckham, "For Whom Were Gospels Written?," in: Bauckham, *The Gospels for All Christians*, 9–48 at 13.

**16** Joseph A. Fitzmyer, *The Gospel according to Luke I–IX: A New Translation with Introduction and Commentary*, AB 28 (New York: Doubleday, 1981), 291–92.

**17** Ulrich Luz, *Studies in Matthew* (Grand Rapids, MI: Eerdmans, 2005), 35.

**18** Stanton, "Fourfold Gospel," 341; and Bauckham, "For Whom Were Gospels Written?," 13.

**19** David C. Sim, "Matthew's Use of Mark: Did Matthew Intend to Supplement or to Replace his Primary Source?," *NTS* 57 (2011): 176–92. In agreement with my position is Richard Last, "Communities that Write: Christ-Groups, Associations, and Gospel Communities," *NTS* 58 (2012): 173–98 at 197.

Pauline polemic has long been on the scholarly agenda. In the middle of the last century, Samuel Brandon mounted an argument that Matthew's very Jewish Gospel contained critiques of Paul and his "liberal" theology at certain points.[20] Brandon's meagre arguments were not especially persuasive, and were mercilessly attacked by William Davies in his magisterial monograph on the Sermon on the Mount.[21] The critique of Davies was so devastating that the whole subject of Matthew's relationship with the Pauline tradition receded into the background for the next three decades or so.[22] Of the few studies that even attempted to address this issue, one of the more instructive is that of Luz.

Luz contends that Matthew contains no anti-Pauline polemic, despite the fact that he disagreed with the apostle over the validity of the Torah and over the issue of the relationship between the Christian tradition and Judaism. While Paul maintained that Judaism stood in sharp contrast to Christianity, Matthew saw no such opposition. In pinpointing the evangelist's Christian theological location, Luz claims that Matthew in fact stood closer to the "Judaisers" who opposed Paul in Galatia than to the apostle himself, and Luz wryly remarks that had the two ever met they would not have been close friends.[23] Yet Luz contends that we should resist the temptation to put Matthew and Paul at opposite ends of the early Christian theological spectrum because they share many areas of agreement – the priority of grace, the theology of works, the interior dimensions of righteousness, love as the core of the Law, and the universality of faith in Christ.[24]

I agree with much in Luz's discussion. He is absolutely right to point out that Matthew and Paul agree with one another on a number of important points. This is not surprising. Both were Christians, followers of Jesus of Nazareth, whom they jointly regarded as messiah and Lord, as crucified and vindicated, as the fulfiller of the ancient prophecies, and now residing in heaven with all power and authority until his triumphant return at the judgement. But we should not allow the many similarities between them to overshadow the issues that separated them. The major issue that divided Paul and Matthew, as Luz acknowledges,

---

**20** Samuel G.F. Brandon, *The Fall of Jerusalem and the Christian Church* (2nd edn.; London: SPCK, 1957), 232–37.

**21** William D. Davies, *The Setting of the Sermon on the Mount* (Cambridge: Cambridge University Press, 1966), 334–40.

**22** See David C. Sim, "Matthew's Anti-Paulinism: A Neglected Feature of Matthean Studies," *HTS* 58 (2002): 767–83.

**23** Ulrich Luz, *The Theology of the Gospel of Matthew*, NTT (Cambridge: Cambridge University Press, 1993), 147–48.

**24** Luz, *Theology of the Gospel of Matthew*, 150–52.

was the role of the Torah in the light of the Christ event, and this was clearly no minor matter. It was the single issue that underlay the apostolic council, the dispute between Peter and Paul in Antioch (Gal 2:11–14) and Paul's conflict in Galatia and probably elsewhere. The place of the Torah in Christian life and practice was still a contentious issue in the late first century and into the second century, as the evidence of the Pastoral epistles, the letter of James and the writings of Ignatius of Antioch attest.[25] I have no doubt that Paul's Christian Jewish opponents in Galatia would have agreed with the apostle over all sorts of theological and christological questions, but they bitterly disputed his understanding of the place of the Torah for Gentile converts and sought to undermine his apostleship and authority because of it. For his part, Paul responds in Galatians with a bitter polemic of his own.[26] The lesson to be learnt here is this. If the point of disagreement is fundamental and serious enough to both parties in a dispute, then it can easily outweigh the many other factors that they may share in common. For this reason, I think Luz's otherwise excellent discussion goes awry by highlighting the agreements between Matthew and Paul at the expense of the absolutely fundamental matter that separated them. If, as Luz correctly claims, Matthew stood theologically close to Paul's "judaising" opponents in Galatia, then it would seem to follow logically that Matthew would have responded to Paul in much the same way as they did. He would have overlooked their agreements and focused his attention on questioning Paul's gospel and his claims to authority and leadership.

The important work of Luz (and others) stimulated my own interest in this area of study, and I found myself drawn to the position of Brandon, although not to his specific arguments. The provisional fruits of my research appeared in my 1998 monograph on the history and social setting of the Matthean community,[27] and I have spent the years since then publishing a number of articles that have refined and expanded that initial work. Let me present a very brief summary of the cumulative argument. The triad of sayings in Matt 5:17–19, whereby Jesus dispels the notion that he has abolished the Torah and affirms that every part of the Law is to be obeyed, is a clear refutation of the Pauline position that the Torah was only a temporary measure that has been brought to an end by Christ (Gal 3:23–25; Rom 10:4).[28] The eschatological scenario in Matt

**25** See David C. Sim, *The Gospel of Matthew and Christian Judaism: The History and Social Setting of the Matthean Community*, SNTW (Edinburgh: T&T Clark, 1998), 172–81, 260–82.

**26** See the chapter by Ian J. Elmer in this volume.

**27** Sim, *Matthew and Christian Judaism*, 188–211.

**28** Sim, *Matthew and Christian Judaism*, 207–209. For a more detailed statement on the very different stances regarding the Torah in both the Pauline and Matthean traditions, see David C.

7:21–23, in which Jesus condemns those who call him Lord because of their lawlessness (ἀνομία), is a strict condemnation of Law-free Christians and recalls Pauline passages such as Rom 10:9–10 and 1 Cor 12:3.[29] Likewise, the material created by Matthew in 13:36–43 makes the point that the Law-free Christian tradition has its origin in Satan and its members will be punished in the fires of Gehenna.[30] The evangelist also confronts the issue of the leadership of the early Christian movement. While Mark presents the future leaders of the Jerusalem church, the disciples and the family of Jesus, in a very poor light, Matthew rehabilitates both groups.[31] In the heavily edited material in 16:17–19, Jesus proclaims the supremacy of Peter as the head of the church using the very language and motifs that Paul employs when referring to his own divine call and mission (Gal 12–17).[32] At the end of the Gospel the risen Christ commissions the disciples to lead and oversee both the Jewish and Gentile missions (28:16–20), which completely undercuts Paul's constant claim to have been appointed the apostle to the Gentiles (e.g., Rom 15:16; Gal 1:16).[33]

The point of these studies was not to show that Matthew simply differed from Paul. Rather, they attempted to demonstrate that in these heavily redacted passages the evangelist was consciously responding to and criticising particular claims and theological positions that can be most easily identified with Paul. On the basis of parallels and intertextual echoes between certain Pauline and Matthean texts, I made a case that the evangelist probably had access to some of the Pauline letters.[34] Yet in arguing in this fashion, I tried to keep the extent of Matthew's anti-Pauline polemic in perspective. The evangelist was motivated to write his story of Jesus by a number of factors and circumstances, and he used his narrative to discredit a number of opponents or contrary views. The most immediate threat to Matthew's community was that posed by Formative Judaism, and for

---

Sim, "Paul and Matthew on the Torah: Theory and Practice," in: *Paul, Grace and Freedom: Essays in Honour of John K. Riches*, eds. Paul Middleton, Angus Paddison, and Karen Wenell (London: T&T Clark, 2009), 50–64.

**29** David C. Sim, "Matthew 7.21–23: Further Evidence of its Anti-Pauline Perspective," *NTS* 53 (2007): 325–43.

**30** Sim, *Matthew and Christian Judaism*, 203–207.

**31** Sim, *Matthew and Christian Judaism*, 188–99.

**32** David C. Sim, "Matthew and the Pauline Corpus: A Preliminary Intertextual Study," *JSNT* 31 (2009): 401–22 at 411–17.

**33** David C. Sim, "Matthew, Paul and the Origin and Nature of the Gentile Mission: The Great Commission in Matthew 28:16–20 as an Anti-Pauline Tradition," *HTS* 64 (2008): 377–92.

**34** Sim, "Matthew and the Pauline Corpus," 402–11.

this reason the scribes and Pharisees receive the most polemical attention,[35] but it is also clear that at certain points in his Gospel Matthew took the opportunity to attack both Paul himself and his version of the gospel.[36] There is more than enough evidence to establish yet another conflict within the Christian canonical texts.

As might be expected, the scholarly reactions to my hypothesis have been divided. In English-language scholarship early and limited support came from a brief discussion of my work by David Catchpole,[37] while Daniel Harrington concluded that while my hypothesis may not convince all, it does at least correctly question the common and canon-influenced tendency to harmonise Matthew and Paul.[38] Much more concrete affirmation came from German-language scholarship. Gerd Theissen made a case for Matthew's anti-Paulinism, which both acknowledged my own contribution to this issue and provided different and supplementary arguments,[39] and the same is true of the recent work of Eric Wong.[40]

Needless to say, such a controversial thesis has attracted a measure of criticism as well. In a study devoted to Matthew and James, Jürgen Zangenberg engaged very briefly with my work, and found it unconvincing.[41] The following year Joel Willitts published a response to my analysis of Matt 28:16–20 as an anti-Pauline tradition, though he made a number of more general observations as well.[42] More recently, in a collection of essays devoted to Paul and the Gospels there were no less than two discussions of the relationship between Matthew's

---

**35** See the definitive study by J. Andrew Overman, *Matthew's Gospel and Formative Judaism: The Social World of the Matthean Community* (Minneapolis, MN: Fortress Press, 1990). Cf. too Sim, *Matthew and Christian Judaism*, 109–63.

**36** On measuring Matthew's perceived threats to his community by the level of his polemic, see David C. Sim, "Polemical Strategies in the Gospel of Matthew," in: *Polemik in der frühchristlichen Literatur: Texte und Kontexte*, eds. Oda Wischmeyer and Lorenzo Scornaienchi, BZNW 170 (Berlin: De Gruyter, 2011), 491–515.

**37** David R. Catchpole, *Resurrection People: Studies in the Resurrection Narratives of the Gospels* (London: Darton, Longman & Todd, 2000), 43–62.

**38** Daniel J. Harrington, "Matthew and Paul," in: Sim and Repschinski, *Matthew and His Christian Contemporaries*, 11–26 at 25–26.

**39** Gerd Theissen, "Kritik an Paul im Matthäusevangelium? Von der Kunst verdeckter Polemik im Urchristentum," in: Wischmeyer and Scornaienchi, *Polemik in der frühchristlichen Literatur*, 465–90. Theissen had signaled his views in an earlier study: Id., "Kirche oder Sekt? Über Einheit und Konflikt im frühen Urchristentum," *ThG* 48 (2005): 162–75.

**40** Eric Kun Chun Wong, *Evangelien im Dialog mit Paulus*, NTOA (Göttingen: Vandenhoeck & Ruprecht, 2011), 107–30.

**41** Zangenberg, "Matthew and James," 120.

**42** Joel Willitts, "The Friendship of Matthew and Paul: A Response to a Recent Trend in the Interpretation of Matthew's Gospel," *HTS* 65 (2009): 150–58.

Gospel and the apostle and his letters, and each was critical of my work in this area. One of these was by Willitts, who expanded his earlier critique, and the other was by Paul Foster.[43] It is not possible here to analyse these studies in detail, but I will highlight a number of their major points and respond briefly to these.

Both Willitts and Foster contend that it is impossible ever to be sure that Matthew was directly attacking Paul. In the view of Willitts any comparison between these two Christian authors is nigh on impossible because they wrote from different social contexts using different genres and different rhetorical strategies and so on. These sorts of issues make it extremely problematic to attempt any comparison or contrast as I had attempted.[44] Foster goes even further by arguing that Matthew never refers to Paul and has no interest in the apostle, since it (the Gospel) "…is primarily written to tell the story of Jesus in order to commend faith in that person as God's Messiah."[45] I would respond to these points by referring to the work of Luz, who has correctly reminded us that the evangelist has written his story of Jesus on two distinct levels; one is the story of Jesus of Nazareth, while the other concerns the history of the Matthean church. Matthew shapes his narrative about Jesus to be meaningful for his intended readers and to address the issues that were most pressing to them at the end of the first century.[46] Most scholars would agree that Matthew's depiction of the conflict between Jesus and the scribes and Pharisees tells us more about the dispute between Matthew's community and Formative Judaism than about Jesus and his scribal and Pharisaic opponents. In the same way we can interpret the sayings of the Matthean Jesus about true and false Christians as much more applicable to the time of the evangelist than to the time of the historical Jesus. On these grounds at least, it is permissible to examine the Gospel for possible or potential references to Paul and his particular gospel.

But these critics have a further argument that is intended to kill stone dead any such possibility; Matthew was produced in an environment where Paul and his gospel were either not known or little known. In the light of this, there would simply be no need to polemicise against Paul. We first find this line of argument

---

**43** Joel Willitts, "Paul and Matthew: A Descriptive Approach from a Post-New Perspective Interpretive Framework," in: *Paul and the Gospels: Christologies, Conflicts, Convergences*, eds. Michael F. Bird and Joel Willitts, LNTS 411 (London: T&T Clark, 2011), 62–85; and Paul Foster, "Paul and Matthew: Two Strands of the Early Jesus Movement with Little Sign of Connection," in: Bird and Willitts, *Paul and the Gospels*, 86–114.

**44** Willitts, "Friendship of Matthew and Paul," 155–56; and Id., "Paul and Matthew," 64–65.

**45** Foster, "Paul and Matthew," 86.

**46** Luz, *Studies in Matthew*, 27–28.

in the work of Zangenberg. Writing in reference to Matthew and the epistle of James, Zangenberg accepts that both must be distinguished from the Pauline tradition and "...that both have developed in a distinctly non-Pauline milieu."[47] This claim of course is not controversial, at least in terms of Matthew. Almost no Matthean scholar would argue that Matthew stood in or even near the camp of Paul; it is well accepted that he belonged to an alternative and independent tradition in the early Christian movement. But Zangenberg continues: "...even if they (Matthew and James) came into contact with strange and suspicious theological positions they might or might not have known as 'Pauline', they commented on them and rejected them on the basis of their own, independently grown convictions."[48] It is clear that for Zangenberg Matthew was written in a location where Paul was either not known or hardly known, and any contradictions between Matthew's theology and Paul's theology are simply coincidental and not deliberate on the evangelist's part.

At the beginning of his article Foster claims that "...it is not possible, due to the limitations of the evidence to postulate whether Matthew was aware of the Pauline mission and the teachings enshrined in his writings."[49] This view is echoed and expanded at the end of his study: "...in fact from the available evidence one could not even infer that Matthew had significant awareness of Paul."[50] Noting that modern readers might be bemused by this contention, Foster believes that his claim can be explained in a number of ways: (1) Matthew was completely isolated theologically and had never heard of Paul; (2) Paul was less significant in the time of Matthew so there was no need to mention him; or (3) Matthew knew of Paul but thought he was irrelevant for his own theological project.[51] The approach of Willitts to this issue is slightly different and more concrete. Willitts makes the claim that my understanding of the Matthew/Paul relationship is necessarily tied in with my view that the Gospel was written in Antioch,[52] and he attempts to undermine this by arguing, in agreement with some other scholars, that the Gospel was perhaps composed in Galilee where Pauline influence was minimal.[53]

---

**47** Zangenberg, "Matthew and James," 120.
**48** Zangenberg, "Matthew and James," 120.
**49** Foster, "Paul and Matthew," 87.
**50** Foster, "Paul and Matthew," 114.
**51** Foster, "Paul and Matthew," 114.
**52** For my arguments favouring Antioch as the location for Matthew, see Sim, *Matthew and Christian Judaism*, 53–62.
**53** Willitts, "Paul and Matthew," 83–84.

How reasonable are these related arguments? Let us first address the issue of Matthew's knowledge of Paul. How plausible is the claim that Matthew was written in a location that had little or no knowledge of the apostle? One might be able to argue in this fashion if Matthew were written in the first century in Chinese for Chinese readers. But Matthew was written in Greek, the common language of the Roman empire, and it must be situated somewhere in that large geographical region. It is of course possible that Matthew was composed in some remote outpost, but this is unlikely given that a number of Christian sources, namely the Gospel of Mark and Q, had made their way into the Matthean community. It is almost impossible to accept that Mark and Q reached Matthew but not the Pauline tradition. I note the evidence of Bauckham that there was extensive communication and interaction between the various Christian communities in the first century,[54] and this makes it extremely difficult to find any part of the Greek-speaking Christian world (or even the Aramaic-speaking Christian world for that matter) that had no knowledge of Paul. Let us consider the following further points.

First, over his thirty-year career as a Christian, Paul was active in a number of Christian centres – three years in the Damascus church (Gal 1:17–18) and some twelve years in the Antiochene church (Gal 1:21; 2:1). After leaving Antioch (c. 49 CE), Paul established churches in Asia Minor and Greece, staying for prolonged periods in Ephesus and Corinth. As a Christian, Paul also travelled to Jerusalem three times (Gal 1:18–20; 2:1–10; Acts 21:17). The much-travelled apostle probably knew personally more followers of Jesus than any other Christian at that time. He was so well-known and so well-connected that he could write with some authority to the church in Rome, even though he had not founded that church and had not visited it. Paul was thus known from Jerusalem to Rome and in all points in between.

Secondly, Paul was a participant at the so-called apostolic council (Gal 2:1–10; Acts 15:1–39). We should not undervalue this fact. So far as we know, the apostolic council was the one and only meeting in the first century that was convened between different churches to iron out a significant difference between them. This meeting involved the major Christian centres in Jerusalem and Antioch, and was called to settle the issue of Law-observance for Gentile Christian converts. Paul and Acts provide two different accounts of this meeting and it is likely that Paul's opponents in Galatia circulated an entirely different ver-

---

**54** Bauckham, "For Whom Were Gospels Written?," 9–48. Accepting this aspect of Bauckham's argument does not entail agreement with his further hypothesis that the Gospels were written for all Christians and not for specific communities. See David C. Sim, "The Gospels for All Christians?: A Response to Richard Bauckham," *JSNT* 84 (2001): 3–27.

sion.[55] Given the importance of the Law issue for Gentile Christians, it must be assumed that many or most of these Christians had heard about the meeting in Jerusalem and Paul's participation in it. Paul would have been widely known for his part in this unique meeting, although whether he was cast as the villain or the hero would vary according to the different versions.

Thirdly, Paul was a very contentious and controversial figure. He claimed to have had an experience of the risen Christ that was the same as those experienced by Peter, James and others in the Jerusalem church (1 Cor 15:3–8), but there were many who did not believe him and who thereby questioned his apostolic credentials.[56] He had a public conflict with Peter in Antioch in the aftermath of the apostolic council (Gal 2:11–14), which led to him leaving Antioch and beginning new missions in Asia Minor and Greece. In those missions he was opposed by Christian Jews with links to Jerusalem who sought to impose the Torah on his Gentile converts. These people questioned Paul's apostolic status and the validity of his gospel. Paul's notoriety would have ensured that he was a well-known and well-discussed figure throughout the early church.

More could be said on this issue, but the above points establish very firmly that Paul, his gospel and his various conflicts and battles must have been very widely known in the early Christian movement during his lifetime. It is reasonable to conclude that most Christians, whether supporters or critics of the apostle, must have known a good deal about his life and his version of the gospel. There is every reason to think that Paul's influence and reputation did not diminish in the decades following his death.

By the end of the first century, Paul's letters were circulating around the Christian world as a distinct corpus[57] and, as noted above, in the early second century Ignatius of Antioch had access to an extensive Pauline collection. Further, the fact that a number of pseudepigraphical letters were composed in the name of Paul towards the end of the first century testifies to the apostle's continuing and widespread influence. There would be little point writing in the name of the apostle, if his name did not carry the utmost authority. In addition Luke wrote the Acts of the Apostles at this time, the second half of which is devoted almost exclusively to the missions of Paul. This hagiographical tradition testifies to the importance of Paul in this period. On the other side of the coin

**55** See Ian J. Elmer, *Paul, Jerusalem and the Judaisers: The Galatian Crisis in its Broadest Historical Context*, WUNT 2.258 (Tübingen: Mohr Siebeck, 2009), 151–54.

**56** David C. Sim, "The Appearances of the Risen Christ to Paul: Identifying their Implications and Complications," *ABR* 54 (2006): 1–12.

**57** See E. Randolph Richards, *Paul and First Century Letter Writing: Secretaries, Compositions and Collection* (Downers Grove, IL: InterVarsity Press, 2004), 156–61, 214–15, 218–19.

and again as discussed earlier, we find in the epistle of James a probable critique, or at least a refinement, of Paul's theology in the same period. This response by the author of James provides concrete evidence that Paul and his letters were well known and influential at this time. If they were not, then there would be no need to criticise or refine his position.

The above evidence indicates strongly that in the latter part of the first century knowledge of Paul and his letters was widespread throughout the Christian world and that the apostle was highly influential in many quarters, but criticised in others. The claim that Matthew was written in a Greek-speaking milieu ignorant of Paul (or largely so) almost beggars belief and can be safely dismissed. Even the attempt by Willitts to follow an emerging trend that locates Matthew in Galilee does not affect this point. The so-called Galilean hypothesis is itself problematic,[58] but given the extensive communication between the various Christian churches in that time it is simply unlikely that Galilean Christians lived in a vacuum that sealed it off from any knowledge of the influential and controversial Paul. No matter where we situate Matthew and his home community, it has to be conceded that they must have known a good deal about Paul's life, gospel and theology.

But even if this is accepted, it could well be the case that Matthew was simply not interested in the apostle, a possibility raised by Foster. Standing in a different Christian tradition, the evangelist may have been completely indifferent to Paul, and saw no need to refer to the apostle or his theology in his own narrative about Jesus of Nazareth. This is the view also of Graham Stanton, who contends that the Gospel shows no pro-Paulinism and no anti-Paulinism but "...is simply un-Pauline."[59] While I expect that many scholars would agree with Stanton, his claim seems to me to be inherently implausible. Apart from the points made above, that Pauline influence was widespread and increasing in the late first century, and that Paul was a highly contentious figure, Matthew's Gospel deals with issues that the apostle was very much involved with during his lifetime. These include the role of the Torah in the Christian community, the terms of the Gentile mission, and the question of leadership and authority of the early church, and on *a priori* grounds we might expect that Matthew would have been extremely

---

**58** See David C. Sim, "Reconstructing the Social and Religious Milieu of Matthew," in: *Matthew, James and Didache: Three Related Documents in Their Jewish and Christian Settings*, eds. Huub van de Sandt and Jürgen Zangenberg, SBLSS 45 (Atlanta: SBL, 2008), 13–32 at 21–24. One of the major problems with this hypothesis is that Galilee was largely Aramaic-speaking, which renders it unlikely that the Greek Gospel of Matthew was written there.

**59** Graham N. Stanton, *A Gospel for a New People: Studies in Matthew* (Edinburgh: T&T Clark, 1992), 314.

interested in Paul's position on these and other matters, and reacted to them in his Gospel narrative.

The arguments of Zangenberg, Willitts and Foster that Matthew either had not heard of Paul or was indifferent to him and his version of the gospel do not stand up to scrutiny. It must be concluded that the evangelist knew a good deal about Paul, certainly from oral traditions about him that were circulating in the late first century and perhaps even from his epistles which were widely distributed and available. Moreover, if Matthew stood theologically near the Christian Jewish tradition that so vehemently opposed Paul in Galatia, then we might expect that he would use his Gospel narrative to discredit the apostle and his understanding of the gospel. If this was indeed the case, then we have a further and extremely important instance of a conflict within the Christian canon.

## 4 Conclusions

Once the Christian canon was finalised and fixed in the late fourth or early fifth century, it took on a life of its own and was characterised by notions of authority, inspiration, inerrancy, and theological unity. Yet, these later views may not have represented the original texts or the intentions of their authors who may indeed have been critiquing and criticising other documents that were later canonised. Even within the church itself voices were raised as to the integrity of the various New Testament texts. While Luther's famous attack on the letter of James is the best-known example, it is not the only case in point. In modern scholarship other instances of inter-canonical conflict have been identified. Scholars have argued, correctly in my opinion, that the three later evangelists were all critical of Mark, and they rewrote and expanded the Marcan narrative in their own ways in order to replace the original Gospel. If that is true, then the fact that Mark stands alongside the Gospels of Matthew, Luke and John in the Christian canon is more than a little ironic.

I have argued in this study that we have a further case of conflict within the canon. There is strong evidence that the Christian Jewish Matthew, who advocated observance of the Torah in addition to faith in Christ, was engaged in a polemic with Paul and his "Law-liberal" gospel. Although critics have attempted to undermine this hypothesis by maintaining that Matthew had perhaps never heard of Paul or would have been indifferent to him, neither of these arguments carries any conviction. Paul was famous (or infamous) during his lifetime, and he was still a figure of contention in the late first century when Matthew was written. His epistles were distributed around the Christian world, and a hagiographical tradition was well established and developing, as evidenced by the Acts of the Apostles and the Deutero-Pauline literature. The epistle of James was one attempt from the other side to stem the flow and correct the Pauline gospel, and Matthew can be seen as a further attempt. If the hypothesis that Matthew was anti-Pauline is correct, as a number of scholars are now suggesting, then it means nothing less than a conflict between the "Gospel of the church" and the greatest theologian in the early church (and arguably in the history of Christianity). What implications might this have in terms of the understanding of the canon in the modern day? While this fascinating question cannot be answered here, its consequences are certainly worth pondering.

Pierluigi Piovanelli

# Rewriting: The Path from Apocryphal to Heretical*

## 1 The function of heresies

Apocryphal production and heresy have always been closely aligned, not least because heretics are well-known for obstinately and consistently going against what the scriptures say,[1] even creating new ones to validate their own ideas. Having dedicated a number of years to the study of both, here I hope to demonstrate the process by which important parts of the memories of the beginnings of Christianity that were handed down and preserved in texts that became, with time, more and more suspect, were in the late-antique period progressively rewritten and updated, a phenomenon that I have been exploring in a series of recent articles.[2] To make my case, I appeal to some examples drawn from the apocryphal literature attributed originally to Mary of Magdala, the "companion" (*koinōnos*)

* Dedicated to François Bovon, a major scholar of texts that are *kanonizomena*, *anagignōskomena* and *psuchōfelē*.

1 Following the definition of heresy ("an opinion chosen by human perception contrary to Holy Scripture, publicly avowed and obstinately defended") attributed to Robert Grosseteste, Bishop of Lincoln (c. 1175 – 1253), the first translator into Latin of the *Testament of the Twelve Patriarchs*. See Shannon McSheffrey, "Heresy, Orthodoxy and English Vernacular Religion, 1480 – 1525," *Past and Present* 186 (2005): 47 – 80 at 47 n. 1; Jonathan Wright, *Heretics: The Creation of Christianity from the Gnostics to the Modern Church* (Boston–New York: Houghton Mifflin Harcourt, 2011), 3 and 306.

2 Pierluigi Piovanelli, "Le recyclage des textes apocryphes à l'heure de la petite 'mondialisation' de l'Antiquité tardive (ca. 325 – 451). Quelques perspectives littéraires et historiques," in: *Poussières de christianisme et de judaïsme antiques. Études réunies en l'honneur de Jean-Daniel Kaestli et Éric Junod*, eds. Rémi Gounelle and Albert Frey, Publications de l'Institut romand des sciences bibliques 5 (Lausanne: Zèbre, 2007), 277 – 295; Id., "The Reception of Early Christian Texts and Traditions in Late Antiquity Apocryphal Literature," in: *The Reception and Interpretation of the Bible in Late Antiquity: Proceedings of the Montréal Colloquium in Honour of Charles Kannengiesser, 11 – 13 October 2006*, eds., Lorenzo DiTommaso and Lucian Turcescu, Bible in Ancient Christianity 6 (Leiden: Brill, 2008), 429 – 439; Id., "*Rewritten Bible* ou *Bible in progress?* La réécriture des traditions mémoriales bibliques dans le judaïsme et le christianisme anciens," *Revue de théologie et de philosophie* 139 (2007): 295 – 310; Id., "De l'usage polémique des récits de la Passion, ou: Là où les chemins qui auraient dû se séparer ont fini par se superposer," in: *La croisée des chemins revisitée. Quand l'Église et la Synagogue se sont-elles distinguées? Actes du colloque de Tours, 18 – 19 juin 2010*, eds. Simon C. Mimouni and Bernard Pouderon, Patrimoines, Judaïsme antique (Paris: Cerf, 2012), 125 – 160.

of Jesus, before it was accorded higher status under the patronage of the "Virgin" (*parthenos*) Mary, his mother. However, before we embark on that path, I turn first to some considerations of a more general nature arising from not just my experience as a philologist and historian, but also from an interest in the sociology and anthropology of Judaism and Christianity, including Ethiopian Christianity.

## 1.1 The social utility of conflict

When considering the dialectical relationship that exists between orthodoxy and heresy, the first general observation that should be made is that in any human group tensions and conflicts of all kinds are quite normal – even indispensible, albeit in small doses –, since, as the sociologists Georg Simmel and Lewis A. Coser have demonstrated, they play an essential role in the definition and redefinition – for better or worse – of a particular group's identity.[3] The history of the advances in identity, indeed the progress in all domains of social and intellectual life, made by the early Christian communities in the wake of the different conflicts that broke out – for example, between the Paul of the authentic epistles, his competitors, and his flock, on the one hand; or between the Paul of the pastorals and the widows of that author's community, on the other; or, again, between Ignatius of Antioch and the prophets of the *Ascension of Isaiah*; between Marcion and his detractors; between Valentinus and his opponents; between "gnostic" Christians (radical mystics?) of all kinds and their less "spiritual" brothers and sisters – is impressive.[4] For that matter, it is precisely the same for the Ethiopian theological controversies of the fifteenth century, and one could adduce numerous examples from other geographic locations and time periods.

3 See in particular Georg Simmel, *Soziologie: Untersuchungen über die Formen der Vergesellschaftung* (Leipzig: Duncker & Humblot, 1908), 247–336; Lewis A. Coser, *The Functions of Social Conflict: An Examination of the Concept of Social Conflict and its Use in Empirical Sociological Research* (New York: Free Press, 1956).

4 The first to apply convincingly the theories of Simmel and Coser to the beginnings of Christianity was John Gager, *Kingdom and Community: The Social World of Early Christianity*, Prentice-Hall Studies in Religion Series (Englewood Cliffs, NJ: Prentice-Hall, 1975), 79–87, 91–92. Their utility in the study of the formation of a specifically Christian identity is recognised, among others, by David G. Horrell, "'Becoming Christian:' Solidifying Christian Identity and Content," in: *Handbook of Early Christianity: Social Science Approaches*, eds. Anthony J. Blasi, Jean Duhaime, and Paul-André Turcotte (Walnut Creek, CA: AltaMira Press, 2002), 309–35 at 313–15, 334.

Such controversies show, in my view, both the extent of the difficulties faced by the early Christians in their attempts to piece together a new identity in relation to Judaism and the variety of solutions explored – a variety that we will also encounter when it comes to the scriptural production of these groups and these communities. Indeed, it may even be that, as argued by Daniel Boyarin,[5] it is precisely due to the construction of the two concurrent orthodoxies of rabbinic Judaism and "patristic" Christianity – to the disquiet of the silent majority of mixed believers – that the two religions gradually separated. In other words, it took the Sages and Fathers to point the finger at heretics, who from the beginning neither did anything wrong nor exhibited any scandalous beliefs, for Judaism and Christianity, as we understand them, to see the light of day.[6]

---

**5** In *Border Lines: The Partition of Judaeo-Christianity*, Divinations: Rereading Late Ancient Religion (Philadelphia, PA: University of Pennsylvania Press, 2004). For the debates to which his arguments have given rise, see the remarks by Virginia Burrus, Richard Kalmin, Hayim Lapin, and Joel Marcus, "Boyarin's Work: A Critical Assessment," *Henoch* 28 (2006): 7–30, and response by Daniel Boyarin, "Twenty-Four Refutations: Continuing the Conversations," ibid., 30–45; Adele Reinhartz, "A Fork in the Road or a Multi-Lane Highway? New Perspectives on 'The Parting of the Ways' Between Judaism and Christianity," in: *The Changing Face of Judaism, Christianity and Other Greco-Roman Religions in Antiquity*, eds. Ian H. Henderson and Gerbern S. Oegema, Studien zu den Jüdischen Schriften aus hellenistisch-römischer Zeit 2 (Gütersloh: Gütersloher Verlagshaus, 2005), 278–93; Simon C. Mimouni, "Les origines du christianisme: nouveaux paradigmes ou paradigmes paradoxaux? Bibliographie sélectionnée et raisonnée," *Revue biblique* 115 (2008): 360–82; Id., "Les identités religieuses dans l'Antiquité classique et tardive: remarques et réflexions sur une question en discussion," in: *Entre lignes de partage et territoires de passage. Les identités religieuses dans les mondes grec et romain. "Paganismes", "judaïsmes", "christianismes"*, eds. Nicole Belayche and Simon C. Mimouni, Collection de la Revue des études juives 47 (Leuven: Peeters, 2009), 485–502; Megan H. Williams, "No More Clever Titles: Observations on Some Recent Studies of Jewish-Christian Relations in the Roman World," *JQR* 99 (2009): 37–55. See also the retrospective reflection by Daniel Boyarin, "Rethinking Jewish Christianity: An Argument for Dismantling a Dubious Category (to which is Appended a Correction of My *Border Lines*)," *JQR* 99 (2009): 7–36, and the combined contributions in: Mimouni and Pouderon, *La croisée des chemins revisitée*.

**6** For Christianity, see the fundamental studies by Walter Bauer, *Rechtglaubigkeit und Ketzerei im ältesten Christentum* (Tübingen: J.C.B. Mohr, 1934; edn. rev. by Georg Strecker, 1964 = *Orthodoxy and Heresy in Earliest Christianity*, trans. Robert A. Kraft and Gerhard Krodel, Philadelphia, PA: Fortress Press, 1971); and Alain Le Boulluec, *La notion d'hérésie dans la littérature grecque, IIᵉ–IIIᵉ siècle*, 2 vols., Collection des Études augustiniennes, Série Antiquité 110–111 (Paris: Études augustiniennes, 1985).

## 1.2 The subjectivity of value judgements

Precisely how is it possible that practices and doctrines that were, up until a certain period, if not admitted, at least tolerated (for example, the belief in "two powers in heaven" among certain mystical branches of late Second-Temple Judaism),[7] could suddenly be rejected, or even condemned? Here again the Ethiopian theological controversies of 1449 CE provide useful lessons. On the one hand, we observe the elimination of one part of the late-antique cultural legacy of the kingdom of Axum[8] that became too archaic and thus obsolete (for example, scriptural texts such as the *Ascension of Isaiah* and the *Shepherd* of Hermas, which up until then had been perfectly canonical; conceivably due to their now obsolete christologies – docetic, in the first instance; pneumatic and adoptionist, in the second[9] –, as well as the pictorial representation of the divine Trinity with anthropomorphic features for a short period later in the seventeenth century).[10] On the other hand, we see that other elements that are just as archaic (for example, the canonicity of *1 Enoch*, *Jubilees* and the *Paralipomena of Jeremiah*, circumcision, the observance of the sabbath, or millennial eschatology)[11]

---

**7** This particular "heresy," studied (from the rabbinic perspective) by Alan F. Segal, *Two Powers in Heaven: Early Rabbinic Reports about Christianity and Gnosticism*, Studies in Judaism in Late Antiquity 25 (Leiden: Brill, 1977), is central to the reconstruction of the theology of an "alternative" Judaism (much closer to certain branches of primitive Christianity) proposed by Boyarin. See esp. Daniel Boyarin, "The *Gospel of the Memra:* Jewish Binitarianism and the Prologue to John," *HThR* 94 (2001): 243–84; Id., "Two Powers in Heaven; or, the Making of a Heresy," in: *The Idea of Biblical Interpretation: Essays in Honor of James L. Kugel*, eds. Hindy Najman and Judith H. Newman, JSJSup 83 (Leiden: Brill, 2003), 331–70; Id., *Border Lines*, 169–272; Id., "Beyond Judaisms: Metatron and the Divine Polymorphy of Ancient Judaism," *JSJ* 41 (2010): 323–65. The identification of this movement has important consequences for the relationship between Second-Temple Jewish apocalyptic, Sethian gnosticism, and the late-antique mysticism of the Merkavah. See, on that point, Nathaniel Deutsch, *The Gnostic Imagination: Gnosticism, Mandaeism, and Merkabah Mysticism*, Brill's Series in Jewish Studies 13 (Leiden: Brill, 1995).

**8** King 'Ezana was officially converted c. 340 CE.

**9** See Pierluigi Piovanelli, "Les aventures des apocryphes en Éthiopie," *Apocrypha* 4 (1993): 197–224 (= "The Adventures of the Apocrypha in Ethiopia," trans. Sarah Waidler, in: *Languages and Cultures of Eastern Christianity: Ethiopian*, ed. Alessandro Bausi, Variorum, The Worlds of Eastern Christianity [300–1500] 4, [Farnham: Ashgate, 2012], 87–109) at 203–206/92–94.

**10** See Pierluigi Piovanelli, "Connaissance de Dieu et sagesse humaine en Éthiopie. Le traité *Explication de la Divinité* attribué aux hérétiques 'mikaélites'," *Le Muséon* 117 (2004): 193–227 at 218–23.

**11** See Pierluigi Piovanelli, "Les controverses théologiques sous le roi Zär'a Ya'qob (1434–1468) et la mise en place du monophysisme éthiopien," in: *La controverse religieuse et ses formes*, ed. Alain Le Boulluec, Patrimoines, Religions du Livre (Paris: Cerf, 1995), 189–228 at 217–21; Id., "Connaissance de Dieu," 223–25.

were, with success, vigorously defended and preserved up to the present day. In an ironic twist, it was the emissaries of the Coptic church and their Ethiopian disciples who drove this updating of its daughter church and it was the head of state, the formidable Emperor theologian Zär'a Ya'qob (1434–1468), who, for reasons of personal faith and politics, fiercely opposed it to the extent that theologians who were considered perfectly orthodox by the rest of Christianity were treated as heretics[12] and persecuted as such in Ethiopia.[13]

This brings us to our second point, namely that the concepts "orthodoxy" and "heresy" have a variety of shapes and forms and are completely subjective. We could say, to paraphrase Robert M. Grant, that "your heresy is my othodoxy, and vice-versa;"[14] or, with Thomas Hobbes, "as they that approve a private opinion, call it Opinion; but they that mislike it, Haeresie" (*Leviathan* 1.11); or, again, as we observe in the Ethiopian example, "yesterday's orthodoxy has become today's heresy, and vice-versa."[15] Categories, like all concepts used to label the actual, are nothing but social constructs, perceptions that vary from one group to another, devoid of any objective content.

In the chapter dedicated to the dichotomy orthodoxy/heresy in their classic work *Le judaïsme et le christianisme antique*, the late Marcel Simon and André Benoît thus had reason to warn their readers of the fact that "the use of these

**12** A task facilitated by the editing in 1424 of the *Book of Mystery* of Giyorgis de Sägla (a catalogue of heresies), on which see Piovanelli, "Les controverses théologiques," 196.
**13** The political dimension to the identification and persecution of the heterodox should not be ignored. Since the late-antique period there has been a general tendency to adopt and impose as the official religion a particular faith, whether Zoroastrianism in Sassanian Persia, the reformed paganism of Diocletian or Julian in the Roman empire, Nicene Christianity in the same territory and in Axum, or a Judaising monotheism in Yemen. On the latter, see Iwona Gajda, *Le royaume de Himyar à l'époque monothéiste. L'histoire de l'Arabie du sud ancienne de la fin du* IV*e* *siècle de l'ère chrétienne jusqu'à l'avènement de l'islam*, Mémoires de l'Académie des Inscriptions et Belles-lettres 40 (Paris: De Boccard, 2009). Regarding the effects of this new synergy between political power and religious authorities, see Polymnia Athanassiadi, *Vers la pensée unique. La montée de l'intolérance dans l'Antiquité tardive*, Histoire 102 (Paris: Les Belles Lettres, 2010).
**14** Robert M. Grant, *Gnosticism and Early Christianity* (New York: Columbia University Press, 1966), 93: "your magic is my miracle and vice versa."
**15** See, e.g., Gerd Lüdemann, *Heretics: The Other Side of Early Christianity*, trans. John Bowden (London: SCM Press, 1996; original German edn., Stuttgart: Radius Verlag, 1995), who calls Paul "the greatest heretic" of early Christianity, i.e., the theologian who initially aroused the most opposition. Regarding the extreme variety that characterised the first two centuries of Christianity, see Heikki Räisänen, *The Rise of Christian Beliefs: The Thought World of Early Christians* (Minneapolis, MN: Fortress Press, 2010).

terms does not imply value judgement."[16] While such reserve is commendable from a methodological point of view, it did not prevent them from concluding the same chapter with a value judgement as unhistorical and inaccurate as: "the victory of orthodoxy is that of consistency over inconsistency, of a certain logic over fanciful imaginings, of a scientifically developed theology over against unorganised doctrines."[17] Forty-five years later, we can not (nor should we) simply repeat, using the same derogatory terms, the judgement of the Fathers against "gnostics," "Jewish-Christians," and other "heretics," real or assumed. To the contrary, we should address the political and social factors behind the triumph of the holders of self-proclaimed "orthodox" ideologies.[18] Despite this, it is precisely this same heresiological rhetoric that certain conservative and/or evangelical theologians (especially in North America) continue to employ against both certain major apocryphal texts (such as the *Gospel of Thomas*, the *Gospel of Peter*, and the *Gospel of Judas*) and the specialists who work on them, to the point that it has been suggested, with good reason, that they be described as modern-day "heresy hunters."[19]

## 1.3 The usefulness of an ideal model

In the end, from the point of view of sociology and anthropology at least, there is clearly no satisfactory answer to questions like "What is orthodoxy?" and "What is heresy?" and, similarly, what is true and false prophecy, magic and miracle, canonical and apocryphal, and so on. The answers to these kinds of questions will, naturally and inevitably, be context-specific and pluriform: a particular concept has a particular meaning for a particular individual or group, at a particular

16 Marcel Simon and André Benoît, *Le judaïsme et le christianisme antique d'Antiochus Épiphane à Constantin*, Nouvelle Clio 10 (Paris: Presses universitaires de France, 1968), 290: "l'usage de ces termes n'implique pas de jugement de valeur."

17 Ibid., 307: "la victoire de l'orthodoxie est celle de la cohérence sur l'incohérence, celle d'une certaine logique sur des élucubrations fantaisistes, celle d'une théologie élaborée de manière scientifique en face de doctrines inorganisées."

18 See, in this regard, Gager, *Kingdom and Community*, 114–48, as well as the somewhat bold, but stimulating reflections of Rodney Stark, *The Rise of Christianity: A Sociologist Reconsiders History* (Princeton, NJ: Princeton University Press, 1996); Id., *Cities of God: The Real Story of How Christianity Became an Urban Movement and Conquered Rome* (New York: HarperOne, 2006); Id., *The Triumph of Christianity: How the Jesus Movement Became the World's Largest Religion* (New York: HarperOne, 2011).

19 See Tony Burke, "Heresy Hunting in the New Millennium," *Studies in Religion* 39 (2010): 405–20.

point in time. Given, however, that all of the above constitute different aspects of the sociology of conflict – deviance, sectarian movements, the construction of reality, and the definition of collective identities – there arises the possibility of developing from the characteristics of such dichotomies as orthodoxy/heresy and obedience/dissent an ideal model in the style of Max Weber, applicable to domains other than theology and religious studies.[20] In that sense, a universal heuristic model in which orthodoxy and heresy constitute two sides of the same coin could prove useful to scholars working in domains as diverse as the study of totalitarian regimes or corporate culture.[21]

# 2 Apocrypha and heresy

Apocryphal texts, in Ethiopia and elsewhere, provide a wealth of fascinating information for historians and theologians who take them seriously. As a result of the work of Julia Kristeva and Gérard Genette, we know that any approach to literary production is based on a cluster of intertextual references and that each new writing is, in reality, a sort of rewriting of works that precede it.[22] With this in mind, I turn first to a brief review of the apocryphal process (perhaps bet-

**20** For religious studies, see the ground-breaking research by John B. Henderson, *The Construction of Orthodoxy and Heresy: Neo-Confucian, Islamic, Jewish, and Early Christian Patterns* (Albany, NY: State University of New York Press, 1998); Id., "The Multiplicity, Duality, and Unity of Heresies," in: *Strategies of Medieval Community Identity: Judaism, Christianity and Islam*, eds. Wout Van Bekkum and Paul Cobb, Mediaevalia Groningana New Series 5 (Leuven: Peeters, 2004), 11–27. Henderson, *The Construction of Orthodoxy and Heresy*, 85, notes, inter alia, that "[a]ll of the orthodox traditions surveyed here attributed to themselves certain qualities, particularly *primacy* (or originality), *a true transmission* from the founder to the present day, *unity*, *catholicity*, and a conception of orthodoxy as a *middle way* between heretical extremes."

**21** Among the few studies that address theoretical issues from the perspective of sociology of religion, see Lester R. Kurtz, "The Politics of Heresy," *American Journal of Sociology* 88 (1983): 1085–1115; George V. Zito, "Toward a Sociology of Heresy," *Sociological Analysis* 44 (1983): 123–30; Jacques Berlinerblau, "Toward a Sociology of Heresy, Orthodoxy, and *Doxa*," *History of Religions* 40 (2001): 327–51. Danièle Hervieu-Léger, "Individualism, the Validation of Faith, and the Social Nature of Religion in Modernity," trans. Michael Davis, in: *Blackwell Companion to Sociology of Religion*, ed. Richard K. Fenn (Oxford: Blackwell, 2001), 161–75 at 168–70, identifies four main types or "regimes" of faith validation: communal, institutional, mutual, and personal, respectively based on the internal coherence of the group, the conformity to the norms fixed by the institution, the authenticity of the individual quest, and the subjective certainty of possessing the truth. While faith validation in pre-Constantinian Christianity seems to depend on a mixture of these four types, the institutional is probably the least critical.

**22** For what follows, see Piovanelli, "*Rewritten Bible* ou *Bible in progress?*," 306–309.

ter described as "the scriptural bent").[23] I then move on to describe the event in the second half of the fourth century that contributed decisively to the official association of the apocryphal texts with authors who are not just misguided but, worse, heretics. Such condemnation, which proved fatal for many texts written before this date, did not, however, put an end to the production of new texts. Finally, I will provide an overview of the resistance strategies adopted by the authors of some texts published after the fateful date of 367 CE.

## 2.1 *E pluribus unam* (more or less)

Initially, there existed (1) passed-down memories of the origins of a people, a clan, a family. Next, there came (2) stories about the exploits of the hero of each of these cultural groups, which one day someone decided to (3) record in writing. Regardless, the existence of one (or more) written text(s) did not prevent the storytellers from continuing to recount their traditional histories; rather, it allowed them to keep better track of their basic versions, which they could (4) consult, from time to time, and even (5) correct, if necessary. However, when someone finally related a story, which (6) constituted a major discrepancy between the oral tales and the written account, which was impossible to resolve, there was no choice but to (7) proceed to a new transcription of the tales, and so on, until someone else, faced with the proliferation of oral and written versions, felt obliged to (8) establish order among all these materials by selecting a single tale (for example, the one that seemed the most beautiful, the most complete or the most faithful) with the intention, again, of writing it down, while (9) the earlier copies were archived or completely destroyed. And so the cycle starts all over again at (4).

I have created this karmic cycle of the passed-down memories of a particular group from the observations of the British anthropologist Jack Goody concerning

23 See esp. Pierluigi Piovanelli, "What is a Christian Apocryphal Text and How Does it Work? Some Observations on Apocryphal Hermeneutics," *Nederlands Theologisch Tijdschrift* 59 (2005): 31–40; Id., "Qu'est-ce qu'un 'écrit apocryphe chrétien', et comment ça marche? Quelques suggestions pour une herméneutique apocryphe," in: *Pierre Geoltrain, ou comment "faire l'histoire" des religions. Le chantier des "origines", les méthodes du doute, et la conversation contemporaine entre disciplines*, eds. Simon C. Mimouni and Isabelle Ullern-Weité, Bibliothèque de l'École des hautes études, Sciences religieuses 128 (Turnhout: Brepols, 2006), 171–84. In these works the apocryphal traditions are treated as passed-down memories ("traditions mémoriales") based on the anthropological approach of Jean-Claude Picard, "Les chemins de la mythologie chrétienne" (1993), in: Id., *Le continent apocryphe. Essai sur les littératures apocryphes juive et chrétienne*, Instrumenta Patristica 36 (Turnhout: Brepols, 1999), 247–64.

the transmission, both oral and written, of creation myths recited at the initiation ceremonies of the Bagre, a cultic association of the LoDagaa, a population of north Ghana (West Africa).[24] Such observations, which match those adduced by the American literary critic Robert Alter,[25] are quite illuminating for understanding the process of perpetual rewriting which is the source of all our scriptural texts, regardless of their subsequent status as canonical or apocryphal.

As Scott Johnson neatly states in his struggle with *The Life and Miracles of Thecla*, a fifth-century rewriting of the *Acts of Paul and Thecla:*

> Both Goody and Alter point to the fact that rewriting is necessarily concomitant with any reception of 'text', be it oral or written, especially when that text has taken on a dominant, self-defining role in a culture. Whether it is the Lo Dagaa Bagre myth, stories from the Hebrew Bible, or the vast Homeric and related mythologies of ancient Greece, *human cognitive response invariably tends towards elaboration and rewriting*, sometimes on a very literal level, as in Hellenistic school exercises. The received text naturally becomes, often without any external pressure, a 'site' or a locus of rewriting and 'play': *this play, of course, has as much to do with refashioning contemporary identity as it does with reformulating ancient mythology.*[26]

In my opinion, this is an analysis that perfectly suits the causes and modalities of the process involved in the spontaneous generation of passed-down memories of ancient Judaism and Christianity, from the beginnings of both up to late antiquity and beyond.

For those who still have doubts about the perfectly natural and recurring character of all scriptural production as part of the evolutionary process of the

---

**24** See Jack Goody, *The Power of the Written Tradition*, Smithsonian Series in Ethnographic Inquiry (Washington, DC–London: Smithsonian Institute Press, 2000), a synthesis based on data collected in the field in 1950–1952 and published in 1972. For a similar approach, inspired by Maurice Halbwach's study of social memory, see April D. DeConick, "Reading the *Gospel of Thomas* as a Repository of Early Christian Communal Memory," in: *Memory, Tradition, and Text: Uses of the Past in Early Christianity*, eds. Alan Kirk and Tom Thatcher, SBL, Semeia Studies 52 (Atlanta, GA: Society of Biblical Literature, 2005), 207–20, as well as the study by Frances Flannery cited in n. 27 below.

**25** See Robert Alter, *Canon and Creativity: Modern Writing and the Authority of Scripture* (New Haven, CT: Yale University Press, 2000).

**26** Scott Fitzgerald Johnson, *The Life and Miracles of Thekla: A Literary Study*, Hellenic Studies 13 (Cambridge, MA: Harvard University Press, 2006), 76 (emphasis added). The Greek text was published by Gilbert Dagron (with Marie Dupré La Tour), *Vie et Miracles de Sainte Thècle. Texte grec, traduction et commentaire*, Subsidia Hagiographica 62 (Bruxelles: Société des Bollandistes, 1978). On the updating of the *Acts of Paul and Thecla* at work in *The Life and Miracles of Thecla*, see also Stephen J. Davis, *The Cult of Saint Thecla: A Tradition of Women's Piety in Late Antiquity*, OECS (Oxford–New York: Oxford University Press, 2001), 39–47.

groups concerned, I would like to recall the highly significant episode of the miraculous reconstitution of the scriptures after their destruction by the Babylonians (i.e., Romans) in *4 Ezra*, a Jewish apocalypse written two or three decades after the destruction of the Second Temple.[27] The work ends with the scribe and prophet Ezra dictating for forty days under divine inspiration not only the twenty-four official books of scripture, that are to be made public ("let the worthy and the unworthy read them"),[28] but also seventy supplementary writings reserved for the wise, "for in them (i.e., the seventy 'esoteric' books) is the spring of understanding, the fountain of wisdom, and the river of knowledge" (14.42–47). But what makes this particular episode illustrative is not so much the reference to a semblance of a canon of biblical writings in Hebrew as the information it provides about seemingly esoteric books: their number is very high, almost three times greater than that of the works that are freely available, and clearly symbolic.

Finally, what about the four biographies of Jesus that eventually made their way into the manuscripts of the New Testament canon? By any logic, one alone would have sufficed (Tatian's *Diatessaron* shows that an attempt was actually made in this direction), two at the most, as in the case of the books Exodus–Leviticus–Numbers and Deuteronomy, Samuel–Kings and Chronicles, Ezra–Nehemiah and *1 Ezra*, all famous biblical "duplicates." But that would be to forget the fact that the early Christian communities – in this regard worthy heirs of a number of Jewish communities from the Second Temple period – produced a large number of scriptural writings, from among which, subsequently, they liberally made their selection.

---

**27** Pending the publication of the proceedings of the sixth Enoch Seminar, *Second Baruch and Fourth Ezra: Jewish Apocalypticism in Late First Century Israel*, Gazzada (Varese), 26–30 June 2011, for an approach to this text informed by anthropological and sociological perspectives, see Frances Flannery, "Esoteric Mystical Practice in Fourth Ezra and the Reconfiguration of Social Memory," in: *Experientia, Volume 2: Linking Text and Experience*, eds. Colleen Shantz and Rodney A. Werline, SBL, Early Judaism and Its Literature 35 (Atlanta, GA: Society of Biblical Literature, 2012), 45–70.

**28** This is most probably an apocalyptic response to the trauma of the abduction of the *Sefer ha-'Azarah*, or "Book of the (Temple) court," the Torah scroll mentioned in the Mishna (Mo'ed Qatan 3.4; Kelim 15.6), which had been written, according to Rashi, by Ezra himself. Concerning such Jewish apocalyptic responses, see now Pierluigi Piovanelli, "*Odio humani generis*. Apocalypticiens messianistes et historiens intégrés à l'époque des Guerres des Judéens," *Laval théologique et philosophique* 69 (2013): forthcoming.

## 2.2 The turning point: *Festal letter* 39 (Easter 367)

To ensure the viability of any social system, it is essential that its natural tendency to disorder be offset by measures designed to reduce the latter and to keep it, wherever possible, under control. Resorting to a principle from thermodynamics, we could say that equilibirum occurs in a social system when the force of its entropy equals that of the constraints to which it is subject; when the force of its entropy exceeds that of its constraints, the potential consequences are mostly adverse. In the case of the excessive production of apocryphal texts, it was Athanasius of Alexandria who undertook to restore order in the libraries of the Egyptian church by giving strict instructions regarding the authorisation or proscription of biblical texts in *Festal letter* 39, circulated on the occasion of Easter in 367.[29]

In his letter, Athanasius attacks the Meletian autonomists of Upper and Middle Egypt and other "heretics" (the Manichaeans, Marcionites, Montanists, and, of course, Arians), whom he accuses of being the true authors of certain writings, "the so-called apocrypha" (§§ 15–16 and 25).[30] According to Athanasius, the only books that are authentically *theopneustoi*, "inspired by God," are those which belong either to the group of *kanonizomena*, those which have been canonised and which thus pose no problem (the "twenty-two books of the Old Testament"

**29** The argument that follows draws on the commentary by Alberto Camplani, *Atanasio di Alessandria. Lettere festali – Anonimo. Indice delle lettere festali*, Letture cristiane del primo millennio 34 (Milan: Paoline, 2003), 82–83, 498–518, 610–12 and 638. See also David Brakke, "Canon Formation and Social Conflict in Fourth-Century Egypt: Athanasius of Alexandria's Thirty-Ninth Festal Letter," *HThR* 87 (1994): 395–419; Id., "A New Fragment of Athanasius's Thirty-Ninth Festal Letter: Heresy, Apocrypha, and the Canon," *HThR* 103 (2010): 47–66 ; Enzo Lucchesi, "Un nouveau complément aux *Lettres festales* d'Athanase," *Analecta Bollandiana* 119 (2001): 255–60; Éric Junod, "Quand l'évêque Athanase se prend pour l'évangéliste Luc (*Lettre festale* XXXIX sur le canon des écritures)," in: *Early Christian Voices in Texts, Traditions and Symbols: Essays in Honor of François Bovon*, eds. David H. Warren, Ann G. Brock, and David W. Pao, Biblical Interpretation Series 66 (Leiden: Brill, 2003), 197–208; Id., "D'Eusèbe de Césarée à Athanase d'Alexandrie en passant par Cyrille de Jérusalem: de la construction savante du Nouveau Testament à la clôture ecclésiastique du canon," in: *Le canon du Nouveau Testament. Regards nouveaux sur l'histoire de sa formation*, eds. Gabriella Aragione, Éric Junod, and Enrico Norelli, Le monde de la Bible 54 (Geneva: Labor et Fides, 2005), 169–95 at 183–95; Gabriella Aragione, "La *Lettre festale* 39 d'Athanase. Présentation et traduction de la version copte et de l'extrait grec," in: ibid., 197–219; Nils Arne Pedersen, "The New Testament Canon and Athanasius of Alexandria's 39th *Festal Letter*," in: *Religion and Normativity: The Discursive Fight over Religious Texts in Antiquity*, ed. Anders-Christian Jacobsen, Acta Jutlandica, Theological Series 1 (Aarhus: Aarhus University Press, 2009), 168–77. As Camplani, *Lettere festali*, 596–97 and 600–602, notes, the letter survives in two fragmentary Coptic manuscripts and an excerpt from the Greek original, preserved in Syriac translation.

**30** All translations are from Brakke, "A New Fragment," 57–66.

and the twenty-seven books of the New Testament, listed at §§ 17–18), or to that of "the *anagignōskomena*, the books 'appointed to be read'," that is, the apocryphal/deuterocanonical books of the Greek Old Testament (the Wisdom of Solomon, Sirach, Esther, Judith and Tobit),[31] to which the patriarch added the *Teaching of the Apostles* (most probably, the *Didache*) and the *Shepherd* of Hermas (§ 20).[32] Because of their inspiration, these books contain all of the dogmatic truths of Christianity on the subject of the Trinity, the incarnation, the resurrection and the last judgement (§§ 19, 24); the only restriction consists in limiting the reading of *anagignōskomena* "to inside the catechetical school under the guidance of a master, an expression of the ecclesiastical hierarchy."[33]

On the other hand, the different apocrypha attributed to Enoch (*1* and *2 Enoch*),[34] to Isaiah (the *Ascension of Isaiah*) or to Moses (*in primis*, *Jubilees*) contain a mix of useful lessons and impiety: this (the category of apocrypha) "is *an invention of heretics*, who write these books whenever they want and then generously add time to them, so that, by publishing them as if they were ancient, they might have a pretext for deceiving the simple folk" (§ 21). Even though he

**31** In fact, since the book of Baruch and Letter of Jeremiah (attached to the book of Jeremiah), and *1 Ezra* (attached to Ezra–Nehemiah) are counted in the number of canonical writings (§ 17), Athanasius accepts here the majority of deuterocanonical and pseudepigraphal books that one could read (to judge by the Codex Vaticanus, Codex Sinaiticus, and Codex Alexandrinus) in the great uncial manuscripts of the fourth and fifth century. However, he makes no mention – with serious consequences – of the four books of the Maccabees (copied in Codices Sinaiticus and Alexandrinus, but absent from not only Codex Vaticanus, but also the ancient Ethiopic version of the Bible) and the *Psalms of Solomon* (whose presence is mentioned in the index to Codex Alexandrinus), nor the *Paralipomena of Jeremiah* (copied following the books Jeremiah–Baruch in the older manuscripts of the Ethiopic Bible).

**32** The *Shepherd* of Hermas, copied in Codex Sinaiticus, was also among the scriptural texts translated from Greek into Ethiopic in the Axumite period (see n. 9 above), while the *Didache* (if that is indeed it), cited here by Athanasius, survives only in a Greek manuscript from Jerusalem copied in 1056, that also contains the *Epistle of Barnabas* (included likewise in Codex Sinaiticus) and *1–2 Clement* (also copied in Codex Alexandrinus). The latter were neither mentioned by the patriarch nor, apparently, translated into Ethiopic.

**33** Camplani, *Lettere festali*, 512 n. 18 (my translation). See also Lance Jenott and Elaine Pagels, "Antony's Letters and Nag Hammadi Codex I: Sources of Religious Conflict in Fourth-Century Egypt," *JECS* 18 (2010): 557–89 at 585. The theme of instructing the faithful in general and catechumens in particular is revisited at the end of the letter (§§ 28 and 32).

**34** The existence of a Greek original of *2 Enoch* has been indirectly but convincingly proved by Joost L. Hagen, "No Longer 'Slavonic' Only: 2 Enoch Attested in Coptic from Nubia," in: *New Perspectives on 2 Enoch: No Longer Slavonic Only*, eds. Andrei A. Orlov, Gabriele Boccaccini, and Jason Zurawski, Studia Judaeoslavica 4 (Leiden: Brill, 2012), 7–34, following his identification of four fragments of a previously unknown Coptic version of *2 Enoch* discovered at Qasr Ibrim in 1972, that contained the remains of a short recension of chapters 36–42.

supplies no further details about the apocryphal books, because "it is even more fitting...not to proclaim anything in them nor to speak anything in them with those who want to be instructed" (§ 23),[35] Athanasius' message seems to me to be sufficiently clear: any book that is not mentioned in the lists of *kanonizomena* or *anagignōskomena* should be considered apocryphal, of heretical origin, and, as a result, proscribed.

It is, certainly, impossible to know the reactions of different Egyptian monastic communities to the reception and reading of *Festal letter* 39. Apparently, to judge from the *Life of Pachomius*, the letter must have had some effect in coenobitic circles.

> Let us be vigilant and take care not to read the books composed by these defiled heretics, atheists, and truly irreverent people, so that we ourselves may not become disobedient to the Lord, who is now saying to our father Athanasius and all those like him and also to those who will succeed him, 'Anyone who receives you, has received me' (Mt 10:40). And we must not lead others astray so that they read them and learn to be disobedient to the commands of the Holy Scriptures which are founded on the orthodox faith our holy fathers taught us.[36]

Some monks thus had to hurry to get rid, by one means or another, of these heretical inventions,[37] while others chose to ignore the instructions of their patri-

---

**35** I deliberately pass over the problem of the Athanasian refutation of the argument that "Paul took a testimony from the apocryphal books when he says, 'What no eye has seen, nor ear heard, things that have not arisen upon the human heart' (1 Cor 2:9)" (§§ 26–27). In reality, it is an extremely complex question, rendered more difficult by the existence of two similar sayings of Jesus, the one in Q (Matt 13:16–17/Luke 10:23–24), the other in the *Gospel of Thomas* (*logion* 17). For an overview of parallel passages and scholarly opinions, ancient and modern, see Enrico Norelli, *Ascensio Isaiae. Commentarius*, CCSA 8 (Turnhout: Brepols, 1995), 590–92; Matteo Grosso, *Vangelo secondo Tommaso. Introduzione, traduzione e commento*, Classici 12 (Rome: Carocci, 2011), 144–45.

**36** Translated by Armand Veilleux, *Pachomian Koinonia, Vol. I: The Life of Saint Pachomius and His Disciples*, Cistercian Studies Series 45 (Kalamazoo, MI: Cistercian Publications, 1980), 231. See Louis Théophile Lefort, "Thédore de Tabennêsi et la lettre pascale de St. Athanase sur le Canon de la Bible," *Le Muséon* 11 (1910): 205–16 at 214; Id., *S. Pachomii Vita Bohairice scripta*, I–II, CSCO 89 and 107, Scriptores Coptici 7 and 11 (Paris: Imprimerie nationale, 1925–1936), vol. 1, 175–78 (text); vol. 2, 114–15 (trans.).

**37** The Pachomian provenance of the Coptic library buried near Nag Hammadi is defended by, among others, James E. Goehring, "New Frontiers in Pachomian Studies," in: Id., *Ascetics, Society, and the Desert: Studies in Early Egyptian Monasticism*, Studies in Antiquity and Christianity (Harrisburg, PA: Trinity Press International, 1999), 162–86 at 173–79; and Tito Orlandi, "Nag Hammadi Texts and the Coptic Literature," in: *Colloque international "L'Évangile selon Thomas et les textes de Nag Hammadi" (Québec, 29–31 mai 2003)*, eds. Louis Painchaud and

arch and continued to read, copy, and translate *1* and *2 Enoch*, *Jubilees*, the *Ascension of Isaiah*, and other similar texts, as if nothing had happened. However, in the space of a few centuries the weight of ecclesiastical institutions eventually got the better of any resistance and the majority of ancient apocryphal texts disappeared from Egyptian libraries. Fortunately, a number of them had already been translated into Ethiopic twenty or thirty years before the circulation of *Festal letter* 39.[38]

## 2.3 The curious case of the two Marys

In other cases, however, in particular those of so-called "gnostic" writings, of which Coptic versions were discovered at Nag Hammadi and elsewhere,[39] the partial preservation of some stories and themes occurred via the medium of rewriting, not to mention recycling. The case study that I would like to present here, in brief, is that of the surprising metamorphosis of the person of Mary of

Paul-Hubert Poirier, BCNH, Études 8 (Quebec–Leuven: Presses de l'Université Laval and Peeters, 2007), 323–34.

**38** The fact that Athanasius cites such biblical figures as Enoch, Isaiah, and Moses, the putative authors of the more important pseudepigraphical texts translated into Ethiopic, is significant. Given the role played by Athanasius in the elevation to the episcopate of Frumentius, the apostle of Ethiopia (Rufinus, *HE* 1.9), indirectly confirmed by the suspicions fed by Emperor Constantius II about a possible collusion between the new bishop of Axum and the patriarch of Alexandria (Athan., *Apol.* 29, 31), it is tempting to imagine that, in writing *Festal letter* 39 Athanasius had in mind not the Meletian dissent, but an attitude more widespread among Egyptian monks and clergy, including those who went to Axum. This supposition supports the likelihood of 367 CE as the *terminus ante quem* for the translation of the entire Bible (including texts that were, in Athanasius' eyes, apocryphal) from Greek into Ethiopic. For the deconstruction of the myth that attributes evangelising activities rather to missionaries of "Syrian" origin, see Paolo Marrassini, "Some Considerations on the Problem of the 'Syriac Influences' on Aksumite Ethiopia," *Journal of Ethiopian Studies* 23 (1990): 35–46; Id., "Ancora sul problema degli influssi siriaci in età aksumita," in: *Biblica et Semitica. Studi in memoria di Francesco Vattioni*, ed. Luigi Cagni, Dipartimento di Studi Asiatici, Series Minor 59 (Naples: Istituto Universitario Orientale, 1999), 325–37 (= "Once Again on the Question of Syriac Influences in the Aksumite Period," trans. Caterina Franchi, in: Bausi, *Languages and Cultures of Eastern Christianity*, 209–19).

**39** Unless otherwise indicated, translations of the Nag Hammadi and related texts are taken from *The Nag Hammadi Scriptures: The International Edition*, ed. Marvin Meyer (New York: HarperCollins, 2007), while those of Christian apocryphal texts are from *New Testament Apocrypha*, ed. Wilhelm Schneemelcher, trans. Robert McL. Wilson, 2 vols. (Cambridge/Louisville, KY: Clarke and Westminster/John Knox Press, 1991).

Magdala,[40] favoured disciple of Jesus and *apostola apostolorum* in the *Gospel of Mary* (BG 1)[41] and other dialogues of "gnostic" revelation such as the *Wisdom of Jesus Christ* (NHC III,4; BG 3), *Dialogue of the Saviour* (NHC III,5) and *Pistis Sophia* (CA),[42] who was destined in the rewritings of late antiquity and the Middle Ages – namely, the *Questions of Bartholomew* and the *Book of the Resurrection of Jesus Christ by the Apostle Bartholomew*, as well as the *Liber requiei* and the various *Dormitions* and *Apocalypses of the Virgin*[43] – to cede the role of recipient of the mysteries of the afterlife to the mother of her Lord.

**40** On the different facets of Mary of Magdala, from the historical woman to the fictional character, see esp. Mary Rose D'Angelo, "Reconstructing 'Real' Women in Gospel Literature: The Case of Mary Magdalene," in: *Women & Christian Origins*, eds. Ross S. Kraemer and Mary Rose D'Angelo (Oxford–New York: Oxford University Press, 1999), 105–28; Jane Schaberg, *The Resurrection of Mary Magdalene: Legends, Apocrypha, and the Christian Testament* (New York– London: Continuum, 2002); Ann G. Brock, *Mary Magdalene, the First Apostle: The Struggle for Authority*, Harvard Theological Studies 51 (Cambridge, MA: Harvard University Press, 2003).

**41** See Anne Pasquier, *L'Évangile selon Marie (BG 1)*, BCNH, Textes 10 (Quebec, Presses de l'Université Laval, 1983); Michel Tardieu, *Écrits gnostiques. Codex de Berlin*, Sources Gnostiques et Manichéennes 1 (Paris: Cerf, 1984), 20–25, 75–82 and 225–37; Karen L. King, *The Gospel of Mary of Magdala: Jesus and the First Woman Apostle* (Santa Rosa, CA: Polebridge Press, 2003); Esther A. de Boer, *The Gospel of Mary: Beyond a Gnostic and a Biblical Mary Magdalene*, JSNTSup 260 (London–New York: T&T Clark, 2004); Christopher Tuckett, *The Gospel of Mary*, Oxford Early Christian Gospel Texts (Oxford: Oxford University Press, 2007).

**42** See Antti Marjanen, *The Woman Jesus Loved: Mary Magdalene in the Nag Hammadi Library and Related Documents*, NHMS 40 (Leiden: Brill, 1996); Silke Petersen, *"Zerstört die Werke der Weiblichkeit!" Maria Magdalena, Salome und andere Jüngerinnen Jesu in christlich-gnostischen Schriften*, NHMS 48 (Leiden: Brill, 1999); F. Stanley Jones, ed., *Which Mary? The Marys of Early Christian Tradition*, SBL, Symposium Series 19 (Atlanta, GA: Society of Biblical Literature, 2003); Gregor Emmenegger, "Maria Magdalena in gnostischen Texten," *Apocrypha* 19 (2008): 56–75. For the literary genre employed, see now Pierluigi Piovanelli, "Entre oralité et (ré)écriture. Le genre des *erotapokriseis* dans les dialogues apocryphes de Nag Hammadi," in: *La littérature des questions et réponses dans l'Antiquité: De l'enseignement à l'exégèse. Actes du séminaire sur le genre des questions et réponses tenu à Ottawa les 27 et 28 septembre 2009*, ed. Marie-Pierre Bussières, Instrumenta Patristica et Mediaevalia (Turnhout: Brepols, 2013), 93–103.

**43** See Simon C. Mimouni, *Dormition et Assomption de Marie. Histoire des traditions anciennes*, Théologie historique 98 (Paris: Beauchesne, 1995); Id., *Les traditions anciennes sur la Dormition et l'Assomption de Marie. Études littéraires, historiques et doctrinales*, Supplements to Vigiliae Christianae 104 (Leiden: Brill, 2011); Michel van Esbroeck, *Aux origines de la Dormition de la Vierge. Études historiques sur les traditions orientales*, Variorum Collected Studies Series 472 (Aldershot: Variorum, 1995); Mary Clayton, *The Apocryphal Gospels of Mary in Anglo-Saxon England*, Cambridge Studies in Anglo-Saxon England 26 (Cambridge: Cambridge University Press, 1998), 6–116; Stephen J. Shoemaker, *Ancient Traditions of the Virgin Mary's Dormition and Assumption*, OECS (Oxford: Oxford University Press, 2003); Jean Longère, ed., *Marie dans les récits apocryphes chrétiens, Tome I. Communications présentées à la 60ᵉ session de la Société Française d'Études Mariales, Sanctuaire Notre-Dame-du-Chêne, Solesmes, 2003*, Études mariales

Mary (of Magdala) is one of the privileged who speak with the Risen Lord in the *Dialogue of the Saviour* (in the company of Matthew, Jude and all the disciples together),[44] in the *Wisdom of Jesus Christ* (with Philip, Matthew, Thomas, Bartholomew and the disciples),[45] and in the *Pistis Sophia* (with all the other disciples).[46] While it is clear that the content of the questions Mary asks the Lord in these texts has no exact equivalent in later apocryphal texts, we can, nonetheless, note some similarities to the tenor of the questions that the apostles direct not just to the Risen Lord, but now to his mother. In the *Questions of Bartholomew*, for example, it is Bartholomew who asks Mary to tell "how [she] conceived the incomprehensible, or how [she] carried him who cannot be carried, or how [she] bore so much greatness" – a mystery, she objects, that cannot be revealed; "fire will come out of [her] mouth and consume the whole earth" (2.4–5), which would, in fact, have occurred, if Jesus had not intervened (2.22).[47] But it could also be that this new curiosity about the mystery of the incarnation is a distant echo of the pressing questions posed by Mary (of Magdala), "who the Savior loved...more than all other women," and who is the subject of the gospel that bears her name (10.1–25). Schematically, in the oldest texts Mary, the disciple of Jesus, is the privileged interlocutor with the Risen Lord, receives revelations separately, and is, in turn, questioned by the other disciples, while in the

(Paris–Montreal: Médiaspaul, 2004); Charles Perrot, ed., *Marie et la Sainte Famille. Récits apocryphes chrétiens, Tome II. 62e session de la Société Française d'Études Mariales, Nevers, septembre 2005*, Études mariales (Paris–Montreal: Médiaspaul, 2006); Enrico Norelli, *Marie des apocryphes. Enquête sur la mère de Jésus dans le christianisme antique*, Christianismes antiques (Geneva: Labor et Fides, 2009).

**44** See, e.g., *Dial. Sav.* 126.17–127.1, 131.19–132.1, 140.14–141.2.

**45** E.g., *Wisd. Jes. Chr.* 114.8–12, 117.12–17.

**46** E.g., *Pist. Soph.* 3.134. This dialogue updates the famous *agraphon* on the approved money-changers, on which see now Curtis Hutt, "'Be Ye Approved Money Changers!' Reexamining the Social Contexts of the Saying and its Interpretation," *Journal of Biblical Literature* 131 (2012): 589–609. Note also, with Ann G. Brock, "Setting the Record Straight – The Politics of Identification: Mary Magdalene and Mary the Mother in *Pistis Sophia*," in: Jones, *Which Mary?*, 43–52, that in the *Pistis Sophia* it is sometimes impossible to identify which of the two Marys – the mother or the disciple of Jesus – takes the initiative in questioning the Lord. In this sense, the text's narrator contributes to the subsequent confusion over the identity of the two women.

**47** A passage from an Ethiopic homily on *The Annunciation by Gabriel to Mary*, which obviously inspired the *Questions of Bartholomew*, is more explicit: "And Bartholomew, one of the Apostles, said, 'Of what kind was the angel who came unto thee, from whom thou couldst not escape? And what said he unto thee, O our Lady? And how is it possible that He Whom the heavens and the earth cannot contain can be carried in thy belly? Is it possible for fire to be mingled with human flesh? O my Lady, there is a torrent of fire in His mouth...'." Trans. by E.A. Wallis Budge, *Legends of Our Lady Mary the Perpetual Virgin and Her Mother Hanna* (Oxford–London: Oxford University Press and H. Milford, 1933), 109.

more recent texts it is the mother of Jesus who takes on the role of intermediary and revealer of the mysteries.[48]

In the *Gospel of Mary*, a text whose degree of "gnosticism" is still debated,[49] the last revelation Mary makes to the other disciples concerns a particular issue, namely the fate of the soul in the first moments following death, which would continue to fascinate minds throughout the entire history of Christianity. In this text, this situation is conceived of and described as a rise through the heavens, during which the soul is questioned bluntly by "the seven powers of Wrath. They interrogated the soul, 'Where are you coming from, human-killer, and where are you going, destroyer of realms?'" (16.12–16). These are conceptual categories of hermetic (the ascent of the soul) and orphic origin (knowledge of the correct answers), which were already well established in Jewish and Christian mysticism (for example, in *Ascension of Isaiah* 9.1–6 or *Gospel of Thomas* 49–50), but are conspicuous by their absence from canonical texts of the Old and New Testament.[50] As we propose in our ideal model (section 2.1), when the ideas defended by certain groups in the first generations of Christianity were gradually marginalised and their scriptural production made apocryphal, the members of other communities could apparently not help but recycle some of

**48** It is also significant that, by circuitous routes, the Virgin Mary also became in some Coptic texts not the "wife" (*hime*), but the "fiancée" (*šeleet*) of Christ, on the basis that it is about Mary that Solomon prophesied: "Arise and come beside me, my bride, my dove, who is beautiful among women" (Cant 1:8; 2:10–14; 5:9; 6:1). See the homily published by Stephen J. Shoemaker, "The Sahidic Coptic Homily on the Dormition of the Virgin Attributed to Evodius of Rome: An Edition from Morgan MSS 596 & 598 with Translation," *Analecta Bollandiana* 117 (1999): 241–83 at 256–59, 270–71; Id., *Ancient Traditions*, 397–407 at 398–99, 403–404.

**49** See in particular Esther A. de Boer, "Followers of Mary Magdalene and Contemporary Philosophy: Belief in Jesus According to the Gospel of Mary," in: *Jesus in apokryphen Evangelienüberlieferungen. Beiträge zu ausserkanonischen Jesusüberlieferungen aus verschiedenen Sprach- und Kulturtraditionen*, eds. Jörg Frey and Jens Schröter, WUNT 1.254 (Tübingen: Mohr Siebeck, 2010), 315–38.

**50** The evidence for such a belief has been re-examined by Einar Thomassen, "Dialogues with the Archons: The Post-mortem Encounters of the Ascending Soul in Gnostic Texts," in: *The Human Body in Death and Resurrection*, eds. Tobias Nicklas, Friedrich V. Reiterer, and Joseph Verheyden, Deuterocanonical and Cognate Literature Yearbook (Berlin: De Gruyter, 2009), 351–69; Simon Gathercole, "*Quis et unde?* Heavenly Obstacles in *Gos. Thom.* 50 and Related Literature," in: *Paradise in Antiquity: Jewish and Christian Views*, eds. Markus Bockmuehl and Guy G. Stroumsa (Cambridge: Cambridge University Press, 2010), 82–100. These two authors stop, however, at the end of the third century, without taking into account later texts such as the *Liber requiei* or the Greek *Apocalypse of Paul*.

these traditions in the (re)writing of new parabiblical texts.[51] Such was the case with several elements from "gnostic" personal eschatology, which were saved from the wreck of "Sethian," Valentinian, and other Christianities to be put to use in the construction of a "routinised" afterlife, which became normative as Christianity matured in the long term.[52]

In the *Liber requiei*, the oldest recension of the *Dormitions of the Virgin*, written in Greek in the fourth century and preserved fully in Ethiopic translation and partially in Coptic, Syriac and Georgian,[53] the "great angel" Jesus/Atodonāwol (i.e., Adonai'el?)[54] reassures his mother that she has nothing to fear from a *post mortem* encounter with the "powers" (37), because he is "the one who will come on the fourth day," together "with all the hosts of the angels," to meet the souls of the deceased righteous "who have kept the Saviour's words," and take them along with their bodies, now incorruptible, "to the Paradise of rest," where they will peacefully await "the day of the resurrection" (10–12, and for the accomplishment of this promise, 67–69 and 88–89). Mary is commissioned to pass on to the apostles this revelation written down in a book that contains "the prayer," the knowledge of which is required for the soul to ascend to heaven (14).[55] As she explains to the relatives and friends gathered in her house,

51 See Guy G. Stroumsa, "The Scriptural Movement of Late Antiquity and Christian Monasticism," *JECS* 16 (2008): 61–77, whose considerations apply equally well to the production of new apocryphal texts.

52 See Pierluigi Piovanelli, "Les origines de l'*Apocalypse de Paul* reconsidérées," *Apocrypha* 4 (1993): 25–64 at 56–57.

53 The Ethiopic version was published by Victor Arras, *De Transitu Mariae Apocrypha Aethiopice*, I–IV, CSCO 342–43 and 351–52, Scriptores Aethiopici 66–69 (Leuven, Peeters, 1973–1974), vol. 1, 1–84 (text); vol. 2, 1–54 (trans.). See also the translations by Mario Erbetta, *Gli apocrifi del Nuovo Testamento, Vol. I.2: Infanzia e passione di Cristo, Assunzione di Maria* (Casale Monferrato: Marietti, 1981), 421–56; and Shoemaker, *Ancient Traditions*, 290–350, who omits, however, the long digression in chapters 105–31 on "acts" of Peter and Paul at Rome and Philippi (on which, see ibid., 347–48 n. 167).

54 Is Jesus here (35, reading of ms. *B*) to be identified with the famous Yaho'el, "the lesser YHWH," identified, for his part, with Enoch/Metatron? On the subject of this high dignitary of the divine court, see Andrei A. Orlov, *The Enoch–Metatron Tradition*, Texts and Studies in Ancient Judaism 107 (Tübingen: Mohr Siebeck, 2005); and Daniel Boyarin, "Beyond Judaisms."

55 Accordings to Shoemaker, *Ancient Traditions*, 299, in chapter 15 the soul also passes a hybrid creature, with the hind parts of a lion and a serpent's tail, reminiscent of some descriptions of a gnostic Demiurge or its officials (ibid., n. 33). It should be noted, however, that the *sabedde'āt* mentioned by the Ethiopic version are, from the context, probably "vipers," i.e., demons that surround human beings in their lifetime in order to draw them into temptation. Moreover, according to Attilio Mastrocinque, *From Jewish Magic to Gnosticism*, STAC 24 (Tübingen: Mohr

> Two angels come to a person, one of righteousness and one of wickedness, and they come with death. And when (death) acts on the soul that is going forth, the two angels come and admonish his body. And if he has good and righteous deeds, the angel of righteousness rejoices because of this, because there is no (sin) that was found upon him. And he calls his other angels, and they come to the soul. And they sing before it until (they reach) the place of all righteous. Then the wicked angel weeps, because he did not find his part in him. And if there are evil deeds that are found in him, that one rejoices. And he takes *seven other angels* with him, and they take that soul and lead it away. The angel of righteousness weeps greatly (40).[56]

The "seven powers of Wrath" seen by the disciple of Jesus have been replaced here by the seven colleagues of the wicked angel who, in the new eschatological system put in place in monastic circles – most probably Egyptian[57] –, are supposed to escort to hell the soul whose body bears clear traces of sins it committed while alive. On the other hand, the soul of the righteous person whose body remained pure is escorted by angels, singing, to the place provisionally destined for it – this is the major innovation derived from the underlying "gnostic" stories, where there can be no place either for friendly angel pyschopomps (because these creatures of the Demiurge can only be hostile)[58] or for a positive evaluation of the human body (because the material from which it is made is just as wicked and doomed to destruction). The connection here between the disciple and the mother of Jesus, who both effectively guarantee such a personal eschatology,

---

Siebeck, 2005), 70–85, Yaldabaoth is usually represented as a god whose features are not *leontopodius*, but *leontocephalus*.

**56** Translated by Shoemaker, *Ancient Traditions*, 313–14 (slightly modified).

**57** The danger of an aerial interception of the souls of the dead by "hostile powers" that cannot be thwarted by the intervention of "holy angels," already present in the thought of Origen, is a topos relatively common in monastic literature as, for example, in the *Life of Antony* (65.2–9), the *Life of Melania the Younger* (64; 70) or the *Homily 22* attributed to Macarius of Egypt and other ps-Macarian writings (see Piovanelli, "Les origines de l'*Apocalypse de Paul*," 46–48 and 57–58 n. 94). The most spectacular narrativisation of such a belief is supplied by the Greek *Apocalypse of Paul* (11–18), where Paul, before attending the death and judgement of a righteous person, a wicked person, and a hypocrite, sees "under the firmament of heaven...angels who were pitiless, who had no compassion; their faces were full of wrath and their teeth projected from their mouths; their eyes flashed like the morning star in the East, and from the hairs of their head and out of their mouth went forth sparks of fire. ...These are those who are appointed for the souls of the wicked in the hour of need" (11, my translation).

**58** See, for example, the ruthless zeal of the "angels" and "customs agents" (*telōnai*) of the fourth and fifth heaven in the Coptic *Apocalypse of Paul* (20.5–22.10), one of the more probable hypotexts of its Greek homologue. However, in the *Pistis Sophia* this problem is bypassed by having Melchizedek, "the great Receiver (*paralēmptōr*) of Light," receive the particles of light emanating from the elect (1.25–26; 2.86; 3.112; 128; 131).

can denote both the change in theological perspective and the validation of a new type of belief, which originally enjoyed no scriptural anchor.

In an earlier study I explored very tenatively the possible intertextual relationships the late apocryphal writings – whose protagonist is Mary, the mother of Jesus – maintain with their "gnostic" predecessors.[59] Six years later, I believe that a set of convergent elements is beginning to emerge and that this hypothesis is increasingly less speculative.[60] On the one hand, the presence of these Magdalenic "gnostic" antecedents potentially allows us to fill a gap in our apocryphal documentation between the traditions concerning Mary regarding the birth of Jesus and those concerning her dormition/assumption.[61] On the other, they provide an eloquent and iconic example of the vitality of aprocyphal writing in the long term and its ability to rise, as it were, from the ashes after changing character and eliminating – to take Athanasius' letter literally – all the impieties of the underlying texts in order to preserve only the useful lesson.

## 3 Conclusion: Texts that are "useful," not just for the soul

The first draft of this present study was almost complete, when I received an offprint of the most recent article of François Bovon, "Beyond the Canonical and the Apocryphal Books, the Presence of a Third Category: The Books Useful for the Soul."[62] It constitutes a significant contribution, in which the Swiss exegete returns to the theological dimension past, present, and future of our apocryphal texts, victims still today of the heresiological prejudices of another time. Inspired by an approach practised in the Middle Ages by certain Byzantine copyists who favoured the preservation of apocryphal texts, Bovon proposes that we view the

59 See Piovanelli, "Le recyclage des textes apocryphes," 280–87.

60 See the similar case of the Coptic *Gospel of the Saviour* and its cognates, the *Discourse of the Saviour on the Subject of the Cross* and the *Dance of the Saviour around the Cross*, examined by Piovanelli, "De l'usage polémique des récits de la Passion," 140–49; Id., "Thursday Night Fever: Dancing and Singing with Jesus in the *Gospel of the Savior* and the *Dance of the Savior around the Cross*," *Early Christianity* 3 (2012): 229–48. These late-antique aprocrypha of the Passion constitute "orthodox" rewritings of an older "gnostic" model, i.e., *Acts of John* 94–102.

61 Analysed, respectively, in chapters 2 and 3 of Norelli, *Marie des apocryphes*, 33–102 and 103–47.

62 Published in *HThR* 105 (2012): 125–37. See also the essays devoted to what he terms the "compagnons apocryphes du Nouveau Testament," assembled in *Dans l'atelier de l'exégète. Du canon aux apocryphes*, Christianismes antiques (Geneva: Labor et Fides, 2012).

latter as works which are neither inspired nor heretical, but simply "useful for the soul" (*psuchōfelē*). It is a strategy both prudent and clever, which, he hopes, will contribute to a change in perception regarding a considerable portion of Christian scriptural literature.

For my part, I will add only that these texts have played a definitive role in the validation and dissemination of numerous beliefs and practices, whose origins one can trace back to the very founder (whether true or imagined is irrelevant!) of Christianity and his closest collaborators, since we must not forget that in every self-respecting pre-industrial culture the innovation that has the greatest chance of being accepted is that which is presented in the guise of a rediscovery.[63] In the process, these texts have contributed to a constant evolution, for the better (the strengthening of identity) and for the worse (the demonisation of the "other," particularly the Jews),[64] of different Christian communities, who were constantly being pulled between the necessity to remain faithful to the spirit of their beginnings and to adapt to what was new. When, with time, certain of these texts became too archaic and, consequently, unusable, even embarrassing, they were set aside, sometimes even condemned by ecclesiastical authorities, but, more often, rewritten, as if it were impossible to give up this particular medium of communication. From that point of view, these are texts of the highest importance and greatest utility for historians of Christianity. But is this also the case for contemporary readers, whether they are believers or not? I am inclined to think "yes," to the degree that these texts give us a glimpse of the extraordinary variety in space and time of identities adopted by the different Christian communities, and to the degree that such awareness could favour the beginning, in this instance, of a process of opening up to the "other." Could they be as or even more (in the case, for example, of the *Gospel of Thomas*) useful than other scriptural texts that were included in the official canon? That is a more delicate question to which each person, each group and each community will supply its own answer. Personally, I wonder whether it would not be better simply to turn the page, here as elsewhere, and finally stop thinking and behaving accord-

---

**63** As in the case of the establishment of a provisional afterlife much better organised than the as yet rudimentary one outlined in the *Liber requiei* (90 – 102), thanks to the discovery of the "original" Greek text of the *Apocalypse of Paul*, on which subject see Pierluigi Piovanelli, "The Miraculous Discovery of the Hidden Manuscript, or the Paratextual Function of the Prologue to the *Apocalypse of Paul*," in: *The Visio Pauli and the Gnostic Apocalypse of Paul*, eds. Jan N. Bremmer and István Czachesz, Studies on Early Christian Apocrypha 9 (Leuven: Peeters, 2007), 23 – 49.

**64** See Piovanelli, "De l'usage polémique des récits de la Passion," 149 – 51.

ing to parameters established, for eminently political reasons, in Alexandria on Easter 367.[65]

65 For a recent example of the persistent influence of Athansius' act see Hans-Christoph Askani, "Comment le canon nous advient. Essai sur le concept de texte, de canon et de texte sacré," *Études théologiques et religieuses* 87 (2012): 145–69.

Alan H. Cadwallader

# Inter-City Conflict in the Story of St Michael of Chonai

The cultivation of conflict between cities under the early principate was part of a strategy of imperial cohesion that included local euergetism and competitive inter-city scrambling for Roman recognition. Whilst it might be argued that the Romans simply brought to a new art-form what had existed previously in inter-*polis* rivalry, their strategy left an indelible mark on ecclesial relationships especially after the Constantinian imperialisation of Christianity. In part the conflict was exacerbated by the hierarchical structuring of church relationships according to metropolitical and suffragan dioceses. Such a mode of administration and management owed not a little to the *conventus* (Greek: διοικήσεις) system of assizes established in the republican period and to the tiers of imperial religious expression cultivated in the first two hundred years of the empire in the Roman province of Asia.[1] The intense conflict between Laodikeia and Kolossai found in the vernacular *Story of St Michael of Chonai* provides a test-case for inter-city and inter-diocesan conflict in the early to mid-Byzantine period.

The story of the archangel St Michael of Chonai is known in three versions. Two tenth-century examples of high Byzantine literature, one by Simeon Metaphrastes and one by Archbishop Sisinnius,[2] do not provide the focus of this chapter, except as a means of highlighting by contrast some of the remarkable intimations of conflict between two neighbouring cities in south western Phrygia. The vernacular story, whilst probably coming to its final recension in the ninth century,[3] contains discernible layers of tradition reaching back into pre-

1 Joseph B. Lightfoot, *Saint Paul's Epistles to the Colossians and to Philemon* (9th edn.; London: Macmillan, 1890), 7; Périclès-Pierre Joannou, ed., *Discipline générale antique (II^e–IX^e s.)*, I.2, *Les canons des synodes particuliers (IV^e–IX^e s.)*, Pontificia commissione per la redazione de le codice di diritto canonico orientale. Fonti. ser. 1 fasc. 9 (Rome–Grottaferrata: Tipografia Italo-Orientale "S. Nilo," 1962), 536–37.

2 Maximilien Bonnet, ed., *Narratio de miraculo a Michaele archangelo Chonis patrato, adjecto Symeonis Metaphrastae de eadem re libello* (Paris: Librairie Hachette, 1890), 20–28, for the former; Joannes Stilting et al., eds., *Acta Sanctorum: Septembris* (Paris–Rome: Victor Palmé, 1869 [1762]), vol. 8, 41C–47C, for the latter.

3 Alan H. Cadwallader, "A Stratigraphy of an Ancient City through its Key Story: The Archistrategos of Chonai," in: *Colossae in Space and Time: Linking with an Ancient City*, eds. Alan H. Cadwallader and Michael Trainor (Gottingen: Vandenhoeck & Ruprecht, 2011), 282–98 at 291.

Christian times.[4] By the time it reached its final form, the site of the sanctuary (and its miraculous deliverance) is titled Chonai.[5] Chonai is the successor name to Kolossai[6] and is indicated tangentially in the text by a blatant punning on the city's Byzantine name (which means "funnels").[7] The punning enables the sanctuary to avoid any precise link with a named city, thereby heightening the David and Goliath inequities of the metropolitical belligerence.

The story begins with the two apostles, John and Philip, cleansing Hierapolis of the putrefaction associated with a triad of related female gods, Artemis, Echidna and Cybele (the "Great Goddess") and promising a healing spring, the gift of the archangel Michael. After a demonstration of the therapeutic qualities of the spring, a sanctuary is established, eventually maintained by an exemplary devotee, Archippos, who hails from a Christian family resident at the now-purified Hierapolis. The particular healing that establishes the fame of the spring is of a mute girl brought to the miraculous waters by her father, a "godless idolater" from Laodikeia. The conversion of his household is set against the reaction of his (former?) city. Laodikeia is portrayed as the centre of resistance to the Christian site. An escalating series of attacks against the holy site finally ushers in a cathartic rescue of the sanctuary, its custodian, and the surrounding region by Michael, the archistrategos of the triune God's heavenly forces. The story concludes with a proclamation that the fame of the site will spread throughout the world.

The story indicates that the site was a touch-stone of the battle between pagan forces, determined to retain it as a talisman of the benefits of the old divinities, and Christians equally determined that it should become a place carved out according to the new dispensation.[8] But there also appears a particular layer of tradition that witnesses to an internecine conflict over the manner in which Christianity would triumph over the gods and their sacred accoutrements – whether by obliteration of pagan history and places or by a negotiated settle-

4 Cadwallader, "Stratigraphy," generally; see also Id., "St Michael of Chonai and the Tenacity of Paganism," in: *Intercultural Transmission in the Medieval Mediterranean: 100–1600 CE*, eds. David W. Kim and Stephanie L. Hathaway (London–New York: Bloomsbury Publishing, 2012), 37–59.

5 All manuscripts attest ἐν ταῖς Χώναις. See also Albert Ehrhard, *Überlieferung und Bestand der hagiographischen und homiletischen Literatur der griechischen Kirche* (Leipzig: J.C. Hinrichs, 1938), vol. 2, 240 n.1. In some menologia the name reverts to Kolossai; see Bonnet, *Narratio*, XVI.

6 Const. Porph., *Them.* 3.24 (*Costantino Porfirogenito De Thematibus*, ed. Agostino Pertusi, Studi e testi 160, Vatican: Biblioteca Apostolica Vaticana, 1952, 68); Nicetas Choniates, *Chron.* 178.19 (*Nicetae Choniatae Historia*, ed. Jan Louis van Dieten, Corpus Fontium Historiae Byzantinae 11, Berlin: De Gruyter, 1975).

7 ἀκοντίσθητε ὑμεῖς ἐν τῇ χώνῃ ταύτῃ καὶ ἔστε χωνευόμενοι ἐν τῷ χάσματι τούτῳ (12.5).

8 Cadwallader, "Tenacity of Paganism," 44.

ment with the past that enabled a measure of continuity to ease ardent devotees from one religious expression to another. The survey conducted by the Canadian Religious Rivalries Seminar is pertinent. Richard Ascough notes, "The overall picture [around the Mediterranean basin] gives a surprising lack of clear evidence for sustained conflict with 'outsiders' and the very clear evidence, spanning a few centuries, for like religious groups competing with one another."[9] Interestingly, the conflict in the St Michael story is portrayed as if it is a battle with "outsiders" when, in reality, it is an infra-ecclesial struggle.

In the massive upheavals in the fourth-century Roman empire, there was no uniform Christian response and the church was as much tested within itself as in its battles with a pagan legacy. One method of dealing with the pluriform issues was for the church to hold councils that would make declarations and "canons" about acceptable and non-acceptable behaviour and thinking.

# 1 The Council of Laodikeia

Right at the beginning of our discussion of this "council," we are beset by critical problems. The manuscripts referring to the council are unusually devoid of any mention of those attending, of any preamble that might have set the motivation for meeting, or of date. Later memory attempted to supply this lack. A sixth- or seventh-century Syriac manuscript for example provides the names of twenty attending bishops, but their middle eastern provenance indicates a confusion between the Laodikeia of Phrygia and that of Syria, and they belong to the list of those who attended the Nicaean Council in 325.[10] This may have been a subtle effort to deflect attention from the disconcerting lack of any reference to Nicaea in the Laodikeian Council,[11] given that Laodikeia was, for much of the middle

---

**9** Richard Ascough, "Religious Coexistence, Co-operation, Competition, and Conflict in Sardis and Smyrna," in: *Religious Rivalries and the Struggle for Success in Sardis and Smyrna*, ed. Richard S. Ascough, SCJ 14 (Waterloo, Ont.: Wilfrid Laurier University Press, 2005), 245–52 at 245.

**10** British Library Add. Ms. 14,528.

**11** Unlike, for example, the roughly contemporaneous Council of Illyricum (c. 375 CE) mentioned by Theodoret, *HE* 4.8 (ed. Leon Parmentier and Günther C. Hansen, GCS NF 5.220–24), or the Council of Serdica; see Ramsay MacMullen, *Voting about God in Early Church Councils* (New Haven, CN–London: Yale University Press, 2006), 105–107. Nicene orthodoxy had to be reasserted in Phrygia, if not Asia. See Neil B. McLynn, *Ambrose of Milan: Church and Court in a Christian Capital*, TCH 22 (Berkeley–Los Angeles: University of California Press, 1994), 92–95.

fourth century, under Arian sway.[12] Arianism is, surprisingly, not one of the named heresies in the canons.[13] The medieval Decretals of Gratian number the attending bishops as thirty-two, though even here the Gratianic manuscripts are divided.[14] Whatever the number, a small gathering is implied.[15] As for the purpose of the council, a twelfth-century church floor mosaic from Bethlehem summarises its concern as directed against "Montanus and the other heresies."[16] Efforts to pin down the date are even more nebulous; placement in the council catalogues between the Council of (Syrian) Antioch (341 CE) and that of Constantinople (381 CE) provide a general period. All this appears to confirm Ramsay MacMullen's observation that "less awe-inspiring councils" were frequently enhanced by manipulated claims about attendance, importance and written texts in an effort to retain or direct desired outcomes.[17]

Overlooked in debates about this council is the close parallel between some of the Laodikeian canons and a direction of the emperor Julian (the Apostate, 361–63 CE). According to Sozomen's transcription, Julian exhorted pagan priests to imitate Christian practice, which included, *inter alia*, that they not attend plays, nor drink at taverns, nor engage in occult arts.[18] Although the letter is not extant in any manuscript of Julian, the sentiments are substantially repeated in a fragmentary letter to a priest (1.296–339). In sum, "the priestly life is to be more reverent than the political life" (1.298), "a pattern of life that ought to speak to the populace of the gods" (1. 322) – Zeus-like philanthropy; orderly management of temple property and ritual; the avoidance of the speech, texts and per-

---

**12** See generally, Soz., *HE* 3.13, 4.12 (eds. Joseph Bidez and Günther C. Hansen, GCS NF 4.117–18, 154). Laodikeia is not listed at the Council of Constantinople in 381, which confirmed the homoousion position. See the discussion in Peter L'Huillier, *The Church of the Ancient Councils: The Disciplinary Work of the First Four Ecumenical Councils* (Crestwood, NY: St Vladimir's Seminary Press, 2000), 210–12. Because the conciliar canons were directed at discipline rather than doctrine, this may have saved the canons for the church.

**13** The named heresies (canons 7 and 8) are Novationism, Photinianism, Quartodecimanism and Montanism; generic references to heretics occur in canons 6, 7, 9, 10, 31, 32–34, 37. The interests of some bishops from Asia in securing uniformity of belief in the church *without* subscription to the Nicene homoousion is mentioned by Sozomen (*HE* 6.12; GCS NF 4.251–52).

**14** Gratian, *Decr.* 16.11; see Brooke Foss Westcott, *A General Survey of the History of the Canon of the New Testament* (Grand Rapids, MI: Baker, 1980 [1889$^{6}$]), 431–32.

**15** A "local synod," claims Archimandrite Ephrem, "Bible," in: *The Blackwell Dictionary of Eastern Christianity*, eds. Ken Parry et al. (Oxford: Blackwell, 2001), 82.

**16** *CIG* 8953. Only canon 8 actually refers to "the heresy of the so-called Phrygians."

**17** MacMullen, *Voting about God*, 107–109.

**18** Soz., *HE* 5.16 (GCS NF 4.217–18). References to the writings of the emperor Julian are to volume and page of the edition by William C. Wright, *The Works of the Emperor Julian*, LCL (Cambridge, MA: Harvard University Press, 3 vols., 1913), here 3.66–73.

formances of lurid poets, playwrights and philosophers; and extreme scruples about interaction in public places and private houses (2.298 – 304, 314 – 18, 324 – 26, 330, 335). He explicitly names "the Galileans" (i.e., Christians) as the competitors (2.336 – 39).[19] Canons 24, 36, 54, and 55 of the Council of Laodikeia address similar matters of discipline, but, of course, directing the behavior of *Christian* clergy. Julian's letters clearly demonstrate that competitive piety was seen as a crucial tactic in harnessing and honing the standing of particular religious adherence.[20]

The canons themselves are terse in their form of expression, almost an epitome,[21] and appear to have two patterns of introduction, one using περὶ τοῦ (canons 1 to 19) and a second, ὅτι δεῖ (canons 20 to 59, with ὅτι οὐ δεῖ for canons 46 – 48) with a sixtieth canon (on the canon of scripture) seemingly tacked on.[22] Sometimes a canon in the former group parallels a canon in the second group (for example, the ban against marriage with heretics in canons 10 and 31).[23] Moreover the canons cover a sweep of concerns from quartodecimanism to Jewish practices, from Montanism to the behaviour of clerics. Accordingly, not only is the date of the council debated (anywhere between 343 and 381, with 360 – 365 the preferred option) but the "council" may be little more than a convenient hook on which to hang a patchwork of decisions made by variously constituted

19 On the asceticism promoted by Julian see Susanna Elm, *Sons of Hellenism, Fathers of the Church: Emperor Julian, Gregory of Nazianzus and the Vision of Rome*, TCH 49 (Berkeley: University of California Press, 2012), 139 – 43.

20 Similarly, N.P. Milner, "Notes and Inscriptions on the Cult of Apollo at Oinoanda," *Anatolian Studies* 50 (2000): 139 – 49 at 144 – 45. From the Christian side see Jn Chrys., *De S. Babyla contra Iulianum* 1 – 23 (*Jean Chrysostome. Discours sur Babylas*, eds. Margaret A. Schatkin, Cécile Blanc, and Bernard Grillet, SC 362, Paris: Les Éditions du Cerf, 1990, 90 – 120); cf. canon 30. This competitive practice was a long-standing topos in philosophical and theological debate; see Seneca, *Nat. quaest.* 4A, Preface 14 – 17; Dio Chrysostom, *Or.* 8.15 – 16; Epictetus 3.22; Paul, 2 Cor 11:21 – 29. How successful was the tactic is another question: see Nicholas Baker-Brian, "The Politics of Virtue in Julian's *Misopogon*," in: *Emperor and Author: The Writings of Julian 'the Apostate'*, eds. Nicholas Baker-Brian and Shaun Tougher (Swansea: The Classical Press of Wales, 2012), 263 – 80 at 265 – 66, 269 – 77. I am grateful to the editors of *Emperor and Author* for allowing me access to the papers prior to published release.

21 Joannou, *Discipline générale*, 128, 501; William A. Jurgens, *The Faith of the Early Fathers* (Collegeville, MN: Liturgical Press, 1970), vol. 1, 315 – 16.

22 The canons are found in three versions in Giovanni D. Mansi, *Sacrorum Conciliorum Nova et Amplissima Collectio* (Florence: 1759), vol. 2, 563 – 614. A translation (of most) is provided by Lawrence Johnson, *Worship in the Early Church: An Anthology of Historical Sources* (Collegeville, MN: Liturgical Press, 2009), vol. 2, 299 – 304.

23 This analysis is found in L'Huillier, *Church of the Ancient Councils*, 210, who has relied on the earlier work of Charles Joseph Hefele, *Histoire des conciles d'après les documents originaux* (Paris: Letouzey et Ané, 1907), vol. 1.2, 993.

synods, councils or episcopal judgement held in the period.[24] Périclès-Pierre Joannou thinks that the canon list reflects the canonical tradition of Phrygia.[25] However, the status of the council appears to have been established early with its canon collection incorporated into collations of various conciliar decisions[26] – although this may itself be part of the collecting process that used a Phrygian metropolitical church as its nominal receiving house.[27] There is one canon however that confirms that there was a Council of Laodikeia precisely because early in the fifth century Theodoret of Cyrrhus directly related canon and council to Kolossai and to the Pauline letter to the Kolossians.

## 2 Anathematising the worship of angels

In contemporary New Testament scholarship, in spite of the apparent anachronism of using a fourth-century record to interpret a first-century text, one Laodikeian canon with strong claims to authenticity becomes prized, utilised to illuminate the deprecation in Colossians 2:8 of the "worship of angels."[28] This appropriation takes various forms, the most valuable being a contribution to the debate over whether θρησκεία τῶν ἀγγέλων is an objective or subjective genitive.[29] But it assumes that the Kolossians were unremittingly obstinate, embracing a

**24** Contra William Tabbernee, *Fake Prophecy and Polluted Sacraments: Ecclesiastical and Imperial Reactions to Montanism* (Leiden–Boston: Brill, 2007), who concludes (301) that the council "must have been a significant one as it formulated sixty canons which have been preserved."

**25** Joannou, *Discipline générale*, 128.

**26** F.J.E. Boddens Hosang, *Establishing Boundaries: Christian-Jewish Relations in Early Council Texts* (Leiden: Brill, 2010), 91.

**27** M. l'abbé Auguste Boudinhon, "Note sur le concile de Laodicée," in: *Congrès scientifique international des Catholiques tenu à Paris du 8 au 13 avril 1888* (Paris: Bureaux des "Annales de philosophie chrétienne," 1889), vol. 2, 420–47. On the numbers variously claimed to be authentic, see Jean-Baptiste Chabot, ed., *Chronique de Michel le Syrien: Patriarche Jacobite D'Antioche (1166–1199)* (Paris: Ernest Leroux, 1910), vol. 4, 265.

**28** See especially Lightfoot, *Saint Paul's Epistles*, 65, and recently, Robert McL. Wilson, *A Critical and Exegetical Commentary on Colossians and Philemon* (London–New York: Continuum, 2005), 52. Frederick F. Bruce, "Jews and Christians in the Lycus Valley," *BSac* 141 (1984): 3–15 at 12, however, reckoned it "most improbable that the practices which incurred the disapproval of the Synod of Laodicea and of Theodoretus bore any direct relationship to those deplored by Paul in his Letter to the Colossians."

**29** See, for example, Darrel D. Hannah, *Michael and Christ: Michael Traditions and Angel Christology Christology in Early Christianity*, WUNT 2.109 (Tübingen: Mohr Siebeck, 1999), 109–10, 112; Charles H. Talbert, *Ephesians and Colossians*, Paideia: Commentaries on the New Testament (Grand Rapids, MI: Baker, 2007), 207–208.

prohibited practice in defiance of apostolic injunction. According to this understanding, canon 35 was designed to restore apostolic injunction. The Laodikeian canon reads,

> Ὅτι οὐ δεῖ Χριστιανοὺς ἐγκαταλείπειν τὴν ἐκκλησίαν τοῦ θεοῦ καὶ ἀπιέναι καὶ ἀγγέλους ὀνομάζειν καὶ συνάξεις ποιεῖν, ἅπερ ἀπηγόρευται. Εἴ τις οὖν εὑρεθῇ ταύτῃ τῇ κεκρυμμένῃ εἰδωλολατρίᾳ σχολάζων, ἔστω ἀνάθεμα, ὅτι ἐγκατέλιπε τὸν κύριον ἡμῶν Ἰησοῦν Χριστὸν, τὸν υἱὸν τοῦ Θεοῦ καὶ εἰδωλολατρείᾳ προσῆλθεν.
>
> Christians shall not forsake the church of God and turn to the worship of angels, thus having gatherings in their honour. This is forbidden. Those who devote themselves to this hidden idolatry, let them be anathema, because they have forsaken our Lord Jesus Christ, the Son of God, and gone over to idolatry.[30]

For all the vehement language of idolatry and anathema, no express mention is made of Kolossai. But early commentators, like recent ones, were in no doubt. In the following century, Theodoret of Cyrrhus twice applied the anathema to the sanctuary of St Michael at Kolossai.[31] A later scholiast on the Laodikeian synod fingered Kolossai.[32] Not only was it manifest to these commentators that canon 35 was directed at one particular ecclesial satellite of the metropolitical church of Laodikeia. It also demonstrated that Kolossai had a long tradition of angel worship, focused at a devotional sanctuary.

The efforts to clarify the nature of this devotion to angels (or an angel) have not yielded scholarly unanimity. The interests of the later Byzantine church (especially one involved in iconoclastic debates) sought to delimit the meaning of ἀγγέλους ὀνομάζειν in canon 35 either to the wrongful use of names for angels or to the multiplication of names beyond biblical warrant.[33] This mis-reads the canon and certainly marginalises how Theodoret of Cyrrhus understood it; moreover it sits uneasily with the elaboration of (named) angels resplendent in

---

**30** Bonnet, *Narratio*, XXV; an expanded text, (ms. Vindobonensis) is reproduced by Joannou, *Discipline générale*, 144–45. The inclusive translation is by Johnson, *Worship in the Early Church*, 2.302; cf. Hefele, *A History of the Councils of the Church*, trans. William R. Clark and Henry N. Oxenham (Edinburgh: T&T Clark, 1876), 317.

**31** *Interpr. ep. ad Col.* (PG 82.613, 620D).

**32** See Wilhelm Lueken, *Michael: Eine Darstellung und Vergleichung der jüdischen und der morgenländisch-christlichen Tradition vom Erzengel Michael* (Göttingen: Vandenhoeck & Ruprecht, 1898), 75.

**33** Charlemagne, *Capitularia Admonitio Generalis* 16 (c. 789 CE) (*Capitularia Regum Francorum*, ed. Alfred Boretius, MGH Leges sec. 2 t.1, Hanover: Hahn, 1960 [1883]). Significantly perhaps, the collating Council of Trullo (691–692) confirmed fifteen of the Laodikeian canons, including canons 36–38, but no explicit mention was made of canon 35: George Nedungatt and Silvano Agrestini, "Concilium Trullanum, 691–692," in: CCCOGD 1.209, 230.

churches such as the Chora Church in Constantinople. But the casuistry of this approach did make it possible to reinstate the cult of angels at the Seventh Ecumenical Council in 787 CE,[34] especially given that (arch)angels had become one of the crucial defences in the battle for the icons.[35]

Because a number of the Laodikeian canons (29, 37, 38, possibly also 16) and the Pauline letter to the Kolossians appear to name Jewish practices explicitly, it has been assumed that the background to canon 35 and Col 2:18 was an aberrant Jewish practice gravitating around the archangel Michael.[36] There may be a hint of this association in Theodoret's commentary on Col 2:18 where he laid the blame for the repudiated cultic practice on those defending the Law by reference to the Law as a gift of angels (cf. Gal 3:19; Acts 7:53).[37] He avoided specific mention of Jews but the allusion is clear, even if threatened by confusion with New Testament writers.[38]

However, caution is advised in deducing Jewish influence or connection with Christians behind the canons or commentary. Thomas Kraabel has convincingly argued that even the explicit reference to Jewish practices in the canons are likely to be no more than Christian use of the figure of the "Jewish other" as a means of identifying and strengthening the boundaries of Christian practice[39] – a critical need in a century where one's orthodoxy as well as one's standing was fraught.[40] Jews of course had no place in Christian councils and had long become the malleable bogey for Christian self-definition; indeed Julian also used the Jews and Jewish religion as a contrast to his own revivalist Hellenic philosophy (Julian 2.312, 3.328). But he had also brought Christians close to the despised Jews in his use of the derogatory term "Galileans" (Julian 3.20 [*Against*

---

**34** See the Letter of the Synod: Erich Lamberz and Johannes B. Uphus, "Concilium Nicaenum II, 787," in: CCCOGD 1.314.

**35** Cadwallader, "Stratigraphy," 282–93.

**36** Pierre Maraval, "The Earliest Phase of Christian Pilgrimage in the Near East," *DOP* 56 (2002): 63–75 at 70; cf. Glenn Peers, "Apprehending the Archangel Michael: Hagiographic Methods," *Byzantine and Modern Greek Studies* 20 (1996): 100–21 at 110–13.

**37** διὰ τούτων [i.e., τῶν ἀγγέλων] λέγοντες δεδόσθαι τὸν νόμον (PG 82.613B).

**38** Compare Theodore of Mopsuestia, who saw this difficulty and navigated around the danger: Rowan A. Greer, *Theodore of Mopsuestia: The Commentaries on the Minor Epistles of Paul*, Writings from the Greco-Roman World (Atlanta, GA: Society of Biblical Literature, 2010), 414.10–32.

**39** Thomas Kraabel, "Synagoga Caeca: Systematic Distortion in Gentile Interpretations of Evidence for Judaism in the Early Christian Period," in: *"To See Ourselves as Others See Us": Christians, Jews, "Others" in Late Antiquity*, eds. Jacob Neusner and Ernest S. Frerichs, Scholars Press Studies in the Humanities (Chico, CA: Scholars Press, 1985), 219–46 at 236–41.

**40** See Gregory of Nazianzus, *Ep.* 130 to Procopius (382 CE) (*Saint Grégoire de Nazianze: Lettres*, ed. Paul Gallay, vol. 2, Paris: Les Belles Lettres, 1967, 20).

*the Galileans*]). Indeed, he manoeuvred Jews ahead of Christians in philosophical and pietistic estimation (3.392–410). In the Laodikeian canons, Jews were not alone in providing the contrastive backdrop for the appearance of Christian orthodoxy; they had to share that place with specified heretics, along with the ill-defined ones and the occasional heathen. But the need for clear distinctiveness is apparent and Julian's polemics provide an illuminating context for this necessity.

But there is a further crucial term in canon 35 that is probably decisive. It receives a doubled emphasis: εἰδωλολατρία ("idolatry"). The word-choice is not coincidental or arbitrary. It had occurred in the Letter to the Colossians (3:5) though not in reference to devotion to angels but rather as an explication of one element in a vice-list (πλεονεξία, "greed"). Here it is claimed as a characteristic that besets the Kolossians, even if it has a quite specific content.[41] Such specificity in usage is not found again in council decisions, even if, by scriptural quote or polemics, the word is used. So, idolatry was scurrilously applied to Jews in Christian polemic that dealt with the dualism of true and false religion, particularly embellishing the invective of Old Testament prophets.[42] But this battle was over and Jews had become a nominal artifice in the rhetoric of Christian supremacy.

If I am right in extending the assumed narrowed time frame for the council (360–365 CE) so as to posit the context following the apostate years of the emperor Julian, then idolatry had become a matter of sensitive political importance for every Christian allegiance to negotiate.[43] It is insufficient to dehistoricise the writings of Christian fathers or councils by positing that they were concerned that the worship of angels was or might readily become idolatrous.[44] Idolatry, the restoration of Greek temples, the repair of statues of the gods, and a revival of Hellenism with an emphatic religious dress all characterised the period of Ju-

---

**41** Theodoret does not turn εἰδωλολατρεία in Col 3:5 towards the worship of angels, restricting it to enslavement to mammon; neither does he use the term in his exposition of Col 2:18 (PG 82.616D–17A, 613).

**42** See, for example, Justin Martyr, *Dial.* 130.4 (*Iustini Martyris Dialogus cum Tryphone*, ed. M. Marcovich, PTS 47, Berlin–New York, 1997, 295); Eusebius, *Comm. in Is.* 2.26 (*Eusebius Werke* IX. *Commentarius in Isaiam*, ed. Joseph Ziegler, GCS, Berlin: Akademie Verlag, 1975, 14–17).

**43** It is worth noting that there are striking examples of conversion from "paganism" during Valens' reign; see Gavin Kelly, "The Roman world of Festus' *Breviarium*," in: *Unclassical Traditions. Volume I: Alternatives to the Classical Past in Late Antiquity*, eds. Christopher Kelly, Richard Flower, and Michael Stuart Williams, Cambridge Classical Journal, Supplementary Volume 34 (Cambridge: Cambridge University Press, 2010), 72–89 at 75–76.

**44** As argued by Boddens Hosang, *Establishing Boundaries*, 104.

lian, as church historians and his own letters indicate.[45] When Julian was attempting to establish Syrian Antioch as a new or pseudo-capital of the eastern empire, most especially through the restoration of Hellenic temples, Christians riveted the anti-idolatry psalms (97, 115) to Julian.[46] His name was punned into εἰδωλιανός ("the Idolian") by Gregory of Nazianzus in an oration delivered shortly after Julian's death.[47] Pseudo-Nonnus in his commentary on Gregory stated the obvious: he is called "the Idolian" because he is an idolater.[48] Subsequent emperors like Valentinian and Valens, in an effort to pacify the tensions inherited from the Julian supernova, pursued a toleration policy that only fostered efforts of religious groups to jockey for position,[49] until Theodosius' edict banned sacrificial practices that reverenced non-Christian gods.[50] "Idolatry" *was* the incendiary word of this period.

Laodikeia had the opportunity to enhance its orthodoxy (regardless of Arianism) by, *inter alia*, defining itself against the Julian years, here pointedly given a localised referent in a Christian neighbour.[51] The irony is that this sort of inter-

---

**45** Theod., *HE* 3 (GCS NF 5.177–206 passim); Socrates, *HE* 3.1 (ed. Günther C. Hansen, GCS NF 1.187–93); Zonaras, *Hist* 13.12 (*Ioannis Zonarae Epitome historiarum*, eds. Charles Du Fresne Du Cange and Ludwig Dindorf, vol. 3, Leipzig: Teubner, 1870, 210–13; trans. Thomas M. Banchich and Eugene N. Lane, *The History of Zonaras: From Alexander Severus to the death of Theodosius the Great*, London–New York: Routledge, 2009, 155). John Malalas, *Chron.* 13.19, tied Julian's soubriquet to his becoming "a Hellene" (*Ioannis Malalae Chronographia*, ed. Joannes Thurn, Berlin: De Gruyter, 2000, 251; trans. Elizabeth Jeffreys et al., *The Chronicle of John Malalas*, Byzantina Australiensia 4, Melbourne: Australian Association for Byzantine Studies, 1986, 178). See Shaun Tougher, *Julian the Apostate* (Edinburgh: Edinburgh University Press, 2007), 48–62.

**46** Soz., *HE* 5.19 (GCS NF 4.226); Theod., *HE* 3.14 (GCS NF 5.190–92).

**47** Greg. Naz., *Or.* 4.77 (*Grégoire de Nazianze. Discours 4–5*, ed. Jean Bernardi, SC 309, Paris: Éditions du Cerf, 1983, 198.20).

**48** Jennifer Nimmo Smith, *A Christian's Guide to Greek Culture: The Pseudo-Nonnus Commentaries on Sermons 4, 5, 39 and 43 by Gregory of Nazianzus*, TTH 37 (Liverpool: Liverpool University Press, 2001), 32.

**49** Compare Theod., *HE* 4.6 (GCS NF 5.217).

**50** *CTh* 16.10.10 (*Code Théodosien. Livre XVI*, ed. Theodor Mommsen, trans. Jean Rougé, SC 497, Paris: Cerf, 2005, 438–40). Note however that "paganism" continued to mount a noticeable showing; see Walter E. Kaegi, *Army, Society and Religion in Byzantium* (London: Variorum Reprints, 1982), V.243–75. See also Robert L. Wilken, "Cyril of Alexandria's *Contra Iulianum*," in: *The Limits of Ancient Christianity: Essays on Late Antique Thought and Culture in Honor of R.A. Markus*, eds. William E. Klingshirn and Mark Vessey (Ann Arbor: University of Michigan, 1999), 42–62 at 44–45.

**51** Julian's initial policy of religious toleration had led to the recall of several exiled bishops – a sign of an effort to depart the ecclesiastical divisiveness of previous years. In the aftermath, however, the strength of the church was viewed as dependent on establishing a theologically

necine conflict was itself cultivated by Julian – "no wild beasts are so hostile to men as are Christian sects in general to one another" was Ammianus Marcellinus' summation of Julian's religious toleration policy.[52] Given that Kolossai was a satellite diocese, Laodikeia not only asserted its own authority in the ongoing competition for recognition that marks the relations of *poleis* from Hellenistic to Byzantine times;[53] it also attempted to make a declared dependent diocese expendable in its game-plan, albeit without expressly naming Kolossai. The "calling upon" or invocation of angels (for this is the sense of ὀνομάζειν,[54] elsewhere as readily used of God)[55] is *not* denounced as Jewish or Judaising in canon 35. Clearly this option was open, given such a pejorative use in other canons (29, 37, 38). I agree with those who argue that there is a pagan (more accurately Greek) frame behind the emphasis on "idolatry;" I propose, more specifically, that the legacy of the Julian years has driven the lexical choice, indeed the very appearance of the canon, albeit for highly complex political reasons on the part of the Laodikeian metropolitan.

Significantly, an eleventh-century catena on scripture, but attributed to the late-fourth-century bishop Severian of Gabala,[56] applied the reference to the distinctly ordered "Greek and Jew" found in Col 3:11.[57] The relevant text reads:

> οἱ ἀπὸ Ἑλλήνων πιστεύσαντες εἶχον καὶ τοὺς Ἕλληνας ἀνθέλκειν εἰς τὰς παρατηρήσεις τὰς Ἑλληνικὰς βουλομένους, καὶ τῶν Ἰουδαίων τοὺς πιστεύσαντας πείθοντας τὸν νόμον τηρεῖν ὡς τῆς χάριτος ἀτελεστέρας οὔσης ἄνευ τοῦ νόμου. Πρὸς τούτοις καὶ Ἕλληνες καὶ Ἰουδαῖοι

---

defended and institutionally reinforced orthodoxy: see Samuel N.C. Lieu, *The Emperor Julian: Panegyric and Polemic*, TTH 2 (2nd edn.; Liverpool: Liverpool University Press, 1989), 41.

**52** Ammianus Marcellinus, *Res gestae* 22.5.4 (*Ammien Marcellin. Histoire*. 3. *Livres XX-XXII*, ed. Jacques Fontaine, Paris: Les Belles Lettres, 1996, 99), translation from John Julian Norwich, *Byzantium: The Early Centuries* (London: Penguin, 1990), 92.

**53** On the competition between cities fostered in the Roman period (republican and imperial), see Anna Heller, *'Les bêtises des Grecs'. Conflits et rivalités entre cités d'Asie et de Bithynie à l'époque romaine (129 a.C.–235 p.C)*, Scripta Antiqua 17 (Bordeaux: Ausonius Éditions, 2006). On the competition between metropolitan and suffragan dioceses (especially through their bishops), see John Cotsonis, "Saints and Cult Centers: A Geographic and Administrative Perspective in Light of Byzantine Lead Seals," *Studies in Byzantine Sigillography* 8 (2003): 9–26 at 17, 19.

**54** See Clement of Alexandria, *Protrepticus* 2.32–41 (ed. Otto Stählin, GCS 12.17–31).

**55** See the Council of Ephesus (431) 19.8 (*Acta conciliorum oecumenicorum*, ed. Eduard Schwartz, Berlin: De Gruyter, 1927, 1.1.5) on worshipping the Emmanuel as God.

**56** John A. Cramer, ed., *Catenae Graecorum Patrum in Novum Testamentum* (Oxford: Academic Typographer, 1844), vol. 6, 292; Karl Staab, *Die Pauluskommentare aus der griechischen Kirche* (Münster: i. W.: Aschendorff, 1933), 315.

**57** See my "Greeks in Colossae: shifting allegiances in the Letter to the Colossians and its context," in: *Attitudes to Gentiles in Ancient Judaism and Early Christianity*, eds. David C. Sim and James S. McLaren (London–New York: Continuum, forthcoming).

τοὺς Κολοσσαεῖς ἔπειθον ἀγγέλοις προσεχεῖν· Ἕλληνες μὲν τοὺς θεοὺς αὐτῶν λέγοντες ἀγγέλους εἶναι· ὅτι τε ὁ μὲν Θεὸς αχώρητος καὶ μέγας οὐκ ἐφικτὸς ἀνθρώποις· διὰ δὲ τῶν ἀγγέλων τούτων ὥσπερ μεσιτῶν, χορηγεῖ τὰς εὐεργεσίας τοῖς δεχομένοις. Οἱ δὲ Ἰουδαῖοι ὅτι "ὁ Θεὸς ἔστησεν ὅρια ἐθνῶν κατ' ἀριθμὸν ἀγγέλων Θεοῦ."

Severian took the worship of angels (here ἀγγέλοις προσεχεῖν) as a major indicator of Greeks at Kolossai being pulled back to the observance of Greek ways and of Jews seeking to uphold the Law; that is, the bipartite internal membership of the church (as he understood it) was falling back into old ways. Greeks, he claimed, asserted that the gods were angels. God, being so great as to be divorced from spatial containment, was inaccessible to human beings. These angels accordingly were mediators through whom God dispensed lavishly to suppliants. In contrast to Theodoret however, Severian claimed the Jews' notion of divine beings maintaining the boundaries of nations contributed to the worship of angels at Kolossai, citing Deut 32:8. He went on to illustrate a number of nations, such as Persia and the Greeks, as each possessing an angelic ruler (ἄρχων) on the basis of the identification of Michael as the ruler of the Jews in Dan 10:20. Even though he identified the Danielic Michael with the Jews, his insight into Greek appropriation of angels is pertinent here precisely because of the collation of angels with gods, albeit subject to the uncontainable God. This, not the collation of nations according to angels, fits the judgement of εἰδωλολατρεία in the Laodikeian canon. Idolatry and the Hellenic heritage are conjoined at this time – a key mark of the Julian period.[58] I have demonstrated elsewhere that the popular story of St Michael of Chonai harnesses the attributes of Greek male deities, notably Zeus, in a synoikism that enabled a measure of continuity with past pagan ways[59] – exactly as Severian suggests here. Severian's particular insight is the rendition of the utter otherness and unapproachability of God. This is precisely what is found in the story of St Michael of Chonai. In the climactic affirmation of his subjection to God, the archangel's role as protective mediator is affirmed: "Even I am not strong enough to gaze upon the awesome and unfathomable glory of divinity...how are mortals going to see God, the one beside whom I stand with trepidation?" (11.6).[60]

---

**58** Socr., *HE* 3.1 (GCS NF 1.191–93); Julian, *Or.* 4 (Wright 1.358–60)

**59** Cadwallader, "The Tenacity of Paganism," cited above.

**60** καὶ τὴν φοβερὰν καὶ ἀνεξιχνίαστον δόξαν τῆς θεότητος...οὐκ ἰσχύω θεάσασθαι...πῶς οὖν μέλλουσιν οἱ βροτοὶ θεὸν ὄψεσθαι ὃν ἐγὼ μετὰ τρόμου παρίσταμαι; The English translation and versification, here and throughout, are from my "The Story of the Archistrategos, St Michael of Chonai," in: Cadwallader and Trainor, *Colossae in Space and Time*, 329.

There was a widespread devotion to angels and to Michael in particular throughout Phrygia. What Theodoret sweepingly dismissed as infecting all of Phrygia and Pisidia, is manifest in inscriptional and artefactual remains.[61] The nexus between angels and the Greek pantheon is crucial in this regard. This had a number of permutations. Angels may be the form under which a god appears; they may be the surrounding cortege for the god; they may be the gods themselves or a companion deity to the eminent god.[62] Such a blurring of distinctions is evident in Julian's polemic against the Christians in his "angel or god" phraseology that deliberately evoked the ambiguity of the Hebrew scriptures (Julian 3.424, 426), even claiming that Moses "called angels gods" (Julian 3.400, cf. 358).[63] This is reminiscent of the famous inscription from Oinoanda in Lycia[64] where Apollo of Claros described himself (either in a plurality of reference or on behalf of a pantheon) as μεικρὰ δὲ θεοῦ μερὶς ἄνγελοι ἡμεῖς ("We are angels, a tiny portion of god" 1.3).[65]

# 3 Regulating Kolossai

Here then were substantial grounds, in a Greek context in the period of and following the Julian era, for the charge that the worship of angels was idolatry. Enough has been shown that this was easily applied to practices at Kolossai, and the canon probably was initiated in response to those practices. The key

61 A.R.R. Sheppard, "Pagan Cults of Angels in Roman Asia Minor," *Talanta* 12–13 (1980–81): 77–101; cf. *CIG* 2895.

62 Ruth M.M. Tuschling, *Angels and Orthodoxy: A study in their Development in Syria and Palestine*, STAC 40 (Tübingen: Mohr Siebeck, 2007), 49–52; Alfons Fürst, "Monotheism Between Cult and Politics," in: *One God: Pagan Monotheism in the Roman Empire*, eds. Stephen Mitchell and Peter van Nuffelen (Cambridge: Cambridge University Press, 2010), 82–99 at 84–89; Angelos Chaniotis, "Megatheism: The Search for the Almighty God and the Competition of Cults," in: ibid., 112–140 at 139–40.

63 Elsewhere Julian can write of "guardian angels" (οἱ φύλακες...ἄγγελοι), referring to Helios and Selene (Julian, *Ep. Ath.*, Wright 2.260).

64 SEG 27.933; cf. *Theosophorum Graecorum fragmenta* 8–9 (ed. Hartmut Erbse, Stuttgart–Leipzig: Teubner, 1995, 4–5); Lactantius, *Div. inst.* 1.7.1 (*L. Caecilius Firmianus Lactantius. Divinarum Institutionem Libri Septem Fasc. 1. Libri I et II*, eds. Eberhard Heck and Antonie Wlosok, Bibliotheca Scriptorum Graecorum et Romanorum Teubneriana, München–Leipzig: K.G. Saur, 2005, 28).

65 See Robin Lane Fox, *Pagans and Christians in the Mediterranean World from the Second Century AD to the Conversion of Constantine* (Harmondsworth: Penguin, 1986), 170–71, who tracks this oracle into Christian texts.

issue then is the question of the relationship between Laodikeia and Kolossai and how that relationship was negotiated.

Laodikeia was the seat of the metropolitical bishop. When the 318 bishops gathered at Nicaea for the decisive council of 325, Bishop Nunechios of Laodikeia was named as the metropolitan head of the thirty-six bishops from Phrygia.[66] After the division of Phrygia into Phrygia Salutaris and Pacatiana some time in the 340s, the number of dioceses under Laodikeia's authority was adjusted, but Hierapolis and Kolossai remained.[67] This authority was certainly asserted by a second Nunechios of Laodikeia at the Council of Chalcedon (451 CE) where he signs "for the absent bishops under him," including one Epiphanios of the city (πόλις) of the Kolossians. Given that Laodikeia's absence from the Council of Constantinople in 381 is explained on the basis of a lingering Arian tendency in its metropolitan if not the region,[68] then one may wonder whether Kolossai was represented at the Council of Laodikeia when a decision seemingly directed against *its* religious practice was made.[69] Some later summations of the council simply referred to "many blessed fathers from various provinces of Asia."[70] It would seem that Laodikeia was using its metropolitical position to assert its authority to make such decisions in full expectation, like the old Roman assizes, that they would be carried out. However, the canons themselves reveal that this was precisely where some difficulty lay. The council felt it necessary to be explicit about the appointment of bishops, tying such to the initiative of the metropolitans (canon 12). Moreover, there was considerable concern that cities (and probably major or capital cities) were to be the well-spring and seat of authority, not the country. Canon 57 repudiated the appointment of bishops "in villages or country districts" (ἐν ταῖς κώμαις καὶ ἐν ταῖς χώραις). One commentator, in an attempt to distill the governing principle guiding all the canons of the council, has argued that the decisions reflected the need to establish hierarchies and clarify positions within the church and in the church's relationship to those

---

**66** Klaus Belke and Norbert Mersich, *Phrygien und Pisidien*, Denkschriften der philosophisch-historischen Klasse 211/Tabula Imperii Byzantini 7 (Vienna: Verlag der Österreichischen Akademie der Wissenschaften, 1990), 323.

**67** Hierocles, *Synekdemos* 664.6–666.16 (*Le Synekdèmos d'Hiéroklès et l'opuscule géographique de Georges de Chypre*, ed. Ernest Honigmann, Brussels: L'Institut de Philologie et d'Histoire Orientales et Slaves, 1939, 24–25), lists thirty-seven dioceses under Laodikeia, some time before 530 CE.

**68** Lightfoot, *Saint Paul's Epistles*, 62. See, for example, Theod., *HE* 4.7 (GCS NF 5.219).

**69** Absenteeism appears as a characteristic of those to be anathematised: see Soz., *HE* 2.32 (GCS NF 4.97–98).

**70** Joannou, *Discipline générale*, 130.

without.[71] Certainly, the upheavals of the fourth century readily explain the attempt to seek a structural rather than a discursive solution to enhance stability.

This sounds simple enough. Gregory of Nazianzus, however, recognised the limitations of these conciliar modes of operation: "I have never seen any council come to a good end, nor turn out to be a solution of evils. On the contrary it usually increases them. You always find here a love of contention and a love of power."[72] Indeed, the canon failed to solve what it saw as an issue at Kolossai.

## 4 The Kolossian resistance

Kolossai was not, at this time, in any position formally to counteract the anathema or the accusation on which it was based. It was officially under the authority of Laodikeia. A different strategy was needed. The defence of her religious practice was found in popular piety armed with a narrative justification. Stories live more powerfully than statutes. The *Acts of Philip*, for example, appears to have been a fourth–fifth century narrative written by an Encratite monk for whom literary fiction was the only available means to resist the repressive marginalisation experienced at the hands of the dominant church. Such writing is frequently characterised by a long period of ongoing development and recensional activity, by allusive references that are clear to sympathisers as well as protective of them, by the construction of the justice and innocence of those against whom the charge is laid and by the evil ruthlessness of opponents. Significantly, in this writing, as in the Chonai story, the defence of the oppressed comes from the archangel Michael and the God whom Michael (and the oppressed community) serves.[73]

The story that divinely authorised the sanctuary as well as the position of Michael the archangel had all but expressly repudiated Laodikeia, even as it evolved later to address other pressures that faced Kolossai/Chonai (especially iconoclasm). The narrative counter-attack upon Laodikeia makes no reference

---

**71** Therese Martin, "The Development of Winged Angels in Early Christian Art," *Espacio* 14 (2001): 13–29 at 22.

**72** Greg. Naz., *Ep.* 130 (ed. Gallay, 19–20). Trans. James Stevenson, ed., *Creeds, Councils and Controversies: Documents Illustrating the History of the Church, AD 337–461* (London: SPCK, 1966), 150.

**73** R.N. Slater, "An Inquiry into the Relationship between Community and Text: The Apocryphal Acts of Philip 1 and the Encratites of Asia Minor," in: *The Apocryphal Acts of the Apostles*, eds. François Bovon, Ann Graham Brock, and Christopher R. Matthews, Harvard Divinity School Studies, Religions of the World (Cambridge, MA: Harvard University Press, 1999), 281–306 at 295–96.

to Jews or Judaism. If the worship of angels in fourth–fifth century Kolossai had been intimated to have been from Jewish infiltration, then one would readily expect the denial to have highlighted the Judaising of the Laodikeian church, given that Laodikeia, unlike Kolossai, is known to have had a substantial Jewish population.[74] Rather, the story accents the city as riddled with idolatry, focused particularly in an unholy Trinity of female gods who are tied to the destructive wiles of the devil, the source of opposition to the holy shrine. The key charge of idolatry in canon 35 becomes the chief characteristic of Laodikeia.[75] What is important is that this idolatry is accented as the idolatry of the Greeks (εἰδωλοθύτεις ἑλλήνες 5.4) not of the Jews.

Clearly Kolossai herself was the arena for battles between Christians and Hellenes over the sacred spring. The Greeks, expressly distinguished in 5.1, receive of the benefits of the healing waters (3.2) even as they were plotting against the Christians and against the Christian control of the site. This battle for place, played out in sacred space and in sacred text, is a key mark of the Julian years, noted by church historians and Julian's writings alike.[76] The story acknowledges this battle for place between Christians and Greeks but swings the locus of the opposition to Laodikeia, thereby constructing the city as the base for Julianesque attacks.

The concentration on a triad of female gods as the means of characterising the evil of Laodikeia in service of the devil has a general and particular reference. At the general level, there is the stereotypical ancient vilification that sees evil or opposition in feminine terms. The Roman practice of representing opponents in disheveled female form bequeathed a resilient legacy.[77] Julian himself made use of the rhetoric (Julian 2.472 [*Misopogon*]). More particularly, though the story opens with Artemis (1.1) who is given a morphing into Echidna by the multiplication of snakes and her carriage by two serpents (1.2),[78] the accent is that "The Greeks even esteemed her as the Great Goddess (θεὰ μεγάλη)" (1.2). Though

**74** For artefactual support to the textual material, see IJO 2.212, 213; Celal Şimşek, *Laodikeia (Laodikeia ad Lycum)* (Istanbul: Yayınları, 2007), 148–49.

**75** 3.2, 5.4, 7.3, 9.1. Most manuscripts use the cognate term εἰδωλθύτης; manuscript P uses εἰδωλολάτρης in 5.4 and 9.1.

**76** E.g., Socr., *HE* 3.11, 15, 18 (GCS NF 1.206, 209, 213–14); Julian, *Misopogon* (Wright 2.474–76).

**77** See Davina C. Lopez, "Before Your Very Eyes: Roman Imperial Ideology, Gender Constructs and Paul's Inter-Nationalism," in: *Mapping Gender in Ancient Religious Discourses*, eds. Todd Penner and Caroline Vander Stichele, Biblical Interpretation 84 (Leiden: Brill, 2006), 115–62.

**78** See Yulia Ustrinova, "Snake-Limbed and Tendril-Limbed Goddesses in the Art and Mythology of the Mediterranean and Black Sea," in: *Scythians and Greeks: Cultural Interactions in Scythia, Athens and the Early Roman Empire (Sixth Century BC – First Century AD)*, ed. David Braund (Exeter: University of Exeter, 2005), 64–79.

Cybele is not expressly named (a familiar practice in Asia Minor),[79] the connection between the goddess and "Greeks" is striking. This, after all, was one of the key accents of Julian's project.[80] Julian was a frequent visitor to Phrygia during his brief rule (Julian 2.216–218, 3.136) and devoted one of his major writings to "the Mother of the Gods." He claimed she was known to the Greeks under many names, not least Deo, Rhea and Demeter (1.442), and was the mother of the gods, including Zeus (for whom she is also spouse and sharer of his throne: 1.462, 500); she subsists as the Great Goddess with the Great Zeus (θεὸς ὑποστᾶσα μεγάλη μετὰ τὸν μέγαν 1.462). Patronage of the Great Mother became a mark of loyalty to Julian (Julian 3.72).[81]

The anonymous writer of the St Michael story severs the connection between the feminine and masculine, a conjunction that Julian had made by way of illustration of the pre-existent reality.[82] Julian may have toyed with the idea of promoting a pagan alternative to the Christian Trinity, claiming an oracle hailing "One is Zeus, One is Hades, One is Helios, these are Serapis; let us hold them in common" (Julian 1.368) but the Christian triumph in the story only allowed such a pagan conjunction to be seen as feminine, riddled with the very snakes that epitomised both the devil and all heresy (1.2).[83] This serpentine idolatrous connection in the story had been eradicated from Ephesos and Hierapolis but imbues Laodikeian antagonism to Kolossai. The story posits the primary battle

**79** Christine Thomas, "The 'Mountain Mother': the other Anatolian Goddess at Ephesos," in: *Les cultes locaux dans les mondes grec et romain. Actes du colloque de Lyon, 7–8 juin 2001*, eds. Guy Labarre and Jean-Marc Moret (Paris: de Boccard, 2004), 249–62; Lynn E. Roller, *In Search of God the Mother: The Cult of Anatolian Cybele* (Berkeley: University of California Press, 1999), 47.
**80** Elm speculates whether the increase of Christian hostility to the cult is directly related to Julian's promotion: *Sons of Hellenism*, 118–19 n. 111. The argument presented here moves beyond speculation.
**81** See, especially, Elm, *Sons of Hellenism*, 118–36.
**82** See J.H.W.G. Liebeschuetz, "Julian's *Hymn to the Mother of the Gods:* The Revival and Justification of Traditional Religion," in: Baker-Brian and Tougher, *Emperor and Author*, 214. Liebeschuetz's recognition of the importance of Julian's *Hymn to King Helios* as a complement to that to Cybele ("different aspects of a divine unity") is probably to be understood in these terms. Perhaps in accent of the St Michael story's rejection of the feminine, there is no Marian presence at all. By contrast, Julian adopts Marian language for Cybele (223–24).
**83** Compare Cyril of Alexandria, *Comm. in Is.* 1.4 (PG 70.176B), *Contra Iulianum* 1.2 (*Cyrille d'Alexandrie, Contre Julien*, eds. Paul Burguière and Pierre Évieux, SC 322, Paris: Éditions du Cerf, 1985, 112). Eusebius used the snake imagery for female-dominated Montanism (*HE* 5.14; *Eusèbe de Césarée. Histoire ecclésiastique (Livres V–VII)*, ed. Gustave Bardy, SC 41, Paris: Éditions du Cerf, 1955, 45).

as an infra-ecclesial dispute veiled beneath a contest between (masculine) Christianity and (feminine) idolatrous Hellenism.[84]

A less than subtle pun is made on the name of the city. We have already seen the punning on the name Chonai at the end of the story. Such punning is familiar in the ancient world, operating at both a textual and visual level.[85] The city name, Laodikeia, is construed as ὁ λαὸς τῆς ἀδικίας ("the lawless mob" 11.10). Later scribes of the vernacular story and later revisions by Sisinnius and Metaphrastes could not accept the blatant invective against Laodikeia that an alpha-privative could bring and made adjustments – either expurgating the offending pun or removing any sense that metropolitical Laodikeia was the city intended in the story.[86] The initial opposition to the sanctuary comes from the Greeks. These are the ones who "gather" (συναχθέντες) from various cities (5000, the story says) to plot against Kolossai. The lexical choice is a transparent reference to those who came to attend the Laodikeian council and to the use of συνάξεις (for those gathered to reverence angels) in the anathematising canon of that council.

The final element in the characterisation of Laodikeia comes in the description of the sinister figure who motivated the whole desperate and ultimately futile attack on Michael's sanctuary. The devil appears to warrant a catalogue of errors that blossoms over time (7.2–3), attracting additions from different periods of conflict. Clearly "the despiser of beauty" (ὁ μισόκαλος) belongs to the later iconoclast controversies, but the one who is "the murderer of saints and persecutor of divine churches...the antagonist of those yearning to be saved" seems to belong to another period. My contention is that the revival of a religiously imbued Hellenism under Julian fits the description neatly.[87] Julian was construed according to snakes, the female goddess, Hellenism and the devil.[88]

---

**84** I explore this gendered dimension of the story in "Tenacity of Paganism" (see n. 4).

**85** See Christopher J. Howgego, "Coinage and Identity in the Roman Provinces," in: *Coinage and Identity in the Roman Provinces*, eds. Christopher Howgego, Volker Heuchert, and Andrew Burnett (Oxford: Oxford University Press, 2005), 1–18 at 12.

**86** Simeon Metaphrastes removes the site to Lycia (c.7). Sisinnius separates Laodikeia from the idol-devotees who gathered there (c.12).

**87** See, for example, Soz., *HE* 5.5, 6 (GCS NF 4.198–201); Greg. Naz., *Or.* 18.32 (PG 35.1025–28).

**88** Greg. Naz., *Or.* 7.11 (*Grégoire de Nazianze. Discour 6–12*, ed. Marie-Ange Calvet-Sebasti, SC 405.206–208); Cyril of Alexandria, *Contra Iulianum* 1.2.15–20 pref. 4.4–5 (SC 322.112).

# 5 Conclusion

The ecclesial battles between metropolitan Laodikeia and satellite Kolossai have been explored in terms of the mechanisms each used to prosecute their cause – a canonical decision of an assembled council being countermanded by a popular story that probably began as a pagan foundation myth for a sacred site.[89] Both were reliant upon written texts; both texts underwent changes over time. But the Kolossian narrative had sprung from widespread, even pre-Christian devotion. Narrow episcopal initiatives that garnered unknown and probably little support do not appear to have attracted popular adherence, at least in regard to its canon 35. However, the conflict between the two Christian centres was engendered and exacerbated by machinations from without that impinged on their individual and inter-related lives. In this sense, little had changed from the tensions between Laodikeia and Kolossai in republican and imperial days.[90] Decisions manifest in imperial politics inevitably elicited responses from each city even if they were not explicitly named or directed. Each negotiated how to represent their own circumstances to best advantage. Julian's Hellenic programme, characterised by Christians as idolatrous, and its highly contentious aftermath in an empire trying to repair its direction, elicited different responses which yet bore the marks of a common reference point. Laodikeia accused Kolossai formally of the very hallmark of the Julian period: idolatry. Kolossai returned the favour without the niceties of either administrative process or textual finesse, but with a more explicit naming of its enemy. The conflict was not resolved by the Laodikeian canon, perhaps because Laodikeia's Arian colouring undercut any action that might be taken against Kolossai. The popular saint's story finally won the day, not of itself at the time, but because of political and theological contests embroiling church and state in later times – preeminently the iconoclastic battles of the eighth and ninth centuries. The narrative was more flexible in its ability to adapt and respond to popular demand and ecclesial directive. The conciliar decision ultimately was rendered ineffective by casuistic re-interpretation long after those whom the Laodikeian council had declared without voice (canon 13: "the multitude") believed themselves vindicated by a higher authority.

**89** See Eran Lupu, *Greek Sacred Law: a Collection of New Documents (NGSL)*, Religions in the Graeco-Roman World 152 (Leiden: Brill, 2005), 33–40.

**90** See my "Aspiring to the *homonoia* of the Gods: Tracking Religion and Identity in the Coins of Colossae," forthcoming.

Raymond J. Laird

# John Chrysostom and the Anomoeans: Shaping an Antiochene Perspective on Christology

By the time John Chrysostom was ordained to the priesthood in 386 CE, various forms of diversion from the Nicene formula had been in existence for half a century. Germane to this study is the fact that several forms of and derivatives from Arianism existed at that time. These were widespread with numerous followers, prospering under the aegis of Constantius II and his successors to the imperial throne. Chrysostom, through his experience of the schism in the churches of his native Antioch,[1] had become acutely aware of the divisions that beset the fourth-century church over the main issue of Nicaea, the assertion of the full deity of Christ.[2] Long before Chrysostom began his preaching–teaching ministry, he had knowledge of and contact with those who held to the Nicene formula of the Son having the "same essence/substance" (ὁμοούσιον) as the Father, and

1 Geoffrey D. Dunn, "The Roman Response to the Ecclesiastical Crises in the Antiochene Church in the Late-Fourth and Early-Fifth-Centuries," in: *Ancient Jewish and Christian Texts as Crisis Management Literature: Thematic Studies from the Centre for Early Christian Studies*, eds. David C. Sim and Pauline Allen, LNTS 445 (London–New York: T&T Clark, 2012), 112–28 at 113–17, provides a succinct account of the schism. Kelley McCarthy Spoerl, "The Schism at Antioch since Cavallera," in: *Arianism after Arius. Essays on the Development of the Fourth Century Trinitarian Conflicts*, eds. Michael R. Barnes and Daniel H. Williams (Edinburgh: T&T Clark, 1993), 101–26 at 111–23, has made a good attempt at fathoming the personal confusion surrounding Meletius, one of the bishops during the schism, by an analysis of his homily on Proverbs 8:22; although, on Meletius' neo-Nicenism, see now Thomas Karmann, *Meletius von Antiochien. Studien zur Geschichte des trinitätstheologischen Streits in den Jahren 360–364 n. Chr.*, Regensburger Studien zur Theologie 68 (Frankfurt am Main: Peter Lang, 2009).

2 Many scholars now argue that the situation in the latter half of the fourth century was much more fluid and complex than had been traditionally held. For typical discussions of this phenomenon and the reasons for revision, see Lewis Ayres, *Nicaea and its Legacy: An Approach to Fourth-Century Trinitarian Theology* (Oxford–New York: Oxford University Press, 2004), esp. 1–7; Michael Slusser, "Traditional Views of Late Arianism," in: *Arianism After Arius*, 3–30, indicates at 13–14 that this wider diversity was recognised at least as early as the seventeenth century by the theologian Dionysius Petavius; Winrich A. Lohr, "A Sense of Tradition: The Homoiousian Church Party," in: *Arianism after Arius*, 81–100 at 81, observes that "There is an increasing awareness in recent scholarship that the traditional designations for church parties – i.e., Nicenes, Homoians, Homoiousians, Anomoians (or Heterousians) – can be very misleading indeed." Nevertheless, as most commentators, including these authors, for the sake of convenience continue to write using the aforementioned labels, I will follow suit.

with those who held to the following diversions: "like in essence" (ὁμοιούσιος), but not the same as the Father; "like" (ὅμοιος), but incomparable to the Father; and the extreme Arian, "unlike" (ἀνόμοιος) the Father, especially in regards to substance and equality, a position known as Anomoean.[3] Chrysostom, apart from the mentoring he received from Meletius, a bishop of Antioch who had held differing positions on the Trinity during his personal development, was trained in exegetical and theological skills in the *asketerion* at Antioch under the able tutelage of Diodore (later Bishop of Tarsus) and Flavian, who eventually became the bishop of Antioch after the death of Meletius in 381, and who ordained Chrysostom as a presbyter. Thus Chrysostom had ample first-hand experience and knowledge on which to formulate his own understanding of and attitude to the Anomoeans. As discussed below, there is no doubt that he saw them as a threat to the Christian faith in general, and to his own congregations in particular. Thus, he was prepared to enter the arena to do battle.

The significant feature of Chrysostom's conflict with the Anomoeans is that he understood it primarily as a defensive action and not as an all-out offensive campaign. This general defensive focus is spelled out clearly by him in *De sacerdotio* ("On the Priesthood"). There it is clear that his approach stems from his understanding of the task of a priest as being first and foremost not the defence of orthodoxy in open debate with the leading proponents of a heretical dogma concerning the nature of God, but rather the protection of the flock in the fold under his care from the ravages of attacking wolves.[4] For him, the healing of the soul sick from false doctrine was but another aspect of ministering to the "security of the household of faith" (τὴν τῶν οἰκείων ἀσφάλειαν) and repelling "the attacks from without" (τοὺς ἔξωθεν πολέμους).[5] His focus, as a shepherd, was on the flock committed to his care. The images used there are quite explicit: as above, a shepherd caring for the flock, the body of Christ, and protecting them from wolves; physicians, coaches, and trainers preparing athletes for their contests;[6] the expert physician healing the invalid;[7] the skilled soldier repelling the attacks of enemies;[8] and the builder of a wall for the fortified city

---

**3** R.P.C. Hanson, *The Search for the Christian Doctrine of God: The Arian Controversy 318–381* (Edinburgh: T&T Clark, 1988), 598–617.

**4** Chrys., *Sac.* 4.4.28–34 (*Jean Chrysostome. Sur le sacerdoce*, ed. Anne-Marie Malingrey, SC 272, Paris: Éditions du Cerf, 1980, 254–56).

**5** Chrys., *Sac.* 4.3.21–25 (SC 272.250).

**6** Chrys., *Sac.* 4.2.106–114 (SC 272.248).

**7** Chrys., *Sac.* 4.3.1–20 (SC 272.248–50).

**8** Chrys., *Sac.* 4.4.1–15 (SC 272.252–54).

to resist raiders and plunderers.[9] All are either defensive or body-building images, emphasising protection on one hand and equipping on the other.

Not that Chrysostom was averse to dealing with doctrine: indeed, he addresses the doctrines of God and of the Person of Christ in his homilies, but they are embedded in the context of his pastoral care of his flocks. Protection and fortifying were the vital elements of his core concerns. Hence, whilst he did take other initiatives against the Anomoeans in the course of his ministry, the main arena in which he entered the lists was in his own churches. The image he uses at the beginning of the third of a series of homilies on the topic, "a wild and uncultivated tree," applies not directly to the Anomoeans themselves, but to the "Anomoean heresy."[10] That heresy, a "fruitless tree," is also a destructive force upon the cultivated plants upon which the farmers have bestowed so much loving care. Hence, we find him encouraging his people to call upon God for the Spirit of God to blow like the wind that aids the farmer in tearing down the uncultivated tree; to assist in tearing up by the roots the Anomoean heresy that threatens to spoil them.[11] It is evident where Chrysostom's aim lies. No doubt, he also counts the Anomoean attendees in his church as plants that have been ravaged by this heresy. His love reaches out to them, but his first concern is his flock, their protection, their growth, their maturity, their fruitfulness.

With this basic approach of Chrysostom in mind, this study will take the following path: to discern Chrysostom's mindset in relation to the Anomoeans; to detect his diagnosis of the Anomoean ailment; to examine the means of healing he employed; to consider the main obstacles in his path; and to assess the outcome of his labours in relation to the development and consolidation of Antiochene christology.

**9** Chrys., *Sac.* 4.4.16–26 (SC 272.254).

**10** *St John Chrysostom, On the Incomprehensible Nature of God*, trans. Paul W. Harkins, FOTC 72 (Washington, DC: Catholic University of America Press, 1984), 3.1. For the most part he refers to them under the nomenclature of "heretics." All citations reference this translation except on those occasions when I comment on the Greek text and wish to add my own insights. Edition of *hom.* 1–5 in *Sur l'incompréhensibilité de Dieu*, ed. Anne-Marie Malingrey, with Jean Daniélou and Robert Flacelière, SC 28bis (Paris: Éditions du Cerf, 1970); of *hom.* 7–12 in *Sur l'égalité du père et du fils*, ed. Anne-Marie Malingrey, SC 396 (Paris: Éditions du Cerf, 1994).

**11** Chrys., *Incomp. hom.* 3.1 (SC 28bis.186–88; trans. Harkins, FOTC 72.95).

## 1 Discerning Chrysostom's mindset toward the Anomoeans

As indicated above, Chrysostom's general mindset in regard to and relationship with Anomoeans is spelt out in *De sacerdotio* 4.2–5 in his references to Arians. On one hand, he classes them as enemies of the true faith as he understood it. As outright subordinationists, rejecting the Nicene ὁμοούσιος (of the same essence) and the equality of the Son with the Father, they are among the wolves and the raiders of the flock. Thus, they are guilty in his eyes of "manic divisibility" (μανιώδη διαίρεσιν)[12] as to the nature of the being of God. They hold, he asserts, to the distinctions of persons in a way which destroys the unity of God in a diversity of substance (οὐσίας).[13] Turning to his homilies, we find much more in the way of negative terminology applied specifically to the Anomoeans.[14] Here, among a large catalogue of names, we find them described as "heretics,"[15] and "infidels."[16] They are "busybodies" and "shameless."[17] As a threat to the church in Constantinople, they are among those whom he describes as a "surging sea, storms, and waves…fires of heresy with their encircling flames."[18] This gives the impression that he had placed them beyond hope, that they were totally outside, far from the fold, totally beyond the pale, and enemies to be destroyed. This was not so, for though Chrysostom speaks of weapons of combat, this and other negative terminology employed in his preaching to and about Anomoeans should not be understood in an absolute sense. This is clear when he states his basic purpose: "I did not take up these weapons to strike my adversaries down but to lift them up as they lie prostrate…These weapons do not inflict wounds; rather they cure those who are sick."[19] Also, it should be noted that John's established practice in contact with them was caution and compassion. He reveals a concern to understand the Anomoeans' mindset: was the door slightly open or totally closed, was there some hope or none at all?

It appears that he usually felt they were winnable. This is evident in three particular ways as witnessed in his homilies. For one thing there is his mention of his hesitation in attacking the beliefs of the Anomoeans in his preaching at

12 Chrys., *Sac.* 4.4.76–77 (SC 272.258).
13 Chrys., *Sac.* 4.4.75–76 (SC 272.258).
14 Chrys., *Incomp. hom.* 2.1, 2, 16 (SC 28bis.140–42, 154; trans. Harkins, FOTC 72.71–72, 77).
15 Chrys., *Incomp. hom.* 1.31 (SC 28bis.124.278; trans. Harkins, FOTC 72.64).
16 Chrys., *Incomp. hom.* 2.1 (SC 28bis.140; trans. Harkins, FOTC 72.71).
17 Chrys., *Incomp. hom.* 1.36 (SC 28bis.128.322–24; trans. Harkins, FOTC 72.66).
18 Chrys., *Incomp. hom.* 11.3 (SC 396.288; trans. Harkins, FOTC 72.271).
19 Chrys., *Incomp. hom.* 1.39 (SC 28bis.130–32; trans. Harkins, FOTC 72.67).

Antioch because of the presence of some of them in his congregation. Apparently these were eager to hear him, and he did not want to frighten them off by a wholesale attack.[20] Only when asked by them to address their position, did he do so. Though he declared them mad, he thought that this "great madness and folly"[21] was not beyond healing. Also to be taken into consideration was the fact that he encouraged his people to pray for them to recover from their illness.[22] Then, too, he urges his people to hold no hatred towards them; rather they must love these who are ill.[23] All this adds up to a basic attitude of compassion in Chrysostom towards them. He uses the striking image of a mother in the anguish of labour to picture his desire to address their ailment and to apply a cure.[24] Another impressive image is his description of them along with other erring Christians in his congregation as "the bone that is out of joint."[25] As such they are seen to be part of the body, but crippled and not functioning as they ought. This corresponds with his view of them as sick rather than dead, as semi-Christian, on the edge within, or close outside the Christian fold, but defective in their understanding.

It is pertinent in discerning John's mindset towards the Anomoeans to compare this with his mindset toward the Jews. Robert Wilken mounts a plausible defence of Chrysostom regarding his use of tropes of invective in his attacks on the Jews, claiming that these customary norms would have blunted the intensity of his language.[26] He notes the customary use of exaggeration, both in use of praise and invective (*psogos*, unrelieved denigration) in normal fourth-century rhetoric. Thus he would excuse Chrysostom's ranting on this basis: that all the listeners would understand his words not as heartfelt, but as the usual means of strengthening his case in order to win them over to his point of view. This is true to a large extent in his use of invective in preaching to the Anomoeans. On the other hand, Chrysostom did view the Jews in a different light to those he considered as Christian or semi-Christian heretics. It appears certain that he regarded the Jews as a far greater threat to the faith as he understood it. From his perspective, the Jews' long and persistent history of rejection and stubbornness, including their rejection in unbelief of their long expected Messiah/

---

**20** Chrys., *Incomp. hom.* 1.38, 39 (SC 28bis.130–32; trans. Harkins, FOTC 72.67).
**21** Chrys., *Incomp. hom.* 3.6 (SC 28bis.192; trans. Harkins, FOTC 72.97).
**22** Chrys., *Incomp. hom.* 3.31 (SC 28bis.214–16; trans. Harkins, FOTC 72.108).
**23** Chrys., *Incomp. hom.* 2.51 (SC 28bis.182; trans. Harkins, FOTC 72.92).
**24** Chrys., *Incomp. hom.* 1.38 (SC 28bis.130.334–40; trans. Harkins, FOTC 72.67).
**25** Chrys., *Incomp. hom.* 10.59–67 (SC 396.276–80; trans. Harkins, FOTC 72.266–68).
**26** Robert L. Wilken, *John Chrysostom and the Jews: Rhetoric and Reality the Late Fourth Century*, TCH 4 (Berkeley: University of California Press, 1983), 112–16.

Christ, demonstrated to him that for the most part they had moved beyond the pale of hope. This applied especially to their religious leaders who displayed an impenetrable hardness of heart that made forgiveness and acceptance of the light of the gospel well-nigh impossible. In the Jews, in his opinion the best of other religious faiths, stands this enigma of Messiah rejection. Commenting on 2 Cor 3:14–15, he says that this should be no surprise, for it has been their history. The veil on Moses' face that hid the glory of God in the Law was indicative of their inability to perceive the Law gifted to them. Chrysostom described this hardness of heart as being γνώμης...ἀναισθήτου καὶ ἀγνώμονος ("...of an insensate and insolent mindset").[27] Some lines later, he attributes this hardness to τὴν τούτων παχύτητα καὶ σαρκικὴν γνώμην ("...their dullness and carnal mindset").[28]

In his homilies on Romans he takes up the issue of Israel's blindness as presented in Romans 11. He opens with the charge that Jewish inconsistency in not accepting the righteousness they sought was a matter of their own insolence or wrong-mindedness (ἀγνωμοσύνη).[29] That a condition or disposition of the γνώμη is in view is made clear in the approach he takes of closing off any loophole for excuse, such as an appeal to nature, by explicitly applying the blame to "the γνώμη of those persons."[30] Little wonder is it, then, that in Antioch he interrupted his attack on the Anomoeans to attend to "our brothers who were sick with the Jewish disease...to snatch them...from the funeral pyre of this illness."[31] He feared that the same hardness of heart, the blindness of the eyes of the soul, would be transmitted to those of his people who, out of friendship with neighbours or business contacts, attended the synagogue and participated in Jewish festivals. This differs from his mindset towards the Anomoeans who had accepted Jesus as the Christ, however deficient their understanding of his deity may have been. Chrysostom attacked their doctrines, but also shows his compassion and concern for them. His interest was in cutting down the Anomoean heresy,[32] and not its sick and deluded followers. It should be noted that although Chrysostom in countering the Anomoeans used similar abuse against the Jews as did

---

**27** Chrys., *In 2 Cor. hom.* 7 (PG 61.445.42–43). See Raymond Laird, *Mindset, Moral Choice and Sin in the Anthropology of John Chrysostom*, Early Christian Studies 15 (Strathfield: St Pauls Publications, 2012), passim, for a full treatment of γνώμη, a critical concept in Antiochene theological anthropology.

**28** Chrys., *In 2 Cor. hom.* 7 (PG 61.446.55–56).

**29** Chrys., *In Rom. hom.* 19 (PG 60.583.25–30).

**30** Chrys., *In Rom. hom.* 19 (PG 60.583.33–35). For fuller discussion, see Laird, *Mindset*, 241–42.

**31** Chrys., *Incomp. hom.* 2.2 (SC 28bis.142.14–17; trans. Harkins FOTC 72.72).

**32** Chrys., *Incomp. hom.* 3.1 (SC 28bis.186.9–14; trans. Harkins FOTC 72.95).

the Cappadocians, it was not with the same motives that Christine Shephardson attributes to the latter, that is, to count the Anomoeans in with Jews in order to stir up hatred against them in line with the anti-semitism of the time.[33]

## 2 Diagnosis

Chrysostom discerned the chief problem of the Anomoeans to be similar to the Jews, a lack of humility, an incredible arrogance – the audacious madness of human beings in all their inadequacy claiming things beyond the scope of their capacities.[34] This refers to their claim that God was totally comprehensible to human beings, a dogma based on a particular theory of language,[35] which ignores the analogical/metaphorical nature of words as used in biblical images.[36] Chrysostom uses his rhetorical skill in his presentation of their arrogance in this assertion:

> Believe me, a holy trembling lays hold of me as I am about to speak of it. I tremble to let my tongue utter the thought they are constantly pondering in their minds. What then is the root

**33** Christine Shepardson, "Defining the Boundaries of Orthodoxy: Eunomius in the Anti-Jewish Polemic of his Cappadocian Opponents," *Church History* 76 (2007): 699–708. At 708 n. 33 she acknowledges the different approach of Chrysostom: "Despite the chronological spread of these Cappadocians' writings against Eunomius, the associations that they make between Eunomius and Judaism remain remarkably consistent, particularly in contrast to Athanasius's and Ephrem's earlier writings and John Chrysostom's later writings."

**34** Chrys., *Incomp. hom.* 1.36: "arrogant presumption;" 2.8: "insolent and reckless;" 2.17: "arrogantly affirm;" 2.19: "mad with pride;" 2.20: "puffed up with arrogance;" 3.4: "arrogant" (trans. Harkins, FOTC 72.66, 74, 77, 78, 79, 96). It is ironic that Eunomius, a leading Anomoean, with a following in Constantinople where he resided at one time, should accuse his detractors of expressing an "arrogant/insolent mindset" (γνώμης ἀγνώμονος), the very terms used by Chrysostom of the Anomoeans. See Eunomius, *Liber apologeticus* 1.1, 2 (*Eunomius: The Extant Works*, ed. R.P. Vaggione, OECT, Oxford: Oxford University Press, 1987, 37–74).

**35** Anthony Meredith, "Orthodoxy, Heresy and Philosophy in the Latter Half of the Fourth Century," *Heythrop Journal* 16/1 (1975): 5–21 at 31. See Kristoffel Demoen, "Incomprehensibility, Infallibility and Untranslatability: The Poverty of Language and the Abundance of Heresy in Fourth Century Greek Patristic Thought," in: *Heretics and Heresies in the Ancient Church and Eastern Christianity: Studies in Honour of Adelbert Davids*, eds. J. Verhegden and H. Teule, Eastern Christian Studies 10 (Leuven–Paris–Walpole, MA: Peeters, 2011), 105–25, esp. 106, 115–17.

**36** Chrys., *Incomp. hom.* 8.4–6 (SC 396.170–72; trans. Harkins, FOTC 72.214–15), for Chrysostom's explanation of the need to search out the meaning of the words.

> of these evils? A mere human has the boldness to say: "I know God as God himself knows himself".[37]

It is this tenet that constituted much of the target of Chrysostom's rhetoric in refuting the Anomoeans and educating his people. For Chrysostom, this was not the God revealed in scriptures. He saw their doctrine as "an offspring of their madness and of their mind swollen with great conceit."[38] In accord with his anthropology, especially his understanding of the psyche, the problem lay in their γνώμη, their mindset. He viewed their mindset as arrogant in their claims as to the capacity of human comprehension. Time and again he emphasises the human incomprehensibility of God; that, as the apostle Paul stated in 1 Cor 13:9, our present knowledge is only in part.[39]

Chrysostom identifies as symptoms of their arrogance an "ungodly curiosity" and their "meddlesome inquisitiveness."[40] These expressions of the vital flaw in their mindset caused Chrysostom to charge them with offending/vexing God with their "curious enquiry."[41] The essence of God is not only ineffable, its nature is impenetrable, and it is not the business of humans to theorise about it.[42]

A second target was the Anomoeans' denial of the consubstantiality of the Son. This issue is taken up in Antioch in the fifth homily of the *Contra Anomoeos* group and is the focus of homilies 7–10. It was also the main issue in the two extant homilies on the Anomoeans given at Constantinople. From these, it is apparent that not only did Chrysostom think that the Anomoeans claimed too much knowledge, but that in regard to the consubstantiality of the Son they were also seriously lacking in it. The crux of the Anomoean argument is that because God is unbegotten (ἀγέννητος), his essence (οὐσία) is not able to be shared with another, for it is not logically possible for the ingenerate to beget the ingenerate. Therefore, according to this theory, the Son, the μονογένητος ("only begot-

---

**37** Chrys., *Incomp. hom.* 2.17 (SC 28bis.154.154–59; trans. Harkins, FOTC 72.77); Socrates, *HE* 4.7.13 (ed. Günther C. Hansen, GCS NF 1.234), also witnesses to this: Ὁ Θεὸς περὶ τῆς ἑαυτοῦ οὐσίας οὐδὲν πλέον ἡμῶν ἐπίσταται, οὐδέ ἐστιν αὕτη μᾶλλον μὲν ἐκείνῳ, ἧττον δὲ ἡμῖν γινωσκομένη.

**38** Chrys., *Incomp. hom.* 2.51 (SC 28bis.182.493–95; trans. Harkins, FOTC 72.92).

**39** Chrys., *Incomp. hom.* 1.12–13; 2.40–42; 4.17–19; 5.33–34 (SC 28bis.104–106, 172–74, 242, 298; trans. Harkins, FOTC 72.55, 87–88, 121–22, 151–52).

**40** Chrys., *Incomp. hom.* 1.36: "curious busybodies;" 2.6, 8: "meddlesome inquisitiveness;" 2.16: "meddlesome inquiries;" 2.18: "meddling...busybody...inquisitive about God;" 2.22, 24: "meddling;" 2.28, 31, 32, 38, 39: "meddle" (trans. Harkins, FOTC 72.66, 73–74, 76–77, 78, 79–80, 82–86).

**41** Chrys., *Incomp. hom.* 2.16 (SC 28bis.154.141–42; trans. Harkins, FOTC 72.76).

**42** Chrys., *Incomp. hom.* 2.13 (SC 28bis.150–52; trans. Harkins, FOTC 72.76).

ten"), cannot be of the same essence as the Father. The Anomoeans were not alone in denying consubstantiality to the Son, but they held to an extreme position that the Son was unlike the Father in many ways, especially in regard to his essence (οὐσία). We find Chrysostom, then, in these homilies piling up examples of Christ's oneness with the Father in all respects. He ranges over the scriptures from Genesis to Revelation to demonstrate the equality of the Son in essence, authority, and power.

Chrysostom held the claim of the Anomoeans "to know God perfectly" to be nothing less than an abuse of the fundamental power of the human person, that of freedom or autonomy (αὐτεξούσιος).[43] In Chrysostom's theology this is none other than the original and ultimate sin, the reiteration of the prototype fall from the soul's natural humility into a state of arrogance. In a passage that addresses Romans 12:3 and discusses at length the value of humility or being lowly of mind (ταπεινοφρονεῖν), Chrysostom associates this virtue with the nobility of nature.

> In this way the soul also, whenever it makes void the essential dignity of its nature that is characterised by humility, receives some weakening habit, becomes cowardly, insolent, and senseless, and eventually may fail to recognise itself.[44]

Such a fall from wisdom results in weakness in the soul and opens the door to habits of weakness, so that the soul ends up in ignorance of its own being. He also contrasts it with ἀπόνοια (senselessness, recklessness or unreasonableness), a recognised folly in the world of Greek παιδεία. Chrysostom compares the soul's loss of its greatness of nature to the loss of condition in the body. The body out of condition becomes a prey to disease. It is the same with the soul. In this regard he applies to the Anomoeans such terms as sickness,[45] sick with disease,[46] "swollen with festering sores,"[47] madness, excessive madness, and ultimate madness.[48] These terms could be taken to provide an excuse

---

**43** Chrys., *Incomp. hom.* 2.32–33 (SC 28bis.166–68; trans. Harkins, FOTC 72.83–84). See Laird, *Mindset*, 85–112.

**44** Chrys., *In Rom. hom.* 20 (PG 60.600.57–61): οὕτω καὶ ἡ ψυχή, ἐπειδὰν τὸ μεγαλοφυὲς ἀπολέσῃ καὶ τὸ ταπεινοφρονεῖν, ἕξιν δεξαμένη τινὰ ἀσθενῆ, καὶ δειλὴ καὶ θρασεῖα καὶ ἀνόητος γίνεται, καὶ ἑαυτὴν ἀγνοήσει λοιπόν. See Laird, *Mindset*, 230–31.

**45** Chrys., *Incomp. hom.* 3.31 (SC 28bis.214.346–47; trans. Harkins, FOTC 72.108–109).

**46** Chrys., *Incomp. hom.* 1.38 (SC 28bis.130–32; trans. Harkins, FOTC 72.67).

**47** Chrys., *Incomp. hom.* 2.20 (SC 28bis.158.181; trans. Harkins, FOTC 72.79).

**48** Chrys., *Incomp. hom.* 1.23, 26, 30, 36; 2.19, 20, 21, 31, 51; 3.2 (SC 28bis.116.188–90, 118.223, 120.233, 124.278, 128.326–27, 156–58, 166.293, 182.491, 188.24; trans. Harkins, FOTC 72.59, 61, 64, 66, 78–79, 83, 92, 96).

for many who had embraced the Anomoean dogma, and thus hold out hope that a cure or healing was at hand. This may look promising until we encounter comments from Chrysostom such as "unpardonable madness."[49] He insists that their sickness and disease is ungodliness (ἀσέβεια), which is "a greater evil than that of any demon. The madness of the possessed has an excuse. The disease of the Anomoeans has nothing to offer in its defence."[50] It would seem that all is lost, that there is no acceptable excuse. As usual, Chrysostom is adamant on the note of personal responsibility. Nevertheless, hope is not dashed: other words of Chrysostom in his preaching to these Anomoeans hold out the promise of deliverance, of healing, of a return to wisdom and health. The point here in his statements in relation to sickness and mania is that Chrysostom, as any competent orator, is tightening the noose in regard to personal culpability. Yes, healing is at hand, but the recognition of personal responsibility is the first step on the path away from arrogance to the humility required to recognise and receive the grace of God. It is this change in mindset that is required.

He promoted and defended Christ's humility as a reminder of a vital virtue to be pursued in conformity to Christ, his aim being to bring his Anomoean hearers to humility in order to make way for a change in their mindset and their theology. So, in his estimation, the deepest reason for their heresy was a very human sin, one which could yield only to the means of grace as granted to and wielded by the Nicene community and its leaders. In his preaching, the appeal of Chrysostom is clear: he pleaded with his hearers (not only, but especially the Anomoeans) to be low and humble in minds and hearts.[51] Failure in this means that the truth is closed to them. Pursue humility, he advised – the kingdom belongs to the servant of all.[52]

# 3 Healing

Although the terms used by Chrysostom referring to the Anomoeans are rather negative, they are suggestive that something may be done to relieve the malady and bring them to health of soul and spirit. In encouraging his people to minister to the Anomoeans, he likens them to a "bone out of joint" and presses upon the congregation the urgency of the task of healing. The longer treatment is delayed,

**49** Chrys., *Incomp. hom.* 2.18 (SC 28bis.154.162; trans. Harkins, FOTC 72.78).

**50** Chrys., *Incomp. hom.* 3.31 (SC 28bis.216.350–52; trans. Harkins, FOTC 72.109).

**51** Chrys., *Incomp. hom.* 7.27 (SC 396.134–36; trans. Harkins, FOTC 72.196–97), in which he cites Matt 11:29, 20:28.

**52** Chrys., *Incomp. hom.* 8.44–48 (SC 396.202–206; trans. Harkins, FOTC 72.230–32).

the more difficult it becomes to put the bone back in its socket.[53] Clearly, he wants them healed, he wants them whole, and he wants his people to want them healed, and he wants his people to be part of the healing process. This points us to one of the images Chrysostom applies to the church. In the first homily in his long Genesis series, he calls the church the ἰατρεῖον...πνευματικὸν ("the medical clinic of the spirit").[54] The church is where the people ought to receive appropriate medicines and apply them to their wounds. As suggested above, this pastoral concern was the main structural element in his homilies. Parallel to the Anomoean situation is the scene Chrysostom paints in another of his Genesis homilies. There he opens his sermon with a discussion of the soul affected by sin under the image of incurable wounds. Although the medicine is applied, it does not benefit the patient, not because of its lack of potency, but because of the lack of desire (μὴ βούλεται) of the patient. The will (προαίρεσις) is not stationary but can change. God has endowed our nature with free will (αὐτεξούσιος), God exhorts and advises us in the depth of our mind (διανοία), but the mindset (γνώμη) is the determining factor. "Everything (τὸ πᾶν) rests upon it."[55] This fits the Anomoeans: healing is available, but everything depends upon their mindset. As he says in one homily in Antioch when addressing them, "These men have at hand the medicine to cure themselves and still they are swollen with festering sores."[56]

The medicine Chrysostom prescribed was the revelation contained in the scriptures which he applied by his preaching, as elucidated in his discussion of the priesthood.[57] Relevant to this is an arresting feature of Chrysostom's con-

---

**53** Chrys., *Incomp. hom* 10.57–60 (SC 396.276–78; trans. Harkins, FOTC 72.265–67).
**54** Chrys., *In Gen. hom.* 1 (PG 53.22.9–12).
**55** Chrys., *In Gen. hom.* 19 (PG 53.159.4). See Laird, *Mindset*, 46–49, for a discussion of γνώμη as the faculty of response in Chrysostom, and where this part of the homily is given fuller treatment.
**56** Chrys., *Incomp. hom.* 2.20 (SC 28bis.156–58; trans. Harkins, FOTC 72.79). Wendy Mayer, "Madness in the works of John Chrysostom: A snapshot from Late Antiquity", in *The concept of Madness from Homer to Byzantium: History and aspects*, ed. Helen Perdicoyianni–Paleologou (Amsterdam: Adolf M. Hakkert, forthcoming), in her analysis of madness in John Chrysostom's usage concludes: "In light of the pathology of madness we have uncovered in John's thought, we should now entertain the suspicion that his discourse of madness when applied to the heterodox operates beyond the level of constructing religious deviancy and defining orthodoxy. It attributes to the heterodox a genuine naturalistic illness of the soul that requires real spiritual therapy in order to restore interior balance." See also Margaret Trenchard–Smith, "Perceptions of Unreason in the Byzantine Empire to the End of the First Millennium", unpub. doctoral diss. (University of California Los Angeles, 2006).
**57** Chrys., *Sac.* 4.3.11–13 (SC 272.250): "after good example there is but one instrument and means of healing: that is preaching."

flict with the Anomoeans. This, as hinted above, is the absence of any philosophically-based treatises directed towards the Anomoean leaders. While other leaders and bishops, such as the Cappadocians, used dogmatic dissertations aimed at the outspoken leading opponents of Nicaea and their supporters, Chrysostom's attack, if we could call it that, was made in homily format in the course of his regular preaching. Even though the pertinent homilies were pointed in reference to the Anomoeans who came to hear him preach, and delivered in their presence at their request, they were vital elements in his strategy of building up his people in their faith. There is a complete rejection of sophistries, philosophy, and the authority of reason. His aim was to protect all his flock regardless of social class from embracing anything but what he saw as revealed truth from the scriptures. His practice was to explain the texts he brought together in order to instruct the flock, to educate the catechumens, and to teach those "meddlesome busybodies" (τὸ περιεργάζεσθαι),[58] the Anomoeans, who attended his preaching. Chrysostom placed his trust in the authority and power of the Christian and Jewish scriptures. By his expositional preaching, he played a vital role at Antioch and Constantinople, and no doubt much more widely through the publication of his sought-after homilies, in shaping mindsets in the Nicene formula, the mindset (γνώμη) being the critical faculty of the soul responsible for sin and answerable to God.[59]

Chrysostom's trust in the power of the preached Word and his disdain of human reason because of its perceived weakness was the working principle of his whole ministry. This is made absolutely clear in these homilies addressing the Anomoean problem. Comparing reason and revelation in *Contra Anomoeos homily* 2, he avers:

> For whenever God makes a revelation, there is no need to stir up the workings of one's reason nor to propose to oneself either a sequence of events, or a necessity rooted in nature, or any such thing. The power of God's revealed word is above all these things;...accept God's revelations on faith.[60]

To trust "the weak processes of their own reason" is madness and folly, and makes them "guilty of great extravagant boasting when they say they...can grasp and define the essence of God who cannot be comprehended by the powers above."[61] As the Anomoean dogma was based on a philosophic position,[62] he

**58** Chrys., *Incomp. hom.* 2.18 (SC 28bis.156; trans. Harkins, FOTC 72.78).
**59** Laird, *Mindset*, 41–51, 239–47.
**60** Chrys., *Incomp. hom.* 2.13–14 (SC 28bis.152; trans. Harkins, FOTC 72.76).
**61** Chrys., *Incomp. hom.* 3.6 (SC 28bis.192; trans. Harkins, FOTC 72.97).

does not rest in reminding them of the weakness of reason, and the danger of dependence upon it. He warned them of what he saw as the fundamental Anomoean error: "bringing down God to fit the limits of your own processes of thought."[63]

It may be asked as to why Chrysostom did not trust human reason. The answer to this is to be sought in his theological anthropology, which is found in a passage commenting on 1 Cor 1:18 – 21, where Chrysostom argues that faith is superior to reason and human wisdom for the knowledge of God and humankind. He sets out his thought on the role assigned to λογισμός (reason) and σοφία (wisdom) prior to the incarnation and concludes:

> This is to say, that in the past, to reason that the one who founded such a so very great world is a God similar to someone who has irresistible and ineffable power, and that through these means to comprehend him, was the function of human wisdom; but now, there is no longer the need for reasonings, but for faith alone.[64]

He understood that the faculty of comprehension or intellect, the διάνοια, was intended to take the evidence presented to it in general revelation in the world, and by the faculty of reasoning, the λογισμός, in dependence upon the Holy Spirit come to the discovery of divine reality.

Chrysostom is adamant that humans, in matters divine, could not reason correctly by themselves alone. If the soul attempts to see without the divine aid of the Spirit of God, it becomes a hindrance to itself.[65] This happened: "The sceptre of knowledge was placed in the hand of independent reasonings,"[66] rather than in the hand of the Holy Spirit. The soul became πανταχοῦ ἄτονος ("absolutely unstrung"),[67] and opened itself to receive τοῖς σφόδρα ἀτόποις ("extreme absurdities").[68] He likens the philosophers who took that path to a metalworker drawing a piece of hardened metal out of the fire without fire tongs and

62 Michel R. Barnes, "The Background and Use of Eunomius' Causal Language," in: *Arianism after Arius*, 217 – 36, in a perceptive analysis of three critical concepts, at 217 – 18, 222 – 25, expresses a preference for the medical tradition of Galen or the philosophical traditions connected with Iamblichus, rejects Aristotelian influence, and recognises that of Julian, Aetius and the contemporary Alexandrian theologians, but wisely chooses not to insist on any source as totally dominant.

63 Chrys., *Incomp. hom.* 2.24 (SC 28bis.160.219 – 20; trans. Harkins, FOTC 72.80).

64 Chrys., *In 1 Cor. hom.* 4 (PG 61.32.42 – 46).

65 Chrys., *In 1 Cor. hom.* 7 (PG 61.60.29 – 31). See Laird, *Mindset*, 247 – 51, for a fuller treatment of this issue.

66 Chrys., *In 1 Cor. hom.* 7 (PG 61.58.57 – 59.3, 60.36 – 37).

67 Chrys., *In 1 Cor. hom.* 7 (PG 61.60.57 – 58).

68 Chrys., *In 1 Cor. hom.* 7 (PG 61.60.41).

with bare hands, an act flagrantly one of "extreme foolishness" (τὴν ἐσχάτην ἄνοιαν).[69] Explicit in this analogy is the point that the philosophers, by counting themselves wise, "disdained faith" (τὴν πίστιν ἠτίμασαν).[70] Then, implicit in the image is the glaring fact that the instrument, not being designed for the task, must be extensively damaged. Λογισμός, διάνοια, and σύνεσις, all part of the reasoning processes, have been so damaged that they no longer can function as was intended. Chrysostom notes that the διάνοια or σύνεσις, the faculty of comprehension that functions as "the eyes of the soul" (τῶν τῆς ψυχῆς ὄψεων) due to its consequent ἀσθενείας ("weakness") and εὐτέλειαν ("poor quality"),[71] has its range severely limited, so that the divine is well beyond it. It is with this in mind that we find him disparaging the Anomoeans' extreme dependence upon reason, and both the utter arrogance and the foolishness of their claims. If they were to be healed they must give attention to his preaching, taking the path of faith in the divine revelation found in the scriptures. It is not surprising, then, that Chrysostom saw the church as a school, a place of learning and instruction.[72] In this regard, we should note his description of the Anomoean heresy as a "fruitless...wild and uncultivated tree."[73] Chrysostom had supreme confidence in the preaching of the scriptures. Teaching would root out the heresy. It would provide the means of healthy growth in the truth.

Prayer was another instrument of healing that Chrysostom called upon his people to apply. His confidence in the power of prayer, especially of united prayer, is evident in his plea to his congregation to go to prayer for the sick, mad, and diseased Anomoeans,[74] and for the "heretics."[75] It is clear that he viewed the Anomoeans as not beyond the grace and the power of God, and thus was confident in the power of prayer to share in the healing of a disorder of their mindset.

Love is another of the instruments whereby the Anomoeans could be healed. Chrysostom called upon his people "to do all we can to prevent hatred between ourselves and those who would be our foes."[76] The life of virtue that he was constantly teaching them was, he stressed, a life of love. They must not show them-

**69** Chrys., *In 1 Cor. hom.* 5 (PG 61.40.20–21).

**70** Chrys., *In 1 Cor. hom.* 5 (PG 61.40.23).

**71** Chrys., *In 1 Cor. hom.* 7 (PG 61.61.29–41). The items cited are at lines 36, 35 and 41.

**72** Chrys., *In Matt. hom.* 17 (PG 57.264). Jaclyn L. Maxwell, *Christianization and Communication in Late Antiquity: John Chrysostom and his Congregation in Antioch* (Cambridge: Cambridge University Press, 2006), 88–117, discusses the importance of preaching as an educational tool in antiquity, and focuses upon Chrysostom's approach to it.

**73** Chrys., *Incomp. hom.* 3.1–2 (SC 28bis.186–88; trans. Harkins, FOTC 72.95).

**74** Chrys., *Incomp. hom.* 3.31 (SC 28bis.214–16; trans. Harkins, FOTC 72.108–109).

**75** Chrys., *Incomp. hom.* 7.56–63 (SC 396.156–60; trans. Harkins, FOTC 72.208–10).

**76** Chrys., *Incomp. hom.* 10.57–68 (SC 396.276–82; trans. Harkins, FOTC 72.265–69).

selves as enemies. They needed to be reconciled without delay so that the dislocated bone might be restored to its place in the body. He elaborates with them on the theme of reconciliation, which "deserves a crown and a hymn of praise."[77] "Love," he said, "is the beginning and end of every virtue."[78] Chrysostom urged them to make friends with the Anomoeans and to share with them what they learned from his homilies.[79] However, this latter was a task only for the strong in the faith. If weak, it is better to flee and not be overcome by their heresies.[80]

These cures – preaching, prayer, love, together with virtue, friendship, and discipling – were the weapons to be employed in the conflict with the Anomoeans. These were the means of healing, the way to dispel the ignorance, to abolish the foolishness, to tame the madness, to replant the wild tree in fertile soil and to provide its proper cultivation. They are not, Chrysostom declared, the war machines of destruction, but rather the implements of truth, peace, and deliverance. These would bring down the strongholds of the devil, the walls of oppression, the proud yet weak reasonings raised up against the knowledge of God.

# 4 Obstacles

It was only when Chrysostom came to Constantinople that he appeared to strike significant problems, so this section deals only with his time in that metropolis. Not all of Chrysostom's efforts to combat the Anomoean influence were limited to preaching in the church. This applied particularly to Constantinople, where as bishop he faced a number of strongholds of Anomoeanism external to his churches. Claudia Tiersch has noted that by 381, when Gregory Nazianzen was appointed bishop there, "the pro-Arian influence of his predecessor had led, unlike Antioch [where each operated without interference], to not only the oppression, but virtually the complete dissolution of the Nicene community."[81] Gregory of Nazianzus, the first bishop of the newly-created community, had described very vividly almost seemingly insurmountable difficulties of this new beginning.

**77** Chrys., *Incomp. hom.* 10.64 (SC 396.280.539; trans. Harkins, FOTC 72.268).

**78** Chrys., *Incomp. hom.* 10.68 (SC 396.282.561; trans. Harkins, FOTC 72.269). See also *In Matt. hom.* 18 (PG 57.265–73); *hom.* 19 (PG 57.276–85); *De proditione Iudae hom.* 1–2 (PG 49.373–92).

**79** Chrys., *Incomp. hom.* 2.51–52 (SC 28bis.182; trans. Harkins, FOTC 72.92).

**80** Chrys., *Incomp. hom.* 2.53–55 (SC 28bis.182–84; trans. Harkins, FOTC 72.92–94).

**81** Claudia Tiersch, *Johannes Chrysostomus in Konstaninopel (398–404): Weltsicht und Wirken eines Bischofs in der Hauptstadt des Oströmischen Reiches*, STAC 6 (Tübingen: Mohr Siebeck, 2002), 114: "Die proarianische Einflußen seiner Vorgänger hatte hier, anders als in Antiochia, nicht nur zur Unterdrückung, sondern zur nahezu völligen Auflösung der nizänischen Gruppierung geführt."

The number of parishioners had thus been whittled away, so that a private home was easily able to accommodate their services.[82]

Of significance was the financial support of some of the wealthier educated elite who were probably followers of Eunomius from the time of his residence there. Another was the presence of Arian Goths living in Constantinople. Then there was the considerable number of Goths in the Roman armies who provided their own distinctive threat to the Nicene faith in the metropolis. The underground Anomoean "churches," the house meetings, provided a challenge, as did the presence of nearby Anomoean bishops. The more distant Goths were a concern to Chrysostom, but not as an immediate obstacle to his labours in Constantinople. The vacillation of imperial and court support was another factor, as was the hostility of some of his clergy, and that of Theophilus, the bishop of Alexandria. As these latter three categories were more in the way of distractions that consumed his time and energy – and ultimately his life – rather than direct opposition to his dealings with the Anomoeans, and as there is considerable analysis of these issues by various authors, along with the distant Goths, they will not be considered in the following comments.[83]

Ongoing support of Anomoean thought by means of house meetings and financial support had been a reality of Constantinopolitan life from the days of the edict *Cunctos populos* of Theodosius I (together with Gratian and Valentinian II), declaring the catholic (Nicene) faith as the religion of the empire, and outlaw-

**82** *Incomp. hom.* 11.1–3 (SC 396.288; trans. Harkins, FOTC 72.270–71), preached by Chrysostom shortly after his arrival to take up the role of bishop in Constantinople some seventeen years later, indicates that the Nicene community was still small.

**83** For a representative corpus of analyses on the pertinent issues, see Timothy E. Gregory, "Zosimus 5,23 and the People of Constantinople," *Byz* 43 (1973): 61–83; Florent van Ommeslaeghe, "Jean Chrysostome en conflit avec l'impératrice Eudoxie. Le dossier et les origines d'une légende," *Analecta Bollandiana* 97 (1979): 131–59; J.H.W.G. Liebeschuetz, *Barbarians and Bishops, Army, Church, and State in the Age of Arcadius and Chrysostom* (Oxford: Clarendon Press, 1991); John N.D. Kelly, *Golden Mouth: The Story of John Chrysostom – Ascetic, Preacher, Bishop* (Ithaca, NY: Cornell University Press, 1995), 115–227; Susanna Elm, "The Dog that did not Bark. Doctrine and Patriarchal Authority in the Conflict between Theophilus of Alexandria and John Chrysostom of Constantinople," in: *Christian Origins. Theology, Rhetoric and Community*, eds. Lewis Ayres and Gareth Jones (London: Routledge, 1998), 66–93; Martin Wallraff, "Le conflit de Jean Chrysostome avec la cour chez les historiens ecclésiastique grecs," in: *L'historiographie de l'église des premiers siècles*, Actes du Colloque de Tours, sept 2000, eds. Bernard Pouderon and Yves-Marie Duval, Théologie historique 114 (Paris: Beauchesne, 2001), 361–70; Tiersch, *Chrysostomus in Konstantinopel*; Wendy Mayer, "John Chrysostom as Crisis Manager: The Years in Constantinople," in: *Ancient Jewish and Christian Texts*, 129–43.

ing others, including the Anomoeans, as heretical.[84] Further to that, Theodosius via the 381 edict *Nullus haereticus* deprived the Anomoeans of their church buildings in Constantinople.[85] Sozomen tells us that Eunomius continued his ministry in private houses,[86] and Socrates reports that Eunomius read his works to those in attendance.[87] Such house meetings of the Anomoeans, without Eunomius who had been exiled long since by Theodosius, were still operating when Chrysostom arrived in Constantinople, although official Anomoean churches were established outside the city walls to which the many followers of Eunomius living in Constantinople repaired for their particular liturgy and worship.[88] In regard to the private churches in the city, Chrysostom recognised their danger and endeavoured to divest the owners of their financial control. Kim Bowes argues that the unpopularity engendered by this action was the prime reason for Chrysostom's demise.[89]

The heretical churches allowed outside the city walls staged regular liturgical processions through the city with antiphonal songs spelling out their dogma and belittling that of the Nicene churches. Chrysostom counted this as a powerful threat, one of the reasons for the weakness of the churches to which he had been appointed for his episcopal care. Thus, with imperial patronage, he instituted liturgical processions of the orthodox, catholic faith. These soon became larger and more frequent than those of the Anomoeans to the extent that the Anomoeans became jealous, resorted to violence and were banned by the emperor.[90] These popular displays of the church, which continued as a permanent feature of its life, proved as effective for the Nicenes as they had done for the Anomoeans, a means of turning many to the truth as Chrysostom perceived and preached it. These spectacles did far more than get rid of the Anomoean processions from the streets of the city. They became a vital ploy in Chrysostom's vision to convert the public spaces of Constantinople into expressions of the heavenly Christian *poli-*

---

**84** *CTh* 16.1.2 (*Codex Theodosianius. Les lois religieuses des empereurs romains de Constantin à Théodose II (312–438)*, vol. 1, *Code Théodosien livre XVI*, ed. Theodor Mommsen, trans. Jean Rougé, SC 497, Paris: Éditions du Cerf, 2005, 114). Cf. the reference to the same law by Bronwen Neil in the opening to her chapter in this volume.

**85** *CTh* 16.5.6 (SC 497.234–36).

**86** Sozomen, *HE* 7.5 (GCS NF 4.306); see *CTh* 16.5.11–13 of 383 CE (SC 497.248–52).

**87** Socrates, *HE* 5.20 (GCS NF 1.294).

**88** Liebeschuetz, *Barbarians and Bishops*, 147–59; See Harry O. Maier, "Dissent, Heresy and Households in Late Antiquity," *VC* 49 (1995): 49–63, esp. 51–53, for a brief summary of the house church movement in Constantinople at that time.

**89** Kim Bowes, *Private Worship, Public Values, and Religious Change in Late Antiquity* (Cambridge: Cambridge University Press, 2008), 118–19; see Tiersch, *Chrysostomus in Konstaninopel*, 152–60, 229–60.

**90** Soz., *HE* 8.8 (GCS NF 4.360–61).

*teia*, over and against the relics of the pagan *politeia* which were used by the court to promote their own power and glory.[91] They were remarkably successful until Chrysostom fell foul of the imperial court. Whilst they lasted, these processions did much to build up the popularity of the Nicene churches and negate that of the Anomoeans.

Another apparent obstacle was the presence of a large number of Goths in the East, mainly in the Roman army, and especially those resident in Constantinople. From Chrysostom's actions toward them, it seems that he thought the threat from that quarter was more apparent than real. This may be because the Goths had accepted an Arian form of Christianity, dating from the work of Ulfilas among them in their homelands earlier in the fourth century. As a consequence of their response to the Christian kerygma in that dress, Arianism had become an element of their ethnic identity.[92] The imperial administration had adopted a pro-German policy toward the Goths, probably because of the need to rely upon them in the army. Chrysostom followed suit, not of necessity, but out of his own conviction. Chrysostom's attitude to barbarians seeking the truth is demonstrated in the visit of some Syrian monks in Antioch when he was speaking on martyrdom. They were talking in their native language, Syriac, and thus to the elite Greeks they would be classed as ignorant barbarians. Chrysostom would have none of it, so he said to his congregation, "Take no notice of their barbarian language, but consider their disciplined intellect. For what is the benefit of a common language if there is a diversity of mindset?"[93] He would not condemn the barbarian who had shown evidence of seeking the truth, but by an accident of geography or circumstances had accepted a dogma that Chrysostom deemed heretical. Such persons were to be encouraged.[94] They may be uncultivated plants, but when given the opportunity to hear the teachings of scripture their mindsets could be shaped into the sound doctrine of the Nicene orthodoxy. This is but one example of his general approach and of his own mindset. Most of the Arian Goths fitted this category, hence his efforts to reach them, to deal kindly with them, and to refrain from barring them from the opportunity to develop

---

**91** See Chrys., *In Matt. hom.* 1 (PG 57.23–24). The πόλις, πολιτεία image starts much earlier in this homily as a contrast to the "absurd city-state," τὴν καταγέλαστον πολιτεῖαν of Plato (PG 57.18.57–58). See Nathanael Andrade, "The Processions of John Chrysostom and the Contested Spaces of Constantinople," *JECS* 18 (2010): 161–89, a perceptive discussion of this aspect and Chrysostom's part in it.

**92** Liebeschuetz, *Barbarians and Bishops*, 153–59.

**93** Chrys., *De sanctis martyribus* (PG 50.646.25–29).

**94** Stanislav Doležal, "Joannes Chrysostomos and the Goths," *Graecolatina Pragensia* 21 (2006): 165–85 at 165–66.

in their understanding of the faith. What then of the Gainas affair and the refusal of Chrysostom to allow the soldiers under him to have their own church within the urban precincts of Constantinople? It should be remembered that Gainas was more than an ordinary Goth soldier. He was intelligent, an officer of status in the Roman army, and had been corresponding with Nilus the hermit about theological matters.[95] Thus he would have been conversant with the doctrines of the various churches. As such, he appears to have been beyond the category that Chrysostom felt was open to the truth, and thus constituted a real threat to the Nicene church in the imperial capital. Also, Chrysostom was a stout defender of the law which had kept Constantinople free of heretical churches inside the city for two decades. On this issue, he was not prepared to take any risks.[96]

These then are the obstacles in the path of Chrysostom in his combat with the Anomoeans and other Arians. He did not let these stand in his way, but turning some of them to advantage, he accomplished much in the mindset-shaping he had set out to do. Other factors cut short his presence in Constantinople, thus limiting, but not ending his influence in the city, as witnessed by his correspondence and the continuing existence and influence of his published homilies and writings.

# 5 Assessment

Chrysostom had given his life to shape the mindset of his congregations. This exhibits his approach to the church: he considered it as a school, a medical clinic, a battle arena, and a shepherd's flock. Chrysostom would not countenance the church as being a philosophical academy. Rather, he saw it as a sphere of divine revelation, a spiritual theatre[97] where the ill, the proud, the uneducated, the mad, the wolf, the enemy, the prisoner, the uncultivated plant and the independent reason were exposed to revelation in the Word as proclaimed and expounded by the preacher who was dependent upon the Spirit of God. In this encounter Chrysostom expected the sick to be cured, the proud to be humbled, the ringing voice of the sophist to be silenced, the mad to be delivered to their senses, the wolf to be tamed, and the enemy to be subdued and to change sides. The rest-

95 Liebeschuetz, *Barbarians and Bishops*, 103.

96 See Justin Stephens, "Religion in the Early Thought of John Chrysostom," in: *The Power of Religion in Late Antiquity*, eds. Andrew Cain and Noel Lenski (Farnham–Burlington, VT: Ashgate, 2009), 181–200 at 181–88, for the suggestion that Chrysostom followed Babylas' approach to the relationship between temporal and spiritual authority.

97 Christoph Jacob, *Das Geistige Theater: Ästhetik und Moral bei Johannes Chrysostomus* (Münster: Aschendorff Verlag, 2010), 69–80.

less, meddlesome patient would find peace; the captive would be released. The plant would be replanted to a place where the gardener could cultivate it, dress it and shape its form and encourage its fruitfulness. All this would be accomplished by the shaping of the mindset which, in its distorted state, lay at the root of the problem.

Chrysostom's confidence in his healing armoury, enhanced as it was by his rhetorical mastery, was a critical factor in establishing his people in Nicene trinitarianism. There is here justification of the pathway chosen by Chrysostom. Opposing Anomoean leaders directly may have been of little effect as their mindsets were so rigid and arrogant in their errors. Seeing the mindset of his congregations as the citadels to be taken and shaped, he thereby stopped leakage from his congregation to the Anomoeans, increased the number of the orthodox, confirmed his flock in the truth as he understood it, made disciplers out of members of his flock, and challenged the curious Anomoeans who came to hear him preach. There is no doubt that he put a large dent in the Anomoean followings in Antioch and Constantinople. Sozomen writes that in Constantinople Chrysostom persuaded many pagans and heretics to unite with him.[98] It would appear that his preaching on the Anomoean issue of their rejection of the consubstantiality of Christ with God the Father had some drawing power. It is evident that he laid a firm base in both cities among the laity in regard to the full deity of the Son, His unity of essence and equality with God the Father. He was committed to the oneness of God in three hypostases, Father, Son and Holy Spirit. He had also spoken about the Person of Christ, holding to His full humanity and His full deity, and significantly, these natures in union without confusion.

As a true pastor, responsibility for the flock entrusted to him was of utmost importance, keeping in mind that he had turned his back upon a career in official and civil public oratory, despising the philosophy of the Greek *paideia*, committing himself to propagation of the Christian *philosophia*, a wisdom which was more than the theory of the sage, or the mere display of the public sophist, but one that focused upon praxis flowing out of the Word of God.[99] In this regard, a

**98** Soz., *HE* 8.5.1–2 (GCS NF 4.357).

**99** Anne-Mare Malingrey, "*Philosophia*": *Étude d'un groupe de mots dans la littérature grecque, des Présocratiques au IVe siècle après J.–C.*, Études et Commentaires 40 (Paris: Kilncksieck, 1961), 263–88, has given a perceptive survey of Chrysostom's usage of φιλοσοφία, esp. the definition at 268: "la foi chrétienne authentiquement vécue au milieu du monde" (Christian life authentically lived in the world). In *In Matt. hom.* 1 (PG 57.18–20) Chrysostom contrasts the Christian φιλοσοφία with that of the pagan philosophers, tracing the weakness of pagan φιλοσοφία not only to their contradictory teachings, but also to their moral failure. In particular, this moral failure was unflattering of the classic παιδεία pointing, in Chrysostom's opinion, to its great weakness.

comparison could be made with what has been observed by Christine Shepardson that:

> Scholars have long recognized that the theological arguments of Basil of Caesarea, Gregory of Nazianzus, and Gregory of Nyssa against their opponent Eunomius helped to shape the development of Christian orthodoxy, and thus Christian self-definition, in the late fourth-century Roman Empire.[100]

What is said here about the Cappadocians at the philosophical dissertation level, could be said about Chrysostom at the level of the congregational homily. His persuasive oratory to the laity ensured that what was becoming orthodox thought was consolidated at the grass roots of the life of the church in two of the larger centres of the Roman empire in the East. Although a rocky road lay ahead, this was a vital contribution that pointed the way forward and prepared a firm base to carry the Nicene faith and its developing christology into the future. Chrysostom had not forgotten some of the lessons he had learned in the Greek *paideia*. The path to real competence in truth and wisdom is a long one.[101] Perhaps he remembered what he had learnt from Xenophon, one of the authors in Libanius' curriculum: "[puppies] if untrained, become useless, crazy, and obstinate (γιγνομένας ματαίους τε καὶ μανιώδεις καὶ δυσπειθεστάτας). It's the same with human beings."[102] Chrysostom was prepared to invest time and energy in ensuring that his congregations were properly educated in the faith. He judged that this was the best way to combat dissenters, and to ensure that his people were not only secure, but also equipped to join the battle with the same grace, zeal, and confidence as he displayed. Whatever failings he may have had, whatever mistakes he may have made, he accomplished the task for which he had taken up his weapons and entered the arena.

**100** Shepardson, "Defining the Boundaries," 699.

**101** Raffaella Cribiore, "Lucian, Libanius, and the Short Road to Rhetoric," *GRBS* 47 (2007): 71–86 at 73, compares the long and the short roads to rhetorical expertise.

**102** Xenophon, *Commentarii* (=*Memorabilia*) 4.1.3 (*Xenophontis opera omnia*, vol. 2, ed. E.C. Marchant, Oxford: Clarendon Press, 1923, 2nd ed., repr. 1971).

Wendy Mayer

# Media Manipulation as a Tool in Religious Conflict: Controlling the Narrative Surrounding the Deposition of John Chrysostom

## 1 Introduction

As we know well from modern events such as the Watergate Scandal, an affair that led to the resignation of a US President,[1] and the Children Overboard Affair in Australia that helped to swing for the Liberal Party and incumbent Prime Minister a critical Federal election,[2] we would be naïve to think that control of the flow of information and the deliberate shaping of the information that the public and key stakeholders receive do not play a critical role in conflicts where obtaining or retaining power is a significant consideration. What is curious is that, while we accept this for the present, the paucity of historical sources for similar events in the distant past often leads us to ignore this principle in our desire to make the best of the few sources that are available. As I argued in an article published in 2008,[3] our reading until now of the key surviving sources surrounding the critical period from John's first exile late in 403 to his posthumous rehabilitation at Constantinople in 438 CE constitutes a particular case in point. By the time that Socrates, Sozomen and Theodoret came to write their ecclesiastical his-

1 Of direct relevance to the topic discussed here see David Greenberg, *Nixon's Shadow: The History of an Image* (New York: W.W. Norton & Company, 2004). Cf. Daniel E. Frick, *Reinventing Richard Nixon: A Cultural History of an American Obsession* (Lawrence, KS: University Press of Kansas, 2008); and Mark Feldstein, *Poisoning the Press: Richard Nixon, Jack Anderson, and the Rise of Washington's Scandal Culture* (New York: Farrar, Straus and Giroux, 2010).

2 For an outline of events see Allison Dellit, "How the 'Children Overboard' Lie Developed," *Green Left Weekly*, issue 483 (6 March 2002) at www.greenleft.org.au/node/25781 (accessed 2 Sept. 2012). Regarding the subsequent senate enquiry and revelations, see the convenient summary at Wikipedia s.v. "Children Overboard Affair" and links (en.wikipedia.org/wiki/Children_Overboard; accessed 2 Sept. 2012).

3 Wendy Mayer, "The Making of a Saint. John Chrysostom in Early Historiography," in: *Chrysostomosbilder in 1600 Jahren: Facetten der Wirkungsgeschichte eines Kirchenvaters*, eds. Martin Wallraff and Rudolf Brändle, AKG 105 (Berlin: De Gruyter, 2008), 39–59. See also Ead., "Biography and Chronology," in: *Chrysostomika II*, ed. Sever Voicu (Rome: Augustinianum, forthcoming).

tories between the late 430s and 450 CE, firstly, a large number of hostile witnesses to events had been suppressed; secondly, a number of documents authored either by John's supporters or by his enemies that had circulated during that period under John's name had become accepted and archived as genuine; and, thirdly, the view of John's supporters, that his role in these events was that of a martyr and saint, had prevailed. The narrative of these events promulgated by modern historians to date, including that of Claudia Tiersch,[4] who fully utilised the funeral oration by ps-Martyrius,[5] is one heavily influenced by the success of the Johannites and rarely gives sufficient weight to the lost narratives. More importantly, it for the most part accepts as genuine works promulgated by others under John's name[6] and, where it does accept that some of these works are inauthentic, dismisses them from consideration.[7] What I wish to argue here is, firstly, that every source from these critical decades, whether authentic or inauthentic, is of equal significance. It is my contention that, when we take the trouble to tease out on which side of the conflict a particular work or the witnesses it utilised fall, a completely different view of the role played in events by these documents comes to light. Secondly, I would argue that it is critical that we recognise that the conflict between John's supporters and his enemies continued

4 *Johannes Chrysostomus in Konstantinopel (398–404). Weltsicht und Wirken eines Bischofs in der Hauptstadt des Oströmischen Reiches*, STAC 6 (Tübingen: Mohr Siebeck, 2002).

5 *Oratio funebris in laudem sancti Iohannis Chrysostomi (Ps.-Martyrius Antiochenus, BHG 871, CPG 6517)*, ed. Martin Wallraff, It. trans. Cristina Ricci, Quaderni della Rivista di Bizantinistica 12 (Spoleto: Fondazione Centro Italiano di Studi sull'alto Medioevo, 2007). Eng. trans. by Timothy Barnes and George Bevan, *On the Death of John Chrysostom. A Funerary Speech*, TTH (Liverpool: Liverpool University Press, forthcoming). Chrysostomus Baur, *John Chrysostom and His Time*, trans. Sr. M. Gonzaga, vol. 1 (Westminster, MD: Newman Press, 1959), xxxii–iii, rejected the work as later in date. Its status as the earliest source (dating to late 407) has been accepted by scholars only since the mid 1990s.

6 This is especially the case with the homilies associated with John's first exile (c. Sept. 403), CPG 4396–4399, in regard to which Emilio Bonfiglio, "John Chrysostom's Discourses on his First Exile. Prolegomena to a Critical Edition of the *Sermo antequam iret in exsilium* and of the *Sermo cum iret in exsilium*", unpub. DPhil diss. (Pembroke College, University of Oxford, 2011), has now adduced convincing proof that only the first three paragraphs of CPG 4396 and CPG 4398 are likely to prove genuine. The authenticity of CPG 4396 in its entirety is accepted by Rudolf Brändle, *Johannes Chrysostomus. Bischof–Reformer–Märtyrer* (Stuttgart: Verlag W. Kohlhammer, 1999), 121; and (cautiously) by John N.D. Kelly, *Golden Mouth. The Story of John Chrysostom – Ascetic, Preacher, Bishop* (London: Gerald Duckworth & Co. Ltd., 1995), 230–31. The latter (236–37) also embraces as genuine CPG 4399, as does Tiersch, *Chrysostomus in Konstantinopel*, 354. See also Kelly, *Golden Mouth*, 239–40, re the anti-Eudoxian sermon attributed to John by Socrates, *HE* 6.18.

7 So Baur, *Chrysostom and His Time*, vol. 2, 268, re CPG 4397 and 4529; Tiersch, *Chrysostomus in Konstantinopel*, 307, re CPG 4528.

to engender narratives about the core events of 403 and 404 until at least 418, when John's name was restored to the diptychs in Constantinople by Atticus, and perhaps even as late as 438, when John's status was completely resolved. That is, the conflict does not conclude with John's death, but up to two decades later, with his rehabilitation.[8] His enemies and supporters continue to manoeuvre throughout this period until both are forced to reconcile, by which time the narrative of one side is beginning to emerge as the victor. My final point is that John's deposition constituted the fall from power of a major player in ecclesiastical politics[9] – that is, that contrary to a modern western view of religious conflict in which there is separation of church and state, in late antiquity ecclesiastical leadership was inescapably political. It is thus inevitable that the partisan interests of his supporters and of his political opponents lie behind the narratives that circulated.

## 2 Including the excluded sources

Critical to an assessment of those partisan interests is the identification and restoration as valid historical sources of a number of letters and homilies promulgated under John's name throughout the first five decades of the fifth century. This is not a straightforward task. Issues of date and the question of how one determines that these sources originated from a partisan camp are complicating factors. Further, it may well prove that not all of the ps-chrysostomica that can be dated to this period can be shown to have a political intent. Regardless, the sources in question potentially fall into two categories: works originally authored by John that were intentionally reframed or altered by others;[10] and works that

**8** A similar reading of events is promoted by Peter Van Nuffelen, "Palladius and the Johannite Schism," *JEH* 64 (2013): 1–19.

**9** It is not insignificant that the two modern examples of media manipulation (Watergate and the Children Overboard Affair) occurred in the lead-up to political elections where the parties in power and their leaders perceived themselves as vulnerable and were manoeuvring to retain power. In the case under discussion here we observe media manipulation at a time when a leader and his party were likewise vulnerable to loss of power. The key differences here are that the election to an office of power was not term-limited, but permanent, and that the manipulation was thus initiated not by the incumbent but by the opponent. For the events immediately surrounding John's deposition (403–407), see Tiersch, *Chrysostomus in Konstantinopel*, 327–414.

**10** Labelled by Sever Voicu, "La volontà e il caso: La tipologia dei primi spuri di Crisostomo," in: *Giovanni Crisostomo: Oriente e Occidente tra IV e V secolo*, Studia Ephemeridis Augustinianum 93 (Rome: Institutum Patristicum Augustinianum, 2005), 106, as "spuri 'preterin-

were not authored by John, but deliberately attributed to him at the time.[11] Where political intent can be demonstrated – that is, where it is clear that the motivation for the creation of such works is connected to the events in question – their value as historical sources dramatically changes. No longer in the pursuit of historical reality are all "inauthentic" works casually to be dismissed from consideration. Rather, it can be argued that some, at least, emerge as key pieces of evidence in a struggle by supporters and enemies alike to control the conflict narrative.

As already mentioned, a cluster of four homilies attributed to the period of John's first exile (CPG 4396–4399), considered a key historical source if authentic, has attracted considerable discussion.[12] The recent work of Emilio Bonfiglio, which minutely examines the manuscript tradition of these homilies and, in particular, previously ignored early translations, leads to the definitive conclusion that paragraphs 4–5 of CPG 4396 (*Sermo antequam iret in exsilium*) are not original, and the strong suspicion that neither CPG 4397 (*Sermo cum iret in exsilium*) nor CPG 4399 (*Sermo post reditum a priore exsilio* 2) is authentic.[13] Bonfiglio was further able to show that in the case of CPG 4397, existing Armenian and Syriac translations witness a different Greek text to that which has survived, of which the present Greek text is a rearrangement, and, more significantly, that both translations are likely to have been produced in the fifth century.[14] That is, it is not unreasonable to attribute the Greek text that both the Armenian and Syriac versions translate to the critical time period. Paragraphs 4–5 of CPG 4396, on the other hand, are unattested before the seventh century,[15] although they bear some relationship to CPG 4397 and may thus either constitute a reworking of the surviving Greek version of CPG 4397 by the author of the *Vita* attributed to George of

tenzionali'." Cf. Id., "L'immagine di Crisostomo negli spuri," in: *Chrysostomosbilder*, 64 ("rescritture antiche [falsi preterintenzionali]").

**11** Labelled by Voicu, "La volontà," 102, as "spuri 'intenzionali';" Id., "L'immagine," 64–65 ("falsi 'intenzionali' legati a Crisostomo").

**12** See n. 6 above; Sever Voicu, "La volontà," 102–106; and Bonfiglio, "Prolegomena," 24–28.

**13** Bonfiglio, "Prolegomena," 227–31, and Id., "[CPG 4396–9]: The Problem of their Authenticity in the Light of the Ancient Armenian, Syriac and Latin Translations", informal talk, Byzantine Studies, Dumbarton Oaks, Georgetown, 23 March 2010; contra Voicu, op. cit., who considers all four homilies to fall into the category of "spuri 'intenzionali'."

**14** Bonfiglio, "Prolegomena," 63–64 and 226–27.

**15** The traditional date of the *Vita Iohannis Chrysostomi* by "George of Alexandria," in which these paragraphs for the first time appear. See, however, Chrysostomus Baur, "Georgius Alexandrinus," *BZ* 27 (1927): 1–16, who argues that the *Vita* draws on the seventh-century *Vita* by Theodore of Trimethis and can only have been produced in the last decades of the seventh century or first three of the eighth.

Alexandria or of the text transmitted by the Syriac and Armenian translations.[16] This complicates their value as an historical source, but does not, as we will see shortly, entirely dismiss them from consideration.

The second of three surviving recensions of a letter attributed to John (*Ep.* 1 [125] *ad Cyriacum* β) bears a clear relationship to CPG 4397 and, more tangentially, para. 4–5 of CPG 4396. A compilation of genuine and additional material (much of the latter hostile towards the empress Eudoxia and Bishop Arsacius, John's successor), it falls into the first of the two categories mentioned above.[17] Its editor assigns it to the narrow window Oct. 404–11 Nov. 405, labels it an intentional falsification, and firmly attributes it to the anti-Johannite camp.[18] Such a well-defined date may be overly confident, and one cannot be certain as to whether there is a degree of dependency between CPG 4397 and *Ep.* 1 *ad Cyriacum* β or they independently draw upon the same sources, but the fact remains that the similarities are sufficiently striking in regard to certain of the material concerning Eudoxia and the accusations against which John is construed as defending himself to suspect that both, at least, emerge from the same camp.[19] That the common point between all three (CPG 4397, the letter,

16 Bonfiglio, "Prolegomena," 225.

17 For a summary of the contents see Panagiotos Nikolopoulos, "Les lettres inauthentiques de saint Jean Chrysostome," in: *SYMPOSION. Studies on St. John Chrysostom* (Thessaloniki: Hidruma Paterikon Meleton, 1973), 126; and Id., *Αἱ εἰς τὸν Ἰωάννην τὸν Χρυσόστομον ἐσφαλμένως ἀποδιδόμεναι ἐπιστολαί* (Athens: Typographeion Georgiou K. Tsiberiotou, 1973), 528. The genuine material derives from Jn Chrys., *epp.* 1 and 3 *ad Olymp.* (CPG 4405) and the treatise *Contra eos qui subintroductas habent virgines* (CPG 4311).

18 Nikolopoulos, *Ἐσφαλμένως ἀποδιδόμεναι ἐπιστολαί*, 528 (edition at 393–411).

19 Cf. *Sermo cum iret* 2 (ed. Bonfiglio, "Prolegomena," 102–103: Λέγουσι δέ μοι· Ὅτι ἔφαγες καὶ ἔπιες καὶ ἐβάπτισας. Εἰ ἐποίησα τοῦτο, ἀνάθεμά μοι ἔστω· μὴ ἀριθμηθείην εἰς ῥίζας ἐπισκόπων, μὴ γένωμαι μετὰ ἀγγέλων, μὴ ἀρέσω τῷ Θεῷ....Καθελέτωσαν καὶ Παῦλον τὸν ἀπόστολον, ὅτι μετὰ τὸ δεῖπνον τῷ δεσμοφύλακι τὸ βάπτισμα ἐχαρίσατο. Καθελέτωσαν καὶ αὐτὸν τὸν Κύριον, ὅτι μετὰ τὸ δεῖπνον τὴν κοινωνίαν τοῖς μαθηταῖς ἐχαρίσατο.) and *Ep.* 1 *ad Cyr.* β 5 (ed. Nikolopoulos, 400–401: Πολλὰ κατ' ἐμοῦ ἐσκευάσαντο καὶ λέγουσιν ὅτι τινὰς ἐκοινώνησα μετὰ τὸ φαγεῖν αὐτούς. Εἰ μὲν τοῦτο ἐποίησα, ἐξαλειφθείη τὸ ὄνομά μου ἐκ τῆς βίβλου τῶν ἐπισκόπων καὶ μὴ ἐγγραφείη ἐν τῇ βίβλῳ τῆς ὀρθοδόξου πίστεως...καθελέτωσαν τὸν Παῦλον, ὃς μετὰ τὸ δειπνῆσαι ὁλόκληρον τὸν οἶκον ἐβάπτισε. Καθελέτωσαν καὶ αὐτὸν τὸν Κύριον, ὃς μετὰ τὸ δειπνῆσαι τοῖς ἀποστόλοις τὴν κοινωνίαν ἔδωκε.); *Sermo cum iret* 8 (Bonfiglio, 104–105: Ἐὰν οὖν ἐξορίσωσί με, τὸν Ἠλίαν μιμοῦμαι. Ἐὰν εἰς βόρβορον βάλωσι, τὸν Ἱερεμίαν. Ἐὰν εἰς θάλατταν, τὸν σύνδουλόν μου καὶ προφήτην Ἰωνᾶν. Ἐὰν εἰς λάκκον, τὸν Δανιήλ. Ἐὰν λιθάσωσι, Στέφανον. Ἐὰν ἀποκεφαλίσωσι, Ἰωάννην. Ἐὰν πρίσωσι, τὸν Ἠσαΐαν·) and *Ep.* 1 *ad Cyr.* β 4 (Nikolopoulos, 399–400: εἴ με βούλεται ἡ βασίλισσα ἐξορίσαι, ἐξορίσει με...Εἴ με βούλεται πρίσαι, πρίσει με· τὸν Ἠσαΐαν ἔχω ὑπογραμμόν. Εἴ με θέλει εἰς τὸ πέλαγος ἀκοντίσαι, τὸν Ἰωνᾶν ὑπομιμνήσκομαι. Εἴ με θέλει εἰς κάμινον ἐμβαλεῖν, τοὺς τρεῖς παῖδας ἔχω τοῦτο πεπονθότας. Εἴ με θέλει τοῖς θηρίοις βαλεῖν, ἔχω τὸν Δανιὴλ ἐν τοῖς λέουσι βεβλημένον. Εἰ θέλει με λιθάσαι,

and CPG 4396 para. 4–5) is John's defence against the allegation (in CPG 4397 and 4396) that he "ate and baptised" (in *Ep.* 1 *ad Cyr.* β, it appears as the variant "ate and shared the eucharist"), with other elements shared in common between CPG 4397 and the letter, on the one hand, and CPG 4397 and 4396 para. 4–5, on the other,[20] may perhaps support an alternative possibility – namely that, rather than a later reworking by "George of Alexandria," para. 4–5 of CPG 4396 derive directly from earlier fabricated material adopted by that author from an archived corpus.

A completely different body of ps-chrysostomic material that circulated at this time is witnessed to in part by the so-called Collection of 38 Latin Homilies and by Augustine's *Contra Iulianum opus imperfectum* (CPL 351). The latter work, which cites a number of "Chrysostom" homilies to which Augustine had access in Latin translation via the Collection, supplies for at least certain versions of the Collection a *terminus ante quem* of c. 420 CE.[21] Of significance to the discussion here is the presence in Latin translation of *In pentecosten* (CPG 4536),[22] one of a cluster of five or so homilies that appear to combine genuine and inauthentic material, promulgated under John's name early in the fifth century.[23] To these can be added a further forty-six non-heterodox category 2 homilies that Sever Voicu identifies as circulating under John's name in the first decades of the

λιθάσῃ με· Στέφανον ἔχω τὸν πρωτομάρτυρα. Εἰ θέλει τὴν κεφαλήν μου λαβεῖν, λάβῃ· ἔχω τὸν Ἰωάννην.).

**20** Particularly the relationship between the reference to Herodias dancing in both CPG 4396 para. 4 and CPG 4397 and in the homily *In decollationem s. Iohannis* (CPG 4570), which by 417 was circulating under John's name. On this point see Sever Voicu, "'Furono chiamati giovanniti...': Un'ipotesi sulla nascita del corpus pseudocrisostomico," in: *Philomathestatos. Studies in Greek and Byzantine Texts Presented to Jacques Noret for His Sixty-Fifth Birthday*, eds. Bart Janssens, B. Roosen, and Peter Van Deun (Leuven: Peeters, 2004), 706.

**21** See PL 44.685–86, discussed by Bonfiglio, "Prolegomena," 35–37. Regarding the Collection see Wolfgang Wenk, *Zur Sammlung der 38 Homilien des Chrysostomus Latinus (mit Edition der Nr. 6, 8, 27, 32 und 33)* (Wien: Verlag der Österreichischen Akademie der Wissenschaften, 1988), esp. 9–13 (list of genuine homilies) and 14–21 (list of spuria); and Sever Voicu, "Le prime traduzioni latine di Crisostomo," in: *Cristianesimo Latino e cultura Greca sino al sec. IV. – XXI. Incontro di studiosi dell'antichità cristiana, Roma, 7–9 maggio 1992* (Rome: Institutum Patristicum Augustinianum, 1993), 397–415.

**22** See Sever Voicu, "'In Pentecosten sermo' 1 (PG 52,803–808; CPG 4536): il problema dell'autenticità," in: *"Historiam perscrutari". Miscellanea di studi offerti al prof. O. Pasquato*, ed. Mario Maritano, Biblioteca di Scienze Religiose 180 (Rome: Ateneo Salesiano, 2002), 849–61, esp. 853 regarding the parallels between this homily and another homily of partial/entirely dubious authenticity, *In illud: Vidi dom. hom.* 4 (CPG 4417.4).

**23** Voicu, "La volontà," 107–12 (CPG 4333.8, 4364, 4528, 4529, 4536).

fifth century.[24] In asking why so many works of other "orthodox" authors were circulating at this time under John's name,[25] Voicu concludes that the reason was political and that they are the product of members of the Johannite party.[26] The cluster of category 1 homilies, in particular, he believes to have emerged from within the Johannite camp in the period prior to John's death (July 404-Sept. 407), while there was still hope that he would achieve rehabilitation.[27]

To the traditionally accepted "legitimate" historical sources the works identified here contribute a substantial body of previously excluded material with the potential to enhance our understanding of events, at least in regard to the jockeying that took place on both sides to secure for each party and their leaders a successful outcome. In a society without newspapers, television, online media, email, twitter and facebook, letters and sermons were important communication media.[28] As the following two sections will show, like contemporary media they could prove to be of especial utility when slanted by partisan interests for the manipulation of public perception.

---

**24** See Voicu, "'Furono chiamati giovanniti...'."

**25** The orthodoxy of the authors raises a question mark, since a predominant reason for the false attribution of original material by one author to a second "orthodox" author is to ensure the survival of heterodox content. Regarding the number of authors in question, see Sever Voicu, "Tracce origeniane in uno pseudocrisostomo cappadoce," in: *Origene e l'alessandrinismo cappadoce (III–IV secolo). Atti del V Convegno del Gruppo Italiano di ricerca su "Origene e la tradizione alessandrina" (Bari, 20–22 settembre 2000)*, eds. Mario Girardi and Marcello Marin (Bari: Edipuglia, 2002), 333–46, who attributes a group of thirty-seven homilies to an author of Cappadocian formation, probably active in Constantinople (for the list see 342–44). For another three authors (two Antiochene, one Constantinopolitan of Antiochene formation), see Voicu, "'Furono chiamati giovanniti...'," 704–705.

**26** Voicu, "'Furono chiamati giovanniti...'," 707–708, where he attributes to the Johannites production of the initial (pre-431) nucleus of ps-chysostomica.

**27** Voicu, "La volontà," 115.

**28** On the importance of letters see Pauline Allen and Bronwen Neil, *Crisis Management in Late Antiquity (410–590 CE)* (Leiden: Brill, forthcoming), esp. chapter 1. Regarding the importance of preaching to the maintenance of charismatic authority and for crisis management see Wendy Mayer, "At Constantinople, how often did John Chrysostom Preach? Addressing Assumptions about the Workload of a Bishop," *Sacris Erudiri* 40 (2001): 83–105; and Ead., "John Chrysostom as Crisis Manager: The Years in Constantinople," in: *Ancient Jewish and Christian Texts as Crisis Management Literature: Thematic Studies from the Centre for Early Christian Studies*, eds. David Sim and Pauline Allen, LNTS 445 (London: T&T Clark, 2012), 136–42.

## 3 Media, politics, and wedge issues

In the Children Overboard Affair the false claims made by the Liberal–National Party that illegal immigrants arriving by boat had thrown their children overboard swiftly gained traction within Australian public perception and were instrumental in helping them to win a marginal federal election precisely because the LNP had latched onto a wedge issue which allowed them to portray the Labour Party as divided. By definition a wedge issue is "a social issue, often of a divisive or controversial nature, which splits apart a population or political group."[29] Wedge issues tend to have cultural or populist themes like race, border and gun control, crime or sexuality. Within the modern discipline of political science the definition of wedge issue is usually specific to election campaigns, where such issues are used to exploit tension within a targeted population, namely the opposition party and its supporters, and to mobilise voting for one's own party. This is achieved by framing the issue as a threat.[30] However, the explicit association between an election and the successful exploitation of a wedge issue can be more fluid. This is seen in the case of the economic threat of the "fiscal cliff" promulgated by the Republican Party in the lead-up to the November 2012 election in the United States. By intentionally delaying the vote until two months after the election, during which time key representatives of the Republican position publicly discredited themselves, it was not, as originally intended, Democratic, but Republican support that was split.

While by modern definition this political tactic cannot explicitly be said to have been exploited by the Johannite and anti-Johannite parties in the case at hand,[31] it provides an initial framework within which the intended purpose of these texts can be viewed. This is particularly the case when we consider that

---

**29** See "Wedge Issue," Wikipedia (en.wikipedia.org/wiki/Wedge_issue; accessed 4 Sept. 2012), where the Tampa Incident, of which the Children Overboard Affair constituted a part, is cited as a case study.

**30** See D. Sunshine Hillygus and Todd G. Shields, *The Persuadable Voter: Wedge Issues in Presidential Campaigns* (Princeton, NJ: Princeton University Press, 2008).

**31** I.e., there is no association with a political election. There are significant differences, however, between modern-western and late-antique political systems, which raises the suspicion that the modern political-science definition is too restrictive. The tactics used by both parties are closely aligned with political power-play, in this case jockeying between the sees of Alexandria and Constantinople for access to imperial favour. See Susanna Elm, "The Dog that did not Bark. Doctrine and Patriarchal Authority in the Conflict between Theophilus of Alexandria and John Chrysostom of Constantinople," in: *Christian Origins. Theology, Rhetoric and Community*, eds. Lewis Ayres and Gareth Jones (London: Routledge, 1998), 66–93. For further similarities in the conditions that governed events see n. 9 above.

there survive hints of the media promulgation in early fifth-century Constantinople of similarly emotive "threats" with the potential to polarise public opinion and mobilise a shift in the support base of the key players involved. These hints are to be found in two "historical" sources, Palladius and Socrates, the first a supporter (Johannite) and intimate of John,[32] the second an ecclesiastical historian writing three to four decades after the events, who importantly utilises, among others, archived documents that constitute hostile (anti-Johannite) witnesses.[33] Both focus at one point or another on the relationship between bishop and empress and the role played by each in John's fall from power. In *Dialogue* 6 Palladius reports that John's enemies "wove false accusations against him by converting certain of his homilies into rash statements against the empress and other members of the imperial court."[34] That John's enemies were deliberately manipulating the reception of his genuine works by misrepresenting them to key parties, the empress Eudoxia in particular, is suggested by Socrates in one instance, and confirmed in another. He reports that the sermon John preached at the time of the consul–eunuch Eutropius' deposition, a genuine work that constitutes a spectacular example of *parrhesia* (frank speech),[35] was received as lacking in compassion and as inappropriately accusatory.[36] On reading this text it is easy to see how the pastoral intent could be suppressed in the reporting and the opening sections read as an insensitive attack on the victim.[37] If John's rhetorical boldness in this instance could be twisted by his detractors to incite negative opinion, one can further see how sermons in which he attacked the vices of women could readily have been misreported verbally to Eudoxia and these negative reports embraced by senatorial women already hostile towards him.[38]

---

**32** See Demetrios Katos, *Palladius of Helenopolis: The Origenist Advocate* (Oxford: Oxford University Press, 2011), 26–97; and Van Nuffelen, "Palladius."

**33** See Mayer, "The Making of a Saint," 40–44.

**34** *Palladios. Dialogue sur la vie de Jean Chrysostome*, eds. Anne-Marie Malingrey and Philippe Leclercq, SC 341, Paris: Éditions du Cerf, 1988, 126.2–7.

**35** See Chrys., *In Eutropium* (CPG 4392; PG 52.391–96).

**36** Socr., *HE* 6.5.2–6 (ed. Günther C. Hansen, GCS NF 1.316–17).

**37** The bulk of the first half of the homily (PG 52.391–93) constitutes a rhetorical tour de force on the contrast between Eutropius' former power and his current circumstances, in which John only twice briefly draws the listener's attention to the purpose behind this (not to kick someone who's down, but to secure the salvation of the observers).

**38** See Soc., *HE* 6.15.2–4 (GCS NF 1.336); Soz., *HE* 8.16.1 (eds. Joseph Bidez and Günther C. Hansen, FChr 73/4.1006), where it is alleged that on Epiphanius' departure John preached a general sermon aimed at women's faults, which was received by the majority as alluding to the emperor's wife. John's enemies bring it to the attention of Eudoxia, who is enraged. Whether one

In fact, we have concrete evidence of a deliberate campaign – either to undermine public approval of John and to cut off imperial support or to demonise the empress Eudoxia and paint her as the villain in the affair – that resulted in the promulgation of inauthentic documents presenting him as publicly attacking or rebuking the empress. This is found in Socrates' famous citation from the archives of the opening lines of what he believed to be a genuine sermon: "Again Herodias rages, again she dances, again she seeks the head of John on a plate".[39] The sermon that preserves these opening lines is inauthentic,[40] as are all other hostile constructions of Eudoxia within the Chrysostomic corpus. So in *Sermo cum iret in exsilium* (CPG 4397) John explicitly crticises the empress, calling her Herodias, Jezebel, the Egyptian whore (i.e., Potiphar's wife), and an enemy of the church.[41] In *Ep.* 1 *ad Cyriacum* β the empress is explicitly said to be the instigator of John's exile,[42] and called an adulteress for having placed Arsacius on the episcopal throne while John is still alive.[43] In the somewhat confused paragraphs 4–5 of CPG 4396, although not explicitly mentioned, the person of the empress is again alluded to via adduction of the examples of Jezebel and Herodias, the latter of whom, while dancing, is said to again seek the head of John.[44]

The demonisation of Eudoxia in these texts has been read by modern scholars as a tactic employed on both sides – as a fabrication of John's supporters seeking a scapegoat for his deposition in the case of the homilies *In decollationem* and CPG 4396–97,[45] and in the case of *Ep.* 1 *ad Cyriacum* β as a fabrication of his enemies seeking to have John brought up on a charge of treason.[46] That the latter tactic was real and enjoyed some success, in that John's alleged slander of the empress as Jezebel did in fact lead to charges of treason being brought, is

believes Socrates or Sozomen's slant on what occurred, it is clear that those hostile to John were by this stage primed to read anti-Eudoxian sentiments into his public statements.

**39** Socr., *HE* 6.18.5 (GCS NF 1.341); cf. Soz., *HE* 8.20.3 (FChr 73/4.1020).

**40** *In decollationem s. Iohannis* (CPG 4570). The opening statement is immediately followed by the claim that again Jezebel is roaming around seeking to snatch Naboth's vineyard (PG 59.485.1–5), another key image in the anti-Eudoxian rhetoric.

**41** Ed. Bonfiglio, 104.45–47 and 105.54–60 (cf. 106.76–79, where she is called "lawless and abominable" and "the new Jezebel").

**42** Ed. Nikolopoulos, 399.35–36; although cf. 401.60–62, where those who are said to have exiled John are referenced in the plural and described as powerful.

**43** Ed. Nikolopoulos, 409.136–40.

**44** *Sermo antequam iret in exsilium* (PG 52.431.31–432.8).

**45** Voicu, "'Furono chiamati giovanniti...'," 706.

**46** Nikolopoulos, *Ἐσφαλμένως ἀποδιδόμεναι ἐπιστολαί*, 528.

indicated by Palladius at the end of *Dial.* 8.[47] Lest we are tempted to think that Voicu is in error, however, and this framing was exclusively employed to undermine John by the anti-Johannite camp, Eudoxia is similarly demonised and blamed as one of two chief instigators of John's deposition by the strongly partisan ps-Martyrius,[48] who produced his funeral oration in the months immediately following John's death (c. Nov. 407).[49] To place this in perspective, the view he promulgates is in distinct contrast to that of the other well-known supporter, Palladius, who, when he writes his legal defence of John a year or more later is restrained in his references to the empress,[50] attributing hostility instead to a cabal of bishops, monks, and senatorial women.[51] To add to the construction of Eudoxia as Jezebel, deriving from the period prior to 438,[52] in the Greek recension of the *Vita Epiphanii* we find the first instance of a more developed narrative based on this image, in which Eudoxia, like the biblical Jezebel, is alleged to have literally misappropriated the vineyard of a Constantinopolitan widow.[53] In this case, it is difficult to determine whether the author adopted or himself embellished a narrative attributable to hostile or favourable witnesses. Whether vilification of Eudoxia is a product of the Johannite or anti-Johannite camp or both, the suspicion that the empress became as much a victim of the manipulation of circulating narratives as John himself is unavoidable. This is especially the case when we take into account Roland Delamire's conclusion, on the basis of anti-Johannite legislation late in 404, that Eudoxia must to some degree have held anti-Johannite interests in check.[54] The ramping up of hostilities against John's supporters following her death betrays these narratives as inimical to her and skewed, making it clear that she cannot have been the instigator of hostilities or personally as hostile towards John as the various sources portray. Most importantly, when we read all of these documents as part of the intentional manipulation by parties on both sides of the conflict of the perception of both John and Eudoxia by the pub-

**47** SC 341.178.240 – 247, where formal affidavits are mentioned.

**48** See *Or. funeb.* 36 (explicit ref. to Jezebel and Naboth), 87 and 120 – 21 (ed. Wallraff, 88, 142, 174 – 76).

**49** Regarding the date see Wallraff, ed., *Oratio funebris*, 14.

**50** Regarding the date see now Van Nuffelen, "Palladius," 14 – 19, who argues for a range between late 408/9 and 418 CE.

**51** *Dial.* 4 (SC 341.94).

**52** On the date of this episode see Claudia Rapp, "The *Vita* of Epiphanius of Salamis – An Historical and Literary Study," unpub. DPhil. diss., 2 vols. (University of Oxford, 1991), 208 – 10.

**53** *V. Epiph.* 61 (*Epiphanii episcopi Constantiae opera*, ed. Wilhelm Dindorf, Bibliotheca Patrum Graecorum et Latinorum, Lipsiae: T.G. Weigel, 1859, vol. 1, 67 – 69 = PG 41.101 – 103).

**54** Roland Delmaire, "Les 'lettres d'exil' de Jean Chrysostome. études de chronologie et de prosopographie," *Recherches augustiniennes* 25 (1991): 71 – 180 at 83.

lic, by those in power, and by the opposing side, the historical truth becomes increasingly elusive and both emerge as the distorted projections of party-political media spin.

This leads to the question: what was the purpose of that spin? How likely are the demonisation of the empress as the arch-villain, on the one hand, and the portrayal of John as treasonous, on the other, to have played successfully on public fears? It may be that, for the anti-Johannites, in a move analogous to the exploitation by the Republican Party of the strongly emotive "patriotism" frame in the United States in the period following the attack on the twin towers of the Trade Center in New York on 11 September 2001 (9/11), portraying John as treasonous was seen as useful for aggravating public hostility and alienating the general populace, driving a wedge between John and the emperor and his court, on the one hand, and between John and popular support, on the other. For the Johannites, portrayal of the empress as the arch-villain (and, by extension, John as her innocent victim) may have been seen as useful for splintering at a single stroke popular support for both imperial authority and the anti-Johannite party – the latter effected via the intimate connection this spin constructed between the empress and its perceived leader, Bishop Theophilus.[55] Even if we cannot reliably assess the effect of these tactics, precisely because, as is now clear, all of our sources for these events are biased and their impact can only with difficulty be inferred, we nonetheless observe here at least some degree of resemblance to the modern media exploitation of wedge issues for political purposes.

It may be, however, that a more useful framework for exploring the intended purpose of these texts is offered by the recent application to political analysis of cognitive psychology. Demonisation and false polarisation of the opposition, for instance, such as we observe here, are documented relationship biases that can be shown to play a significant role in the escalation and/or perpetuation of conflict.[56]

---

**55** Eudoxia and Theophilus are explicitly linked in the earliest Johannite source, ps-Martyrius. See *Or. funeb.* 36 (ed. Wallraff, 88). Just as Eudoxia is Jezebel and Herodias, Theophilus is the Egyptian Pharaoh, likewise hostile to John, in *Antequam iret in exs.* (ed. Bonfiglio, 104.37–41).
**56** See Ifat Maoz, "Social-Cognitive Mechanisms in Reconciliation," in: *From Conflict Resolution to Reconciliation*, ed. Yaacov Bar-Siman-Tov (Oxford: Oxford University Press, 2004), 225–237, esp. 230 and 234. On the utility of social psychology for the analysis of religion, see Joanna Collicutt, "Bringing the Academic Discipline of Psychology to Bear on the Study of the Bible," *JTS* n.s. 63 (2012): 1–48 at 28–29.

## 4 Cognitive frames and conceptual metaphors

Sever Voicu identifies a cluster of five homilies that he describes as mosaic in character – that is, they contain what can be identified as genuine material mixed with material that is inauthentic.[57] To these can be added a sixth homily, whose authenticity has been challenged and whose opening paragraphs bear thematic and stylistic similarities to one of the five mixed homilies.[58] On the surface, none of these six refers to the conflict in question, but I would like to expand on Voicu's idea that these homilies, and in particular *In pentecosten sermo* 1 (CPG 4536), which promotes John as in good standing with the emperor, may have played a role.[59] Here I turn to George Lakoff's theory of cognitive framing,[60] a theory currently used by him to explain the tactics used by political and religious conservatives in the United States. As Lakoff states, his theory is "based on results from the cognitive and brain sciences on how reason about social and political issues really works – primarily in terms of morally-based frames, metaphors, and narratives, and only secondarily, if at all, in terms of policy, facts, and logic."[61] This is because morality and politics are embodied ideas that operate not at the rational, but at the subconscious level.[62] Conservative intimidation by framing, he goes on to argue,

57 See n. 23.

58 *In illud. Vidi dom. hom.* 4 (CPG 4417.4). Its authenticity has been defended by Pierre Augustin, "La pérennité de l'Église selon Jean Chrysostome et l'authenticité de la IV^e^ Homélie *Sur Ozias*," *Recherches augustiniennes* 28 (1995): 95–144; but see Voicu, "'In Pentecosten'," 853, and Id., "La volontà," 106.

59 See Voicu, "'Furono chiamati giovanniti...'," 707.

60 The broader theory from which it derives is Conceptual Metaphor Theory (CMT), first outlined in George Lakoff and Mark Johnson, *Metaphors We Live By* (Chicago–London: University of Chicago Press, 1980). For an assessment of current developments in the field, see Raymond W. Gibbs Jr, "Evaluating Conceptual Metaphor Theory," *Discourse Processes* 48/8 (2011): 529–62. For the utility of its application to the study of religion and morality, see Omar Sultan Haque, "Moral Creationism: The Science of Morality and the Mutiny of Romantic Relativism," *Journal of Cognition and Culture* 11/1 (2011): 151–87.

61 Used by Lakoff to describe the theory behind his recent books in "The Use of 9/11 to Consolidate Conservative Power: Intimidation via Framing," *Huffington Post* (11 Sept. 2011) at www.huffingtonpost.com/george-lakoff/the-use-of-911-to-consoli_b_955954.html (accessed 6 Sept. 2012). Prior to applying CMT to politics Lakoff was concerned primarily with its application in the fields of cognitive science, philosophy and linguistics. See Id., *Moral Politics: How Liberals and Conservatives Think* (2nd ed.; Chicago: The University of Chicago Press, 2002), 11.

62 Id., *The Political Mind: Why You Can't Understand 21st-Century American Politics with an 18th-Century Brain* (New York: Viking, 2008), 10–11.

> does not use violence. It uses media. When conservatives, using their moral system, are able to frame the main values that define public discourse, the media follows suit, because that is how 'mainstream' public discourse has been defined. The media, encountering more conservative language, picks up on that language and uses it. Since conservative language evokes conservative frames and values, which are carried with it, the media (liberal or not) winds up helping conservatives. Even arguing against conservatives, liberal pundits in the media first quote what they say. Liberals in the media help the conservatives by quoting their language, even to argue against it.[63]

In the case of the Johannite–anti-Johannite conflict, Lakoff would point out that it doesn't matter who actually claimed that John framed Eudoxia as Jezebel or Herodias, and who denied the claims,[64] the framing and language stick;[65] once they started to circulate, because of the implicit moral values (Jezebel and Herodias were already framed in both Hebrew and Christian scripture as enemies of the true religion) the point of view would quickly have become entrenched and almost impossible to defeat. The repeated metaphoric application to John within these same partisan sources of a defined array of Old and New Testament heroes (e.g., Daniel, Elijah, Joseph, John the Baptist) can be viewed as part of this same successful discourse.[66]

A not unrelated moral framework, which is likely to have enjoyed success (and indeed underwrote the eventually triumphant narrative of the Johannite party, with its construction of John as martyr and saint),[67] lies with the framing by the Johannite party of themselves as the persecuted, yet unassailable, orthodox church.[68] For much of *In pentecosten sermo* 1 and the opening paragraphs of *In illud: Vidi dominum hom.* 4 this narrative dominates. Each frames the dis-

63 Lakoff, "Use of 9/11."

64 See Id., *Don't Think of an Elephant! Know your Values and Frame the Debate* (White River Junction, VT: Chelsea Green Publishing, 2004), 3: "When we negate a frame, we evoke a frame."

65 Ibid., 73: "Frames once entrenched are hard to dispel." On the science behind this, see Id., *The Political Mind*, 24–28, 99–110, and 236–237.

66 See ps.-Chrys., *In decoll. s. Iohannis* (PG 59.486.9–487.20): Daniel, Jonah, Sampson, Elijah, John the Baptist, Adam, David, Solomon, Joseph; *Ep.* 1 *ad Cyr.* β (ed. Nikolopoulos, 399–400): Isaiah, Jonah, Daniel, Stephen, John the Baptist; *Cum iret in exs.* (ed. Bonfiglio, 104.45–105.53): Elijah, John the Baptist, Joseph, Jeremiah, Jonah, Daniel, Stephen, Paul, Isaiah; CPG 4396 para. 4–5 (PG 52.431.31–432.8): Elijah, John the Baptist. One of the simple narratives (a frame-based scenario with extra structure) based on standard metaphors that Lakoff, *The Political Mind*, 22–24, describes is the Rescue narrative, with its variant the Self-Defence narrative, both of which involve Hero, Villain, and Victim. What we observe in these particular ps-Chrysostomic sources is a narrative in which John is the Hero-Victim and Eudoxia the Villain.

67 See Mayer, "The Making of a Saint."

68 Lakoff, *Moral Politics*, 71–76 and 100, characterises this as the metaphor of "moral strength."

course slightly differently but shares language in common. The eleven apostles, sans Judas, are sheep circled by wolves,[69] echoing John's own language when talking about the heterodox-embattled church;[70] the church is attacked, but never defeated;[71] it has been attacked by emperors, whose names have been forgotten, while the church surpasses the heavens.[72] Matt 25:34: "Heaven and earth shall pass away, but my words shall not pass away" is cited in both.[73] Additionally, in *In pentecosten sermo* 1 the dominical assertion "You are Peter and on this rock I build my church" is exegeted at length and becomes a persistent refrain.[74] Significantly, we find this same assertion made by John himself at a time of crisis in the opening, probably genuine paragraphs of *De capto Eutropio* (CPG 4528).[75] There, as I have argued, he deliberately invokes this scriptural mandate to assert his episcopal authority at a time when it was under threat.[76] More subtle, perhaps, is the adduction in *In illud: Vidi dom. hom.* 4 of the exemplum of Herod and John the Baptist,[77] and in *In pentecosten sermo* 1 the claim that neither exile nor martyrdom are anything to fear.[78] There are a lot of question marks

---

**69** *In pent. sermo* 1 (PG 52.805.40 – 66; for the number eleven, 806.43 – 45); *In illud: Vidi dom. hom.* 4 (*Jean Chrysostome. Homélies sur Ozias (In illud, Vidi Dominum)*, ed. Jean Dumortier, SC 277, Paris: Éditions du Cerf, 1981, 144.12 – 20). Cf. *Ep.* 1 *ad Cyr.* β (ed. Nikopolopoulos, 409.136 – 37): Arsacius is a wolf in sheep's clothing; and *De s. Phoca* (PG 50.702.57 – 59): if a heretic fox enters the church, John converts it into a sheep; if a wolf, into a lamb. On the location of the latter homily among the "mosaic" ps-chrysostomica that emerge in this period, see Voicu, "La volontà," 108 – 109 (in large part authentic, but reworked).

**70** E.g., Chrys., *Contra anomoeos hom.* 11 (*Jean Chrysostome. Sur l'égalité du père et du fils. Contre les Anoméens homélies VII-XII*, ed. Anne-Marie Malingrey, SC 396, Paris: Éditions du Cerf, 1994, 288.18 – 27); *Adv. Iud. hom.* 4 (PG 48.871.8 – 11 ab imo); and esp. *In Matt. hom.* 33/34 (PG 57.389.8 – 45).

**71** *In pent. sermo* 1 (PG 52.806.27 – 42); *In illud: Vidi dom. hom.* 4 (SC 277.144.13 – 21).

**72** *In pent. sermo* 1 (PG 52.808.8 – 10): Claudius, Augustus, Nero, Tiberius; *In illud: Vidi dom. hom.* 4 (SC 277.142.4 – 144.9): Augustus, Tiberius, Gaius, Claudius, Nero. Cf. *Contra Iudaeos et gentiles quod Christus sit Deus* (CPG 4326; PG 48.833), which Augustin, "La pérennité," 97, believes to be authentic, but which Voicu, "La volontà," 106, locates in the same category of ps-chrysostomica as *In illud: Vidi dom. hom.* 4.

**73** *In pent. sermo* 1 (PG 52.806.51 – 53, repeated at 806.62 – 64); *In illud: Vidi dom. hom.* 4 (SC 277.144.25 – 27).

**74** *In pent. sermo* 1 (PG 52.807.13 – 32).

**75** PG 52.397.24 – 26.

**76** Mayer, "Chrysostom as Crisis Manager," 138.

**77** SC 277.138.28 – 30. This may have been sufficient in itself to evoke the Herodias frame.

**78** *In pent. sermo* 1 (PG 52.805.77 – 806.5). Significantly the same scriptural citation in response to exile (LXX Ps 23:1) is adduced in *Ep.* 1 *ad Cyr.* β (ed. Nikolopoulos, 399.36 – 37: εἴ με βούλεται ἡ βασίλισσα ἐξορίσαι, ἐξορίσει με· τοῦ Κυρίου ἡ γῆ καὶ τὸ πλήρωμα αὐτῆς); cf. PG 52.805.77 – 78: Ἀλλ' ἐξορίζει σέ τις; Τοῦ Κυρίου ἡ γῆ, καὶ τὸ πλήρωμα αὐτῆς).

that attach to this argument, but what I would like to suggest is that in these homilies promulgated under John's name subjects that are superficially innocuous – the historic persecution of the apostles and of the Christian church – take on contemporary significance and are intentionally adduced to frame the Johannite cause as upholding the one true faith in a conflict in which, in objective terms, orthodoxy is not in dispute.[79] That both sermons are products of the Johannite camp is supported, on the one hand, by the opening paragraph of *In illud: Vidi dominum hom.* 4, with its exaggerated praise of the faithful Constantinopolitan laity,[80] and on the other, by the concluding statements of *In pentecosten sermo* 1, in which the piety of the current emperor Arcadius is highlighted.[81] One point on which the sources all agree is that at Constantinople John enjoyed a large popular support base,[82] while as Voicu has already pointed out in the second case, exempting Arcadius from criticism as a persecutor of the church was critical to the Johannite cause, if they wished to uphold the image of themselves as the persecuted true church, while maintaining that John was innocent of treason.[83]

What this brief analysis of the language of a small number of the category 1 homilies demonstrates is the strong probability that it was not just overt polemic, of the kind explored in section 3, but also superficially ordinary language placed in the mouth of John that played a role in the Johannite–anti-Johannite conflict. In this latter respect, analysis through the mapping of cognitive frames and metaphors of the less than obvious language employed in media engendered by the conflict can be seen also to have utility. As Lakoff himself points out, "wedge issues are stand-ins for the whole of a moral system."[84] Moral sys-

**79** On this latter point see Elm, "The Dog that did not Bark," who defines the conflict as administrative. Objectively, both parties are orthodox and both represent "the one, true church."

**80** SC 277.136–42. Augustin, "La pérennité," 129–37, argues that these paragraphs address the city of Antioch, based on an argument for the homily's authenticity that assumes that, if authentic, its provenance is the same as that of the other five homilies *In illud: Vidi dom.* (CPG 4417). If one assumes, however, that this first part of the homily is a Johannite product of Constantinopolitan milieu, then the necessity that the paragraphs describe Antioch is removed, as are any problems concerning their reference to the city's senate and consuls (Antioch possessed neither).

**81** PG 52.808.24–29.

**82** See his own exaggerated claims in Chrys., *De regressu* 1–10 (CPG 4394; ed. Antoine Wenger, "L'homélie de saint Jean Chrysostome 'à son retour d'Asie'," *REByz* 19 [1961]: 114–18); ps-Mart., *Or. funeb.* 78–80, 111–12 (ed. Wallraff, 130–34, 166–68); Socr., *HE* 6.4.8, 6.16 (GCS NF 1.316, 338–39); Soz., *HE* 8.5.1–2, 8.18, 8.22 (FChr 73/4.972, 1012–16, 1026–28).

**83** Voicu, "'Furono chiamati giovanniti...'," 707; Id., "La volontà," 107–108.

**84** *Don't Think of an Elephant*, 101.

tems (= frames) themselves underlie and are evoked by metaphors, while metaphors can be both consciously and unconsciously employed.[85] What we have touched upon here is only the tip of the iceberg. Only a thorough and systematic analysis of the corpus to which these homilies belong will show how accurate is the suspicion raised here: that the seemingly innocuous language of this particular class of (probably) Johannite products is strategic and that its borrowings from key metaphors that John himself employed were intended to resonate at a subconscious level with its audience.

# 5 Implications

To sum up, what I hope to have shown is that in late antiquity religious conflict on this scale was inescapably political and that in consequence it generated media spin. This finding has both positive and negative consequences. When we view religious conflict in this light, all of the surviving sources, no matter how manipulated, fabricated or seemingly innocuous, take on value, increasing the available pool of historical documents. The problem lies not in "inauthentic" documents themselves, but in how we categorise and approach them. On the negative side, what we gain in sources, and consequently in our understanding of the tactics of the parties engaged in conflict, comes with a price. The more we understand about the manipulation of the narrative of the conflict, the further any attempt to retrieve the historical reality at the centre of the conflict slips from our grasp. It is only when we let go of that desideratum that we can fully value in their own right the sources generated by such conflicts.

In the specific case of the conflict that surrounded the deposition of John Chrysostom, this study opens up new avenues for the investigation of such sources, as well as raising a number of significant questions. Given the nature of the surviving documents generated by this dispute, in our search for fruitful avenues of analysis theoretical approaches from the fields of political science, media/journalism studies, and cognitive psychology offer a natural starting point. In explaining these texts, some approaches will prove more successful than others, although one suspects that cognitive analyses, which have the capacity to explain the connection between thoughtworld/ideology and action (that is, between an idea and its social consequences), may prove particularly effective. Whatever approach is applied, however, needs to address a number of funda-

**85** See ibid., 100 – 101, on the difference between frames that occur normally and the deliberate manipulation of frames (spin and propaganda).

mental questions and associated problems. How can we determine with certainty which side – Johannite or anti-Johannite – produced which document, without succumbing to circularity of argument? This is particularly problematic in the case of the kind of document discussed in section 3, when we consider that the written source is more likely the end product of what may have been a process of accretion, in which verbal slander and rumour circulated and underwent both spontaneous morphing and deliberate shaping progressively.[86] The emergence of the narrative concerning Eudoxia and the widow's vineyard preserved in the *Vita Epiphanii*, for instance, may be indicative of the complexity of such a process. On the other hand, in some cases, as in the documents studied in section 4, the type of manipulation involved can have served only one side in the dispute, while in the case of the sources discussed in section 3 their production could equally have served the interests of either party. In the latter case, who generated the documents may in fact prove to be of less importance than the issue of their impact or how the other side in the conflict exploited the opposition's tactic for their own purposes. These issues in turn raise the questions of breadth of audience, dissemination, and at what phase in the evocation and promulgation of a conceptual frame a particular document was employed. These questions lead to the equally problematic issue, given the nature of our sources, of the precise relationship between the documents that survive and the full range of media and tactics that were employed. The sources mentioned in section 3 above already suggest that in some cases the misinformation was verbal and quite target specific (that is, aimed at women of the court and imperial household who were not present when a particular homily was orally delivered and thus unable to verify the truth of the intentionally reframed report for themselves). The documents that survive are thus not just partisan, but biased at another level, in that they represent only a small number of possible tactics within a much larger media campaign. In fact, the more we consider these sources in this light, the more methodological concerns are raised and the more intriguing these neglected sources become. The implications extend well beyond expanding our understanding of a single early fifth-century religious conflict.

---

**86** I am indebted to fellow Chrysostom scholar, Chris de Wet (University of South Africa), and to my colleague in the Centre for Early Christian Studies, Alan Cadwallader, for raising a number of these issues in their review of this chapter.

Geoffrey D. Dunn

# Zosimus and the Gallic Churches

The Roman empire was never a static entity; its external boundaries changed frequently, as did its internal provincial ones, particularly under Diocletian, when not only were provinces divided, but grouped to form civil dioceses, which later were combined into several praetorian prefectures.[1] Changes did not end with Diocletian. Even within the early fifth-century *Notitia dignitatum* we find continuing modifications.[2]

Christian communities found the imperial provincial pattern a convenient one for structuring the church and determining a hierarchy of responsibilities. We find recognition of this emerging pattern in the canons of the First Council of Nicaea in 325 CE with the acknowledgement of metropolitans, who were to ratify the election of bishops within their province.[3] The hierarchicalisation of the

---

**1** Lactantius, *De mort. pers.* 7.4 (ed. Städele, FChr 43.104–106); Zosimus, *Hist. noua* 2.33 (*Zosime. Histoire nouvelle*, t. 2/1, ed. François Paschoud, Collections des Universités de France, Paris: Les Belles Lettres, 1971, 105–107). See A.H.M. Jones, *The Later Roman Empire 284–602: A Social, Economic, and Administrative Survey* (Oxford: Basil Blackwell, 1964), 42–52, 100–104; Ronald T. Ridley, *Zosimus: New History. A Translation with Commentary*, Byzantina Australiensia 2 (Sydney: Australian Association for Byzantine Studies, 1982), 158–59, n. 77; Stephen Williams, *Diocletian and the Roman Recovery* (New York–London: Routledge, 1985), 102–14; Roger Rees, *Diocletian and the Tetrarchy*, Debates and Documents in Ancient History (Edinburgh: Edinburgh University Press, 2004), 24–36; Bill Leadbetter, *Galerius and the Will of Diocletian*, Roman Imperial Biographies (London–New York: Routledge, 2009), 71–72; Paul Stephenson, *Constantine: Unconquered Emperor, Christian Victor* (London: Quercus, 2009), 236–41; Timothy D. Barnes, *The New Empire of Diocletian and Constantine* (Cambridge, MA–London: Harvard University Press, 1982), 123–74, 209–25; Paul S. Barnwell, *Emperor, Prefects, and Kings: The Roman West, 395–565* (Chapel Hill, NC–London: University of North Carolina Press, 1992), 58–67; Christopher Kelly, "Bureaucracy and Government," in: *The Cambridge Companion to the Age of Constantine*, ed. Noel Lenski (Cambridge: Cambridge University Press, 2006), 183–204; and R. Malcom Errington, *Roman Imperial Policy from Julian to Theodosius* (Chapel Hill, NC: University of North Carolina Press, 2006), 80–87.

**2** F.S. Salisbury, "On the Date of the Notitia Dignitatum," *JRS* 17 (1927): 102–106; Peter Brennan, "The User's Guide to the *Notitia Dignitatum:* The Case of the *Dux Armeniae* (*ND Or.* 38)," *Antichthon* 32 (1998): 34–49; and Michael Kulikowski, "The Notitia Dignitatum as a Historical Source," *Historia* 49 (2000): 358–77.

**3** First Council of Nicaea, can. 4 (CCCOGD 1.21–22). See Geoffrey D. Dunn, "Canonical Legislation on the Ordination of Bishops: Innocent I's Letter to Victricius of Rouen," in: *Episcopal Elections in Late Antiquity*, eds. Johan Leemans, Peter Van Nuffelen, Shawn W.J. Keough, and Carla Nicolaye, AKG 119 (Berlin: De Gruyter, 2011), 145–66 at 155–59.

imperial provincial system (with prefectures, dioceses, and provinces) certainly encouraged a similar hierarchicalisation of church leadership.[4]

In this chapter I examine how religious conflict within the church could arise from the fluctuations of Roman imperial provincial organisation. As my example, I consider the situation in Gaul in the early decades of the fifth century when the praetorian prefect relocated from Trier to Arles and how this contributed to years of rivalry and disagreement among the Gallic bishops, and how eventually it led Zosimus, bishop of Rome between 417 and 418, to become involved in such a way that the relationship between Rome and the Gallic churches was called into question and became part of the conflict. I suggest that sociological Conflict Theory helps us understand what kind of authority Zosimus was trying to exercise, and why that exacerbated rather than ameliorated the situation in Gaul, as we identify the goals and interests of the participants.

## 1 Transfer of praetorian prefect from Trier to Arles

Trier (ancient Augusta Treuerorum in the province of Belgica Prima in the diocese of Galliae) had been an imperial residence under Constantine and his family.[5] After the imperial court departed, Trier remained the residence for the praetorian prefect of the Gauls until he moved to Arles[6] (ancient Colonia Iulia Paterna Arelatensium Sextanorum or simply Arelate in the province of Viennensis in the diocese of Viennensis, which was renamed Septem Prouinciae at some point around this time).[7] Some have dated this move to about 395,[8] others to about

---

**4** See Geoffrey D. Dunn, "The Development of Rome as Metropolitan of Suburbicarian Italy: Innocent I's *Letter to the Bruttians*," *Augustinianum* 51 (2011): 161–90 at 166–68.

**5** Barnes, *New Empire*, 68–87.

**6** On Arles see Claude Sintés, "L'Évolution topographique de l'Arles du haut-empire à la lumière des fouilles récentes," *Journal of Roman Archaeology* 5 (1992): 130–47; and Edwin Mullins, *Roman Provence: A History and Guide* (Oxford: Signal Books, 2011), 88–91.

**7** According to *Notitia dignitatum* the diocese of Septem Prouinciae was the only one in today's France and consisted of seventeen provinces instead of seven. See Alexander Willem Byvanck, "Notes batavo-romaines. X. La Notitia dignitatum et la fronti re septentrionale de la Gaule," *Mnemosyne* 9 (1940–41): 87–96. André Chastagnol, "Le diocèse civil d'Aquitaine au Bas-Empire," *Bulletin de la société nationale des antiquaires de France* (1970): 272–92 at 279, dates the renaming to before 381, and on 287–88 claims that the vicar resided at Bordeaux since 355. On the division of provinces in Gaul see *Notitia Galliarum* (*Chronica Minora saec. IV. V. VI. VII.* 1, ed. Theodor Mommsen, MGHAA 9, Berlin: Weidmann, 1892, 552–600).

**8** Joseph Zeller, "Das concilium der Septem Provinciae in Arelate," *Westdeutsche Zeitschrift* 24 (1905): 1–19; Jean-Rémy Palanque, "La date du transfert de la préfecture des Gaules de Trèves à Arles," *Revue des études anciennes* 36 (1934): 358–65; Charles Munier, ed., *Concilia Galliae a. 314*

407, as a response to the Great Invasion of barbarians at the end of 406.[9] Michael Kulikowski convincingly dates it to about 407, with a more formal establishment in the years after Flavius Constantius – Honorius' *magister utriusque militiae* who would marry the emperor's half-sister, Galla Placidia at the start of 417 and who would, for a few short months before his death in 421, be Constantius III – had recaptured the city in 411 from the British usurper Constantine III, who had based himself there with his praetorian prefects, Apollinaris and Decimus Rusticus.[10]

This change in fortune for Arles was going to place pressure on the status of bishops within the area.[11] This is what we witness. At the centre of this conflict is

---

– *a. 506*, CCSL 148 (Turnhout: Brepols, 1963), 52; Elie Griffe, *La Gaule chrétienne a l'époque romaine*, vol. 2, *Des origines chrétiennes à la fin du IV*e *siècle* (Paris: Letouzey et Ané, 1964), 337; Jean-Rémy Palanque, "Du nouveau sur la date du transfert de la préfecture des Gaules de Trèves à Arles," *Histoire de la Provence et civilisation médiévale: Provence Historique* 23, fasc. 93–94 (1973): 29–38; Ralph W. Mathisen, *Ecclesiastical Factionalism and Religious Controversy in Fifth-Century Gaul* (Washington, DC: Catholic University of American Press, 1989), 19; William E. Klingshirn, *Caesarius of Arles: The Making of a Christian Community in Late Antique Gaul*, Cambridge Studies in Medieval Life and Thought (Cambridge: Cambridge University Press, 1994), 53; and J.H.W.G. Liebeschuetz, *The Decline and Fall of the Roman City* (Oxford: Oxford University Press, 2001), 88.

**9** André Chastagnol, "Le repli sur Arles des services administratifs gaulois en l'an 407 de notre ère," *Revue historique* 249 (1973): 23–40; Charles Pietri, *Roma Christiana. Recherches sur l'église de Rome, son organisation, sa politique, son idéologie de Miltiade à Sixte III (311–440)*, Bibliothèque des Écoles Françaises d'Athènes et de Rome 224 (Rome: École Française de Rome, 1976), 974–75; Christopher Chaffin, "The Application of Nicaea Canon 6 and the Date of the Synod of Turin," *Rivista di Storia e Letteratura Religiosa* 16 (1980): 257–72 at 261; Walter Goffart, *Rome's Fall and After* (London: Hambledon Press, 1989), 37; David Frye, "Bishops as Pawns in Early Fifth-Century Gaul," *JEH* 42 (1991): 349–61 at 350; Simon T. Loseby, "Arles in Late Antiquity: Gallula Roma Arelas and urbs Genesii," in: *Towns in Transition: Urban Evolution in Late Antiquity and the Early Middle Ages*, eds. Neil Christie and Simon T. Loseby (Aldershot: Scolar Press, 1996), 45–70; and John Matthews, *Western Aristocracies and Imperial Court AD 364–425* (rev. edn.; Oxford: Clarendon Press, 1998), 333. On the incursion of Vandals, Alans, and Suevi see Prosper of Aquitaine, *Epit. chron.* 1230 (MGHAA 9.465). Although Michael Kulikowski, "Barbarians in Gaul, Usurpers in Britain," *Britannia* 31 (2000): 325–45 at 327, suggested a date of 31 December 405, in Id., *Rome's Gothic War: From the Third Century to Alaric*, Key Conflicts in Classical Antiquity (Cambridge: Cambridge University Press, 2007), 171, he questioned his own argument for revising the date from the end of 406.

**10** On Flavius Constantius see PLRE 2.321–25 (Constantius 17); Michael Kulikowski, "Two Councils of Turin," *JTS* n.s. 47 (1996): 159–68 at 163–64; and Ian N. Wood, "Arles," in: *Late Antiquity: A Guide to the Postclassical World*, eds. Glen W. Bowersock, Peter Brown, and Oleg Grabar (Cambridge, MA: Harvard University Press, 1999), 315.

**11** Griffe, *La Gaule chrétienne*, 2.146–64; and Raymond Van Dam, *Leadership and Community in Late Antique Gaul*, TCH 8 (Berkeley: University of California Press, 1985), 166.

Patroclus, bishop of Arles from 411, whose claims to an extensive authority exacerbated an already fractious relationship among a number of Gallic bishops. Although Peter Norton argues that there is little evidence of the church imitating civil administrative structures beyond the provincial level, I am arguing that what we find in southern Gaul is such an example.[12]

## 2 The context of religious conflict in Viennensis in the early fifth century

There were several cities within the province of Viennensis where this religious conflict would be played out: Arles, Vienne (ancient Vienna), and Marseille (ancient Massalia), whose bishop was in dispute with his colleague in Aix-en-Provence, the capital of the recently detached province of Narbonensis Secunda, over who had metropolitan rights in that new province. We may distinguish three phases in this conflict: an initial one prior to Patroclus (including the First Synod of Turin), a second phase from 411 culminating in the Second Synod of Turin, and the final phase where Zosimus of Rome became involved.

Patroclus inherited tension within Arles. His predecessor, Heros, a follower of Martin of Tours (ancient Ciuitas Turonum in the province of Lugdunensis Tertia),[13] had become bishop, probably installed in 408 by the usurper Constantine III.[14] Heros left Arles soon after Constantine fell in 411, abandoning his church voluntarily, according to Zosimus, but driven out unjustly by the people, accord-

**12** Peter Norton, *Episcopal Elections 250–600: Hierarchy and Popular Will in Late Antiquity*, OCM (Oxford: Oxford University Press, 2007), 118–19.

**13** Martin and Ambrose of Milan had opposed the execution of Priscillian in Trier in 386, although the local bishop, Felix, had supported it. See Ambrose, *Ep.* 68.3 (CSEL 82/2.169–70); Sulpicius Severus, *Chron.* 2.50.1–2 (SC 441.340–42); 2.51.3 (SC 441.344); and Gregory of Tours, *Hist. franc.* 10.31 (*Gregorii episcopi Turonensis Historiarum libri X*, ed. B. Krusch, MGHSRM 9, 2nd edn., Hannover: Hahn, 1942, 527–28). As a result Martin refused to attend any further Gallic synods (Sulpicius Severus, *Dial.* 3.13; CSEL 1.211). Mathisen, *Ecclesiastical Factionalism*, 14–15, identified Martin as an anti-Felician, those who supported outside intervention in church affairs in Gaul. See David G. Hunter, "Vigilantius of Calagurris and Victricius of Rouen: Ascetics, Relics, and Clerics in Late Roman Gaul," *JECS* 7 (1999): 401–30 at 419. However, with regard to Heros, we would have to note that, unlike Martin, he was not a supporter of Roman imperial intervention but of the more local management of problems. Perhaps the terms Felician and anti-Felician should not refer so much to an attitude towards outside intervention but more to a sympathy towards Priscillianism.

**14** On Constantine III see PLRE 2.316–17 (Constantinus 21); and John F. Drinkwater, "The Usurpers Constantine III (407–411) and Jovinus (411–413)," *Britannia* 29 (1998): 269–98.

ing to Prosper.[15] In his place Patroclus, a friend of Constantius, was made bishop. While most scholars think that this was at the initiative of Constantius, I would argue that a reading of Prosper could suggest equally that it was Patroclus who sought to exploit his friendship with Honorius' general in securing his appointment.[16] Since Zosimus was opposed to Heros, it was only natural that the Roman bishop was favourably disposed to Patroclus, and, since Heros had the support of a number of his fellow Gallic bishops, it was only natural that they became opponents of Patroclus.

If Constantine had been seen in Gaul not as a tyrant but as one who provided opportunity for the local aristocracy to win high office, which they had not had under Honorius' regime,[17] then we may conclude that many would have turned to the bishop of Arles, in whose city an emperor and a praetorian prefect then resided, eager to seek his help in gaining access to the imperial ear, in much the same way that Ambrose's position had been augmented by him being located in a city that hosted an imperial court.[18] Since Constantius did not stay long in Arles, Patroclus was not going to enjoy the influence and rapport Heros had with locals and favour seekers alike. Thus, we find the political rivalry between Constantine III and Flavius Constantius contributing to a conflict within the church of Arles between its bishop and his community and between its bishop and his colleagues.

We may next turn to the tensions involving Patroclus with other churches in the province, beginning with Vienne. Although the praetorian prefects were based in Arles from about 407 onwards, Vienne remained the provincial capital of Viennensis and its bishop retained his rights as metropolitan. However, before 417 the provincial governor had relocated from Vienne to Arles, as Honorius' constitution *Saluberrima magnificentiae* makes clear.[19] So, if the imperial provincial model were followed slavishly, the church of Vienne then should have surrendered its metropolitan status to the church of Arles.

---

**15** Zosimus, *Ep.* 3.3 (PL 20.657) = *Collectio Avellana*, *Ep.* 46.6 (CSEL 35.104); and Prosper of Aquitaine, *Epit. chron.* 1247 (MGHAA 9.466).

**16** Mathisen, *Ecclesiastical Factionalism*, 35–36; Frye, "Bishops in Early Fifth-Century Gaul," 354.

**17** Frye, "Bishops in Early Fifth-Century Gaul," 351.

**18** Van Dam, *Leadership and Community*, 38–39; Mathisen, *Ecclesiastical Factionalism*, 27–28; and Frye, "Bishops in Early Fifth-Century Gaul," 351. On Ambrose, see Neil B. McLynn, *Ambrose of Milan: Church and Court in a Christian Capital*, TCH 22 (Berkeley: University of California Press, 1994); and Timothy D. Barnes, "Ambrose and Gratian," *AntT* 7 (1999): 165–74.

**19** *Collectio Arelatensis*, *Ep.* 8 (*Epistolae Arelatenses Genuinae*, ed. Wilhelm Gundlach, MGHEpp 3, Munich: Monumenta Germaniae Historica, 1978, 13–15). See Kulikowski, "Two Councils of Turin," 166.

Simplicius was bishop in Vienne (his dates are unclear), and he was not prepared to relinquish his authority. We learn of this conflict with Arles in the canons of a Synod of Turin, which was held on 22 September; the question is about the year. In 1904 Babut identified two synods held in Turin, the second of which, the one on 22 September, he dated to 417.[20] Duchesne disagreed, maintaining there was only one synod, dated to 400.[21] Palanque modified Duchesne's date to 398, but maintained the idea of a single synod.[22] More recently, Frye has argued for two synods, the second in 417, which Zosimus attended.[23] Rather than support this novel solution, I adopt Kulikowski, wherein the first synod is dated to somewhere between 397 and 411 and the second somewhere between 407 and 416 (with no Zosimus).[24] I think we can narrow that second date range to between 412 and 416.[25] This places it after both prefect and governor had moved to Arles and shows that we are dealing with a clash between Patroclus and Simplicius in the second phase of the conflict.

The second synod discussed the conflict between Arles and Vienne. The canons report that their dispute was over who had primacy, and the synod resolved that the one who could prove his city was metropolitan would hold it.[26] They then state that, since there was doubt and since peace needed to be preserved, the bishop of Vienne should be responsible for ordaining bishops in that part of the province near him and the bishop of Arles should be responsible for the

---

**20** Ernest-Charles Babut, *Le Concile de Turin. Essai sur l'histoire des Églises provençales au Ve siècle et sur les origines de la monarchie ecclésiastique romaine (417–450)* (Paris: A. Picard et fils, 1904), 17–23. Chastagnol, "Le repli sur Arles," 23–30, supported Babut.

**21** Louis Duchesne, "Le Concile de Turin," *Revue Historique* 87 (1905): 278–302. Ernest-Charles Babut, "Le date du concile de Turin et le développement de l'autorité pontificale au V^e siècle. Réponse à Mgr. Duchesne et à M. Pfister," *Revue Historique* 88 (1905): 57–82, responded.

**22** Jean-Rémy Palanque, "Les dissensions des Eglises des Gaules à la fin du IV^e siècle et la date du Concile de Turin," *Revue d'Histoire de l'Église de France* 21 (1935): 481–501. Munier, *Concilia Galliae*, 52; Elie Griffe, "La date du Concile de Turin (398 ou 417)," *Bulletin de littérature ecclésiastique* 74 (1973): 289–93; and Chaffin, "The Application of Nicaea Canon 6," 257–72, supported Palanque.

**23** Frye, "Bishops in Early Fifth-Century Gaul," 356.

**24** Kulikowski, "Two Councils of Turin," 161–62.

**25** Geoffrey D. Dunn, "Did Zosimus Travel to Turin in 417?," forthcoming. See n. 37 below.

**26** Second Synod of Turin, can. 2 (CCSL 148.55–56): "Illud deinde inter episcopos urbium Arelatensis et Viennensis qui de primatus apud nos honore certabant, a sancto synodo definitum est, ut qui ex his approbauerit suam ciuitatem esse metropolim, is totius prouinciae honorem primatus obtineat, et ipse iuxta canonum praeceptum ordinationum habeat potestatem."

rest,[27] effectively dividing the province in two temporarily. The bishops reveal that they supported the notion that the structures of the church ought to imitate those of the empire. They also reveal that there was confusion about which city was the provincial capital, which must mean that the synod met soon after the provincial governor moved to Arles and before the move was made permanent.[28] It also shows Gallic compromise and Patroclus' lack of sway over his fellow bishops. The conflict would escalate when Patroclus rejected the compromise.

We may now consider Marseille. In the first phase of the conflict, at the first Synod of Turin, which we know about only from Zosimus of Rome's account, and on other occasions, we discover that Brice (Brictius) of Tours, Martin's successor and former antagonist, was accused of unspecified crimes by Lazarus, possibly a presbyter or monk of Tours, and a follower of Martin. In turn, at the synod Lazarus was accused of making false accusations by Proculus, who had been bishop of Marseille for some time, and was condemned.[29] This would make the first synod something of a victory for Felicians.[30] Sometime later Proculus changed his mind about Lazarus and, reading between the lines in Zosimus' hostile version, after having engineered violently the departure of (the unnamed) Remigius from Aix-en-Provence (ancient Aquae Sextiae in the province of Narbonensis Secunda, capital since the province was detached recently from Viennensis) following charges of adultery and the connivance of Constantine III,[31] he succeeded in having Lazarus installed as bishop in Aix-en-Provence.[32] This made Lazarus a metropolitan, and suggests a date of about 408.

---

**27** Second Synod of Turin, can. 2 (CCSL 148.56): "Certe ad pacis uinculum conseruandum hoc consilio utiliore decretum est, ut si placet memoratarum urbium episcopis, unaquaeque de his uiciniores sibi intra prouinciam uindicet ciuitates, atque eas ecclesias uisitet quas oppidis suis proximas magis esse constiterit, ita ut memores unanimitatis atque concordiae, non alter alterum longius sibi usurpando quod est alii proprium inquietet."

**28** I reject the interpretation of Frye, "Bishops in Early Fifth-Century Gaul," 357–58, that the two parts of the canon reflect changes made during the course of the synod.

**29** Zosimus, *Epp.* 3.3 (PL 20.656) = *Collectio Avellana, Ep.* 46.5 (CSEL 35.104); and 4.2 (PL 20.662–63 = Pierre Coustant, *Epistolae Romanorum Pontificum et quae ad eos scriptae sunt a S. Clement I usque ad Innocentum III*, t. 1, Paris: L.-D. Delatour, 1721, cols. 956–57) = *Collectio Arelatensis, Ep.* 2 (MGHEpp 3.7) = JK 331.

**30** Frye, "Bishops in Early Fifth-Century Gaul," 352.

**31** *Chron. Gallica ad a. ccccclii* 60 (Richard Burgess, "The Gallic Chronicle of 452: A New Critical Edition with a Brief Introduction," in: *Society and Culture in Late Antique Gaul: Revisiting the Sources*, eds. Ralph W. Mathisen and Danuta Shanzer, Aldershot: Ashgate, 2001, 74). I wonder how much of this was instigated by Constantine. I think it more likely that Proculus was the driving force.

**32** Zosimus, *Ep.* 3.3 (PL 20.656) = *Collectio Avellana, Ep.* 46.5 (CSEL 35.104).

With the fall of Constantine III Lazarus suffered the same fate in Aix-en-Provence as Heros did in Arles: he was driven out, voluntarily departing, Zosimus would have us believe from one letter, or ordered out, according to comments made in another letter.[33] Remigius returned to his old church in 412 and found in Patroclus an ally, just as Proculus was an opponent to both because of his connection with Lazarus and therefore with Heros.[34]

At the second Synod of Turin, in the next phase, we find the bishops discussing a conflict between Proculus of Marseille and Remigius of Aix-en-Provence over the validity of episcopal ordinations performed by Proculus. He had been acting throughout the province of Viennensis for some time as though he were metropolitan, and this continued when the province of Narbonensis Secunda was created.[35] While Lazarus probably would not have complained about the activities of the man responsible for elevating him to the episcopal rank, Remigius did.[36] At the second Synod of Turin Proculus claimed that he ought to be recognised as metropolitan of Narbonensis Secunda, while the bishops of the province rejected the idea of a provincial outsider as their metropolitan. The synod decided as a compromise that Proculus' position as metropolitan ought to be recognised, but only for his lifetime.[37] Mathisen suggests that Proculus, with his many non-Gallic contacts, might have been anti-Felician, while Remigius was Felician, suggesting an explanation for inherited antagonism.[38] The second synod was something of a victory for the anti-Felicians.[39] So we may now consider Zosimus' role in Gallic affairs in the third phase of the conflict as he became involved in a situation that was plagued already with animosity.

**33** Ibid.; and *Ep.* 4.2 (PL 20.663) = *Collectio Arelatensis, Ep.* 2 (MGHEpp 3.7).

**34** Zosimus, *Ep.* 19 (Friedrich Maassen, *Geschichte der Quellen und der Literatur des canonischen Rechts im Abendlande bis zum Ausgange des Mittelaters*, Gratz: Leuschner and Lubensky, 1870, 955).

**35** See Griffe, *La Gaule chrétienne*, 1.337; and Chastagnol, "Le diocèse civil," 273–79.

**36** For this reason I refine the date of the second Synod of Turin to between 412 and 416.

**37** Second Synod of Turin, can. 1 (CCSL 148.55): "Haec igitur ipsi tantum in die uitae eius forma seruabitur, ut in ecclesiis prouinciae secundae Narbonensis quas uel suas parrocias uel suos discipulos fuisse constiterit ordinatos, primatus habeat dignitatem."

**38** Mathisen, *Ecclesiastical Factionalism*, 24.

**39** Second Synod of Turin, can. 6 (CCSL 148.57–58), welcomed anti-Felicians back into communion, as proposed by the now deceased Ambrose and Siricius of Rome.

## 3 Zosimus and Patroclus

On 22 March 417, only four days after his election, Zosimus wrote *Placuit apostolicae* to the Gallic bishops of both civil dioceses announcing that Patroclus of Arles was to have the authority in ordaining bishops throughout the provinces of Viennensis, Narbonensis Prima, and Narbonensis Secunda.[40] Further, no cleric of any grade was to appeal to Rome without having obtained permission from Patroclus.[41]

Many think that Patroclus was in Rome at the time of the election, with Frye even going so far as to argue that this letter implements Constantius' plans to deal with bishops he could not remove while he had been in Gaul, and this was Zosimus' way of repaying Constantius for having secured his election, since the Roman bishop was little more than his puppet.[42] Something certainly prompted Zosimus to deal with this matter immediately after his election, but we do not know why. Frye's argument is not one I accept, since the evidence for such a connection between Zosimus and Constantius is just not there. Maybe Innocent I, Zosimus' predecessor, was preparing to deal with Gaul but died before any letter could be sent. I am inclined to agree with Kulikowski that Patroclus was not in Rome until later in 417.[43]

However, Kulikowski is not completely clear when he writes: "The bishop of Arles was therefore necessarily the metropolitan bishop [after the move of the

**40** Zosimus, *Ep.* 1.II.2 (PL 20.644 = Coustant, *Epistolae Romanorum Pontificum*, col. 936) = *Collectio Arelatensis*, *Ep.* 1 (MGHEpp 3.6) = JK 328: "Iussimus autem praecipuam, sicuti semper habuit, metropolitanus episcopus Arelatensium ciuitatis in ordinandis sacerdotibus teneat auctoritatem. Viennensem, Narbonensem primam et Narbonensem secundam prouincias ad pontificium suum reuocet."

**41** Zosimus, *Ep.* 1.I.1 (PL 20.642–43) = *Collectio Arelatensis*, *Ep.* 1 (MGHEpp 3.5): "Placuit apostolicae sedi, ut si quis exqualibet Galliarum parte, sub quolibet ecclesiastico gradu, ad nos Romam uenire contendit, uel alio [MGHEpp = ad alia] terrarum ire disponit, non aliter proficiscatur, nisi metropolitani Arelatensis episcopi formatas acceperit, quibus sacerdotium suum, uel locum ecclesiasticum quem habet, scriptorum eius adstipulatione perdoceat."

**42** Duchesne, "Le Concile de Turin," 281; Louis Duchesne, *Fastes épiscopaux de l'ancienne Gaule*, 3 vols. (Paris: Albert Fontemoing, 1907), 1.98; Pierre Batiffol, "Les Églises Gallo-Romaines," *Revue d'Histoire de l'Église de France* 8 (1922): 145–69 at 160; Émilienne Demougeot, "À propos des interventions du pape Innocent Ier dans la politique séculière," *Revue historique* 212 (1954): 23–38; Georg Langgärtner, *Die Gallienpolitik der Päpste im 5. und 6. Jahrhundert. Eine Studie über den apostolische Vikariat von Arles* (Bonn: P. Hanstein, 1964), 26; Griffe, *La Gaule chrétienne*, 2.146–64; Stewart Irvin Oost, *Galla Placidia Augusta: A Biographical Essay* (Chicago–London: University of Chicago Press, 1968), 148–89; Pietri, *Roma Christiana*, 1005–6; Mathisen, *Ecclesiastical Factionalism*, 49; and Frye, "Bishops in Early Fifth-Century Gaul," 354–55.

**43** Kulikowski, "Two Councils of Turin," 165.

prefect and governor there]. Zosimus recognized this, and entrusted to Patroclus the highest powers in southern Gaul."[44] The first part is unquestionable. By 417 the enduring status of Arles as provincial capital and permanent base of the praetorian prefect would have been well established, and thus the provisional decision made at Turin needed correcting, and one could imagine that Patroclus had written to Rome asking for such a statement of support for his proposal to make it explicit that Arles alone was the metropolitan church in the province of Viennensis. Certainly creating Arles as the conduit through which appeals to Rome were to be channelled paralleled what existed in the prefecture of Illyrium Orientale, where the bishop of Thessaloniki (ancient Thessalonica in the province of Macedonia Prima) enjoyed such responsibility, and was designated to hear appeals from the other churches of the prefecture, at least under Innocent I, if not earlier.[45] However, the second part of Kulikowski's statement needs clarification. To extend Patroclus' metropolitan authority (in particular, the right of ordaining the bishops of a province) over other provinces was unprecedented.[46] Innocent I, by contrast, had reminded Rufus of Thessaloniki not to harm the primacy of metropolitans within their own provinces.[47]

Was it accepted that the Roman bishop had the authority to order ecclesiastical reorganisation in churches outside Italy or outside the Italian prefecture? Was Zosimus in fact ordering this or merely endorsing a claim made by Patroclus to revive the ancient, widespread authority of Trofimus, the first bishop of Arles, over a large part of southern Gaul? Certainly "iubeo" admits of shades of meaning. Even if Zosimus was ordering it, did anyone accept that he had such authority?

Leading bishops in the affected provinces reacted negatively to Zosimus' decree, indicating that they did not believe he did have such authority to order changes in Gaul, and conflict between Gaul and Rome erupted.

---

**44** Kulikowski, "Two Councils of Turin," 167.

**45** Geoffrey D. Dunn, "Innocent I and Anysius of Thessalonica," *Byz* 77 (2007): 124–48; and Geoffrey D. Dunn, "Innocent I and Rufus of Thessalonica," *Jahrbuch der Österreichischen Byzantinistik* 59 (2009): 51–64.

**46** Zosimus, *Ep.* 1.III (PL 20.644–45) = *Collectio Arelatensis*, *Ep.* 1 (MGHEpp 3.6), justified this by appealing to the first bishop of Arles, Trofimus, whose see must have been believed to have extended over all this region.

**47** Innocent I, *Ep.* 13.3 (PL 20.516 = Coustant, *Epistolae Romanorum Pontificium*, col. 817) = JK 300: "...saluo earum primatu curam...."

## 4 Zosimus in conflict with Gallic bishops

We hear of the reaction to Zosimus' announcement in March in a series of letters, many of them concentrated in a two-week period at the end of September and beginning of October 417. As the information comes from Zosimus it is impossible to gauge accurately the Gallic perspective.

Proculus of Marseille carried out what Zosimus described as "ordinationes nonnullorum,"[48] including those of Ursus and Tuentius to the newly created dioceses of Citharista and Gargaria, churches which Zosimus specifically had announced should be under Patroclus' authority in his letter of March 417 and which scholars think must have been under control of Marseille until then.[49] Zosimus' letter, *Cum aduersus*, directed to the African, Gallic, and Spanish episcopates on 22 September 417, after a synod in Rome, announced the excommunication of Ursus and Tuentius.[50] Proculus had failed to attend this synod even though summoned,[51] and we know from Zosimus' letter, *Quid de Proculi*, of 26 September, that Proculus was condemned by the Roman synod, the one I believe Patroclus attended.[52]

Simplicius of Vienne was another opposed to the new arrangement. He had the least to complain about since Arles was in the same province and, if one accepted the notion that the move of the governor legitimised a swap in status between Vienne and Arles, then all he had to suffer was a legitimate loss of power and prestige due to the downgrade of Vienne. Patroclus' authority over Vienne was to be nothing extraordinary since it was within the province. However, influ-

---

**48** Zosimus, *Ep.* 5 (PL 20.665 = Coustant, *Epistolae Romanorum Pontificum*, col. 959) = *Collectio Arelatensis*, *Ep.* 5 (MGHEpp 3.11) = JK 334.

**49** Zosimus, *Ep.* 4.1–2 (PL 20.661–63) = *Collectio Arelatensis*, *Ep.* 2 (MGHEpp 3.7). See Duchesne, *Fastes épiscopaux*, 1.98; Batiffol, "Les Églises," 161–62; Griffe, *La Gaule chrétienne*, 1.408–9; and Mathisen, *Ecclesiastical Factionalism*, 53–54. After attacking Proculus' failure to abide by the new procedure, Zosimus attacked the characters of the two new bishops, accusing them of Priscillianism and accusing Proculus of making Ursus a bishop, whom he had condemned previously (as a presbyter?), as he had done with Lazarus.

**50** Zosimus, *Ep.* 4.4 (PL 20.664) = *Collectio Arelatensis*, *Ep.* 2 (MGHEpp 3.8). In Frye, "Bishops in Early Fifth-Century Gaul," 357, this took place in Turin with Zosimus present, an interpretation I do not accept. What Frye does not explain is how a synod in Turin could issue can. 1, which was favourable to Proculus, and also could have Zosimus issuing his stinging rejection in *Multa contra*. His statement (358) that "the council did not comply with the pope's wishes" surely must be rejected; one cannot imagine Zosimus being party to a meeting at which he did not get his way. It would be an unparalleled example of a Roman bishop travelling to a synod.

**51** Zosimus, *Ep.* 5 (PL 20.665) = *Collectio Arelatensis*, *Ep.* 5 (MGHEpp 3.11).

**52** Zosimus, *Ep.* 7.1 (PL 20.668 = Coustant, *Epistolae Romanorum Pontificum*, cols. 961–62) = *Collectio Arelatensis*, *Ep.* 4 (MGHEpp 3.10).

enced by Proculus, Simplicius complained that he should not be denied what had been granted him at Turin. Zosimus considered Turin to have been an illegitimate synod, as he expressed in his letter, *Multa contra*, to the bishops of Viennensis and Narbonensis Secunda, dated 29 September 417. Zosimus appealed to the Trofimus story again to justify Arles' position.[53] If one accepts that *Epistula* 18 of 3 October, *Reuelatum nobis est*, is a forgery, then there is no evidence that Simplicius ever accepted Zosimus' declaration.[54]

Another bishop involved, although we have not mentioned him previously, was Hilary of Narbonne (ancient Colonia Narbo Martius in the province of Narbonensis Prima). He had written to Zosimus complaining that bishops ought not to be ordained by one from another province, which is what would in effect happen with Patroclus of Arles' new responsibilities. It would appear his letter arrived while the synod was still in session in Rome. Hilary protested that his authority as metropolitan was being usurped. Zosimus responded on 26 September with his letter, *Mirati admodum*, again resorting to the Trofimus story to argue that Arles had a wide authority by virtue of its original boundaries. Any claims that the church of Narbonne had been recognised by Rome in a previous generation as a metropolitan church were both deceitful and now rescinded (if this is not contradictory!).[55] Trofimus again justified this and Hilary was threatened with excommunication if he persisted with exercising what he believed were his metropolitan rights.[56]

There is evidence that Hilary had been a supporter of Constantine and an opponent of Constantius in those turbulent years of the Great Invasion. Indeed, Frye goes as far as to argue that Hilary survived Constantine's downfall because Constantius was unable to remove him.[57] However, it is hard to believe that a ruthless general could not have found a way to remove a difficult bishop.

Lazarus seems to have been back in Gaul in 417 and was involved in ordaining a bishop with no regard to Patroclus.[58] Lazarus' replacement in Aix-en-Pro-

---

**53** Zosimus, *Ep.* 5 (PL 20.665) = *Collectio Arelatensis*, *Ep.* 5 (MGHEpp 3.11).

**54** Zosimus, *Ep.* 18 (PL 20.704 = Coustant, *Epistolae Romanorum Pontificum*, appendix cols. 111–12) = *Collectio Viennenses spuriae*, *Ep.* 7 (MGHEpp 3.90). See Mathisen, *Ecclesiastical Factionalism*, 58 n. 72.

**55** Zosimus, *Ep.* 6.1 (PL 20.666–7 = Coustant, *Epistolae Romanorum Pontificum*, col. 960) = *Collectio Arelatensis*, *Ep.* 3 (MGHEpp 3.9). Langgärtner, *Die Gallienpolitik der Päpste*, 25, argues that there was no metropolitan in this province until 417.

**56** Zosimus, *Ep.* 6.2 (PL 20.667) = *Collectio Arelatensis*, *Ep.* 3 (MGHEpp 3.9–10).

**57** Frye, "Bishops in Early Fifth-Century Gaul," 354.

**58** Zosimus, *Ep.* 4.2 (PL 20.663) = *Collectio Arelatensis*, *Ep.* 2 (MGHEpp 3.7). See Columba Stewart, *Cassian the Monk*, Oxford Studies in Historical Theology (Oxford: Oxford University Press,

vence, Remigius, however, was a supporter of the new arrangement and took advantage of it. He claimed back territory Proculus had appropriated, and in this he was supported by Zosimus' letter of 3 October, *Licet proxime.*[59]

In March 418 Zosimus wrote again to Gaul. In *Non miror* to the church of Marseille Zosimus revealed that Proculus had taken no notice of Zosimus' excommunication, which the Roman bishop issued a second time.[60] The bishop of Rome seems to have had little success in directing church life in southern Gaul. On the same day he wrote another letter, *Cum et praesenti*, this time to Patroclus, criticising the lack of result the bishop of Arles was having in implementing the new arrangements.[61] Zosimus' frustration is evident in his criticism of the local bishop he had trusted. Zosimus died shortly afterwards with the situation unresolved.

Zosimus' criticisms of this group of Gallic bishops obviously did not bother others terribly much. In 418, a group of African bishops, including Aurelius of Carthage and Augustine of Annaba (ancient Hippo Regius) wrote to Proculus informing him that they had received a presbyter, Leporius, in Africa after he had been expelled from Gaul, rightly they hastened to add, in order to correct his errant theological opinions about the nature of Christ.[62] The Africans also saw Lazarus as a friend and colleague.[63]

# 5 Zosimus and Gaul from the perspective of Conflict Theory

Does Conflict Theory help us understand the situation in late-antique Gaul any more clearly? In a recent definition, Bartos and Wehr have suggested that social conflict is to be understood "as a situation in which *actors use conflict behavior against each other to attain incompatible goals and/or to express their hostility.*"[64]

1998), 16 and 151 n. 133. The evidence from Zosimus needs to be added to indicate that Lazarus returned to Gaul.

**59** Zosimus, *Ep.* 19 (Maassen, *Geschichte der Quellen*, 955).

**60** Zosimus, *Ep.* 11 (PL 20.674–75 = Coustant, *Epistolae Romanorum Pontificum*, col. 973) = *Collectio Arelatensis*, *Ep.* 7 (MGHEpp 3.13).

**61** Zosimus, *Ep.* 10 (PL 20.673–74 = Coustant, *Epistolae Romanorum Pontificum*, cols. 971–72) = *Collectio Arelatensis*, *Ep.* 6 (MGHEpp 3.12).

**62** Augustine, *Ep.* 219 (NBA 23.614–18).

**63** Augustine, *De gest. Pel.* 1.2 (NBA 17/2.22).

**64** Otomar J. Bartos and Paul Wehr, *Using Conflict Theory* (Cambridge: Cambridge University Press, 2002), 13.

Weber defined conflict (*Kampf*) as a situation where "action is oriented intentionally to carrying out the actor's own will against the resistance of the other party or parties."[65] Conflict and competition are both forms of rivalry but the former is targeted directly at an opponent rather than at a third party for something neither of the competitors possesses.[66] Conflict behaviour includes both rational and non-rational considerations (depending upon the extent to which one evaluates consequences), while conflict action is limited to rational ones. The behaviour or action is coercive if it forces opponents to do something they do not wish to do by threatening or inflicting injury, which could be violent (as in physical injury) or non-violent (as in deprivation of resources) or symbolic (in that it is usually more emotional). If not coercive, the behaviour or action could be co-operative when both parties search for new goals to keep everyone happy. Along this axis one could locate persuasion, where one attempts to convince an opponent that one's goals should be theirs as well.[67] Goals are incompatible when both parties cannot achieve what they want simultaneously. They may involve contested resources (wealth, power, prestige)[68] – which may be contested because of feelings of injustice[69] or simply belligerent personality –, incompatible roles (whether vertically[70] or horizontally different), or incompatible values, particularly when one considers one's identity undervalued by others or where communal values clash with individualistic ones.[71] Besides incompatible goals, conflicts may arise also from feelings of hostility, which do not involve goal incompatibility. Conflicts often lead to the formation of groups as the frequency of interaction between individuals who like each other and share similar beliefs results in bonding directed against a shared opponent, which often arises from

---

**65** Max Weber, *Economy and Society: An Outline of Interpretive Sociology*, eds. Guenther Roth and Claus Wittich (2nd Eng. edn.; Berkeley: University of California Press, 1978), 38.

**66** Louis Kriesberg, *Social Conflicts* (2nd edn.; Englewood Cliffs, NJ: Prentice-Hall, 1982), 17. Weber, *Economy and Society*, 38, saw competition as non-violent conflict, not a position endorsed by Bartos and Wehr.

**67** Bartos and Wehr, *Using Conflict Theory*, 19–28.

**68** C. Wright Mills, *The Power Elite* (2nd edn.; Oxford: Oxford University Press, 2000), investigated the elite in contemporary American society, defining them (9) as those who possessed more of these resources and whose positions in institutions enabled them to acquire such resources because they "are able to realize their will, even if others resist it."

**69** George C. Homans, *Social Behavior: Its Elemental Forms* (New York: Harcourt, 1974).

**70** Ralf Dahrendorf, *Class and Class Conflict in Industrial Society* (Stanford: Stanford University Press, 1959). Weber, *Economy and Society*, 54, stated that in a hierocratic organisation order is maintained through the "psychic coercion by distributing or denying religious benefits.…" This implies a vertical relationship.

**71** Bartos and Wehr, *Using Conflict Theory*, 29–49; Jürgen Habermas, *The Theory of Communicative Action*, vol. 2, *Lifeworld and System* (Boston: Beacon Press, 1987).

common grievances and frustration (conflict solidarity).[72] Conflicts often escalate either unilaterally or reciprocally (as in retaliation).[73]

In his posthumously published *Economy and Society*, Max Weber outlined how to understand repeated human action: *Brauch* is simply repeated usage, *Sitte* is custom, and *Zweckrational* is self-interested action.[74] For the sociologist custom has no external sanction, but depends upon legitimate order (*Geltung*) that is either based upon convention or law.[75] Authority can be either legal, traditional, or charismatic.[76]

In terms of the background context, we can identify political conflict for the resource of power in Gaul between Constantine III and Honorius (represented by Flavius Constantius) and the incompatible value of local versus Roman focus. Since armies were involved, we are talking about violent coercion. One of the ways the conflict escalated was through the broadening of the conflict solidarity as those military leaders forged relationships with church leaders, reinforcing existing divisions among the Gallic bishops (Felicians and anti-Felicians). In Arles and Aix-en-Provence we have evidence of conflict between some bishops (Heros and Lazarus) and their people, particularly as political fortunes changed and those bishops became a liability for the fortunes of the local Christians.

The relocation of praetorian prefect and governor from Trier to Arles instigated a new phase of conflict, but one built upon existing tensions. The agitation of Patroclus of Arles to upgrade his church to metropolitan status at the expense of Simplicius of Vienne was a rivalry based upon Patroclus' feeling of injustice at the incompatible goal of both churches wanting the power and prestige of metropolitan status. There was vertical differentiation in roles between bishops and metropolitan, and the conflict was about who had that superior role. Something similar was happening between Marseille and Aix-en-Provence, where the bishops of Narbonensis Secunda felt aggrieved that Proculus, now an external bishop, was acting like a metropolitan (not that he had that status even before the provincial changes). Here it was not so much an incompatible goal as an incom-

---

**72** Bartos and Wehr, *Using Conflict Theory*, 70–82.

**73** Bartos and Wehr, *Using Conflict Theory*, 98–121.

**74** Weber, *Economy and Society*, 29. See Donald N. Levine, "The Continuing Challenge of Weber's Theory of Rational Action," in: *Max Weber's "Economy and Society": A Critical Companion*, eds. Charles Camic, Philip S. Gorski and David M. Trubek (Stanford: Stanford University Press, 2005), 101–26, especially 108–14.

**75** Weber, *Economy and Society*, 31–36.

**76** Weber, *Economy and Society*, 215–54. Of particular interest is his discussion (271–84) of collegiality as a limitation upon legal and traditional authority.

patible value – that of having a metropolitan living in the province and being the bishop of the provincial capital.

The Gallic bishops addressed their conflict in this second phase through the Second Synod of Turin, a generally non-coercive form of conflict action, where persuasion was used to reach the two compromises that emerged. There was an incompatible value of Patroclus not respecting the decision of the synod, thus he escalated the matter by involving Rome in what was a third phase of conflict. I suspect that he first appealed to the ancient supposed custom of the geographically extensive authority of Trofimus. What was asked for and/or endorsed by Zosimus was far more than a resolution of the metropolitan identity of a church in the province; it involved the extension of power over other provinces. Why this goal was introduced we cannot tell, but it seemed to be a deliberate endorsement of the ecclesiastical imitation of political boundaries, on the one hand, and a rejection of those Diocletianic boundaries, on the other, by harking back to an earlier provincial structure. I suspect that Zosimus saw an opportunity to tie the Gallic churches more closely to Rome, thereby increasing his own power and prestige, even though appeals to Rome did take place already, as *Placuit apostolicae* makes evident. The mention of Trofimus is as an example of how the self-interest of both Patroclus and Zosimus was disguised by an appeal to custom (in terms of ancient precedent). This clashed with the self-interest of a significant number of Gallic bishops and the Trofimus tradition was rejected. Zosimus' hierocratic coercion failed because the Gallic bishops did not see the benefits he was denying them as being particularly important. Without legal or traditional authority (due most likely to a strong sense of shared episcopal collegiality rather than extra-prefecture hierarchy), Zosimus' charismatic authority failed him because of his abrasive personality and the entrenched Gallic self-interest.

Zosimus succeeded in uniting the hitherto disparate Gallic bishops into conflict solidarity against him. They believed that neither the Roman bishop nor Patroclus had the *Geltung* to order such a change. Zosimus implemented non-violent injury in his excommunication of bishops after the Roman synod to which he had summoned some of his opponents from Gaul. The Gallic bishops did not seem concerned by this, revealing that they did not hold Zosimus' conventional *Geltung* in high regard.

While the death of Zosimus might have defused the situation, it certainly did not resolve the issues, as later letters of Boniface I and Celestine I to Gaul attest, but which cannot be considered here.

# 6 Conclusion

The use of Conflict Theory to examine the letters of Zosimus of Rome dealing with the appointment or recognition (an important but unresolved question) of Patroclus of Arles as metropolitan not only of his province of Viennensis but of several others as well makes the scholar of early Christianity focus on issues of goals, roles, and values. Some of the values can be identified, but some remain elusive. The conflict arising from the impact of changes in Roman provincial arrangements on the hierarchy among bishops escalated as quickly as it did because it was built upon years of tension and division within the Gallic churches. Zosimus' failure to appreciate this meant his intervention was doomed to fail.

Contrary to the novel suggestions of Frye, I conclude that the Second Synod of Turin was not attended by Zosimus and that it showed a Gallic willingness for compromise, but that Patroclus rejected it in his all-or-nothing bid for power and prestige. The Gallic bishops did not appreciate Roman involvement in this matter and the argument that the geographically broad authority of Trofimus as first bishop of Arles ought to be reinstated for Patroclus was rejected. Conflict Theory helps us appreciate that, while Zosimus was right to insist that confusion no longer existed about the provincial capital of Viennesis and that Patroclus ought to be recognised as the sole metropolitan in the province, as imitation of the Roman provincial system would suggest, he was being provocatively innovative in downgrading the metropolitan authority of other leading bishops across several provinces. That Zosimus started excommunicating Gallic bishops who disobeyed his directives shows that he believed he had extensive authority in Gaul, but this claim to vertical differentiation was disputed by those affected. Zosimus' involvement turned this from being an internal rivalry among the Gallic churches to a conflict about the role of Rome in Gallic affairs.

Pauline Allen

# Religious Conflict between Antioch and Alexandria c. 565–630 CE

One of the periods in late antiquity most fraught with religious conflict is that between the death of Emperor Justinian in 565 CE and the first three decades of the seventh century. This was an era that witnessed the separation of the anti-Chalcedonian churches and the creation of their own clergy and hierarchy,[1] with concomitant conflict with the Chalcedonian church. At the same time serious tensions developed within the anti-Chalcedonian party itself, tensions which ended up in fully-blown, long-standing conflicts, particularly between the patriarchates of Antioch and Alexandria on the doctrine of tritheism. On the one hand, for events during this seventy-year period we have a remarkable source at our disposal for the years 564 to 581; on the other hand, from 581 to the 630s the sources are sparser and to some extent contradictory. However, to a large degree we can construct the causes and effects of religious dissent and outright conflict during these years, as well as the subtext of tritheism and the significance of the conflict for the eastern church.

## 1 Introducing the first two decades of conflict and a key source

For evidence of religious conflict between anti-Chalcedonian groups in the East between the years 564 and 581, particularly the patriarchates of Antioch and Alexandria, we have a remarkable dossier of forty-five letters, written mostly by bishops, which encompasses at least five letter-types.[2] In this collection, published by Jean-Baptiste Chabot,[3] we find five synodical letters (that is, letters

---

1 On this topic see Volker L. Menze, *Justinian and the Making of the Syrian Orthodox Church*, OECS (Oxford: Oxford University Press, 2008).

2 For a wider discussion of religious crises and conflicts in the fifth and sixth centuries, to which parts of this paper make a contribution, see Pauline Allen and Bronwen Neil, *Crisis Management in Late Antiquity (410–590 CE). A Survery of the Evidence from Episcopal Letters*, Supplements to VC (Leiden–Boston–Cologne: Brill, forthcoming).

3 *Documenta ad origines monophysitarum illustrandas*, CSCO 17, Scr. Syr. 17 (Paris: E Typographeo Reipublicae, and Leipzig: Otto Harrassowitz, 1908; repr. Louvain: Secrêtariat du CSCO, 1962). This work and its translation (CSCO 103, Scr. Syr. 52, Louvain: E Typographeo Marcelli Istas, 1933; repr. Louvain: Secrêtariat du CSCO, 1965) are designated henceforth as *DM*. See the

written by new bishops or patriarchs in which they publish their confession of faith to other bishops),[4] one widely-disseminated encyclical letter which accompanied a theological discourse,[5] one canonical letter (so called, obviously, because it had canons appended to it),[6] two *entolika* or *mandata* of a hortatory nature in letter-form,[7] and four letters designated as *syndoktika* or *edicta*, which encompass agreed statements of a theological or disciplinary nature.[8]

Apart from a shortage of clergy and bishops in the anti-Chalcedonian churches of Syria and Egypt, three converging conflicts gave rise to this anonymously compiled dossier. The first was the doctrine of tritheism, which in its sixth-century form[9] arose in the 550s among anti-Chalcedonians and was an attempt to solve christological differences by positing that, just as we distinguish three hypostases in the Trinity, so too must we distinguish three natures, substances, and godheads.[10] The theological niceties of this mostly nominal tritheism do not concern us here, except for the fact that the doctrine caused a bitter

---

analysis of the *DM* in Albert Van Roey and Pauline Allen, *Monophysite Texts of the Sixth Century*, OLA 56 (Leuven: Uitgeverij Peeters and Departement Oriëntalistiek, 1994), 265–303.

**4** *DM* nrs. 1, 2, 13, 14, and 44. On this epistolographical genre see Pauline Allen, *Sophronius of Jerusalem and Seventh-Century Heresy. The* Synodical Letter *and Other Documents*. Introduction, Texts, Translations, and Commentary, OECT (Oxford: Oxford University Press, 2009), 47–51.

**5** *DM* nr. 3.

**6** *DM* nr. 6.

**7** *DM* nrs. 18 and 19.

**8** *DM* nrs. 26, 27, 29, and 31.

**9** On the various manifestations of tritheism in the early church see Basil Studer, art. "Tritheism," in: *Encyclopedia of the Early Church*, ed. Angelo Di Berardino, Eng. trans. Adrian Walford, vol. 2 (Cambridge: James Clarke & Co., 1992), 853.

**10** On sixth-century tritheism see Giuseppe Furlani, *Sei scritti antitriteistici in lingua siriaca*, PO 14/4 (Paris: Firmin-Didot, 1920; repr. Turnhout: Brepols, 2006); Henri Martin, "La Controverse trithéite dans l'empire byzantine au VIe siècle," diss. Louvain, 1960; on the history of sources treating it, see Van Roey in: Van Roey and Allen, *Monophysite Documents*, 122–24; further, Albert Van Roey, "La Controverse trithéite depuis la condemnation de Conon et Eugène jusqu'à la conversion de l'évêque Elie," in: *Von Kanaan bis Kerala. Festschrift für Prof. Mag. Dr. Dr. J.P.M. van der Ploeg O.P. zur Vollendung des siebzigsten Lebensjahres am 4. Juli 1979.* Überreicht von Kollegen, Freunden und Schüler, Alter Orient und Altes Testament, eds. Wilhelm C. Delsman et al., Veröffentlichungen zur Kultur und Geschichte des Alten Orients und des Alten Testaments 211 (Neukirchen–Vluyn: Neukirchener Verlag, 1981), 487–97; Albert Van Roey, "La Controverse trithéite jusqu'à l'excommunication de Conon et d'Eugène (557–569)," *OLP* 16 (1985): 141–65; Rifaat Y. Ebied, Lionel R. Wickham, and Albert Van Roey, *Peter of Callinicum. Anti-Tritheist Dossier*, OLA 10 (Leuven: Uitgeverij Peeters and Departement Oriëntalistiek, 1981); Van Roey and Allen, *Monophysite Texts*, 105–263; Alois Grillmeier, *Jesus der Christus im Glauben der Kirche* 2/3. *Die Kirche von Jerusalem und Antiochien*, ed. Theresia Hainthaler (Freiburg: Herder, 2002), 279–91.

split among the anti-Chalcedonians particularly in the patriarchates of Antioch and Alexandria and is the subject of various letters in the *DM*. This doctrinal conflict prompted Bishop Theodosius, agreed leader of the anti-Chalcedonian party after the death of Severus of Antioch in 538, to write his *Theological Discourse* against tritheism, which he perceived as heresy, a work that is considered the touchstone of orthodoxy in the *DM*. The conflict over tritheism was complicated by a rift between its leaders, Bishops Conon of Tarsus and Eugenius of Seleucia, on the one hand, and the tritheist Aristotelian philosopher from Alexandria, John Philoponus (d. c. 565), on the other, particularly with regard to the doctrine of the resurrection.[11] A second point of doctrinal conflict was the popularity of the Agnoetai, who were found initially among anti-Chalcedonians but later also among Chalcedonians. In yet another attempt to achieve christological balance during this time, the Agnoetai upheld the existence of human ignorance in Christ, a position that probably grew out of the argument that Patristic *testimonia* regarding Christ's ignorance and knowledge were contradictory.[12] The third conflict was related to the tritheist controversy and concerned the succession of anti-Chalcedonian patriarchs in Antioch. This had been waiting in the wings for some time, but took centre-stage in 564 when the anti-tritheist Paul, nicknamed "the Black," was ordained to that office. We shall have to look at Paul's career briefly to understand the depth and width of this conflict,[13] caused at least in part by his personality – he was a colourful *enfant terrible*.

---

**11** For the remains of John's writing in favour of tritheism, see Albert Van Roey, "Les Fragments trithéites de Jean Philopon," *OLP* 11 (1980): 135 – 63. On John's activities more generally see Theresia Hainthaler in: Aloys Grillmeier, *Christ in Christian Tradition*, vol. 2, *From the Council of Chalcedon (451) to Gregory the Great (590 – 604)*; part 4, *The Church of Alexandria with Nubia and Ethiopia after 451* (London–Louisville, KY: Mowbray and Westminster John Knox Press, 1996 = English trans. by O.C. Dean of *Jesus der Christus im Glauben der Kirche*, Band 2/4 [Freiburg i. Breisgau: Herder, 1990]), 107 – 46 (131 – 35 on tritheism); Uwe M. Lang, *John Philoponus and the Controversies over Chalcedon in the Sixth Century: A Study and Translation of the Arbiter* (Leuven: Peeters, 2001).

**12** See further Van Roey and Allen, *Monophysite Texts*, 3 – 15.

**13** On Paul see Theodor Hermann, "Patriarch Paul von Antiochia und das Alexandrinische Schisma von Jahre 575," *ZNW* 27 (1928): 263 – 304, corrected by Ernest W. Brooks, "The Patriarch Paul of Antioch and the Alexandrine Schism of 575," *BZ* 30 (1930): 468 – 76; Ernest Honigmann, *Évêques et évêchés monophysites d'Asie antérieure au VIe siècle*, CSCO 127, Subsidia 2 (Louvain: Secrétariat du CSCO, 1951), 195 – 205; William H.C. Frend, *The Rise of the Monophysite Movement. Chapters in the History of the Church in the Fifth and Sixth Centuries* (Cambridge: Cambridge University Press, 1972), 291 – 93, 318 – 28. Cf. Lucas Van Rompay, "Pawlos of Beth Ukome," in: *Gorgias Encyclopedic Dictionary of the Syriac Heritage*, eds. Sebastian Brock, Aaron Butler, George Kiraz, and Lucas Van Rompay (Piscataway, NJ: Gorgias Press, 2011), 322 – 23. The main sources for Paul's biography, apart from the evidence in the *DM*, are the *Ecclesiastical History* of

The anti-Chalcedonian patriarchate of Antioch was vacant after the death of Sergius in c. 560 until in 564 Paul, an Alexandrian archimandrite and *syncellus* (patriarchal secretary) living in Constantinople, was elevated to the position. This was engineered by his patriarch, Theodosius of Alexandria, but it ran counter to the wishes of the influential leader of the eastern churches, Jacob Baradaeus, who probably wanted the position himself, and additionally went against the will of the Syrian bishops, who had not been consulted and would not have wanted a nominee of the patriarch of Alexandria. Paul thus started his episcopal career in an invidious position from which he was never to recover, attributable in no small measure to the polarisation between his followers and those of Jacob.[14] As we shall see, the repercussions of Paul's consecration and the conflict it caused between the sees of Antioch and Alexandria were to continue well into the seventh century.[15]

On Theodosius' death on 22 June 566, Paul was left as the heir of the deceased's property, which he used to try to buy his way into the position of patriarch of Alexandria against his rival, the tritheist monk Athanasius, a grandson of the late Empress Theodora. When this attempt was unsuccessful, Paul retired first to Syria, then to the Arabian camp of his protector, the anti-Chalcedonian Arab sheik al-Harith.[16] In 570 we find him debating against tritheists in Constantinople, where in the next year he subsequently accepted the edict of union designed by Emperor Justin II[17] and communicated with Chalcedonians. With other bish-

John of Ephesus and the *Chronicle* of Michael the Syrian (which for the most part follows John). See the chronological table by Adrian Fortescue in: Jean Maspero, *Histoire des patriarches d'Alexandrie depuis la mort de l'empereur Anastase jusqu'à la reconciliation des églises jacobites (518–646)* (Paris: Librarie ancienne Édouard Champion, 1923), 352–53.

**14** Cf. Grillmeier, *Jesus der Christus im Glauben der Kirche* 2/3. *Die Kirchen von Jerusalem und Antiochien*, ed. Theresia Hainthaler (Freiburg i. Breisgau: Herder, 2002), 199: "Damit beginnt eine leidvolle Geschichte."

**15** The anti-Chalcedonian bishop John of Ephesus, an eye-witness of many of the events, emphasises the violence and confusion that occurred, not only in Egypt and Syria but also throughout the eastern empire: *HE* 4.10, 12, 16, 19, 20 (*Iohannis Ephesini Historiae Ecclesiasticae Pars Tertia*, ed. and trans. Ernest W. Brooks, CSCO 105 [text], Scr. Syr. 54, Louvain: Secrĕtariat du CSCO and Paris: E Typographeo Reipublicae, 1935, 191, 194–97, 201–202, 205–206, 207; CSCO 106 [trans.], Scr. Syr. 55, Louvain: Secrĕtariat du CSCO, 1936, repr. 1964, 154, 143, 147, 151, 155).

**16** On the role of these Ghassanid Arabs in the ecclesio-political life of early Byzantium see Irfan Shahîd, *Byzantium and the Arabs in the Sixth Century*, vol. 2, pt. 1, *Toponymy, Monuments, Historical Geography and Frontier Studies* (Washington, DC: Dumbarton Oaks Research Library and Collection, 2002).

**17** Text in Evagrius, *HE* 5.4 (*The Ecclesiastical History of Evagrius with the Scholia*, ed. Joseph Bidez and Leon Parmentier, London: Methuen & Co., 1898; repr. Amsterdam: Adolf M. Hakkert, 1964, 197–201); cf. Michael the Syrian, *Chronicon* (*Chronique de Michel le Syrien Patriarche*

ops Paul withdrew from communion and was incarcerated as a result, upon which the group communicated again. Since by now Paul was regarded as a security risk by the imperial government, he was kept in prison and the eastern synod broke off relations with him, although in 574 he was able to escape to the camp of al-Moundhir, the successor of al-Harith, from where he went to Egypt disguised as a soldier. In 575[18] the candidature of the moderate Theodore, a Syrian archimandrite resident in Egypt, was proposed for the patriarchate of Alexandria, a man who would have supported Paul at a time when his stocks were very low. One of the consecrating bishops was Bishop Longinus of Nubia, a former *apocrisiarius* of Paul. The manipulation of this election of an outsider enraged the Alexandrians, who refused to recognise Theodore and proceeded to incite violence and tumult.[19] They put forward their own candidate, Peter, who lost no time in claiming his rights as ecumenical patriarch and deposing Paul uncanonically, initiating what we now call the Alexandrine schism of 575. Jacob Baradaeus travelled to Egypt to assess the situation, but ultimately decided in favour of Peter and against the absent Paul. Forced to retire to Constantinople, like many out-of-favour anti-Chalcedonians, Paul lived in hiding until his death in 581. He was buried in a convent under cover of darkness with a false name and no funeral.

## 2 The conflict from the perspective of the dossier

The compiler/compilers of the *DM* was/were quite obviously supporters of Paul and defenders of his divisive career, but beyond that it is difficult to be more precise. The first part of the dossier (letters 1 – 2) contains the synodical letter which Theodosius sent to the exiled Severus of Antioch in 535, and Severus' reply.[20] These are included to highlight Theodosius' authority over the Chalcedonian church given Severus' continuing exile in Egypt (518 – 538), as well as the latter's approval of Theodosius' consecration as patriarch. The seal of approval which

*Jacobite d'Antioche [1166 – 1199]*, ed. and trans. Jean-Baptiste Chabot, 4 vols., Paris: Ernest Leroux, 1899 – 1910; repr. Brussels: Culture et Civilisation, 1963), here *Chron.* 10. 4 – 5 (ed. Chabot, vol. 2, 295 – 300). There is considerable emphasis in the edict on the correct formulation of trinitarian theology, indicating that the conflict which Justin was trying to resolve was not simply that between the two sides of the Chalcedonian divide, but also between adherents and opponents of tritheism.

**18** On the following events see Brooks, "The Patriarch Paul of Antioch," 473 – 74.

**19** John of Ephesus, *HE* 4.10, 11 (ed. Brooks, 191 – 94/143 – 45).

**20** See Van Roey and Allen, *Monophysite Texts*, 271 – 72.

the great Severus gave to Theodosius is, moreover, a guarantee of the validity of Theodosius' future actions, two of the most important of which, from the perspective of the compiler(s) of the *DM*, were his condemnation of tritheism and his appointment of Paul as patriarch. The second part (letters 3–7)[21] deals with the tritheist dispute, in which the *Theological Discourse*, designed to manage and indeed end the conflict, assumes an important place;[22] letters 8–17[23] are concerned with Paul's consecration as patriarch of Antioch. Within the latter group letters 8 and 9 are confidential communications from Theodosius to the bishops of the East explaining why he wants Paul to fill the vacancy left by Sergius' death, and enjoining them to consecrate Paul clandestinely and have him send his synodical letter as soon as possible. Letter 10, addressed to Theodosius by the consecrating bishops Jacob Baradaeus, Eugenius of Seleucia (leader of the tritheists), and Eunomius of Amida, confirms that they have carried out his instructions. (The inclusion of Eugenius in the consecrators is perhaps significant – was this an attempt to diffuse the conflict with the tritheists?) In reply, Theodosius writes an encomium of Paul (letter 10): he is the right man for difficult times and will bring peace to the church – probably the resolution of the tritheist dispute is meant here. Paul has already dispatched his synodical letter, which follows in the dossier (letter 13). In this, his first official communication as patriarch, he complains that Theodosius has deceived him, just as Abraham deceived his son Isaac (cf. Gen 22), by having him consecrated (if this is not a modesty *topos*, we might assume that Paul knew already the difficulties that lay ahead of him), but nonetheless presents his confession of faith, including the Councils of Nicaea, Constantinople I, Ephesus, Cyril's *Twelve Anathemata* against Nestorius, the *Henotikon* or instrument of union promulgated by Emperor Zeno in 482, and Theodosius' *Theological Discourse* itself. Paul condemns tritheism explicitly, leaving no doubt where he stands on the issue, and additionally rejects the doctrine of the Agnoetai. In reply (letter 14) Theodosius makes a similar confession of faith, and for his part too condemns tritheism and Agnoetic doctrine. The next three letters in this group are not from bishops but rather from archimandrites and monks, two to Theodosius sent by Jacob Baradaeus (letters 15 and 17) and one to Paul (letter 16), expressing their approval of

21 See Van Roey and Allen, *Monophysite Texts*, 272–74.

22 For the text and translation of this document and related pieces see Van Roey and Allen, *Monophysite Texts*, 144–263.

23 See Van Roey and Allen, *Monophysite Texts*, 275–78.

Paul's consecration. From Jacob's involvement at this juncture it seems that he was putting his moral and charismatic authority behind Paul's appointment.[24]

By now elderly and still in exile in Constantinople, Theodosius decided in 565 to manage his Egyptian patriarchate through the medium of Paul, to whom he gave the mandate to go there and perform ordinations in his stead. The fourth group of letters in the *DM* (letters 18 – 22),[25] all written by Theodosius, relate to this mission.[26] When Theodosius died on 22 June 566, the conflict between tritheists and anti-tritheists began in earnest, and is documented in the sixth part of the *DM* (letters 25 – 41).[27] As explained in letter 25, written by six anti-Chalcedonian bishops residing in Constantinople to the church in the East, while Theodosius was alive people subscribed to his *Theological Discourse*; after his death, however, some retracted their signatures and openly championed tritheism. The episcopal writers try to bring this divisive situation under control by documenting the chain of events on the basis of four *syndoktika*, one anathema, and two letters, the texts of which the compiler then gives in full (letters 26 – 31).[28] In these documents it is alleged that Jacob Baradaeus and Bishop Theodore of Arabia are being touted as tritheists and Paul the Black is being opposed and defamed as patriarch. The conflict around tritheism appears particularly virulent in the eastern monasteries. In letter 33 Paul writes to Jacob and Theodore about these allegations, claiming that he is attacked verbally and in writing for his opposition to tritheism. Because his detractors claim that Jacob and Theodore are not only tritheists but also opposed to him, Paul requests that the two bishops make known in writing their commitment to Theodosius' *Theological Discourse* and to him. Letter 34 is the reply of Jacob and Theodore, acceding to this request and stating that they abide by everything that was done by Theodosius (this implicitly includes Paul's consecration). The extent of Jacob's authority in the East, particularly in the face of the unpopularity of Paul's consecration, can be seen from the next three letters (letters 35 – 37).[29] The first of these, written by the eastern archimandrites to the anti-Chalcedonian clergy in Constantinople, relates that there is peace, thanks to the intervention of

---

**24** On Jacob's authority, which was not canonical, see David D. Bundy, "Jacob Baradaeus. The State of Research, a Review of Sources and a New Approach," *Le Muséon* 91 (1978): 45 – 86; Grillmeier, *Jesus der Christus* 2/3, 197 – 200.

**25** See Van Roey and Allen, *Monophysite Texts*, 278 – 79.

**26** By contrast, the two letters in the fifth bracket (letters 23 and 24) are out of chronological order because they concern Paul's consecration.

**27** See Van Roey and Allen, *Monophysite Texts*, 281 – 90.

**28** See Van Roey and Allen, *Monophysite Texts*, 283 – 85.

**29** See Van Roey and Allen, *Monophysite Texts*, 287 – 88.

Jacob, who, however, has informed the archimandrites that conflict has arisen over the consecration of Paul. The writers accept Paul as patriarch. From this point as far as letter 41, the emphasis is on managing the conflict over tritheism, which culminated in the excommunication of the leaders of the doctrine, Bishops Conon of Tarsus and Eugenius of Seleucia, in 569. It seems that Conon and Eugenius wrote to Jacob, and that letter 36 is Jacob's reply to them, in which he asks them to end the scandal of tritheism either by being reconciled with their opponents or else coming to the East to discuss the matter with him. In any case, Jacob states that nothing done by Theodosius can be changed (this again implicitly includes Paul's consecration) and that opposition to them is growing in Alexandria and elsewhere. Again taking the initiative in resolving the double conflict of the tritheist controversy and the unpopularity of Paul, in letter 37 Jacob writes to the anti-Chalcedonian bishops residing in Constantinople, asking them to forgive Eugenius and his followers if they renounce their heresy, but once more stating that he accepts all that Theodosius did, namely the condemnation of tritheism and the consecration of Paul. In the following letter (38) from the bishops in the East to those in Constantinople we read again of Theodosius' condemnation of tritheism. The writers allege that, while the tritheists maintain that they accept Theodosius and his *Theological Discourse*, in fact they do not, and they ask the recipients to sign the letter if they are in communion with them. For their part, the bishops of the East accept everything that Theodosius did (including yet again, no doubt, Paul's consecration). Letters 39–41 deal with the increasing episcopal intervention in the case of Conon and Eugenius. In letter 39 the synod of bishops in Constantinople writes to the anti-Chalcedonian church at large about their concerted endeavours and those of the eastern archimandrites to bring the tritheite leaders to heel, recounting how they had drawn up an encyclical (the previous letter) in which they carefully did not mention the attacks of Conon and Eugenius against orthodoxy or against Paul and other bishops. Even with this concession and the insistence of al-Harith, the tritheists refused to sign, as appears from a letter sent to them by Jacob and other bishops, which is transcribed in letter 39. All interventions having failed, Conon and Eugenius were condemned.

The seventh group of documents (letters 42 and 43)[30] comprises an outright defence of Paul the Black composed by a certain Sergius, a hermit in a monastery of Nicaea. The *Defence* itself (42), written in letter-form, moves away from the tritheist debate and Paul's part in it to deal in particular with two of the most contentious events in his career: his part in the consecration of Theodore as pat-

**30** See Van Roey and Allen, *Monophysite Texts*, 291–98.

riarch of Alexandria in 575 and his communion with the Chalcedonians after the promulgation of the edict of Emperor Justin II in 571. In the course of the long *Defence*, Sergius cites from no fewer than seventeen documents, mostly episcopal letters, including an *Apology* written by Paul himself which is attested to only here. It is not clear whether this piece was composed in letter-form. In any case, the entire *Defence* is a tribute to the scholarly, if partisan, activity of Sergius and his access to impeccable sources. On the basis of this document Honigmann[31] concluded that Sergius was the compiler of the whole dossier, but the hermit is designated explicitly as author only in letter 42.[32] In the following letter (43) it is revealed that the author, presumably Sergius, agrees to meet with a certain priest, John the Lame, to discuss the case of Paul (who by this time, November 580,[33] was in hiding in or around Constantinople).

In the eighth and last bracket of letters (44 – 45)[34] we jump back to the short-lived consecration of Theodore as patriarch of Alexandria in 575 and the synodical letter which he wrote to Paul on that occasion (44). Paul's reply is contained in letter 45.[35] It is very probable that these last two letters in the dossier were added by Sergius the hermit, who was exercised by Theodore's consecration and Paul's supposed role in it[36] – rightly so, for this incident ushered in the schism between the sees of Alexandria and Antioch that was to last at least until 616. If it is the case that Sergius was responsible for the addition of these two letters, it would strengthen the argument for his compilation of the dossier as a whole.

While the picture of religious conflict documented in the episcopal letters and other pieces in the *DM* has to be supplemented by the first-hand account provided by John of Ephesus, which dwells on the violence that was provoked by the tritheist dispute and the role of Paul in it, and to a lesser extent by the record preserved by the twelfth-century chronographer, Michael the Syrian, the dossier is a masterful defence of the controversial patriarch of Antioch. All the parts of this picture illustrate the extent to which the conflict aroused by trithe-

**31** *Évêques et évêchés*, 201.

**32** In letter 43 the name of the writer is missing, but it appears to be the work of Sergius. See further Van Roey and Allen, *Monophysite Texts*, 297 n. 47.

**33** On the date see Van Roey and Allen, *Monophysite Texts*, 297 with n. 48.

**34** See Van Roey and Allen, *Monophysite Texts*, 298 – 300.

**35** This epistolary exchange is reported by John of Ephesus, *HE* 4.10 (ed. Brooks, 191/143).

**36** For this speculation see the references in Van Roey and Allen, *Monophysite Texts*, 300 with n. 52.

ism influenced ecclesiastical politics in the East from the 550s to the 580s.[37] As we shall see, this conflict did not end here.

## 3 Relations between Alexandria and Antioch after 581 CE

The tritheist schism continued to dog the patriarchates of Damian of Alexandria (578–606) and Peter of Antioch (formerly of Callinicum; 581–591),[38] although, as stated at the outset of this chapter, our sources are patchier and more disparate than those concerned with the conflict that broke out specifically over Paul the Black. It is a telling fact that the synodical letter which Damian wrote in 578 on his ordination to the patriarchate, preserved by Michael the Syrian, stresses his opposition to tritheism, and after his signature ends with the prayer that the unity of the Trinity be preserved indissolubly.[39] Originally friends – indeed one source claims that Damian ordained Peter to the patriarchate[40] – the two patriarchs fell out over Damian's rebuttal of tritheist doctrine, which Peter considered had gone too far in the opposite direction, namely Sabellianism. It was but a small step for Peter himself to be considered a tritheist and to feel compelled to write in his own defence. The conflict between the two sees was characterised

37 See further Pauline Allen, "Episcopal Succession in Antioch in the Sixth Century," in: *Episcopal Elections in Late Antiquity*, eds. Johan Leemans, Peter Van Nuffelen, Shawn W.J. Keough, and Carla Nicolaye, AKG 119 (Berlin–Boston: De Gruyter, 2011), 23–38, for the suggestion that tritheism lay behind many of the episcopal elections and depositions in the patriarchate of Antioch, on both the anti-Chalcedonian and Chalcedonian sides.

38 See Rifaat Y. Ebied, "Peter of Callinicum and Damian of Alexandria: The End of a Friendship," in: *A Tribute to Arthus Vööbus: Studies in Early Christian Literature and its Environment*, ed. Robert H. Fisher (Chicago, IL: Lutheran School of Theology at Chicago, 1977), 277–82; Ebied, Wickham, and Van Roey, *Peter of Callinicum. Anti-Tritheist Dossier*; Rifaat Y. Ebied, Lionel R. Wickham, and Albert Van Roey, eds. and trans., *Petrus Callinicensis: Tractatus contra Damianum*, CCSG 29, 32, 35, and 54 (Turnhout: Brepols, 1994, 1996, 1998, and 2004).

39 *Chron.* 10.14 (ed. Chabot, vol. 2, 325–332, signature and ending at 332). There is a (different) Coptic version in Herbert E. Winlock, Walter E. Crum, and Hugh G. Evelyn-White, *The Monastery of Epiphanius at Thebes*, pt. 2 (New York: Metropolitan Museum of Art. Egyptian Expedition, 1926), plate XV and 331–37.

40 Anon., *Chronicon ad annum Christi 1234 pertinens* (ed. Jean-Baptiste Chabot, CSCO 82, Scr. Syr. 3, 15, Paris: E typographeo reipublicae, 1920, 256 [text]; trans. Albert Abouna, CSCO 354, Scr. Syr. 154, Louvain: Secrétariat du CorpusSCO, 1974, 193). See the discussion in Ebied, Wickham, and Van Roey, *Peter of Calliniucum. Anti-Tritheist Dossier*, 5.

by futile and tempestuous meetings between Damian and Peter until the latter's death on 22 April 591.[41]

About Peter's successor, Julian (591–595), we know only the little relayed to us by Michael the Syrian:[42] Julian was a monk of a monastery in Qennesrin (Chalcis) and had been Peter's *syncellus*. Perhaps he was also anti-tritheist, like Peter. The same doctrinal leanings may hold true for Julian's successor, the Syrian Athanasius Gammal or Camel-driver (595–634), who was a monk in the same monastery in Qennesrin,[43] perhaps an indication that the conflict around tritheism had become part-and-parcel of the abysmal relations between the patriarchates of Antioch and Alexandria. During his long patriarchate Athanasius devoted a great deal of energy to ending the long-standing religious conflict between the anti-Chalcedonian churches in Antioch and Alexandria – unsuccessfully, as it turned out.

It was Emperor Heraclius who attempted to broker a deal between the two patriarchates through the offices of the imperial official Nicetas. Athanasius travelled to Egypt in the company of a number of his bishops and signed a document of union with Damian's successor, Anastasius (604–619). This union, traditionally dated to 616, has recently been assigned more probably to the second half of 617;[44] it was ratified by a synodical letter drawn up by both patriarchs in which considerable attention is paid to proper trinitarian formulations. Our most important source for this event is Michael the Syrian,[45] although supplementary in-

---

**41** On the evidence in the sources for the date see Ebied, Wickham, and Van Roey, *Peter of Callinicum. Anti-Tritheist Dossier*, 8 n. 33. For the details of the meetings, actual, attempted, and aborted, see ibid., 34–43.

**42** *Chron.* 9.27 (ed. Chabot, vol. 2, 234, 373, 375). See Allen, "Episcopal Succession in Antioch in the Sixth Century," 34.

**43** For the sources and the possible origin of his soubriquet see Allen, "Episcopal Succession in Antioch in the Sixth Century," 35 with n. 44.

**44** On the union see Mich. Syr., *Chron.*, 10.26 (ed. Chabot, vol. 2, 381–94); Friedhelm Winkelmann, "Ägypten und Byzanz vor der arabischen Eroberung," *Byzantinoslavica* 40 (1979): 161–82 at 168; David Olster, "Chalcedonian and Monophysite: The Union of 616," *Bulletin de la Société d'Archéologie Copte* 27 (1985): 93–108; Walter E. Kaegi, *Heraclius, Emperor of Byzantium* (Cambridge: Cambridge University Press, 2003), 214; Allen, *Sophronius of Jerusalem*, 11, 24–26, 59, 60, 62, 145. On the new date of 617 see Marek Jankowiak, "Essai d'histoire politique du monothéletisme à partir de la correspondence entre les empereurs byzantins, les patriarches de Constantinople et les papes de Rome," diss. Paris–Warsaw, February 2009, 18–23, forthcoming as *La Controverse monothélite. Une approche politique*, Travaux et Mémoires, Centre d'Histoire et Civilisation de Byzance (Paris). I am very grateful to Dr Jankowiak for putting an electronic copy of his thesis at my disposal. His dating is discussed and accepted by Phil Booth, *Moschus, Sophronius, Maximus: Asceticism, Sacrament and Dissent at the End of Empire*, forthcoming.

**45** *Chron.* 10.26 (ed. Chabot, vol. 2, 381–94).

formation is found in an anonymous chronicle[46] and in the chronography of the eighth/ninth-century pro-Chalcedonian, Theophanes. Theophanes or his source ridicules the rapprochement as "wishy-washy" (ὑδροβαφῆ),[47] and indeed it was of short duration, possibly not least because of the death of Anastasius in 619. There is a hint in another anonymous chronicle of a union with the "sect of Conon and Eugenius" in 618/9,[48] perhaps meaning between the followers of John Philoponus and the main tritheist body, who, as mentioned above, had fallen out over Philoponus' tritheist interpretation of the resurrection.[49]

A well-documented meeting between Athanasius Gammal and Emperor Heraclius at Mabbug in 629/30 illustrates, however, that a decade later the focus was not on tritheism but on monoenergism.[50] Both Theophanes[51] and Michael the Syrian[52] recount that on that occasion the question of one activity (ἐνέργεια) in Christ was at the centre of discussions, and Michael reports that when emperor

---

**46** *Chronicon miscellaneum ad annum 724 pertinens* (ed. Ernest W. Brooks, trans. Jean-Baptiste Chabot, *Chronica Minora* 1, CSCO 1, Scr. Syr. 1, Louvain: Sécretariat du CorpusSCO, 1960, 146/113): "uniti sunt Damiani asseclae." Cf. Jankowiak, "Essai d'histoire," 18–23.

**47** AM 6121 (ed. Carolus de Boor, Leipzig: Teubner, 1883, 330.5–11; trans. and annotated by Cyril Mango and Roger Scott, with the assistance of Geoffrey Greatrex, *The Chronicle of Theophanes Confessor: Byzantine and Near Eastern History AD 284–813*, Oxford: Clarendon Press, 1997, 461). This pejorative designation of the union appears also in recension 2 of the *Life of Maximus* (PG 90.77C), and in recension 3 (ed. and trans. Bronwen Neil and Pauline Allen, *The Life of Maximus the Confessor: Recension 3*, Early Christian Studies 6, Strathfield: St Pauls Publications, 2003, 54–55).

**48** *Chronicon ad annum 724 pertinens* (ed. Brooks, 146, trans. Chabot, 113). English trans. in Andrew Palmer, *The Seventh Century in the West-Syrian Chronicles*, introduced, translated and annotated by Andrew Palmer, including two seventh-century Syriac apocalyptic texts, introduced, translated and annotated by Sebastian Brock, with added annotation and an historical introduction by Robert Hoyland, TTH 15 (Liverpool: Liverpool University Press, 1993), 17. Cf. Jankowiak, "Essai d'histoire," 20–21.

**49** See Hainthaler, in: Grillmeier, *Christ in Christian Tradition* 2/3, 138–41; cf. Albert Van Roey, "Une Traité cononite contre la doctrine de Jean Philopon sur la résurrection," in: *ΑΝΤΙΔΩΡΟΝ 1. Hulde aan Dr. Maurits Geerard bij de voltooiing van de* Clavis Patrum Graecorum/ *Hommage à Maurits Geerard pour célébrer l'achèvement de la* Clavis Patrum Graecorum, eds. Jacques Noret et al. (Wetteren: Cultura, 1984), 123–39.

**50** See now Christian Lange, *Mia Energeia. Untersuchungen zur Einigungspolitik des Kaisers Heraclius und des Patriarchen Sergius von Constantinopel*, STAC 66 (Tübingen: Mohr Siebeck, 2012), esp. 531–622.

**51** *Chron.*, AM 6121 (ed. de Boor, 320–30; trans. Mango and Scott, 460–61).

**52** Mich. Syr., *Chron.* 11.3 (ed. Chabot, vol. 2, 412).

and patriarch failed to reach agreement about Chalcedon, Heraclius set an anti-Chalcedonian persecution in train.[53]

# 4 Concluding observations

The first stage of the religious conflict between Antioch and Alexandria between c. 565 and 630 is dominated by the controversial personality of Paul the Black and documented precisely, if polemically, by a carefully constructed dossier. It is not often that the historian is able to have recourse to such a valuable tool. For both the earlier and later phases of the conflict it is clear that the problem of tritheism was never far from the surface, although our disparate sources often make it difficult to reconstruct the precise implications of the doctrinal dispute. It is also obvious that the conflict between the sees of Antioch and Alexandria and the consequent splintering of the anti-Chalcedonian party were intolerable frustrations for the imperial government, hence the decisive interventions by Emperor Heraclius. However, after c. 619 the fifty-year old conflict, with its subtext of tritheism, no longer dominated ecclesiastical politics in the East. Rather it was wider issues that commanded attention: the occupation and repulse of the Persians,[54] the rise and demise of the doctrines of monoenergism and monotheletism which went hand in hand with the rapid advances of the Muslims,[55] and a new dynamic in church relations between Constantinople and Rome, illustrated most fully by the activities of Maximus the Confessor.

**53** Mich. Syr., *Chron.* 11.3 (ed. Chabot, vol. 2, 412 – 13). On the meeting see Jan Louis van Dieten, *Geschichte der Patriarchen von Sergios I. bis Johannes VI (610 – 715)*, Enzyklopädie der Byzantinistik 24 (Amsterdam: Verlag Adolf M. Hakkert, 1972), 219 – 32; Wolfgang Hage, "Athanasios Gammala und sein Treffen mit Kaiser Herakleios in Mabbug," in: *Syriaca II: Beiträge zum 3. deutschen Syrologen-Symposium in Vierzehnheiligen 2002*, ed. Martin Tamcke, Studien zur Orientalischen Kirchengeschichte 33 (Münster: LIT Verlag, 2004), 165 – 74; Lange, *Mia Energeia*, 553 – 66; Booth, *Moschus, Sophronius, Maximus*, forthcoming.

**54** On which see, e. g., Clive Foss, "The Persians in the Roman Near East (602 – 630 AD)," *Journal of the Royal Asiatic Society of Great Britain & Ireland* 13 (2003): 149 – 70 (arguing against the negative and destructive role usually assigned to the Persians); Kaegi, *Heraclius, Emperor of Byzantium*, passim.

**55** As argued by Wolfram Brandes, "'Juristische' Krisenbewältigung im 7. Jahrhundert? Die Prozesse gegen Martin I. und Maximos Homologetes," *Fontes Minores* 10 (1998): 141 – 212 at 146 – 51; and Booth, *Moschus, Sophronius, Maximus*, forthcoming.

Sarah Gador-Whyte

# Christian-Jewish Conflict in the Light of Heraclius' Forced Conversions and the Beginning of Islam

Religious conflict of various sorts plagued the Byzantine Empire. In particular, doctrinal disputes between different Christian groups divided the empire and caused headaches for a succession of emperors. The earliest and most long-lasting religious dispute, however, was between Jews and Christians. Jews perceived Christians as heretics, as misguided Jews or, worse, as Gentiles, who had been deceived by a false messiah and persisted in their mistake, refusing to keep the Law or honour the Sabbath. For Christians, the continuing presence of Jews seemed to contradict prophecies about the advent of the Messiah; all Jews should have converted to Christianity after the resurrection. Treatment of Jews by Christian emperors varied, but conditions gradually deteriorated, with successive emperors removing certain rights previously enjoyed by Jews.[1] In the fifth century CE Theodosius restricted the rights of Jews to hold public office (Novella Th.3).[2] The emperor Justinian went further. In 553, in his Novella 146, he prohibited the use of Hebrew scriptures in Jewish synagogues, declaring that the scriptures must be read in Greek.[3] This was an attempt to remove the perceived power Jews had over Christians by reading the scriptures in the original language, and by having their own religious language which Christians generally did not understand. In this novella the Jews are presented as troublemakers who are stubborn and deaf to the truth.[4] Justinian's revision of the legal code

1 On Jews in the Byzantine empire, see, for example, Elli Kohen, *History of the Byzantine Jews* (Lanham, MD: University Press of America, 2007); Andrew Sharf, *Byzantine Jewry from Justinian to the Fourth Crusade*, The Littman library of Jewish civilization (London: Routledge & K. Paul, 1971); Nicholas R.M. de Lange, "Jews and Christians in the Byzantine Empire: Problems and Prospects," in: *Christianity and Judaism*, ed. Diana Wood (Oxford: Blackwell, 1992), 22–23.

2 *CTh*, vol. 3, *Novellae*, eds. Paul Krüger, Theodor Mommsen, and Paul M. Meyer (Berlin: Weidmann, 1902; repr. Hildesheim: Georg Olms Verlag, 1990), Novella III: *De Iudaeis Samaritanis haereticis et paganis*. See also Fergus Millar, *A Greek Roman Empire: Power and Belief under Theodosius II (408–450)*, Sather Classical Lectures (Berkeley: University of California Press, 2006), 128.

3 *Corpus Iuris Civilis*, vol. 3, *Novellae*, eds. Rudolf Schoell and Wilhelm Knoll (Berlin: Weidmann, 1895), 714–18.

4 Leonard V. Rutgers, "Justinian's Novella 146: Between Jews and Christians," in: *Jewish Culture and Society under the Christian Roman Empire*, eds. Richard Lee Kalmin and Seth Schwartz (Leuven: Peeters, 2003), 389.

also removed many of the legal and religious rights of Jews and, in fact, removed Theodosius' statement about the legality of Judaism.[5] Jewish and Samaritan dissatisfaction with their treatment expressed itself in riots and revolts in the fifth and sixth centuries. In 556, for example, Jews and Samaritans in Caesarea attacked and killed Christians, including the governor, and destroyed churches.[6] In the seventh century, the emperor Heraclius decreed that all Jews in the empire should be forcibly baptised.

The *Doctrina Iacobi nuper baptizati* or "The Teaching of Jacob, the newly baptised one" is a dialogue, written in Greek around 634 CE, between Jews who have been forcibly baptised as a result of this decree of the emperor Heraclius.[7] The ostensible setting for the dialogue is that one of the Jews, Jacob, has become convinced of the truth of Christianity and sets out to convince the others. The dialogue is carefully situated within its historic context by the author, unlike other *adversus Iudaeos* literature, making it an important source for religious conflict in the seventh century.[8] This chapter situates the text in the context of increasing religious tensions and explores what it can tell us about Christian-Jewish interactions in the period.

## 1 A century of conflict

Seventh-century Byzantium was marked by violence and political strife. The first decade saw imperial murders and usurpations: the emperor Maurice was slaughtered by supporters of the usurper Phocas in 602;[9] in 610 Heraclius led a rebellion and, once he was successful, had Phocas killed and his body mutilated.[10]

---

5 Nicholas R.M. de Lange, "Jews in the Age of Justinian," in: *The Cambridge Companion to the Age of Justinian*, ed. Michael Maas (Cambridge: Cambridge University Press, 2005), 420.

6 Kohen, *History of the Byzantine Jews*, 31.

7 Some scholars date the dialogue slightly later, but, given that there is no mention at all of the Arab invasions, it seems unlikely that it could have been written much later than 634 or 635. See Patricia Crone and Michael Cook, *Hagarism: The Making of the Islamic World* (Cambridge: Cambridge University Press, 1977), 3 n. 3.

8 Stephen J. Shoemaker, *The Death of a Prophet: the End of Muhammad's Life and the Beginnings of Islam*, Divinations: Rereading Late Ancient Religion (Philadelphia, PA: University of Pennsylvania Press, 2012), 21–22.

9 Agapius, *Universal History*, ed. and trans. Alexander A. Vasiliev, PO 8 (1912), Part 2.2, 447–48.

10 The different versions of this tale as recorded by various chroniclers are presented together in Robert G. Hoyland, *Theophilus of Edessa's Chronicle and the Circulation of Historical Knowledge in Late Antiquity and Early Islam*, TTH 57 (Liverpool: Liverpool University Press, 2011), 59–61.

Heraclius then (and for almost his whole reign) had to contend with numerous invasions of Byzantine territory.[11] By 619 many of the eastern regions (Mesopotamia, Syria, Palestine and Cilicia) had been lost to the Persians,[12] including, most significantly, Jerusalem. The Persians had destroyed the Church of the Holy Sepulchre and stolen the relic of the True Cross.[13]

The loss of Jerusalem to the Persians, and with it the Church of the Holy Sepulchre and the True Cross (with all its connotations of Christian triumph), signalled, to Jews and Christians alike, the end of the Roman empire.[14] Christian apocalyptic literature had previously stated, based on the vision of the four beasts in the book of Daniel, that the Roman empire should be the last remaining empire, and that it would triumph over all others before the advent of the antichrist and the second coming of the Messiah.[15] The victories of the Persians thus threatened Christian concepts of the *eschaton* and, for some Jewish communities in Jerusalem, gave credence to Jewish theology.[16] The Jewish apocalyptic work *Sefer Zerubbabel*, written just after the Persian conquest of Jerusalem, expresses the Jewish hope that this victory signalled the end of Christian hegemony and the coming of the Jewish Messiah.[17] For example, there are contemporary stories of Jews assisting the Persian invaders and taking up arms against

**11** There were only about five years in Heraclius' reign in which the empire was not at war. See Frank R Trombley, "Military Cadres and Battle During the Reign of Heraclius," in: *The Reign of Heraclius (610–641): Crisis and Confrontation*, ed. Gerrit J. Reinink and Bernard H. Stolte (Leiden: Peeters, 2002), 241–60 at 241.

**12** Gerrit J. Reinink, "Heraclius, the New Alexander: Apocalyptic Prophecies during the Reign of Heraclius," in: *The Reign of Heraclius*, 81–94 at 81.

**13** Ibid., 81–82.

**14** See Hans J.W. Drijvers, "Heraclius and the *Restitutio Crucis:* Notes on Symbolism and Ideology," in: *The Reign of Heraclius*, 175–76; Robert L. Wilken, *The Land Called Holy: Palestine in Christian History and Thought* (New Haven, CN–London: Yale University Press, 1992), 203.

**15** Paul Julius Alexander, *The Byzantine Apocalyptic Tradition*, ed. Dorothy deF. Abrahamse (Berkeley: University of California Press, 1985), 151. This idea is based on chapter 7 of the book of Daniel, in which four beasts come one after another. The fourth is the most terrible and powerful and will take over the whole earth; it was believed to be the Roman empire.

**16** Wilken, *The Land Called Holy*, 203.

**17** The text can be found in Israel Lévi, "L'apocalypse de Zorobabel et le roi de Perse Siroès," *Revue des Études Juives* 68 (1914): 129–60 at 131–44. See also Martha Himmelfarb, *The Apocalypse: A Brief History* (Chichester: Wiley-Blackwell, 2010), 118–19; Wilken, *The Land Called Holy*, 207–15.

the Roman soldiers, in the belief that they were assisting the end of Christian rule and bringing in the *eschaton.*[18]

This Jewish optimism was, however, short-lived. When, in 628, Heraclius reconquered Jerusalem, it was portrayed as a great victory of Christianity and a confirmation of Christian eschatological thought.[19] His triumphal entry into the city and restoration of the relic of the True Cross dramatised Christianity's victory and emphasised the Christian belief in God's salvific support of the Roman empire.[20] It looked like the Roman empire was indeed going to conquer all others, as had been predicted. It was shortly after this reconquest that Heraclius issued his decree that Jews in the empire should be forcibly baptised.

There were good reasons, both theological and political, to issue this decree. The Persians had benefitted from the dissatisfaction of Jewish groups, who had been willing to support their military efforts against the Christian Romans.[21] Heraclius is unlikely to have thought that forcible baptisms would eradicate such subversive acts, but this religious persecution of Jews aimed to weaken their position and served as a sign of his commitment to imperial unity based on religious uniformity. This political program was only strengthened by a growing anticipation of the *eschaton*, as a result of the events of the preceding decades, the political upheaval and intense military conflicts. In this context, Heraclius was seen to have an important role to play in preparing the empire for the second coming of the Messiah, stamping out disputes between Christian groups and ensuring that all those who lived in the empire were Christian.[22] Heraclius, at the same time as he was trying to unite different Christian groups by his proposal of the "one will" and "one energy" of Christ,[23] also considered it his responsibility to ensure that the remnant of troublesome Jews, who should have converted when the Messiah first appeared, were brought into the fold.

---

**18** See Gilbert Dagron and Vincent Déroche, "Juifs et chrétiens dans l'Orient du VII$^{e}$ siècle," *Travaux et Mémoires* 11 (1991): 17–273 at 22; Wout Jac. van Bekkum, "Jewish Messianic Expectations in the Age of Heraclius," in: *The Reign of Heraclius*, 95–112 at 103 ff.

**19** See Drijvers, "Heraclius and the *Restitutio Crucis*," 178–79, 186–90.

**20** On this restoration and the various connotations of the triumphal ceremony, see ibid., 175–90.

**21** See Dagron and Déroche, "Juifs et chrétiens dans l'Orient," 28; Wilken, *The Land Called Holy*, 206; Vincent Déroche, "Polémique anti-judaïque et émergence de l'Islam (7e–8e siècles)," *REByz* 57 (1999): 141–61 at 145.

**22** Dagron and Déroche, "Juifs et chrétiens dans l'Orient," 30.

**23** See Drijvers, "Heraclius and the *Restitutio Crucis*," 184; Pauline Allen and Bronwen Neil, eds., *Maximus the Confessor and his Companions: Documents from Exile*, OECT (Oxford: Oxford University Press, 2002), Introduction, 2–21.

The decree does not seem to have been carried out systematically or effectively except in Carthage. Nor was it met with universal approval by contemporary Christians. A letter survives, attributed to Maximus the Confessor, in which he expresses his concerns about the ramifications of such a decree.[24] The letter is addressed to Sophronius the Monk (probably the Sophronius who shortly thereafter became patriarch of Jerusalem),[25] and in it Maximus sets out his three main objections to the forced baptisms: first, he feared that, by forcing people who were not properly prepared for it to be baptised, this decree was in danger of desecrating the sacrament of baptism; second, he expressed fear for the spiritual well-being of these people who were in reality maintaining their Jewish faith while ostensibly being Christian; and finally, that these new initiates, having been brought into close connection with believing Christians, would be better able to spread discord and disbelief amongst the people. While the Jews remained outside the church, their views could be side-lined and ordinary Christians need not be exposed to them. It would be an entirely different matter once these Christ-deniers were brought inside the church. Maximus begs Sophronius to explain why he should not fear the consequences of this move by Heraclius. Unfortunately we do not have Sophronius' reply.

The *Doctrina Iacobi nuper baptizati* (hereafter *Doctrina Iacobi*) is plausibly interpreted in the context of such debates over forced baptism. It can be understood as responding to the concern that forced baptisms would bring a new group of heretics into the church who would endeavour to lead true Christians astray. This reading sees the text as a sort of manual for Christians who are faced with Jewish questions, a list of potential questions and appropriate answers, even answers which should appeal to Jews, having been drawn primarily from the Jewish scriptures (see further below). The way in which this text is structured, the brief questions and long answers followed by statements of belief, makes it more plausible that it is designed to be useful for combatting similar

---

**24** The letter was edited in Robert Devreesse, "La fin inédite d'une lettre de Saint Maxime: un baptême forcé de Juifs et de Samaritains à Carthage en 632," *Revue des Sciences Religieuses* 17 (1937): 25–35. For the following, see Joshua Starr, "St Maximos and the Forced Baptism at Carthage 632," *Byzantinisch-Neugriechische Jahrbücher* 16 (1940): 192–96. There is some dispute about the authenticity of this letter. See Wolfram Brandes, "Heraclius between Restoration and Reform: Some Remarks on Recent Research," in: *The Reign of Heraclius*, 17–40 at 38. I follow the editors of the *Doctrina Iacobi* in considering the letter genuine or at least contemporary.

**25** On Sophronius see Pauline Allen, ed. and trans., *Sophronius of Jerusalem and Seventh-Century Heresy. The* Synodical Letter *and Other Documents*, OECT (Oxford: Oxford University Press, 2009); Phil Booth, *Moschus, Sophronius, Maximus: Asceticism, Sacrament and Dissent at the End of Empire* (Berkeley: University of California Press, forthcoming).

such questions, rather than being a genuine attempt at dialogue leading to conversion.

Throughout, and in opposition to Maximus, the author seems to argue for the program of forced baptism. The text attempts to justify the Christian use of violence in baptising the Jews. Although Jacob himself draws attention to the violence, he claims he is glad that he was forcibly baptised (I.7), and Justus says he is sorry that he was not (IV.5).[26] The length to which the author goes to show that these Jews can be convinced of the truth of Christianity is in stark contrast to many contemporary anti-Judaic texts which claim that the Jews are too stubborn and are therefore unable to be converted.[27] Most such polemics exclude Jews completely from those who are to be saved. The Jews are not part of God's new creation. The author of the *Doctrina Iacobi*, by contrast, seems to argue that the forced baptisms are part of the divine plan of salvation and that they have taken place at the right time (i.e., that the *eschaton* is near). In response to the prefect's declaration that all the Jews must be baptised, they respond that the time for baptism has not yet come (I.3).[28] But, by the end of their conversation with Jacob, they believe that the time has indeed come, and they are glad to have been baptised. Thus this text counters one aspect of Maximus the Confessor's concerns,[29] arguing that the *eschaton* is at hand and that the time for mass baptism of non-Christians has arrived, while at the same time providing Christians with the necessary tools to combat the questions of newly converted Jews.[30]

Such seventh-century tensions provide the historical context for the *Doctrina Iacobi*. Anti-Jewish political policies were extended and hardened in draconian religious persecution in the context of Christian apocalyptic speculation

---

**26** The edition used is from Dagron and Déroche, "Juifs et chrétiens dans l'Orient," 70–219. The translations are my own.

**27** David M. Olster, *Roman Defeat, Christian Response, and the Literary Construction of the Jew*, Middle Ages series (Philadelphia, PA: University of Pennsylvania Press, 1994), 164.

**28** This part is missing from the Greek original, but the Arabic version preserves the Jewish response that it is not time for baptism yet. See the French translation: Dagron and Déroche, "Juifs et chrétiens dans l'Orient," 72.

**29** See Robert G. Hoyland, *Seeing Islam as Others Saw It: A Survey and Evaluation of Christian, Jewish and Zoroastrian Writings on early Islam* (Princeton, NJ: Darwin Press, 1997), 55.

**30** See Averil Cameron, "The Byzantine Reconquest of North Africa and the Impact of Greek Culture," *Graeco-Arabica* 5 (1993): 153–65 at 162. See also Reinink, "Heraclius, the New Alexander," 93–94, who thinks that the *Doctrina Iacobi* was aimed at Christians who feared a Jewish alliance with Arabs. The presentation of the Saracens, discussed in detail below, also suggests that the author intended readers (and both Jews and Christians) to see the new Arab prophet as a false one, and his rising popularity as a threat to the truth of Christianity.

strengthened by external religious pressures. That the forced baptisms were not universally praised by Christian thinkers provided the author of the *Doctrina Iacobi* with opportunities to explore aspects of minority discourses (the extent to which he does is weighed further below). But the dialogue is clearly generated in part by these general pressures and should be read in the context of other contemporary anti-Judaic tracts as well as the broader tradition of apocalyptic literature.

## 2 The *Doctrina Iacobi* and religious conflict

The dialogue is set in Carthage, although some of the discussion is about events taking place in Ptolemaïs in Palestine (which is arguably where it was written).[31] Its popularity is attested to by the fact that, as well as the Greek version, versions or fragments survive in Slavonic, Syriac, Arabic and Ethiopian. It is ostensibly written by a recently baptised Jew called Joseph, who secretly records the conversation which Jacob has with him and a group of other recently baptised Jews, and then with a non-baptised Jew, Justus. There were many polemical texts circulating during this period, but this is the only one which is ostensibly written by a Jew who was forcibly baptised as a result of Heraclius' decree.

Although generally referred to as a dialogue, the *Doctrina Iacobi* is a closed dialogue and, as I have already suggested, is in many ways more like question and answer literature.[32] Understanding the text as a type of question and answer literature makes sense in the context of the letter attributed to Maximus. The lack of openness in the dialogue is soon apparent. The group of Jews, often referred to as "the circumcised" (οἱ ἐκ περιτομῆς), asks Jacob brief questions and then is silent while he gives detailed and long answers, drawing on a large range of scriptural passages to make his case. Occasionally there is a follow-up question, but often the Jews quickly say they believe and then move on to another problem point. Towards the end of the dialogue another Jew turns up, an acquaintance of Jacob and cousin of one of the other Jews, who has escaped the forced baptisms because he was in Palestine at the time (this suggests that the governor of Carthage, George, was more effective in carrying out Heraclius' decree than others elsewhere in the empire). Justus is set up as a more difficult opponent, learned in the scriptures, whose father taught Jacob, and he does bring up new questions

---

**31** Crone and Cook, *Hagarism*, 3.

**32** On this genre, see Annelie Volgers and Claudio Zamagni, *Erotapokriseis: Early Christian Question-and-Answer Literature in Context* (Leuven: Peeters, 2004).

for Jacob to deal with, but he is also quickly convinced of the truth of each answer and in fact it is his cousin Isaakios' wife and mother-in-law who maintain their disbelief for the longer period (III.12). The text thus does not present a real dialogue or argument, but rather a series of questions and detailed answers. The dialogue seems to have been written as an *erotapokrisis*, designed to give Christians plausible answers to the types of questions Jews might ask about Christianity.

The dialogue (or question and answer text) thus seeks to aid Christians in conflict with Jews. Alongside this discursive violence, the text also figures religious conflict in several interrelated ways.

## 2.1 Fear

The dialogue emphasises the fear of both the Jewish and the Christian communities felt by the group. They fear the Christians because the prefect George had decreed that any Jews who had been forcibly baptised should then be forced to attend catechetical classes and to listen to sermons to ensure they truly believed.[33] These Jews are meeting because they do not believe, and fear the consequences if they are discovered. Isaakios, for example, fears being burned by the Christians (I.43). Likewise, the group fears being treated as Christians by non-baptised Jews, who would consider them unclean because of their baptism.

The characters in the text meet secretly and promise not to record the conversation or to tell outsiders about the discussion or the membership of the group (I.43). Naturally the author then has to justify the fact that the dialogue has been written down word for word. Joseph (the supposed author) goes to great lengths to record it, stationing his son at the window in the next house so that he could take notes from what he could overhear through the open windows, and every so often dashing out to inform his son about the goings-on (I.43). Twice he explains what he did and twice records that one of the Jews (first Isaakios and then Justus) questioned him about it (I.43; III.4). He hides his true purpose by claiming to have diarrhoea. All of this seems very staged, but it serves to highlight the fear which such a group of Jewish converts would feel, and therefore the strength of the conflict between Christian and Jewish groups in this period.

33 Dagron and Déroche, "Juifs et chrétiens dans l'Orient," 262.

## 2.2 Violence

Violence is a major aspect of Jewish-Christian interaction in the text, and it is violent on both sides of the conflict. According to the Arabic version of the text (there is a lacuna in the Greek text at this point), Jacob was imprisoned for one hundred days for refusing to be baptised and, when he still refused, was baptised by force (I.3). At the end of the dialogue Justus is willing to endure torture and death for his new-found Christian beliefs (V.17).

Violence of the Jews towards Christians is also treated in the dialogue. Jacob admits to brutal behaviour towards Christians in his youth (I.40). He says he hated Christ (ἐμίσουν τὸν Χριστόν) and did terrible things to Christians (καὶ τοῖς Χριστιανοῖς κακὰ ἐνέδειξα). His behaviour is linked to the (often violent) conflict between the circus factions, which he used to his advantage, changing sides when he saw an opportunity to brutalise Christians (I.40):

> Καὶ ὅτε ἐβασίλευσε Φωκᾶς ἐν Κωνσταντινουπόλει, ὡς πρασίνους παρεδίδουν τοῖς βενέτοις τοὺς Χριστιανούς, καὶ Ἰουδαίους καὶ μαμζίρους ἀπεκάλουν. Καὶ ὅτε οἱ πράσινοι ἐπὶ Κρουκίου ἔκαυσαν τὴν Μέσην...ὡς βένετος, φησί, πάλιν ἐκύλλωνα τοὺς Χριστιανούς, ὡς πρασίνους ὑβρίζων καὶ καυσοπολίτας ἀποκαλῶν καὶ Μανιχαίους.

> And when Phocas was ruling in Constantinople, I handed over Christians to the Blues as if they were Greens, and called them Jews and bastards (*mamzirs*). And when the Greens, under orders from Kroukis, burned the Mese...as a Blue, I say, again I brutalised Christians, insulting them as Greens and stigmatising them as arsonists and Manichaeans.

There is some attempt to justify the Christian use of violence in baptising the Jews. Although Jacob himself draws attention to the violence, he claims he is glad that he was forcibly baptised (I.7), and Justus expresses regret that he was not (IV.5). Similarly, Justus' willingness to die for his new-found beliefs is treated very positively (V.17). By contrast, the author does not justify the Jewish use of violence; Jacob says he was young and thoughtless and is now sorry for his actions (I.40).

The ways in which violent conflict between Jews and Christians is presented in this dialogue point to a Christian author. Christian brutality is mentioned, but justified; Jewish violence is given in more detail and is presented in terms of devilry and mistaken hatred of Christ (I.40). Jacob admits that he refused to pay attention to what the prophets say about Christ (I.40).

## 2.3 Rationality of Jews

However, despite this rhetorical violence, Jews are not presented in an entirely negative fashion, perhaps suggesting an author with Jewish sympathies. Unlike other contemporary Christian polemics, the dialogue does not present Jews as stubborn and unable to be converted to the truth.[34] By contrast, the Jews in the text are rational beings, able to be swayed by reasoned arguments. Lay Jewish intellectual life is presented as vibrant and engaging, arguably suggesting that the author had some experience of such theological conversations in the Jewish community.[35] Jacob expresses lack of comprehension about the Christian tendency to excommunicate those with different opinions about certain doctrinal matters (II.5). Excommunication was not practised by Jewish leaders, nor was it unusual for different interpreters of scripture to have entirely different views.[36]

The questions in the *Doctrina Iacobi* express particularly Jewish concerns about Christian doctrines, and the answers draw heavily on the Old Testament to make their case. At one point (I.12) the Jews ask why Moses said to live by the Law, whereas Jacob has said it is not necessary anymore to be Jewish or observe the Sabbath. They are conflicted: "We want to observe the Sabbath and believe in Christ" (Ἡμεῖς καὶ σαββατίζειν θέλομεν καὶ τῷ Χριστῷ πιστεύειν I.12). Jacob responds by arguing that the Sabbath and the Laws are like the moon and the stars: they are good, but their light is still surpassed (and in fact hidden) by that of the sun (Christ). In his answer he explicitly draws on Deuteronomy, Malachi, the Psalms, Genesis and Isaiah. He also makes use of 1 Timothy and 1 Thessalonians, but he does not draw attention to these as he does to the Old Testament texts.

Other Jewish questions are dealt with in turn. Why does God reject the synagogue, which is supposed to be the place in which the people come to know God (I.32)? Jacob replies that Judaism has reached its full term, and draws on the prophet Isaiah to argue that Christ surpasses the old and that the way to know God now is through Christ and his resurrection.

Why did Christ die the death of a criminal (I.33)? Jacob replies that the prophets had decreed that the Messiah would save humanity through his crucifixion. He uses texts from Deuteronomy, Numbers, Jeremiah, Isaiah and the

---

**34** On the stubbornness of Jews in contemporary Christian writings, see, for example, Yossi Soffer, "The View of Byzantine Jews in Islamic and Eastern Christian Sources," in: *Jews in Byzantium: Dialectics of Minority and Majority Cultures*, eds. Robert Bonfil, Oded Irshai, Guy G. Stroumsa, and Rina Talgam (Leiden: Brill, 2012), 845–70 at 853.

**35** The view of Olster, *Roman Defeat*, 160.

**36** Ibid., 163.

Psalms which refer to the Messiah being placed on wood in pain, and to his outstretched arms and to his pierced hands and feet. In such examples, which could be multiplied, the questions are either generated from within Judaism or draw on resources that would be most rhetorically effective amongst a Jewish audience. The discursive violence against Jews that I have already outlined is somewhat softened in this regard, as the author displays an understanding of key Jewish concerns. The *Doctrina Iacobi* is not merely a closed and triumphalist text; it recognises the reality of the Jewish "other" to some degree and attempts to come to terms with it, albeit within a larger aim of conversion.

After each such Jewish question and appropriate response, and occasionally following a related question and response, the group of Jews believes that Jacob tells the truth, and makes a declaration such as this (I.31):

> Ὄντως, κύρι Ἰάκωβε, ἀληθῆ εἰσιν πάντα ἃ ἐλάλησεν ὁ Θεὸς διὰ τοῦ στόματός σου σήμερον.
>
> Truly, brother Jacob, everything is the truth which God has said today by your mouth.

The conflict between Christianity and Judaism is thus presented as one of rational argument – a conflict in which dialogue is fruitful and brings people to the truth. Gradually, every point of dispute between Jews and Christians (according to the author and his characters) is dealt with satisfactorily, and the Jews convert to Christianity. This particular interreligious conflict evaporates and Jews and Christians are united under the banner of Christ. Reason is figured as a way of overcoming conflict. Yet the standards of rationality are carefully controlled and constructed by the author of the text, and while this move does present the Jews as capable of reason, the reason they are capable of is strictly Christian. The dialogue form in this register is a rhetorical mechanism for overcoming conflicting rationalities by writing them out of the discourse.

Yet despite this Christian totalising discourse (and the fact that all the Jews in the text come to believe in the truth of Christianity), Christians themselves are not presented very positively. The Jews still do not want to marry Christians or associate with them, and Jacob at one point suggests that the converted Jewish race would remain separate from the wider Christian population.[37] Jacob describes his forced baptism as violent (I.3) and all the characters are extremely fearful of the Gentile Christian population (I.43). Violence by Christians towards Jews is not a prominent theme in pro-Christian polemical literature of this period, leading scholars such as David Olster to argue that this text could only have been written to convert Jews or to strengthen Jewish-Christian identity, rather

**37** Ibid., 167.

than merely using them as the traditional enemy to prove "Christianity's integrity."[38]

Yet all of these points can be read as supporting the reading Olster rejects. The term *mamziros* (taken by Olster as a distinctively Jewish insult), for example, is well-attested in the bible, so it is not necessary to infer from its use here that the author was familiar with contemporary Jewish insults.[39] The topos of the purity of the Jewish race, here expressed in the group's desire to remain separate from the Christian population, was important for Christians too, since it ensured that Jesus was the direct descendant of David, and could also be used to marginalise their opponents and set appropriate boundaries around specifically Christian identity. The fear of Gentile Christians is an important aspect of characterisation in the dialogue. And, although Christians are not necessarily presented very positively, as I suggested above, the violence of Jews towards Christians is also prominent: Jacob was involved in various riots against Christians (I.40). He is hardly presented as a model of peace and godly behaviour. This reading, emphasising the way in which Jews are used in the text to demarcate Christian values and identity, harmonises with the general discursive violence we have been tracing.

## 2.4 Conflict with Saracens

Further interreligious conflict is explored towards the end of the dialogue, when the prophet Muhammad is mentioned (although not by name, but simply as the prophet among the Saracens) (V.16). According to Abraham, the brother of the character Justus, this prophet caused many in the Jewish community to rejoice, believing him to be their awaited prophet who would foreshadow the Jewish Messiah (V.16):

> Καὶ ἔσχαμεν οἱ Ἰουδαῖοι χαρὰν μεγάλην. Καὶ λέγουσιν ὅτι ὁ προφήτης ἀνεφάνη ἐρχόμενος μετὰ τῶν Σαρακηνῶν καὶ κηρύσσει τὴν ἔλευσιν τοῦ ἐρχομένου Ἠλειμμένου καὶ Χριστοῦ.
>
> And the Jews greatly rejoice. And they say that the prophet has appeared, coming among the Saracens, and announces the advent of the coming anointed one and Christ.

The author presents the Jewish community as hopeful and expectant, anticipating the arrival of their awaited prophet. And yet he also depicts them as divided

**38** Ibid., 158.
**39** Déroche, "Polémique anti-judaïque," 148 n. 30.

in their reaction to Muhammad. Abraham consults a Jewish wise man, who denies that Muhammad is the one the Jews are waiting for (V.16):

> Πλάνος ἐστίν. Μὴ γὰρ οἱ προφῆται μετὰ ξίφους...ἔρχονται;
>
> He is a false prophet. For do prophets come with swords?

Rather, the holy man says that Christ was the one they were looking for, and the Jews rejected him.

In this conflict we see the apocalyptic frame to the text shaping religious conflict. As I argued above, political persecution of Jews was partly motivated and justified by Christian apocalyptic thought. The *Doctrina Iacobi* is evidence for ways in which the advent of Islam reshaped Christian apocalyptic.[40] The coming of the prophet raised the possibility that the new age that Christianity claimed had been inaugurated by Christ was in fact a sham, and that Muhammad would instead initiate a new age. The rejection of Muhammad within this text points to contested apocalyptic visions and goes towards explaining the urgency of Christian attempts to impose their own apocalyptic worldview across the empire.

Hence the author of the *Doctrina Iacobi* makes it clear that the Jews should think of this new prophet as false, focusing their attention instead on the true Messiah, Jesus Christ, whose advent and status they had misinterpreted as false (V.16). As we have seen, the author argues that there should be no conflict between Jews and Christians, since all Jews should (and can) become Christians. His learned character, Justus, is truly converted by the arguments of Jacob and declares that he wants all his family to become Christian (V.17). At this point Jacob asks (V.17):

> Καὶ ἐὰν ἀναστρέψῃ σε ὁ ἀδελφός σου ἢ οἱ Ἰουδαῖοι οἱ μιγέντες μετὰ τῶν Σαρακηνῶν, τί ποιοῦμεν;
>
> And if your brother turns away from you or the Jews, who are mingled with the Saracens, what will we do?

In passages such as these, the text is witness to the alliances between Jews and Arabs I identified above. These Jews who have joined with the Arabs will cause serious problems for Jews newly converted to Christianity. Justus replies (V.17):

**40** As O'Sullivan points out, it is too early to be considered a polemic against Islam. See Shaun O'Sullivan, "Anti-Jewish Polemic and Early Islam," in: *The Bible in Arab Christianity*, ed. David Thomas, The History of Christian–Muslim Relations 6 (Leiden: Brill, 2007), 63.

Πίστευσον τῷ Θεῷ, κύρι Ἰάκωβε, ὅτι ἐὰν πιάσουσί με οἱ Ἰουδαῖοι καὶ οἱ Σαρακηνοὶ καὶ κομμάτια κομμάτια κατακόψουσι τὸ σῶμά μου, οὐ μὴ ἀρνήσομαι τὸν Χριστὸν τὸν Υἱὸν τοῦ Θεοῦ.

Trust in God, brother Jacob, that even if the Jews and Saracens press upon me and cut my body into tiny, tiny pieces, I will not deny Christ the Son of God.

The Jews and Saracens are presented as an allied and violent force. Justus expects (and possibly seeks) violence from the Jewish community and links them very closely with the Arabic community. This is the group against which Justus wishes to fight and die in the cause of Christianity, if necessary. By these means the author presents the Arabs (or Saracens) as the correct enemy for both Christians and Jews. Whereas the Jews should recognise their wrongs and join the Christians, he argues that both Christians and Jews should see the Arabs and their new prophet as their common enemy, again leaving traces of violently contested apocalyptic in the text.

# 3 Conclusion

Discursive violence in the *Doctrina Iacobi* witnesses to the religious conflict of the seventh century, a period in which wars with the Persians and the advent of Muhammad and subsequent Arab invasions led both Christians and Jews to think apocalyptically and reconsider their conceptions of the *eschaton*. At no place in the text is a genuinely free Jewish voice allowed to be heard. At each point, even when Jewish values are used in an attempt to bridge the gap between Christians and Jews, Christian discourse triumphs and functions to support the violent imperial attempts to suppress religious difference and bolster Christianity. Yet unlike many Christian polemics, this text argues that Jews can become part of God's new creation. The question and answer format, and the assumption that rational argument is capable of convincing opposed groups and leading to conversion also gives Jews agency as rational thinkers, although the dominant rationality, for all its attempt to bridge difference through the use of shared Old Testament texts, is Christian. Throughout, the text champions the cause of Christianity and argues that the *eschaton* is imminent, while presenting Christians with the means to counter particularly Jewish concerns about Christianity.

Bronwen Neil

# The Earliest Greek Understandings of Islam: John of Damascus and Theophanes the Confessor

## 1 Introduction

On 28 February 380 CE, Emperor Theodosius issued his famous edict on religious observances in the empire:[1]

> It is our will that all the peoples who are ruled by the administration of Our Clemency shall practice that religion which the divine Peter the Apostle transmitted to the Romans, as the religion which he introduced makes clear even unto this day...[W]e shall believe in the single Deity of the Father, the Son, and the Holy Spirit, under the concept of equal majesty and of the Holy Trinity. We command that those persons who follow this rule shall embrace the name of Catholic Christians. The rest, however, whom We adjudge demented and insane, shall sustain the infamy of heretical dogmas, their meeting places shall not receive the name of churches, and they shall be smitten first by divine vengeance and secondly by the retribution of Our own initiative...

This edict sums up the dilemma faced by Byzantine Christians when confronted by the rise of Islam some 250 years later. In the view of Christians such as John of Damascus, those Arabic-speaking tribesmen who followed the prophet Muhammad seemed to embrace a deviant form of Christianity, one which did not "believe in the single Deity of the Father, the Son, and the Holy Spirit." Their meeting places were not called churches, and Christians fully expected them to be smitten by divine vengeance, and to be the victims of imperial retribution. As a model, the Byzantines could recall the defeat of the Persians in the first decades of the seventh century, when – on the pretext of recovering the True Cross, which had been taken from Jerusalem by Shah Chosroes II in 614 CE – the Persians were defeated in a series of campaigns from 624 to 628.[2] However, in the clash with Arab forces in Syria and Palestine, the opposite occurred, and Byzantine armies led by Emperor Heraclius (610 – 641) were defeated, most notably at

1 *CTh* 16.1.2 (*Code Théodosien. Livre XVI*, ed. Theodor Mommsen, trans. Jean Rougé, SC 497, Paris: Éditions du Cerf, 2005, 114; Eng. trans. Clyde Pharr, *Theodosian Code*, Princeton, NJ: Princeton University Press, 1952, 326).

2 See Barbara Baert, "*Exaltatio crucis.* De Byzantijnse keiser Heraclius (610 – 641) en het middeleeuwse Westen," *Bijdragen. Tijdschrift voor filosofie en theologie* 60 (1999): 147 – 72.

the Battle of Yarmuk (636), which brought to an end 300 years of Byzantine rule in Syria. In the wake of their defeats, Christians were forced to reassess their initial opinion of this "heresy," and its relationship with divine providence. Could the people of the prophet Muhammad themselves be instruments of divine vengeance? In the fourth century, Lactantius had portrayed the Persians in just this way, in his tract *De mortibus persecutorum*, which described the murder of pagan Roman emperors (namely, Valerian) by King Sapor as an act of divine punishment for their sacrilege.[3] Tim Briscoe argues that as Rome became Christianised from the fourth century, historical sources – which were discourses of legitimacy – became more "Christian" and religion became a key factor in the justification of wars.[4] By the time of the Byzantine conflict with Chosroes II, the religious rhetoric was quite specific: Heraclius' defeat of the Persians was depicted as a victory over God's enemies, and the salvation of the Christians of Persia.[5] Extending this idea one step further, I suggest that for John of Damascus and to a lesser extent Theophanes, the conflict of Byzantium with Islam was one of orthodox Christianity threatened by heretics, who in the absence of any better analogy, were deliberately likened to Arians.[6]

Religion and history intersected in complex ways in early contacts between Muslims and Christians. This was felt most keenly in Constantinople, the new capital of Christianity since its foundation by Constantine in 331. With the establishment of Islam as a contestant to the power of the Byzantine and Persian empires in the early eighth century, Christian writers felt obliged to respond to this threat to their cultural hegemony. Most reacted negatively, refusing even until the ninth century to concede that Muhammad's increasingly popular message con-

3 Lactantius, *Mort.* 5 (ed. and trans. John L. Creed, Oxford: Oxford University Press, 1984, 107). This was one of the sources from the third to seventh centuries discussed by Tim Briscoe, "Rome and Persia: Rhetoric and Religion," Australasian Society for Classical Studies conference, 5–7 February, 2012, Hellenic Centre, Melbourne.

4 Ibid.

5 John W. Watt, "The Portrayal of Heraclius in Syriac Historical Sources," in: *The Reign of Heraclius (610–641): Crisis and Confrontation*, eds. Gerrit J. Reinink and Bernard H. Stolte (Leuven: Peeters, 2002), 63–79, esp. 68–69, where he cites eastern Syrian chronicles.

6 The fourth-century Alexandrian priest and theologian Arius advocated the teaching of Christ's subordination to God the Father, being neither begotten out of time, nor equal to God. While trinitarian orthodoxy was imposed at the Ecumenical Councils of Nicaea (325) and Constantinople (381), with the affirmation in the Niceno-Constantinopolitan Creed of Christ as "eternally begotten of the Father, begotten not made," Arianism or Homoean Christianity continued to cause religious dissension in the West, where it was embraced by the newly-converted Germanic tribes. See further Rowan Williams, *Arius: Heresy and Tradition* (2nd edn.; Grand Rapids, MI: W.B. Eerdmans, 2002).

stituted a rival monotheistic religion. While Greek reactions to the rapid spread of early Islam were largely negative, their responses being conditioned by the circumstances of the Persian invasions and the widespread adoption in the Christian East of monothelitism, some commentators gave more neutral responses in which Muslims played a role in God's providential plan for humanity. Previous research in English has focused on the later, western mediaeval period of Christian–Muslim relations, whose representations of Muslims were drawn from earlier stereotypes.[7] This chapter analyses some of the earliest responses preserved in the sources, starting with John of Damascus, and the sources used by Theophanes Confessor in the early ninth century.[8]

## 2 John of Damascus' defence of Christianity

John of Damascus was born some time after 650 CE and died in 749.[9] From a wealthy Syrian family, John probably served in the Ummayad administration of Damascus, where he was born. At some stage, early in the eighth century, John moved to Palestine where he joined the monastery of Mar Sabas, near Jerusalem. It is not certain where he composed his theological works, but Andrew Louth argues for their composition in Palestine.[10] Sidney Griffith demonstrates from his survey of the textual evidence of the ninth and tenth centuries that, while there was a steady stream of refugees (and therefore information) from Palestine and Syria to Constantinople from the mid-eighth century onwards, there

**7** Norman Daniel, *Islam and the West: The Making of an Image* (2nd edn.; Oxford: One World, 1993); John V. Tolan, ed., *Medieval Christian Perceptions of Islam* (New York: Garland, 1996; repr. London–New York: Routledge, 2000); Id., *Saracens: Islam in the Medieval European Imagination* (New York: Columbia University Press, 2002); John V. Tolan and Philippe Josserand, *Les relations entre les pays d'Islam et le monde latin du milieu du X^eme^ siècle au milieu du XIII^eme^ siècle* (Paris: Bréal, 2000).

**8** An updated survey of texts from 600 to 900 CE is found in *Christian–Muslim Relations: A Bibliographical History 700–900*, eds. David Thomas and Barbara Roggema, A History of Christian-Muslim Relations 11 (Leiden: Brill, 2009). See also James Howard-Johnston, *Witnesses to a World Crisis: Historians and Histories of the Middle East in the Seventh Century* (Oxford: Oxford University Press, 2010); Peter Sarris, *Empires of Faith. The Fall of Rome to the Rise of Islam, 500–700* (Oxford: Oxford University Press, 2012).

**9** Karl-Heinz Uthemann, "Johannes von Damaskus," in: *Biographisch-Bibliographisches Kirchenlexikon* 3 (Herzberg: Bautz, 1992), 331–36.

**10** Andrew Louth, *St John Damascene: Tradition and Originality in Byzantine Theology*, OECS (Oxford–New York: Oxford University Press, 2002), 8–10. On the Damascene synthesis, see Basil Studer, *Die theologische Arbeitsweise des Johannes von Damaskus*, Studia Patristica et Byzantina 2 (Ettal: Buch-Kunstverlag, 1956).

was little or no traffic from Byzantium to the world of Islam.[11] The unilateral direction of information had a substantial impact on relations between the two worlds, and meant that Byzantine sources were unable to be read or contradicted by Christians or Muslims in the East.

John's polemic against Islam is contained in *De haeresibus*,[12] an appendix to his tract *De fide orthodoxa*.[13] The work dates to around the turn of the seventh to eighth centuries, as Theophanes testifies.[14] We have not treated here the *Disceptatio Christiani et Saraceni* whose authorship is contested, but certainly could have been written by John, as Daniel Sahas contests, though perhaps not in its present form.[15] The *Disceptatio* does, however, date to the eighth century.

## 2.1 Precursor of the Antichrist

John introduces Islam, his one hundredth heresy, as "the superstition of the Ishmaelites, which to this day prevails and keeps people in error, being a precursor of the Antichrist."[16] In describing Islam in this way, he was repeating a charge he had leveled in *De fide orthodoxa* at the fifth-century patriarch of Constantinople, Nestorius.[17] In the same work he defined the Antichrist as "any man who does not confess that the Son of God came in flesh, is perfect God and became perfect

11 Sidney Griffith, "Byzantium and the Christians in the World of Islam: Constantinople and the Church in the Holy Land in the Ninth Century," *Medieval Encounters* 3/3 (1997): 231–65.

12 *De haeresibus* (PG 94.677–780; *Die Schriften des Johannes von Damaskos*, IV, ed. Bonifatius Kotter, PTS 22, Berlin: W. de Gruyter, 1981, 19–67).

13 *De fide orthodoxa* (*Die Schriften des Johannes von Damaskos*, II, ed. Bonifatius Kotter, PTS 12, Berlin: W. de Gruyter, 1973, 7–239). This in turn was part of a larger work called *The Fount of Knowledge*.

14 Theophanes, *Chronographia*, AM 6234, a. 741/2 (ed. Carolus de Boor, *Theophanis Chronographia*, Leipzig: Teubner, 1885; repr. Hildesheim, NY: Georg Olms, 1980, vol. 1, 417). This dating is accepted by Louth, *St John Damascene*, 80. Cf. Daniel J. Sahas, *John of Damascus on Islam. The "Heresy of the Ishmaelites"* (Leiden: E.J. Brill, 1972), 54, who dates the work to 743 or immediately afterwards, linking it to the murder of Peter, bishop of Maiuma, for his condemnation of Muhammad and his mythography in 741/2.

15 Sahas, *John of Damascus on Islam*, 60 and 99; with an English translation in Appendix 2; ed. Kotter. *Die Schriften des Johannes von Damaskos* IV, 427–38. Louth, *St John Damascene*, 81, considers John's authorship of the work as it is preserved today "unlikely." The *Disceptatio* is listed under *Dubia* in CPG 8075. I return to Peter of Maiuma below in the discussion of Theophanes Confessor's *Chronographia*.

16 *Haer.* 100 (ed. Kotter, IV, 60.1–2 = PG 94.764 A).

17 *De fide orthdoxa* 56 (ed. Kotter, II, 135 = PG 94.1032 A).

man while at the same time being God."[18] He used the "precursor of the Antichrist" to dismiss the anti-Chalcedonians or miaphysites in Syria, and the iconoclast emperors Leo III and Constantine V. It was especially apt for those who were suspected of Arianism, that is, of denying the true divinity of Christ, as exemplified in the fourth century by Athanasius of Alexandria's use of the epithet to attack the emperor Constantius for his support of the Arians.[19]

John attributes the origins of Muhammad's heresy to the malign influence of an Arian monk, who inspired him to devise his own heresy.[20] John refers to a *hadith* that identifies the Syrian monk as Bahîrâ, who predicted Muhammad's prophetic powers. After a brief explanation of the origins of the Ishmaelites or Saracens, John critiques the Qur'an's account of the origins of Christ and his apparent but not real crucifixion. Muhammad's statement that Christ never claimed to be the Son of God is one of the many "extraordinary and quite ridiculous things in this book which he boasts was sent down to him by God,"[21] a claim for which John insists there is no evidence or any witnesses. Nor are there any witnesses that Muhammad was a prophet from God.[22] There were no forerunners to announce him, in contrast with Christ who had John the Baptist to announce his advent.

## 2.2 Associators and idolaters

According to John, Muslim accusations against Christians consist of two charges: that Christians are associators and idolaters. The first accusation John puts down to their misunderstanding of the doctrine of the Trinity. Muslims call Christians "associators" (*hetaeriasts*) because they make Christ an associate or partner of God, by claiming him to be both the Son of God and God.[23] John retorts by calling them "mutilators of God:" by avoiding the association of Christ with God – for they confess that Christ is the Word and Spirit of God – they deprive God of Word and Spirit. In this way they mutilate the Trinity, by isolating the three persons of the Godhead from each other.

---

**18** *De fide orthodoxa* 99 (ed. Kotter, II, 232 = PG 94.1216 A). Trans. Sahas, *John of Damascus on Islam*, 63.
**19** Athanasius, *Historia Arianorum* (PG 25.773).
**20** *Haer.* 100 (ed. Kotter, IV, 60.12–13 = PG 94.765 A).
**21** *Haer.* 100 (ed. Kotter, IV, 61.32–33 = PG 94.765 C).
**22** *Haer.* 100 (ed. Kotter, IV, 61.34–62.35 = PG 94.765 C).
**23** *Haer.* 100 (ed. Kotter, IV, 63.61–62 = PG 94.768 B).

Second, John explains that Christians are called "idolaters" because they venerate the Cross. In response, John accuses Muslims of litholatry, harking back to Saracen practices of pre-Islamic times, as described by Jerome, Bede, and Isidore of Seville, among other Christian writers.[24] He poses this question in his mock interrogation of an unnamed Saracen: "How is it then that you rub yourselves against a stone in your Khabar and kiss and embrace it?"[25] This was an ingenuous rhetorical move on John's part, since he had earlier conceded that the idolatrous worship of the black stone which represented Aphrodite had ceased with Muhammad's arrival in Mecca.[26] John continues with the oral tradition: "Then some of them say that Abraham had relations with Agar upon it [the rock] but others say that he tied the camel to it, when he was going to sacrifice Isaac."[27] John is offended by the gratuitous reference to a camel at the sacrifice of Isaac – he notes that Abraham left his donkeys (not camels) behind with the servants before the sacrifice.[28]

## 2.3 *The Camel of God*

The Damascene's lampoon of the Qur'an targets four books (suras) of the Qur'an,[29] which John must have read in Arabic if he read them at all, as the Islamic scriptures were not yet available in a Greek translation in his day.[30] It is not clear whether John knew Arabic, which only replaced Greek as the language of Arabic administration from the second year of the caliphate of al-Walīd (705–715) onwards.[31] I focus here only on the fourth book, *The Camel of God*, because

**24** The early western sources, including the Latin Byzantine–Arab Chronicle of 741 and the Hispanic Chronicle of 754, are discussed by Tolan, *Saracens*, 72–78; Robert Hoyland, *Seeing Islam as Others Saw It. A Survey and Evaluation of Christian, Jewish and Zoroastrian Writings on Early Islam*, Studies in Late Antiquity and Early Islam 13 (Princeton, NJ: The Darwin Press, 1997), 216–19 and 423–27.
**25** *Haer.* 100 (ed. Kotter, IV, 64.79–80 = PG 94.769 A).
**26** *Haer.* 100 (ed. Kotter, IV, 60.7–10 = PG 94.764 B).
**27** *Haer.* 100 (ed. Kotter, IV, 64.80–82 = PG 94.769 A).
**28** Cf. Gen 22:3.
**29** *Haer.* 100 (ed. Kotter, IV, 64–67 = PG 94.769–73).
**30** On the question of the earliest Greek translation of the Qu'ran, see Erich Trapp, "Gab es eine byzantinische Koranübersetzung?," *Diptycha* 2 (1980/1981): 7–17. There seems to have been a translation available by the ninth century: Griffith, "Byzantium," 259.
**31** Theoph., *Chron.* AM 6199 [706/7 CE] (ed. de Boor, vol. 1, 376). Sahas, *John of Damascus on Islam*, who uses the earlier edition of Theophanes by Classen and Bekker, locates these events six years earlier than does de Boor. Cyril Mango and Roger Scott, trans., *The Chronicle of Theophanes the Confessor. Byzantine and Near Eastern History, AD 284–813* (Oxford: Clarendon

it is not a sura of the Qur'an as it has been handed down to us, although several Qur'anic passages refer to it.[32] There is a she-camel mentioned in the Qur'an (96.13), an animal that was given as a sign to test the people of Thamud (Petra).[33]

> She and the people were to drink from the river on alternate days. The people were to let the camel feed, and not harm her, lest punishment fall on them. Certain men maltreated her, and hamstrung her, and destruction followed. Other features of the story as given by our author are oral tradition.

John's version of *The Camel of God* raises the question of whether he had any firsthand knowledge of Islam, or whether his knowledge came simply from books. John Merrill argues against any firsthand knowledge, pointing to two errors in John's account. First, there are not three rivers in Paradise, but four, consisting of water, wine, milk, and honey (47.15/16, 17). Second, John of Damascus' jest that men should become drunk from drinking unmixed wine in Paradise "is impossible, for the wine of Paradise does not intoxicate."[34] However, neither of these criticisms discounts the possibility that John had knowledge of an oral tradition that was not included in the written version of the Qur'an.

John subjected his version of *The Camel of God* to a mock Trinitarian analysis, as though he was trying to reveal a hidden Arian message. John introduces into the narrative a baby camel of semi-divine status, "which when the mother had been done away with, called upon God and God took it to himself." John continues his interrogation of the text thus:[35]

> And we say to them: 'Where was that camel from?' And they answer that (she was) from God. And we say: 'Was there any other camel coupled with her?' And they say: 'No.' 'How then,' we say, 'was the offspring begotten? For we see that your camel is without father and without mother and without genealogy, and when she gave birth she was met, instead, with evil. Neither is it evident who bred with her, nor (where) the little camel was taken up. So why did not your prophet, with whom, according to what you say, God

Press, 1997), lxiv–lxvii, explain how Theophanes' dating was one year behind the indiction from some time after 603, during the reign of Phocas (602–610) until at least 659.

**32** 91.13; 26.155–57; 54.27, 28; 17.61/69; 11.64–66/67, 68; and 7.73/71. The other suras are *On Woman*, *The Table*, and *The Heifer*, usually known as *The Ox*.

**33** John E. Merrill, "Of the Tractate of John of Damascus on Islam," *The Muslim World* 41 (1951): 88–97 at 94. All references to the Qur'an come from the standard English translation by Abdullah Yusuf Ali (6th edn.; Elmhurst, NY: Tahrike Tarsile Qur'an, 2003) available online at http://www.credoreference.com/entry/quran (accessed 11 Sept. 2012).

**34** Merrill, "Of the Tractate," 94, citing sura 37.47/46.

**35** *Haer.* 100 (ed. Kotter, IV, 65.121–66.130 = PG 94.772 A). Trans. Sahas, *John of Damascus on Islam*, 139–41 (modified).

> spoke, find out about the camel – where it grazed, and who got milk by milking it? Or did she possibly, like her mother, meet with evil people and get destroyed? Or did she enter into paradise before you, so that you might have the river of milk that you so foolishly talk about?'

John's suspicion of an Arian basis for Islamic christology is apparent from his description of the mother camel as "the forerunner," a term usually reserved for John the Baptist.[36] All this buffoonery is aimed at contesting the prophetic authority of Muhammad, who cannot explain the allegory of the camel and its offspring adequately.[37] He finished his account of the heresy of the Ishmaelites with a list of practices that were contrary to Jewish and Christian law. Muhammad advocated male and female circumcision, renouncing the Sabbath, refusal of baptism, and abstinence from wine and some foods, "while he ordered them to eat some of the things forbidden by the Law."[38] One of the forbidden foods which Muhammad ordered them to eat, or at least allowed them to eat, was camel meat, though there is some debate still in Muslim circles about whether this abrogates food pollution laws, with modern commentaries on the text (*hadiths*) pointing both ways.[39]

## 3 Theophanes the Confessor's *Chronographia*

Around a century later, Theophanes the Confessor (d. 818), resident in Constantinople, sought to compose a Greek chronicle in annalistic style to cover the centuries from the reign of Diocletian up to his own time. Unfortunately Theophanes had no access to Byzantine histories in Greek for Constans II's rule (641–668),[40] a key period in the development of Muhammad's following. Instead, he was obliged to Syriac sources, especially the so-called "eastern source" that has com-

36 *Haer.* 100 (ed. Kotter, IV, 66.132–35 = PG 49.772 B): "If your forerunner the camel is outside of paradise, it is obvious that she has dried up out of hunger and thirst, or that others are going to enjoy her milk." Trans. Sahas, *John of Damascus on Islam*, 141.

37 Ibid.: "...and so your prophet is boasting in vain that he talked with God, since there was not revealed to him the mystery about the camel." Trans. Sahas, *John of Damascus on Islam*, 141.

38 *Haer.* 100 (ed. Kotter, IV, 67.152–56 = PG 49.777 A).

39 The *Islam Question and Answer* of Sheik Muhammed Salih Al-Munajjid at http://islamqa.info/en/ref/7103 (accessed 25 Sept. 2012) is a convenient collection of ancient and modern hadiths on the question of whether eating camel meat, cooked or raw, nullifies ablution (*wudoo'*) and requires purification.

40 Mango and Scott, *Chronicle*, lxxxix.

monly been identified with Theophilus of Edessa's *Chronicle.*[41] Historical sources for the early Arab period from 630 to the 750s were scarce in general.[42] Other sources for the later period used by Theophanes included Greek date-lists of rulers and patriarchs; a contemporary Greek *bios* of the iconoclast Emperor Leo III (714–741); and an anti-monothelite tract that drew from Anastasius of Sinai.[43] By contrast with John Damascene, Theophanes' representation of the followers of Muhammad is startlingly neutral. This is at least in part due to the generic constraints of the chronicle, and his attempts as a Christian historiographer to explain how their military successes fitted into God's providential plan for the Byzantine empire.[44] In the early centuries of Arab military triumphs over eastern and western Christendom, the spread of Islam certainly appeared to be divinely ordained, to Muslims and Christians alike. Early Christian writers, on the other hand, with the exception of Augustine, embraced a model of divinely-ordained domination rather than passive submission. Thus one popular Christian explanation of Muslim success was that God was punishing Byzantine Christians for their flirtation with monotheletism, the doctrine of one will in Christ (rather than two, a human and a divine will). Islamic military victories over Emperors Heraclius and his grandson Constans II from the 640s to late 660s were directly

---

**41** Robert G. Hoyland, *Theophilus of Edessa's Chronicle and the Circulation of Historical Knowledge in Late Antiquity and Early Islam*, TTH 57 (Liverpool: Liverpool University Press, 2011), 4–6. Hoyland comments (6) that this identification is an over-simplification. Further contributions to the debate about the identity of Theophanes' eastern source(s) for 630 to the 740s have been made by Muriel Debié, "Théophile d'Edesse, le fantôme de l'historiographie syriaque," and Maria Conterno, "The Chronicle of Theophanes: Sources, Composition and Transmission," papers presented to *Theophanes Confessor. An International Workshop*, 14–15 September 2012, Paris (forthcoming).

**42** On the other historical sources that were available for this period, see Hoyland, *Theophilus*, 14–19; on Theophanes' dependence on an eastern source in general, ibid., 7–13, and for information on the Arab conquests in particular, ibid., 23–24.

**43** Mango and Scott, *Chronicle*, lxxxvii. The anti-monthelite tract was based partially on Anastasius of Sinai's *Sermo III in 'secundum imaginem'* (CPG 7749).

**44** The use of chronicles to defend or attack the religious agenda of the current regime is well-established. See for example Roger Scott, "The Treatment of Religion in Byzantine Chronicles and Some Questions of Religious Affiliation," in: *Between Personal and Institutional Religion: Self, Doctrine, and Practice in Late Antique Eastern Christianity*, eds. Brouria Bitton-Ashkelony and Lorenzo Perrone, Cultural Encounters in Late Antiquity and the Middle Ages 15 (Turnhout: Brepols, forthcoming); Philippe Blaudeau, "Ordre religieux et ordre public: observations sur l'histoire de l'Église post-chalcédonienne d'après le témoignage de Jean Malalas," in: *Recherches sur la chronique de Jean Malalas*, II, eds. Sandrine Agusta-Boularot et al., (Paris: Association des amis du Centre d'histoire et civilisation de Byzance, 2006), 243–56.

linked to imperial sponsorship of the heresy, which was not officially condemned until the Ecumenical Council of 680/81.

## 3.1 Theophanes' approach to Islam

Theophanes embraces this spiritualised explanation of history in his *Chronographia*. He first mentions Muhammad in his entry for 626/7 CE, the year of Siroes' accession as Persian emperor: "At which time also Moamed, leader of the Arabs, that is, the Saracens, living under the Persians, was in his sixth year out of a total of nine."[45] Theophanes records the uprising of the Muslims, whom he called Amalekites, in 628/9 CE:[46]

> After [Pope] Martin's exile, Agathon was ordained Pope of Rome, who, being moved by a divine zeal, also convened a holy synod and rejected the monothelete heresy, while proclaiming the two wills and energies.[47] And while the church at that time was being troubled thus by emperors and impious priests, Amalek rose up in the desert, smiting us, the people of Christ, and there occurred the first terrible downfall of Palestine, Caesarea and Jerusalem, then the Egyptian disaster, followed by the capture of the islands between the continents and of all the Roman territory, by the complete loss of the Roman army and navy at Phoinix, and the devastation of all Christian peoples and lands, which did not cease until the persecutor of the church had been miserably slain in Sicily.

The "persecutor of the church" was the monothelite emperor Constans II, who was murdered in his bath in Sicily in 668, while fleeing the Muslim raids on the East. Theophanes reports that in 741/2, Peter of Maiuma, chartulary of the public taxes, was sentenced to death for his public condemnation of Islam

---

**45** Theoph., *Chron.* AM 6119 (ed. de Boor, vol. 1, 327). An interpolation in some codices is noted by de Boor, ibid., line 16, and supported by Anastasius' text: "quando et Moamed, Arabum seu Saracenorum princeps sub Persis degens sectum agebat annum perventurus ad nonum." There is one earlier mention of Muhammad in a short coda to the entry for AM 6116 which de Boor, ibid., 314, rejected as inauthentic, relegating it to his *apparatus criticus* (line 26): "Mamed, leader of the Arabs, 9 years." This line did not appear in Anastasius' Latin version.
**46** *Chron.* AM 6121 (ed. de Boor, vol. 1, 332; trans. Mango and Scott, 462).
**47** Synod of Rome (680). Theophanes has skipped a couple of decades of papal history: Pope Martin (649–653) was taken to Constantinople for trial and died in exile in the Chersonese in 655; see *Narrationes de exilio sancti papae Martini* 25–28 (ed. and trans. Bronwen Neil, *Seventh-century Popes and Martyrs: the Political Hagiography of Anastasius Bibliothecarius*, Studia Antiqua Australiensia 2, Sydney–Turnhout: Brepols, 2006, 214–21). Martin's successor, Eugenius, was ordained in 654. See discussion in Bronwen Neil, "From *Tristia* to *Gaudia:* the Exile and Martyrdom of Pope Martin I," in: *Martyrdom and Persecution in Late Antique Christianity*, ed. Johan Leemans, BETL 241 (Peeters: Leuven, 2010), 179–94.

and Muhammad.[48] According to Theophanes, Peter had summoned prominent Arab friends and anathematised their “false prophet and precursor of the Antichrist,” because he “does not believe in the Father, Son, and Holy Ghost, the consubstantial and life-giving Trinity within a unity.”[49] Here the purported association between Islam and Arianism is made very clear, in common with John of Damascus.

## 3.2 Muhammad and his successors

Theophanes relates that Muhammad brought back his ideas from Palestine “where he consorted with Jews and Christians and sought from them certain scriptural matters.”[50] Theophanes is at pains to point out that Muhammad’s tribe, the Amanites or Homerites, did not trade cattle like the other Arab tribes, but rather “traded on their camels.” The destitute and orphaned Muhammad married a rich widow, Chadiga, after first working for her as a hired labourer “with a view to trading by camel in Egypt and Palestine.” He tried to hide his epilepsy from his wife by pretending that his fits were trances induced by visitations from the angel Gabriel, which implies a Jewish or Christian influence.

According to Theophanes, Muhammad’s death occurred in 629/30 CE, after he had appointed his kinsman Abū Bakr as his successor.[51] Theophanes’ catalogue of Arab caliphs, from the advent of Muhammad’s immediate successor, Abū Bakr, in 630 (actually 632) to the death of the ‘Abbasid Caliph al-Amīn in 813, contained some inaccuracies, but the number of years from Muhammad’s starting point in 622 CE correctly totals 191 years.[52] Abū Bakr’s rule over two and a half years was marked by significant clashes with Byzantine and Persian forces. He sent four generals against the Christians in Arabia, then took Hera and

**48** Maiuma has been identified both as Gaza and Mimas, a monastery near Emesa. On the possible coincidence of this event with John’s composition of *Fount of Knowledge*, see n. 14 above.

**49** Theoph., *Chron.* AM 6234 (ed. de Boor, vol. 1, 416–17; trans. Mango and Scott, 577). Cf. Mango and Scott, *Chronicle*, 579 n. 5 on the identification of Peter of Maiuma with Peter of Capitolias in Transjordan.

**50** Theoph., *Chron.* AM 6122 [629/30 CE] (ed. de Boor, vol. 1, 333–34).

**51** Theoph., *Chron.* AM 6122 (ed. de Boor, vol. 1, 333). Islamic sources are agreed that Muhammad actually died in 632. Cf. the argument of Stephen J. Shoemaker, *The Death of a Prophet: the End of Muhammad’s Life and the Beginnings of Islam* (Philadelphia, PA: University of Philadelphia Press, 2012), 73–117, that this date was of symbolic significance, making Muhammad a Moses-type figure.

**52** Mango and Scott, *Chronicle*, lxxi.

the territory of Gaza. After what Theophanes describes as a "brilliant victory" over the patrician Sergius, the generals returned home with many captives and much booty. There is an ambiguous reference to idol worship in Theophanes' account of the four emirs' attack on Christian Arabs. This was meant to occur "on the day when they sacrificed to their idols." It is unclear from the text whose sacrifice is intended: whether the Muslims were accusing the Christians of idolatrous worship, or whether Theophanes is referring to idolatrous Muslim sacrifices.[53] Abū Bakr's successor, Umar, captured Bostra, then won a significant victory at the battle of Yarmuk in 633/4 in which combined Byzantine forces numbering 40,000 men were overthrown. On the back of this victory, they took Damascus "as well as the country of Phoenicia."[54] Some settled there while others proceeded against Alexandria, which was governed by the monothelite patriarch Kyros, who negotiated a treaty with them but was then accused before Emperor Heraclius of giving gold to the Saracens. Arab forces took up arms against Byzantine troops, led by the prefect of Egypt, Manuel. With Manuel's forces defeated, they then imposed taxes on Egypt in retribution.

## 3.3 Umar and Sophronius

In c. 638, Umar stood at the gates of the holy city of Jerusalem and demanded that the patriarch, Sophronius, hand over the keys to the city. In Theophanes' account of this confrontation we find the first Byzantine acknowledgement that Islam was a rival religion, and not a heretical offspring of Judaism or Christianity.[55]

> Oumaros entered the Holy City dressed in filthy garments of camel-hair and, showing a devilish pretence, sought the Temple of the Jews – the one built by Solomon – that he might make it a place of worship for his own blasphemous religion. Seeing this, Sophronios said,

---

53 Modern scholars have taken up both sides of the argument, with Mango and Scott following Krikov in opting for the latter interpretation, and Conrad arguing for the former: Mango and Scott, *Chronicle*, 467 n. 4; Lawrence I. Conrad, "Theophanes and the Arabic Historical Tradition: Some Indications of Intercultural Transmission," *Byzantinische Forschungen* 15 (1990): 1–44 at 23–26.

54 Theoph., *Chron.* AM 6126 (ed. de Boor, vol. 1, 338; trans. Mango and Scott, 470). See Daniel J. Sahas, "The Face to Face Encounter Between Patriarch Sophronius of Jerusalem and the Caliph 'Umar Ibn Al-Khattab: Friends or Foes," in: *The Encounter of Eastern Christianity with Early Islam*, eds. Emmanouela Grypeou, Mark N. Swanson, and David Thomas, History of Muslim-Christian Relations 5 (Leiden: Brill, 2006), 33–44.

55 Theoph., *Chron.* AM 6127 [634/5 CE] (ed. de Boor, vol. 1, 339; trans. Mango and Scott, 471).

'Verily, this is the abomination of desolation standing in a holy place, as has been spoken through the prophet Daniel.'[56]

The "abomination of desolation" or Antichrist motif was to have a long life in anti-Muslim polemic in the West, where the Islamic conquest was seen as a precursor of the Antichrist and the end of the age.[57] Here, again, it is the camel-hair cloak that particularly offends the Christian patriarch. Sophronius begs him to take from him a "kerchief and a garment" to wear, but he refused. Eventually he consented to borrow some clothes until his had been washed. Sophronius, after striking this great blow for Byzantine sartorial standards, died and left his city open to the raiders. His struggle against the monothelite heresy of Heraclius and his companions Sergius and Pyrrhus, patriarchs of Constantinople, is duly noted by Theophanes.[58]

# 4 Conclusion

It might seem from this short survey of Theophanes' account of the first ten years of Islam's development that the worst thing the early Byzantine Greeks could say about Muhammad and his followers was that they had a disgusting association with camels. However, behind Theophanes' superficial criticism of Islamic standards of dress and dietary preferences, there lies a profound ambivalence. Muslims were both agents of divine chastisement and the "abomination of desolation," or Antichrist. God had delivered them brilliant victories to chasten the monothelite heretics, but at the same time Byzantine Christians were called to stand clear of the "blasphemous religion" of the Saracens.

John of Damascus showed considerably more confidence than Theophanes in his defence of Christianity, especially in his refutation of the charges of association of the persons of the Trinity, and of idolatry in their worship of the cross. John retorted that Muslims mutilated God by trying to cut off the Son of God and the Holy Spirit from God the Father. He sought to make Muhammad's revelation sound ridiculous, thereby calling into question his prophetic authority. John's satirical commentary on the legend of a mother camel and her offspring points to an early association of Muslims with heresy, particularly that of the Homoians.

**56** Cf. Dan 11:31.

**57** See Tolan, *Saracens*, 45–50, and Brett Whalen, *Dominion of God. Christendom and Apocalypse in the Middle Ages* (Harvard: Harvard University Press, 2009), 145–46.

**58** Theoph., *Chron.* AM 6127 (ed. de Boor, vol. 1, 339).

Changed political realities might account for the somewhat more subdued critique of Theophanes in 813, the very year that the Islamic caliphate reached the zenith of its power with the taking of the city of Baghdad, its future capital. Theophanes was not to know that this was the highpoint of Islamic rule, at least until the Ottoman empire took power in the fifteenth century, and that the caliphate was doomed to self-destruct in the ninth century. The usefulness of Theophanes' *Chronographia* as a source on the early Islamic conquest is clearly compromised by its overtly religious agenda. Nor were Theophanes' sources particularly reliable. With no access to contemporary Byzantine historical sources for the early Arab conquest, Theophanes had to make do with Syriac authors, possessed of their own dyothelite and iconophile biases.

Scholars of religious history are fortunate to possess in *De haeresibus* and the *Chronographia* two unique witnesses to the beginnings of an extremely significant religious conflict, both reflecting early Greek understandings of Islam, but written in different genres and from totally different perspectives. The differences between them should alert us to the dangers of characterising early Islam on the basis of evidence provided by Greek Christians, even if they were near-contemporaries of the events they sought to understand and represent.

Damien Casey

# Muhammad the Eschatological Prophet

It is clear from Stephen Shoemaker's study of traditional narratives of the origins of Islam and the life of Muhammad that these were heavily theologised in order to account for Islam's distinctiveness.[1] Initially the Believers' movement led by Muhammad was an inclusive one concerned for the reform of monotheistic belief in the God of Abraham in preparation for the imminent arrival of the Day of Judgement. Muhammad's followers did not initially distinguish themselves from other Abrahamic monotheists. "Because many, if not most, of the people of the Near East were already ostensibly monotheists, the original Believers' movement can best be characterised as a monotheistic reform movement, rather than as a new and distinct religious confession."[2] Rather, "convinced of the imminence of the Last Judgment, and, feeling themselves surrounded by corruption and sin, they strove to form themselves into a righteous community so as to attain salvation on Judgment Day."[3] One might say that Muhammad had no more intention of establishing a new religion than did Jesus. As with time the Jesus movement felt a need to distinguish itself from its Jewish foundations, so it was with Muhammad's community of believers. And just as Paul would distinguish between the legal requirements of Gentile and Jewish Christians, Muhammad's followers were expected to follow Qur'anic law but Jews could also follow the Torah and Christians the gospel. This chapter will trace an interesting parallelism in the self-understanding of both Jesus and Muhammad as eschatological prophets who would herald the coming of the reign of God and the Day of Judgement.

## 1 Prophets, religious beginnings, and revision

### 1.1 The Jesus movement

What the search for the historical Jesus uncovered was the absolute centrality of the notion of Jesus as an eschatological prophet, leading Albert Schweitzer to

1 Stephen J. Shoemaker, *The Death of a Prophet: The End of Muhammad's Life and the Beginnings of Islam* (Philadelphia, PA: University of Pennsylvania Press, 2012).

2 Fred M. Donner, *Muhammad and the Believers. At the Origins of Islam* (Cambridge, MA: Belknap Press of Harvard University Press, 2010), 87.

3 Ibid., 67.

conclude that "The historical Jesus will be to our time a stranger and an enigma."[4] This is a position that most biblical scholars would hold to this day. However, there remains a tendency among many scholars of the historical Jesus to portray Jesus as a social and ethical reformer in a reflection of the scholar's own values.[5] The same can be said of western scholars who have attempted to present a sympathetic portrait of Muhammad and of Islam to the West.[6] But the idea of Muhammad as an eschatological prophet is just as strange and unfamiliar as is the similar apocalyptic portrait of Jesus. Just as the urgency of Jesus' eschatological message became diminished and reinterpreted with time, so it was with Muhammad's community of believers.

## 1.2 Hagarism

The current revisionism in the study of Islamic origins can trace its beginnings to Patricia Crone and Michael Cook's landmark study *Hagarism*,[7] which although often methodologically flawed has raised questions about the received history of Islam that will not go away. Despite the perceived inadequacy of Crone and Cook's account, its basic thesis seems to stand, putting in doubt the claim that Islam was born in "the full light of history"[8] as the suspicion emerges that traditional historiography was in fact heavily theologised history.

One key indication that early Islamic history has been theologised is its chronology of the Prophet's death, just as in the canonical gospels, where the precise day of Jesus' death makes a theological point. While the synoptic gospels narrate that Jesus died on the day of the Passover so that the Last Supper may be a Passover meal, the Gospel of John describes Jesus' death on the day before, while the Passover lambs are being slaughtered, in order to identify Jesus as the Passover lamb. Similarly with the death of Muhammad, traditional accounts of the life of Muhammad relate that Muhammad died before entering the prom-

---

4 Albert Schweitzer, *The Quest of the Historical Jesus: A Critical Study of its Progress from Reimarus to Wrede*, trans. W. Montgomery (London: A. & C. Black, 1910), 399.

5 E.g., John Dominic Crossan, *The Historical Jesus: The Life of a Mediterranean Jewish Peasant* (San Francisco, CA: HarperSanFrancisco, 1991); Burton L. Mack, *Who Wrote the New Testament? The Making of the Christian Myth* (San Francisco, CA: HarperSanFrancisco, 1995); and Marcus Borg, *Meeting Jesus Again for the First Time* (San Francisco, CA: HarperSanFrancisco, 1995).

6 In particular one thinks of the works of Karen Armstrong, including *Muhammad: Prophet For our Time* (London: Harper, 2006).

7 Patricia Crone and Michael Cook, *Hagarism: The Making of the Islamic World* (Cambridge: Cambridge University Press, 1980).

8 Arnold J. Toynbee, *A Study of History*, vol. 12 (Oxford: Oxford University Press, 1961), 464.

ised land, suggesting a strong parallel with Moses. The identification is not accidental, considering that Moses is the prophet mentioned more than any other in the Qur'an. As Shoemaker notes: "Muhammad is frequently modeled directly after the life of Moses, in an effort to shape Muhammad's biography according to the pattern of a biblical prophet."[9] The same tendency is evident in Matthew's portrayal of Jesus as the new Moses handing down the perfection of the Law at the Sermon on the Mount.[10]

## 2 Eschatology in early witnesses to the Believers' movement

Apart from the so-called *Constitution of Medina* there is no extant documentary mention of Muhammad in Arabic for the first seventy years of the Islamic era. According to Donner, the earliest dated inscription mentioning Muhammad is an Egyptian tombstone bearing the date 71 AH.[11] As for the traditional dating of the death of Muhammad, Shoemaker argues that "eleven different sources" from the seventh and eighth centuries, "including one from the Islamic tradition itself, indicate Muhammad's continued survival at the beginnings of Near Eastern conquests."[12]

Although there is a dearth of early texts witnessing to the rise of Islam, those few that we do have from outside of the Islamic tradition give credence to the eschatological character of the early movement. Three of these will be considered below, in very different genres: a Greek apology for Christianity directed at Jews, *The Teaching of James, recently baptised*; a Jewish apocalyptic text, *The Secrets of Rabbi ben Yohai*; and the Armenian *History* of Sebeos. The eschatological content of these Christian and Jewish texts will be compared with the account of the Qur'an.

---

**9** Shoemaker, *The Death of a Prophet*, 114.

**10** The five discourses found in Matthew chapters 5, 6, and 7 do not seek to do away with the Torah, but can be understood as a thoroughly rabbinic practice as expressed at the beginning of the mishnaic text *Pirkei Avot 1.1* or *Ethics of the Fathers:* "Make a fence for the Torah," the basic thinking being this maxim is to go beyond the Law in order to increase the likelihood that one will not inadvertently infringe upon the Law. "So be perfect, just as your heavenly Father is perfect" (Matt 5:48).

**11** Fred M. Donner, "From Believers to Muslims: Confessional Self-Identity in the Early Islamic Community," *Al-Abhath* 50 – 51 (2002 – 2003): 9 – 53 at 41.

**12** Shoemaker, *The Death of a Prophet*, 13.

## 2.1 *The Teaching of James, recently baptised*

The *Doctrina Jacobi nuper baptizati* is the earliest extant non-Muslim text that refers to the upheaval of the Arab conquests.[13] It is a Greek apologetic written in response to the forced baptism of Jews ordered by Heraclius. Its author argues for the appropriateness of forced conversions, making the case that the Jews should persist in their adopted religion, Christianity. Of special interest here is its record of a supposed discussion between Jacob, a forced convert, with other Jews on recent events within the Byzantine Empire.

> When the *candidatus* was killed by the Saracens, I was at Caesarea and I set off by boat to Sykamina. People were saying 'the *candidatus* has been killed,' and we Jews were overjoyed. And they were saying that the prophet had appeared, coming with the Saracens, and that he was proclaiming the advent of the anointed one, the Christ who was to come. I, having arrived at Sykamina, stopped by a certain old man well-versed in scriptures, and I said to him: 'What can you tell me about the prophet who has appeared with the Saracens?' He replied, groaning deeply: 'He is false, for the prophets do not come armed with a sword. Truly they are works of anarchy being committed today and I fear that the first Christ to come, whom the Christians worship, was the one sent by God and we instead are preparing to receive the Antichrist. Indeed, Isaiah said that the Jews would retain a perverted and hardened heart until all the earth should be devastated. But you go, master Abraham, and find out about the prophet who has appeared.' So I, Abraham, inquired and heard from those who had met him that there was no truth to be found in the so-called prophet, only the shedding of men's blood. He says also that he has the keys of paradise, which is incredible.[14]

That the prophet should claim to be the keeper of the keys (cf. Matt 16:19) reflects an early Islamic tradition, Shoemaker suggests.[15] The Jews looked with hope to a deliverer. We shall see this supported by *The Secrets of Rabbi Simon ben Yohai*, to be discussed below. The seventh century was a time of escalating polemic against the Jews, beginning with the conflict with Persia, but reaching a new plateau in response to the Muslim conquests. After all, it was not yet clear that Islam was a new religious threat.[16] Neither does it seem, according to the testimony of some sources, that Muslims considered Christians a religious adversary. According to the Nestorian patriarch Isho'yahb III, writing in 650, "The Arabs not

13 See the more detailed treatment of this text in Sarah Gador–Whyte's chapter in this volume.
14 *Doctrina Jacobi* V.16, in Gilbert Dagron and Vincent Déroche, "Juifs et chrétiens dans l'Orient du VIIe siècle," *Travaux et Mémoires* 11 (1991): 17–248 at 209. Cited and translated by Robert G. Hoyland, *Seeing Islam as Others Saw It: A Survey and Evaluation of Christian, Jewish and Zoroastrian Writings on Early Islam* (Princeton, NJ: Darwin Press, 1997), 57.
15 Shoemaker, *The Death of a Prophet*, 23.
16 See the chapter by Bronwen Neil in this volume.

only do not fight Christianity, they even recommend our religion, honour our priests and saints of our Lord, and make gifts to monasteries and churches."[17] The Jews, on the other hand, were an old enemy and the similarities between Jewish and Muslim practices were noted.

Explaining how the Saracens had their descent from Sara, Sozomen had almost two centuries earlier observed that:

> Such being their origin, they practice circumcision like the Jews, refrain from the use of pork, and observe many other Jewish rites and customs. If, indeed, they deviate in any respect from the observances of that nation, it must be ascribed to the lapse of time, and to their intercourse with the neighboring nations.[18]

Consequently, those things that Jew and Muslim held in common, such as circumcision, the direction of prayer, and the veneration of certain objects, were the dominant concerns of Christian anti-Muslim tracts.[19] This is clear from a text attributed to Maximus the Confessor who, although troubled by the forced conversion of the Jews, nonetheless fulminates against those "who announce by their actions the presence of the antichrist," as if they were the reason for the turn of events. "What is more terrifying, I say, for the eyes and ears of Christians than to see a cruel and alien nation authorized to raise its hand against the divine inheritance? But it is the multitude of sins committed by us that has allowed this."[20]

In the wake of the Arab conquest Christianity's version of the doctrine of manifest successes needed to be reversed, and anti-Jewish volleys were part of this new arsenal, even while it maintained its triumphalist tone.[21] The Jews were the punching bag used to help the Christians salvage some semblance of

---

**17** Isho'yahb Patriarcha III, *Liber Epistolarum* (CSCO, Scriptores Syri, ser. III/64, 251). Cited by Donner, "From Believers to Muslims," 49.

**18** Sozomen, *HE* 6.38.11 (eds. Joseph Bidez and Günther C. Hansen, GCS NF 4.299; trans. Chester D. Hartranft, *Nicene and Post-Nicene Fathers, Second Series*, vol. 2, eds. Philip Schaff and Henry Wace, Buffalo, NY: Christian Literature Publishing Co., 1890, online at http://www.newadvent.org/fathers/26026.htm).

**19** Hoyland, *Seeing Islam*, 82, notes the presence of these three themes in a number of works, including the late seventh-century Greek apology, *Trophies of Damascus*, and John of Damascus, *De fide orthodoxa* 4.12, 16 and 25.

**20** Maximus, *Ep.* 8. Cited by Hoyland, *Seeing Islam*, 78. This text is dubious. See the comments by Sarah Gador-Whyte in her chapter at n. 24.

**21** As Hoyland, *Seeing Islam*, 80, notes, the *Trophies of Damascus* begins with the words: "Of the divine and invincible church of God." On the notion of invasion as God's punishment, see Abdul-Massih Saadi, "Nascent Islam in the Seventh Century Syriac Sources," in: *The Qur'ān in its Historical Context*, ed. Gabriel Said Reynolds (London: Routledge, 2008), 217–22 at 219.

self-esteem. The Jewish interlocutor of the mid to late seventh-century anti-Jewish tract *Trophies of Damascus* ripostes: "If things are as you say, how is it that enslavements are befalling you? Whose are these devastated lands? Against whom are so many wars stirred up? What other nation is [so much] fought as the Christians?"[22] To which Anastasius of Sinai could be replying in his *Dialogue against the Jews:*

> Do not say that we Christians are today afflicted and enslaved. This is the greatest thing, that though persecuted and fought by so many, our faith stands and does not cease, nor is our empire abolished, nor are our churches closed. But amid the peoples who dominate and persecute us, we have churches, we erect crosses, found churches and engage in sacrifices.[23]

## 2.2 *The Secrets of Rabbi ben Yohai*

For our purposes the most significant work of Jewish apocalyptic literature of the seventh century is that attributed to one of the great rabbis of the second century, Simon ben Yohai. Two versions of *The Secrets of Rabbi ben Yohai* are incorporated into the *Prayer of Rabbi Simon ben Yohai*, which dates to the Crusades, and into another midrash entitled Ten Kings.[24] As for *The Secrets* themselves, Bernard Lewis is convinced that the events and rulers referred to are those of the Umayyad Caliphates.[25] The *Prayer of Rabbi Simon* simply reused the older tradition of the Ishmaelite conquest and reapplied it to the Crusades.

According to *The Secrets*, Rabbi Simon ben Yohai had been hiding in a cave from the Roman emperor when he prayed standing for forty days and nights, beseeching God: "Lord God, how long wilt Thou be angry against the prayer of Thy servant?" (cf. Ps 80:5). It is here that the vision begins. Rabbi Simon is shown two empires: the Kenite, associated with Rome, and Ishmael, with the Arabs.

> He saw the Kenite. When he saw the kingdom of Ishmael that was coming, he began to say: 'Was it not enough, what the wicked kingdom of Edom did to us, but we must have the

22 *Trophies of Damascus* II.3.1.220. Cited by Hoyland, *Seeing Islam*, 79.

23 Anastasius of Sinai, *Dialogue against the Jews* (PG 89.1221 C–D). Cited by Hoyland, *Seeing Islam*, 81.

24 Bernard Lewis, "An Apocalyptic Vision of Islamic History," *Bulletin of the School of Oriental and African Studies, University of London* 13/2 (1950): 308–38 at 309.

25 Lewis, ibid. For Graetz's argument, see Heinrich Graetz, *Geschichte der Juden von den ältesten Zeiten bis auf die Gegenwart: aus den Quellen neu bearbeitet*, vol. 5, *Geschichte der Juden vom Abschluß des Talmud (500) bis zum Aufblühen der jüdisch-spanischen Kultur (1027)* (Magdeburg: Druck und Verlag von Albert Falckenberg & Co., 1860), Note 16 at 489–97.

> kingdom of Ishmael too?' At once Metatron the prince of the countenance answered and said: 'Do not fear, son of man, for the Holy One, blessed be He, only brings the kingdom of Ishmael in order to save you from this wickedness. He raises up over them a Prophet according to His will and will conquer the land for them and they will come and restore it in greatness, and there will be great terror between them and the sons of Esau.'[26]

The revelation continues as Rabbi Simon asks Metatron: "How do we know that they are our salvation?" Metatron responds by referring Rabbi Simon to the prophet Isaiah's vision of the two riders (Isa 21:6–7) as a prophecy of messianic deliverance through this Ishmaelite prophet. Metatron also cites Zechariah's prophecy that Israel's salvation shall come riding on an ass (Zech 9:9). Muhammad is clearly identified therefore with the fulfillment of Jewish messianic hopes and corroborates the report of *Doctrina Jacobi* that "the prophet had appeared, coming with the Saracens, and that he was proclaiming the advent of the anointed one, the Christ who was to come."[27] Shoemaker makes an interesting observation that the grammatical ambiguities in the Hebrew text do not make it clear whether it is God or the prophet who is to conquer the land. Shoemaker argues persuasively that Lewis is simply following tradition in ascribing the conquest to God, but that based on the text alone it would be more reasonable to ascribe the conquest to the prophet.[28]

## 2.3 The *History* of Sebeos

Our third text of interest is the Armenian history attributed to Sebeos, bishop of the Bagratunis, writing around the year 660. Sebeos is the first non-Muslim author to present an exposition of the rise of Islam that "pays attention to what Muslims themselves thought they were doing."[29] Hoyland cites as evidence of Sebeos' trustworthiness as a chronicler his occasional use of documentary material and his apparent access to privileged information.[30] Sebeos sees the Arab conquests as part of the salvation history. As descendents of Abraham, Muhammad

---

**26** Adolf Jellinek, *Bet ha-Midrasch*, vol. 3 (Leipzig: Vollrath, 1855), 78. Cited and translated by Lewis, "An Apocalyptic Vision," 321–322.

**27** *Doctrina Jacobi* V.16, 209. Cited by Hoyland, *Seeing Islam*, 57.

**28** Shoemaker, *The Death of a Prophet*, 27–30.

**29** Hoyland, *Seeing Islam*, 128.

**30** Hoyland, *Seeing Islam*, 125–26.

and his followers could rightly lay claim to the promised land.[31] "I shall speak of the stock of Abraham, not of the free one but of that born from the handmaiden concerning which the divine word was fulfilled: 'his hands on all, and the hands of all on him'."[32] Sebeos believed the kingdom of Muhammad and his followers to be the fourth of the successive kingdoms prophesied by Daniel.[33] In this he differs from the more widespread Christian view that saw the sons of Hagar as a tool of God's wrath for the chastisement of Christians.[34]

Sebeos describes how the Jews gathered in the city of Edessa after the departure of the Persians and were subsequently besieged by Heraclius' army. Realising that they could not hold out, the Jews negotiated their peaceful departure. Theophilus of Edessa (695–785), writing a century after Sebeos, gives us a slightly different account, although Hoyland clearly finds his reconstructed account of Theophilus more convincing than that of Sebeos, which he describes as "garbled."[35] The sources using Theophilus describe how Shiroi (Siroes), having murdered his father the Shah Khosrau and become emperor himself, made peace with Heraclius and agreed to restore all Byzantine lands seized by Persian troops. Heraclius and his brother Theodore were marching to Syria to reclaim those cities. When Theodore reached Edessa and informed them of what had happened, the Persians replied: "We do not know Shiroi and we will not surrender the city to the Romans." The Jews of Edessa, standing on the walls with the

---

**31** See the commentary by Howard-Johnston in *The Armenian History attributed to Sebeos*, Robert W. Thomson and James Howard-Johnston, with Tim Greenwood, TTH 31, 2 vols. (Liverpool: Liverpool University Press, 1999), vol. 2, 238.

**32** Sebeos, Ch. 42 (trans. in Thomson and Howard-Johnston, *The Armenian History*, vol. 1, 95). Sebeos is here citing Gen 16:12, which continues with the statement that Ishmael "shall be a wild ass of a man."

**33** Ibid., 239. Dan 2:36–45, elaborated as the four beasts of the last judgement in Daniel 7.

**34** John bar Penkāyē writes from Mesopotamia: "We should not think of the advent (of the children of Hagar) as something ordinary, but as due to divine working. Before calling them, (God) had prepared them beforehand to hold Christians in honour, thus they also had a special commandment from God concerning our monastic station, that they should hold it in honour...God put victory into their hands in such a way that the words written concerning them might be fulfilled, namely: 'one man chased a thousand and two men routed ten thousand' (Deut. 32.30). How otherwise could naked men riding without armour or shield have been able to win, apart from divine aid, God calling them to destroy by them 'a sinful kingdom' (Amos 9.8) and to bring low through them the proud spirit of the Persians." Trans. Sebastian Brock, "North Mesopotamia in the Late Seventh Century: Book XV of John bar Penkāyē's Rish Melle," *Jerusalem Studies in Arabic and Islam* 9 (1987): 51–75 at 57–58.

**35** Hoyland, *Seeing Islam*, 635 n. 28. In an excursus (631–71), Hoyland explains that his reconstruction of the lost chronicle of Theophilus of Edessa is based on the agreement of extant authors who seem to have used his text as their main source for the history of the period.

Persians, taunted the Christians, thereby provoking Theodore's assault on the city. Persian resistance was crushed, leading them to accept a pledge of safe return to their country. A Jew by the name of Joseph, fearing for his people, escaped from the city in order to find Heraclius, whereupon he successfully urged the king to forgive his fellow Jews and to send an envoy to restrain his brother from extracting vengeance.[36]

In Sebeos' account the Jews then went to the sons of Ishmael and informed them of their blood relationship through the testament of scripture, asking for aid. But although the Muslims were persuaded of their close relationship, yet they were unable to agree amongst themselves, because their cults were divided from each other. At this point Muhammad enters the narrative:

> At that time a certain man from among those same sons of Ismael whose name was Mahmet, a merchant, as if by God's command appeared to them as a preacher [and] the path of truth. He taught them to recognize the God of Abraham, especially because he was learned and informed in the history of Moses. Now because the command was from on high, at a single order they all came together in unity of religion. Abandoning their vain cults, they turned to the living God who had appeared to their father Abraham. So Mahmet legislated for them: not to eat carrion, not to drink wine, not to speak falsely, and not to engage in fornication. He said 'With an oath God promised this land to Abraham and his seed after him forever. And he brought about as he promised during that time while he loved Israel. But now you are the sons of Abraham, and God is accomplishing his promise to Abraham and his seed for you. Love sincerely only the God of Abraham, and go and seize your land which God gave to your father Abraham. No one will be able to resist you in battle because God is with you'.[37]

Just as Rabbi Simon understood the rise of the kingdom of Ishmael as divine providence, Jewish messianic expectations were encouraged by Arabs building on the Temple Mount. According to Sebeos, the Jews, "after gaining help from the Hagarenes for a brief while, decided to rebuild the temple of Solomon. Finding the spot called Holy of Holies, they rebuilt it with base and construction as a place for their prayers. But the Ishmaelites, being envious of them, expelled them from that place and called the same house of prayer their own."[38]

Jerusalem and especially the Temple Mount were of high significance to the believers due to the expectation that the key scenarios of the Day of Judgement would take place at the Temple Mount. It was on the Rock that "God had chosen

---

**36** *Chronicle* 1234 1.235–36 (trans. in *Theophilus of Edessa's Chronicle and the Circulation of Historical Knowledge in Late Antiquity and Early Islam*, trans. Robert G. Hoyland, TTH, Liverpool: Liverpool University Press, 2011, 80–81). See also Hoyland, *Seeing Islam*, 635.

**37** Sebeos, 135. Ch. 42 (trans. Thomson and Howard-Johnston, vol. 1, 95–96).

**38** Sebeos, 139. Ch. 43 (trans. Thomson and Howard-Johnston, vol. 1, 102).

as His throne and from which He ascended to Heavan (sic). On this Rock, God will judge mankind and on this Rock, the Scales will be placed."[39] Given then the centrality of Jerusalem for eschatological expectation, its conquest was especially significant.[40]

## 3 The Qur'an: The prophet of the Hour

The Qur'an abounds in eschatological imagery. Sura 16 begins with the pronouncement that "The command of Allah is coming"[41] or, more literally, the rule or reign of God is coming. Although only Allah knows the hour "It may be that the Hour is nigh" (33.63). It is possibly even "nearer" than a "twinkling of the eye" (16.77). It is Muhammad's mission to "warn them of the Day" (40.18); for "The threatened Hour is nigh" (53.57); "the Hour is surely coming" (20.15). Of that "there is no doubt" (22.7). "The doom of thy Lord will surely come to pass" (52.7). "Their reckoning draweth nigh for mankind, while they turn away in heedlessness" (21.1) for "most of mankind believe not" (40.59). People will not recognise the signs for what they are. "The Hour has come near, and the moon has split [in two]. And if they behold a portent they turn away and say: 'Prolonged illusion'" (54.1–2). "The judgment will indeed befall" (51.6), "casting down some and exalting others" (56.1–3); and when it does "the disbeliever will cry: 'Would that I were dust!'" (78.40). To those who disregard the warning the Qur'an threatens that "they behold that which they were promised" (19.75). Some of the most poetic texts in the Qur'an describe the Day of Judgement, accompanied and anticipated by a range of astronomical phenomena and terrestrial cataclysms.

---

**39** Meir Jacob Kister, "Sanctity Joint and Divided: On Holy Places in the Islamic Tradition," *Jerusalem Studies in Arabic and Islam* 20 (1996): 18–65 at 62.

**40** As Donner, *Muhammad and the Believers*, 143–44, writes: "The Believers' ambition to establish the writ of God's word as widely as possible was apparently given special urgency by the conviction that the Last Judgement was imminent. The mood of apocalyptic expectation – in which presumably, they followed the lead of Muhammad himself – made it important to get on with the business of creating a righteous order so that, when the End came, those who would be counted amongst the Believers would attain paradise. This may also explain the early Believers' desire to extend their domains to Jerusalem, which many apocalyptic scenarios depicted as the place where the events of the Last Judgment would be played out. They may also have believed that the *amir al-mu'minin* as leader of this new community dedicated to the realization of God's word, would fulfil the role that expected the 'last emperor' who would, on the Last Day, hand earthly power over to God."

**41** Translations from the Qur'an are by Marmaduke Pickthal.

> When the sun is overthrown, and when the stars fall. When the hills are moved, and when the camels big with young are abandoned, and when the wild beasts are herded together, and when the seas rise, and when souls are reunited, and when the girl-child that was buried alive is asked for what sin she was slain. And when the pages are laid open when the sky is torn away, and when hell is lighted, and when the Garden is brought nigh, (then) every soul will know what it hath made ready. (81.1–14)

It seems likely that Muhammad expected to see the Day of Judgement in his own lifetime. The problem here is that sura 3.144 of the Qur'an states that the prophet would die. However Al-Tabarī's history describes an episode that suggests that this text might be a later interpolation. Ibn Ishaq's *Life of the Prophet* recounts the episode as follows, with Umar (who will be the second Caliph) protesting at the news that the prophet has died.

> Some of the disaffected will allege that the prophet is dead, but by God he is not dead: he has gone to his Lord as Moses b. Imran went and is hidden from his people for forty days returning to them after it was said that he had died. By God, the apostle will return as Moses returned and will cut off the hands and feet of men who allege that the apostle is dead.[42]

Clearly Umar believes that the prophet will not die before the Day of Judgement arrives. But Abū Bakr (who is about to become the first Caliph) rebukes Umar saying:

> 'O men, if anyone worship Muhammad, Muhammad is dead; if anyone worship God, God is alive and immortal.' Then he recited this verse: 'Muhammad is nothing but an apostle. Apostles have passed away before him. Can it be that if he were to die or be killed you would turn back on your heels? He who turns back does no harm to God and God will reward the grateful.' (3.144) By God, it was as though the people did not know this verse (concerning the apostle) had come down until Abū Bakr recited it that day. The people took it from him and it was (constantly) in their mouths.[43]

Al-Tabarī gives an alternative account whereby after Abū Bakr's recitation of sura 3.144 prompted some of the companions of the prophet to affirm "that they had never heard those verses before Abū Bakr spoke them on that day."[44] Shoemaker argues that "In all likelihood, the alarmingly unfamiliar Qur'anic verse placed in Abū Bakr's mouth at Muhammad's death was in fact a later interpolation de-

**42** Alfred Guillaume, *The Life of Muhammad: a translation of Ibn Ishaq's* Sirat Rasul Allah (Oxford: Oxford University Press, 1967), 682.

**43** Guillaume, *Life of Muhammad*, 683. Cf. Al-Tabarī, *The History of Al-Tabarī*, trans. Ismail K. Poonawal, vol. 9 (Albany: State University of New York Press, 1990), 184–85.

**44** Al-Tabarī, *The History of Al-Tabarī*, vol. 9, 187–88.

signed to adjust the early community's eschatological calendar around their leader's unanticipated passing."[45] There are in fact a number of *hadith* that suggest that Muhammad's ministry was intimately connected with the Hour's imminent arrival. This finds expression in the tradition cited by Ibn Hanbal that Muhammad explained to his followers that "'The hour has come upon you; I have been sent with the Hour like this', and he showed them his two fingers, the index finger and the middle finger,"[46] joined so as to indicate their concurrence. Al-Tabarī's history reconciles the two-finger tradition by observing that the index finger is shorter than the middle finger, calculating that from the total length of the world's existence the Hour would arrive 500 years after the prophet.[47]

Just as the urgency of Jesus' eschatological message became diminished and reinterpreted with time, so it was with Muhammad's community of believers. I follow Donner in his argument that the followers of Muhammad did not initially see themselves as constituting a distinct confessional identity. Muhammad's own self-understanding is that of a reformer of monotheism. What mattered to the Believers was not a person's confessional identity, but whether he or she shared their belief in the One God, Creator of the World and Judge at the end of time, and their conviction that the Day of Judgement was near, or at least rapidly nearing. To ensure their salvation in the face of the imminent Day of Judgement, the Believers strove to create a community (*umma*), submitting themselves to a life of piety lived in strict accordance with the divine law that had been revealed repeatedly throughout history. What was essential was belief in the one God of Abraham and in the Last Day. Otherwise Muhammad's followers did not initially distinguish themselves from other Abrahamic monotheists.[48]

> Lo! those who believe, and those who are Jews, and Sabaeans, and Christians – Whosoever believeth in Allah and the Last Day and doeth right – there shall no fear come upon them neither shall they grieve. (Sura 5.69)

This is affirmed by the *Constitution of Medina*,[49] which only mentions one set of religious beliefs in which it states that "it is not lawful for any *Mu'min* who has

45 Shoemaker, *The Death of a Prophet*, 183.

46 Ibn Hanbal, *Musnad* 3.310–11. Cited by Shoemaker, *The Death of a Prophet*, 174–75.

47 Shoemaker, *The Death of a Prophet*, 173.

48 See Donner, *Muhammad and the Believers*, 69 ff.

49 R.B. Serjeant, "The 'Sunnah Jāmi'ah,' Pacts with the Yathrib Jews, and the 'Tahrīm' of Yathrib: Analysis and Translation of the Documents Comprised in the So-Called 'Constitution of Medina'," *Bulletin of the School of Oriental and African Studies, University of London* 41/1 (1978): 1–42 at 8, describes the *Constitution of Medina* as consisting of "treaties establishing the confederation between the Quraysh Muhajiriin seeking protection at Yathrib and the tribal Sup-

affirmed what is on this sheet and/or believes in God and the Last Day, to support or shelter an aggressor or innovator."[50] The *Constitution of Medina* gives witness to the inclusion of Jews as a distinct group within the community. The only doctrinal requirement of the *Constitution* is belief "in God and the Last Day." Thus Christians and Jews could continue to follow their own scriptures under Islamic rule. While some Jews and Christians seem to have joined Muhammad's community while retaining their confessional identities, others clearly rejected it, or did not live up to the Qur'anic standard of piety, or rejected the imminence of the Day of Judgment.[51]

The Nestorian monk John bar Penkāyē of northern Mesopotamia, writing in the late 680s, confirms that the Arab raiders demanded tribute, but were content for each of the subject peoples to remain in their faith of choice. He also suggests that there were Christians, both monophysites and Nestorians, amongst the raiders.[52] Furthermore, recent evidence suggests that some of the earliest mosques were established on the place of worship of "the people of the book," the best known being the Church of St John in Damascus but also, it would seem, in part of the Church of the Holy Sepulchre, before a mosque was established on the Temple Mount.[53] Of course the anti-Trinitarian polemic remains an obstacle for the inclusion of Christians, as Trinitarian faith was seen as a threat to Islamic monotheism. Most early Muslim believers, however, probably had little knowledge of the Qur'an.[54] Doctrinal clarity became more significant later as the identity of the community of believers evolved.[55]

All of this is consistent with what we know about the first community of believers at Yathrib, which included at least some "people of the book" (*al-kitāb*), certainly some Jews. Patricia Crone and Michael Cook note that "the Jews appear in the 'Constitution of Medina' as forming one community *(ummha)* with the be-

---

porters (Ansar) of Muhammad [that] have been lumped together with later agreements and transmitted as a single document known to European scholars as the 'Constitution of Medina' – a misnomer in that it relates the treaties to a locality rather than to tribes. From the historical view-point it is not less in importance than the Qur'an itself and, though slightly jumbled in transmission, it is patently authentic."

**50** C3a. Translation by Serjeant, "The 'Sunnah Jāmi'ah'," 23.

**51** Shoemaker, *The Death of a Prophet*, 208.

**52** Text of John bar Penkāyē in: Alfons Mingana, *Sources Syriaques* (Leipzig: Otto Harrassowitz, for Imprimerie des Peres Dominicains a Mossoul, 1907–8), vol. 1, 147, lines 1–6. Cited by Donner, "From Believers to Muslims," 44.

**53** Ibid., 51.

**54** Donner, *Muhammad and the Believers*, 77.

**55** Shoemaker, *The Death of a Prophet*, 209–210.

lievers despite the retention of their religion."[56] The question of whether any other groups of monotheists belonged to Muhammad's community is unable to be answered as clearly by traditional sources.[57] According to the *Constitution of Medina:* "The Jews of Band 'Awf are a confederation (ummah) with the Mu'minuin, the Jews having their religion/law (din) and the Muslimūn/Mu'miniin having their religion/law, their clients (mawali) and their persons, excepting anyone who acts wrongfully (zalama) and commits crime/acts treacherously/breaks an agreement, for he but slays himself and the people of his house."[58] Similarly, the *Constitution* further affirms that "the Jews of the Aws, their clients and themselves, are on the same (basis) as the people of this sheet."[59]

We find some intriguing confirmation of the inter-confessional nature of the first community of believers in an unlikely source two centuries later. We have in the teachings of Ahmad ibn Hanbal (d. 855), founder of the conservative Hanbali school of religious law (*fiqh*), reports that the question of whether the early community (*umma*) included Jews and Christians remained a matter of great concern. Ibn Hanbal responded with vehemence to the repeated questions on this issue, exclaiming: "This is a filthy question, and one must not discuss it." Ibn Hanbal seems utterly perplexed when the question continues to come up and is surprised to learn that anyone could possibly claim such a thing.[60]

In the wake of Islamic rule messianic hopes ran high amongst all the conquered peoples. But even when Islam began to establish clear boundaries between its own identity and that of other monotheists, as exemplified by the anti-Trinitarian inscriptions in the Dome of the Rock – a monument to victory over the Christians[61] – the eschatological strain began to reassert itself in new ways. Amongst those marginalised within Islam we can see the development of the same messianic expectation of the Mahdī, "the rightly guided one," the restorer of religion and justice who, according to a widely held Muslim belief, will rule before the end of the world.[62] The concept of the Mahdī first appeared in the contexts of sectarian rivalries and confessional disputes of the first civil war when the title was applied variously to the caliphs Uthman, Ali, and Ali's

---

**56** Crone and Cook, *Hagarism*, 7.

**57** Donner, "From Believers to Muslims," 29.

**58** C2a (trans. Serjeant, "The 'Sunnah Jāmi'ah'," 27).

**59** G6 (trans. Serjeant, 33).

**60** Al-Khallāl, *Ahl al-milal* 1:54–55. Ibn Hanbal's *responsa* on this topic occupy 1:53–62 of this collection. Cited by Shoemaker, *The Death of a Prophet*, 216.

**61** Donner, *Muhammad and the Believers*, 200.

**62** Wilferd Madelung, "al-Mahdī," in: *Encyclopaedia of Islam, Second Edition*, Brill Online, 2013, http://referenceworks.brillonline.com/entries/encyclopaedia-of-islam-2/al-mahdi-COM_0618 (accessed 14 Feb. 2013).

son al-Husayn, by their supporters.[63] After the death of Muʿāwiya, the term came first to be used for an expected ruler who would restore Islam to its original perfection.[64] An interesting variation on the role of the Mahdī that reflects an earlier inclusiveness can be found in a tradition attributed to Ka'b al-Ahbār, an early Yemenite Jewish convert to Islam who, al-Tabarī relates, accompanied Umar to Jerusalem in 636 and revealed to him the site of the Temple Mount.[65] According to this tradition, the Mahdī was so called because he would find the original texts of the Torah and the gospel concealed in Antioch. As transmitted by Abdullah Bishr al-Kathami from Kufa:

> The Mahdī will send (an army) to fight the Rūm, will be given the knowledge of ten, and will bring forth the Ark of the Divine Presence from a cave in Antioch in which are the Torah which God sent down to Moses and the Gospel which he sent down to Jesus, and he will rule among the People of the Torah according to their Torah and among the People of the Gospel according to their Gospel.[66]

## 4 Conclusion

In considering the earliest sources documenting the rise of Islam I am struck by parallels in the development of both Christianity and Islam. Both founding figures understand themselves to be the prophet who would usher in the *eschaton.* Both movements originally sought to be as inclusive as possible within the constraints of what was considered the necessary requirement of preparation for the Day of Judgement. When the *eschaton* failed to arrive and the fires of the apocalyptic imagination died down, both communities adjusted their expectations and self-understanding. They constructed their identities by consolidating a tradition and developing institutions by which to maintain and nourish what was new and distinct in each. Both communities were supercessionalist in the manner in which they established boundaries and constructed a clear identity from the other from which they emerged. The Christian church, divorced from the synagogue, sought to distance itself ever further from Judaism even as it claimed Ju-

---

**63** Hayrettin Yücesoy, *Messianic Beliefs and Imperial Politics in Medieval Islam: The Abbasid Caliphate in the Early Ninth Century* (Columbia, SC: The University of South Carolina Press, 2009), 19.

**64** Madelung, "al-Mahdī."

**65** Shari Lowin, "Ka'b al-Ahbār," in: *Encyclopedia of Jews in the Islamic World*, exec. ed. Norman A. Stillman, Brill Online, 2013, http://referenceworks.brillonline.com/entries/encyclopedia-of-jews-in-the-islamic-world/kab-al-ahbar-SIM_0012450 (accessed 14 Feb. 2013).

**66** Madelung, "al-Mahdī."

daism's legitimacy as heir of the covenant for itself. Islam, similarly, as the instrument of God's justice, sought to distinguish itself from the embarrassment of feuding factions of monotheisms by establishing itself as *the* straight path.

# List of Contributors

**Pauline Allen**
is Founding Director of the Centre for Early Christian Studies at Australian Catholic University, and internationally renowned for her work on Evagrius Scholasticus, Maximus the Confessor, Severus of Antioch, John Chrysostom, late-antique bishops and letter-writing, and the Council of Chalcedon. Her most recent books include *Crisis Management in Late Antiquity (410–590 CE): A Survey of the Evidence from Episcopal Letters*, co-authored with Bronwen Neil, and *John Chrysostom. Homilies on Philippians*, the founding volume in a new translation series of Chrysostom's New Testament exegetical homilies. Together she and Bronwen Neil are editing *The Oxford Handbook to Maximus the Confessor.* Professor Allen is also Research Associate in the Department of Ancient Languages, University of Pretoria.

**Alan Cadwallader**
is Senior Lecturer in Biblical Studies at Australian Catholic University in Canberra and a member of the Centre for Early Christian Studies. His research interests are in archaeology of the Roman and Byzantine period in Asia Minor, in the politics of bible translation and in contemporary hermeneutics. He is co-editor with Michael Trainor and main contributor for the collection, *Colossae in Space and Time: Linking to An Ancient City* (Göttingen: Vandenhoeck & Ruprecht, 2011) and is working on a critically annotated translation of the texts of St Michael of Chonai.

**Damien Casey**
is Lecturer in Systematic Theology at Australian Catholic University and a member of the Centre for Early Christian Studies. His research interests are in theological pluralism, in philosophies of dialogue and difference, and in soteriology. Recent publications include: "The Dangerous Idea of the Domestic Church," in: *The Household of God and Local Households. Revisiting the Domestic Church*, eds. T. Knieps-Port Le Roi, G. Mannion, and P. De Mey (Leuven: Peeters, 2013); "The spiritual valency of gender in Byzantine society," in: *Questions of Gender in Byzantine Society*, eds. Bronwen Neil and Lynda Garland (Farnham: Ashgate, 2013); and "Divine Pedagogy as Skilful Means. Theological Pluralism in the Early Church," *Patristica*, supplementary vol. 3 (2011): 1–16.

**Geoffrey D. Dunn**
is Senior Research Fellow in the Centre for Early Christian Studies, Australian Catholic University, where he received his PhD in 2000, and is a presbyter of the Catholic Diocese of Cairns. Between 2007 and the end of 2011 he was an Australian Research Fellow, funded by the Australian Research Council, working on the letters of Innocent I of Rome. His publications include *Tertullian* in the series Early Church Fathers, *Cyprian and the Bishops of Rome: Questions of Papal Primacy in the Early Church* in the series Early Christian Studies and *Tertullian's Aduersus Iudaeos: A Rhetorical Analysis* in the North American Patristics Society Patristic Monograph series.

**Ian Elmer**
is Lecturer in Biblical Studies, Assistant Head of the National School of Theology, and a member of the Centre for Early Christian Studies at Australian Catholic University, with research interests in first-century Christian movements and the letters of Paul. In addition to his monograph *Paul, Jerusalem and the Judaisers. The Galatian Crisis in Its Broadest Historical Context*, WUNT 2.258 (Tübingen: Mohr Siebeck, 2009), recent publications include: "Family Feud: Paul's Response to the Internecine Crisis in Galatia," in: *Ancient Jewish and Christian Texts as Crisis Management Literature: Thematic Studies from the Centre for Early Christian Studies*, eds. David C. Sim and Pauline Allen (London–New York: T&T Clark, 2012), 46–61; and "Pillars, Hypocrites and False Brothers. Paul's Polemic against Jerusalem in Galatians," in: *Polemik in der frühchristlichen Literatur. Texte und Kontexte*, eds. O. Wischmeyer and L. Scornaienchi (Berlin: De Gruyter, 2011), 123–54.

**Sarah Gador-Whyte**
is a post-doctoral research associate in the Centre for Early Christian Studies and tutor in the Faculty of Theology and Philosophy at Australian Catholic University. She has published several articles on Romanos the Melodist and other aspects of late-antique history. Her article "Changing Conceptions of Mary in Sixth-Century Byzantium: the Kontakia of Romanos the Melodist" will appear this year in *Questions of Gender in Byzantine Society*, eds. Bronwen Neil and Linda Garland (Farnham: Ashgate, 2013).

**Raymond Laird,**
an ordained Baptist minister and Honorary Fellow in the Centre for Early Christian Studies at Australian Catholic University, has been involved in theological education for over thirty years, lecturing in Church History and Theology. He served as Principal of two colleges, latterly the Bible College of South Australia (1991–2000) followed by five years as Dean of the South Australian Graduate School of Theology (2001–2006). His main publication has been *Mindset, Moral Choice and Sin in the Anthropology of John Chrysostom*, ECS 15 (Strathfield: St Pauls Publications, 2012). In 2012 he was awarded the Medal of the Order of Australia (OAM) for service to the study of theology.

**James S. McLaren**
is Professor of Ancient History and Biblical Studies in the Faculty of Theology and Philosophy, Associate Dean of Research for that Faculty and a member of the Centre for Early Christian Studies at Australian Catholic University. He is the author of several books and numerous papers on various aspects of first-century CE history. He is co-editor of *Attitudes towards Gentiles in Ancient Jewish and Christian Literature* (London: Continuum, 2013) and a member of the Brill Josephus Project team.

**Wendy Mayer**
is a Research Fellow in the Centre for Early Christian Studies at Australian Catholic University, known internationally for her ground-breaking work on the homilies of John Chrysostom and his biography. In addition to numerous journal articles, book chapters, and several books on those topics, including translations of his homilies on the cult of the saints, her most recent book is *The Churches of Syrian Antioch (300–638 CE)* (Leuven: Peeters, 2012), co-authored with Pauline Allen.

**Bronwen Neil**
holds the Burke Senior Lectureship in Ecclesiastical Latin at Australian Catholic University and is Assistant Director of the Centre for Early Christian Studies. She has published widely on Maximus the Confessor, Pope Martin I, Anastasius Bibliothecarius and Pope Leo I, as well as poverty and welfare in Late Antiquity. She is a Fellow of the Australian Academy of the Humanities and President of the Australian Association for Byzantine Studies. In addition to the books edited and co-authored with Pauline Allen, listed above, her latest work includes a translation of the papal letters of Gelasius, and the *Brill Companion to Gregory the Great*, co-edited with Matthew Dal Santo.

**Pierluigi Piovanelli**
is Professor of Second Temple Judaism and Early Christianity at the Département d'études anciennes et de sciences religions/Department of Classics and Religious Studies, Université d'Ottawa/University of Ottawa, Ottawa (Ontario), a specialist of Jewish and Christian apocryphal texts, the historical Jesus, Jewish/Christian relations in Late Antiquity, and Ethiopian history. He has extensively published, contributing to academic journals and collective volumes, with more than one hundred essays written in English, French, and Italian.

**David C. Sim**
is an Associate Professor in the School of Theology and a member of the Centre for Early Christian Studies at Australian Catholic University. He is a co-editor (with Pauline Allen) of *Ancient Jewish and Christian Texts as Crisis Management Literature* (London-New York: T&T Clark, 2012), and a co-editor (with James S. McLaren) of *Attitudes to Gentiles in Ancient Judaism and Early Christianity* (London: Continuum, 2013).

**Michael P. Theophilos**
is Lecturer in Biblical Studies and Ancient Languages within the Faculty of Theology and Philosophy and a member of the Centre for Early Christian Studies at Australian Catholic University. He is a council member of the Australian Institute of Archaeology and has edited a number of Oxyrhynchus papyri based at the Papyrology Rooms, Oxford University. His most recent monograph is *The Abomination of Desolation in Matthew 24:15*, LNTS 437 (London: T&T Clark, 2012).

# Index of Names and Places

# General Index

www.ingramcontent.com/pod-product-compliance
Lightning Source LLC
Chambersburg PA
CBHW070026100426
42740CB00013B/2605